Books for Development

Rethinking Canada in the World

SERIES EDITORS: IAN MCKAY AND SEAN MILLS

Supported by the Wilson Institute for Canadian History at McMaster University, this series is committed to books that rethink Canadian history from transnational and global perspectives. It enlarges approaches to the study of Canada in the world by exploring how Canadian history has long been a dynamic product of global currents and forces. The series will also reinvigorate understanding of Canada's role as an international actor and how Canadians have contributed to intellectual, political, cultural, social, and material exchanges around the world.

Volumes included in the series explore the ideas, movements, people, and institutions that have transcended political boundaries and territories to shape Canadian society and the state. These include both state and non-state actors, and phenomena such as international migration, diaspora politics, religious movements, evolving conceptions of human rights and civil society, popular culture, technology, epidemics, wars, and global finance and trade.

The series charts a new direction by exploring networks of transmission and exchange from a standpoint that is not solely national or international, expanding the history of Canada's engagement with the world.

http://wilson.humanities.mcmaster.ca

Books for Development

*Canada in the
Late Twentieth-Century World*

JODY MASON

McGill-Queen's University Press
Montreal & Kingston · London · Chicago

© McGill-Queen's University Press 2026

ISBN 978-0-2280-2701-0 (paper)
ISBN 978-0-2280-2702-7 (ePDF)
ISBN 978-0-2280-2703-4 (ePUB)

Legal deposit first quarter 2026
Bibliothèque et Archives nationales du Québec

Printed in Canada on acid-free paper that is 100% ancient-forest-free, containing 100% sustainable, recycled fibre, and processed chlorine-free.

This book has been published with the help of a grant from the Federation for the Humanities and Social Sciences, through the Awards to Scholarly Publications Program, using funds provided by the Social Sciences and Humanities Research Council of Canada.

Funded by the Government of Canada | Financé par le gouvernement du Canada | | Canada Council for the Arts | Conseil des arts du Canada

We acknowledge the support of the Canada Council for the Arts.

Nous remercions le Conseil des arts du Canada de son soutien.

McGill-Queen's University Press in Montreal is on land which long served as a site of meeting and exchange amongst Indigenous Peoples, including the Haudenosaunee and Anishinabeg nations. In Kingston it is situated on the territory of the Haudenosaunee and Anishinaabek. We acknowledge and thank the diverse Indigenous Peoples whose footsteps have marked these territories on which peoples of the world now gather.

Library and Archives Canada Cataloguing in Publication

Title: Books for development : Canada in the late twentieth-century world / Jody Mason.

Names: Mason, Jody, 1976– author

Series: Rethinking Canada in the world ; 15.

Description: Series statement: Rethinking Canada in the world ; 15 | Includes bibliographical references and index.

Identifiers: Canadiana (print) 20250306344 | Canadiana (ebook) 20250306395 | ISBN 9780228027010 (paper) | ISBN 9780228027027 (PDF) | ISBN 9780228027034 (EPUB)

Subjects: LCSH: Economic development – Developing countries – History – 20th century. | LCSH: Books and reading – Economic aspects – Developing countries – History – 20th century. | LCSH: Books and reading – Social aspects – Developing countries – History – 20th century. | LCSH: Canadian literature – Economic aspects – History – 20th century. | LCSH: Canada – Foreign economic relations – Developing countries. | LCSH: Developing countries – Foreign economic relations – Canada.

Classification: LCC HC59.72 .M37 2026 | DDC 338.91/7101724 – dc23

This book was designed and typeset by Peggy Issenman in 11/14 Minion Pro. Copyediting by Rachel Taylor.

McGill-Queen's University Press
Suite 1720, 1010 Sherbrooke St West, Montreal, QC, H3A 2R7

Authorized safety representative in the EU: Mare Nostrum Group BV, Mauritskade 21D, 1091 GC Amsterdam, the Netherlands, gpsr@mare-nostrum.co.uk

Development

blue,

and
bluer

still,

and
bluer,

still.

– Cameron Anstee

Contents

Tables and Figures   ix

Acknowledgments   xiii

Abbreviations   xv

Introduction: Books in the "Age of Development"   3

1 "Famine of Books": Late Colonial Book Development and Margaret Wrong in Africa (1929–48)   25

2 The Department of External Affairs and Postwar Uses of the Book, 1945–59   57

3 "Not Even Bread Itself": Nongovernmental Book Development in Late Twentieth-Century Canada   90

4 Developing Africa and Late Twentieth-Century Anglophone Settler Nationalism   129

5 The Fourth World Challenge to Developmentalism   187

Conclusion   224

Appendix A: Selections for the Canadiana Program (1948–59), by Category   231

Appendix B: Selections for the Special Book Presentation Programme, by Language   241

Notes 251

Bibliography 301

Index 327

Tables and Figures

Tables

A.1 Publications selected for the Annual "Canadiana" Book Presentation Program (1948–59), by category and year of first publication.   231

B.1 English-language publications selected for the Special Book Presentation Programme for Colombo-Plan Area Countries (1956–59).   241

B.2 French-language publications selected for the Special Book Presentation Programme for Colombo-Plan Area Countries (1956–59).   246

Figures

1.1 *King Khama*. Box 40, ICCLA-SOAS.   31
1.2 Photograph of Margaret Wrong, Rev. S. Moore, and three teacher trainees, 10 April 1948. Box 001P, file 05, GMW-UT.   36
1.3 Margaret Wrong at a local market in Nyasaland, 1936. Album 2, box 8, ICCLA-SOAS.   37
2.1 John D. Robins, ed., *A Pocketful of Canada* (Collins, 1952).   73
3.1 Canada Information Service, *Canada from Sea to Sea* (E. Cloutier, King's Printer, 1947), 2–3.   96
3.2 "Canada's March of Books for War Devastated Libraries," vol. 1, file titled "Reports and Minutes of the Executive

	and Operating Committees, 1950–1951 (1)," Canadian Council for Reconstruction Through UNESCO fonds, Library and Archives Canada. 97
3.3	Overseas Book Centre, "You Can Help," vol. 95, file 22, "Overseas Book Centre to: 1973, 1967–1973," ICAE-LAC. Image reproduced with the permission of CODE. 116
3.4	Overseas Book Centre, "Books and Educational Aids for Developing Countries," undated, vol. 108, file 13, "ICAE (International Council for Adult Education) General Files 1976–80 International Organizations – Society for International Development 1976–80 Overseas Book Centre, 1976–80," ICAE-LAC. Reproduced with the permission of CODE. 118
4.1	*A Tree for Poverty* (Eagle Press, 1954). Reproduced with the permission of the estate of Margaret Laurence. Courtesy of Rare Books and Special Collections, McGill University Library. 145
4.2	Dorothy Livesay's Federation of Northern Rhodesia and Nyasaland Residence Permit. Box 9, folder 4, "UNESCO and Africa Teaching, 1958–63: Correspondences, Reports, Documents," MSS 37, DL-UM. Reproduced with the permission of the estate of Dorothy Livesay. 150
4.3	Dorothy Livesay at her residence at Kitwe Training College, ca. 1960. Box 3, folder 8, "Dorothy Livesay Photograph Collection, Northern Rhodesia Photographs," PC 43, DL-UM. Reproduced with the permission of the estate of Dorothy Livesay. 151
4.4	Play program for *Androcles and the Lion*. Box 10, folder 1, "UNESCO and Africa Teaching, 1958–63: Teaching-Related Material," MSS 37, DL-UM. Reproduced with the permission of the estate of Dorothy Livesay. 160–1
4.5	"SUCO et Vous," vol. 50, file 20, "CUSO and You / SUCO et Vous, 1965," CUSO/SUCO-LAC. Reproduced with the permission of CUSO International. 171
4.6	Godfrey, Dave. *Death Goes Better with Coca-Cola*. Press Porcépic, 1973. Reproduced with the permission of the estate of Dave Godfrey. Courtesy of Archives and Special Collections, Carleton University, Ottawa. 182

5.1 "CUSO Volunteer Wants More Indians to Go Overseas," *CUSO/ SUCO Bulletin*, December 1968, p. 9, vol. 103, file 2, "CUSO Bulletin, 1967–1971," CUSO/SUCO-LAC. Reproduced with the permission of CUSO International.   204

Acknowledgments

I'm a settler of British and Irish ancestry originally from the territory of the Haldimand Treaty, signed in 1784. Since 2007, I've worked in Ottawa on the unceded territory of the Algonquin Nation, and I live as a guest in Montreal, site of the traditional territories of both Anishinaabe and Haudenosaunee Peoples. This book is rooted in these places and in their complex histories.

It was my privilege to work with the research assistants who moved this project from an article about postwar cultural diplomacy to a book about late twentieth-century book development. Many thanks to Dessa Bayrock, Noah Bendzsa, Sarah Dorward, Dana Mitchell, Sarah Pelletier, Meghan Tibbits-Lamirande, and Daisy Sheps.

I've drawn on resources from both scholarly and NGO communities. The historian Ruth Compton Brouwer generously pointed me to Margaret Wrong, a tip that helped me connect the late colonial and postwar elements of book development. Scott Walter, the former executive director at Canadian Organization for Development Through Education (CODE), kindly scanned anniversary materials for me and chatted about CODE's history. A fleet of skilled archivists helped me navigate complicated fonds and finding aids: thanks especially to Nicole Aminian at the University of Manitoba; Gillian Dunks at McMaster University; Lauren Williams of Rare Books and Special Collections at McGill University; Michael Moir at the Clara Thomas Archives and Special Collections, York University; and the archival staff at Library and Archives Canada in Ottawa. I'm grateful that CODE, CUSO International, Ellen Godfrey, and the estates of Margaret Laurence and Dorothy Livesay were willing to assist with image permissions.

Many thanks to Jonathan Crago and the team at McGill-Queen's University Press and to the assessors of this manuscript. Many people have good reason to say no to peer review these days; I'm grateful that the readers who stepped up in this case did not. Their smart deliberation shaped the published book. Rachel Taylor's editorial insights made this book better than it otherwise would have been. Thanks to Catherine Marjoribanks for her attentive work on the index.

Part of chapter 2 originally appeared as a journal article in *Canadian Literature* no. 240 (2020). The Canadian Network on Humanitarian History opened their blogspace to my thoughts about J.R. Kidd and the Overseas Book Centre, and Active History published my blog about Fourth World critiques of developmentalism. Kyle Wyatt at the *Literary Review of Canada* offered me a place to think through my initial ideas about cultural diplomacy in the creative-economy era. The longer work that came from that seed (not part of this manuscript) was published in *Book History* 26, no. 2 (Fall 2023). I'm thankful to those who gave me an opportunity to talk about this project as it was emerging: the Society for the History of Authorship, Reading and Publishing; the Canadian Historical Association; and Sarah Krotz, former director of the Centre for Literatures in Canada / Centre de littératures au Canada at the University of Alberta. The work of organizing research talks and conferences is unjustly undervalued in the twenty-first-century Canadian university. Thanks to those who do it nonetheless.

Thank you to Cameron Anstee of the marvellous Apt. 9 Press in Ottawa, who gave me permission to reprint his poem "Development" (first published in *Sky Every Day*, Gaspereau Press, 2024). I like how its polyptoton comments on the late twentieth-century preoccupation with universal modes of progress and improvement: "blue" and "bluer" are one and the same; the latter is not an improved version of the former.

Finally, un très gros merci to Pascal Bikorimana; Yvette, Jean Paul, Sandra, Viecoslaves, Dilan, and Keva Mugisha; and Joselyne Nyirahabimama. You were part of a journey that has produced important things for me, including this book.

Abbreviations

CAAE	Canadian Association for Adult Education
CCRU	Canadian Council for Reconstruction Through UNESCO
CIDA	Canadian International Development Agency
CIS	Canadian Information Service
CMS	Christian Missionary Society
CUSO	Canadian University Service Overseas
EALB	East African Literature Bureau
EWLP	Experimental World Literacy Programme
ICAE	International Council for Adult Education
ICCLA	International Committee on Christian Literature for Africa
IPA	Independent Publishers' Association
NARP	Native Alliance for Red Power
NFB	National Film Board
NGOS	nongovernmental organizations
NIB	National Indian Brotherhood
OBC	Overseas Book Centre
OECD	Organisation for Economic Co-operation and Development
OIC	Overseas Institute of Canada
UN	United Nations
UNESCO	United Nations Educational, Scientific, and Cultural Organization
UNIP	United National Independence Party
USAID	United States Agency for International Development
USIA	United States Information Agency
WIB	Wartime Information Board

Books for Development

Introduction

Books in the "Age of Development"

Announcing the creation in 2018 of the Canadian Ombudsperson for Responsible Enterprise (CORE), Canada's then–international trade minister François-Philippe Champagne equated the Canadian brand with "a set of values based on dignity, respect, diversity, and tolerance." According to Champagne, the brand "conveys extraordinary commercial advantage" but also comes with "extraordinary responsibilities." Yet as journalist Tavia Grant's 2023 investigation makes clear, CORE is a toothless office that has failed to complete a single investigation of the human rights and environmental abuses allegedly committed by Canadian companies operating abroad. The Canadian brand will not forever withstand such contradiction, particularly in the context of current shifting of the international order, but how did the values Champagne so confidently identified in 2018 become so durably attached to the nation?[1]

This study argues that we might look to the book – as object, as symbol, as idea – for some answers to these questions. The work of book historians, sociologists of literature, and literary scholars has shown how, since the end of the twentieth century, settler Canadian book culture has been associated in both domestic and international contexts with a moralizing rhetoric that associates reading with an enlightened liberal tolerance for difference; but what is the history of this set of meanings, and how were they generated?[2]

Books for Development: Canada in the Late Twentieth-Century World argues that we must consider the meanings of the book within the late twentieth-century development paradigm – what Wolfgang Sachs calls the "age of development" (1950–90) – to see how this set of meanings was constructed and then deployed both within Canada and internationally. Between 1945 and the end of the 1970s or so we can track the ways the book, which came to function as a key representative of settler exceptionalism, was used within the context of the development paradigm to express solidarity with newly decolonized nations, to argue for the importance of Canadian leadership in the new international order, and to consolidate settler liberal rule at home.[3]

The five chapters that follow argue that books functioned in the decades of the last half of the twentieth century as particularly good instruments for concealing settler-colonial antinomies – the contradictory relation of the nation's external self-presentation to its settler-colonial realities. The confluence of books and a national "brand" was shaped during these decades by a liberal internationalism that privileged the book, and the associated skill of literacy, as fundamental instruments of development. The development paradigm associated with these years consistently disavowed the fact that underdevelopment was and is linked to the ways that colonialism and capitalism engender inequality, focusing instead on symbolically rich objects such as the book and the individual improvement it stands for. This development paradigm served Canadian interests well, displacing attention from domestic structures of dispossession, namely internal colonization, while emphasizing the nation's status as recently "colonized," an argument that positioned Canada as uniquely equipped to be a "trusted broker" in international affairs.

The arguments of this study are situated at the intersection of two emergent fields of inquiry: the work of historians on Canadian development assistance, and sociological and book historical studies of the role of the book in the late twentieth-century development paradigm. Building on this scholarship, *Books for Development: Canada in the Late Twentieth-Century World* is the first study to account for the role that developmentalism – and more specifically book development – played in legitimating settler-colonial rule in the second half of the twentieth century.

The Development Paradigm

There is general agreement in histories of the international development paradigm that it did not emerge, ex nihilo, a bright vision from the ashes of the Second World War. Mike Davis contends that the making of the Third World and the concepts that came to accompany it in the postwar years – development and underdevelopment among them – must be dated to the era of high imperialism. The "new vulnerability" to catastrophes such as famine that one finds in nineteenth-century South Asia and southern Africa, among other places, is attributable to changes wrought by colonial rule: "With few exceptions, the forcible incorporation of peasant production into commodity financial circuits ultimately controlled from the metropolis radically exacerbated the instability of subsistence agriculture." Moreover, Victorian imperialism "impeded state-level developmental responses" that might have buffered the negative effects of drought-induced famine. Davis's broad conclusion is that the postwar development paradigm, which cast the nations of South Asia and elsewhere as famine-prone, helpless, and in need of western aid, occludes the fact that long histories of colonial rule and subjugation contributed to conditions that were later apprehended as the natural tendencies of impoverished nations.[4]

The reading of the development paradigm that this book constructs builds on the work of post-development theorists, who began in the last decade of the twentieth century to write development's obituary, arguing that its basic premise – that under a capitalist world system the so-called Third World could ever catch up to the so-called First World – is false. This book also explores, where relevant, the emergence of development in colonial and late colonial contexts. As early as 1961, decolonial thinkers such as Frantz Fanon were decrying the very premises of the development paradigm, calling out a tendentious benevolence and urging its recognition as payment of what was owed by the world's former colonial powers to newly independent nations. Scholars such as Gilbert Rist and Gustavo Esteva understand the postwar development paradigm – consonant with Sachs's "age of development" – as part of an older western European episteme associated with a linear conception of history and an idea of progress that is universally available and not subject to limits. Rist further identifies clear continuities between the "openly asymmetrical, hierarchical and non-egalitarian relationship" of colonies to European metropoles and the postwar development paradigm. Practices and policies associated with the training of colonial administrators and with colonial systems of education, for instance, "clearly anticipate measures taken in the second half of the twentieth century." However, if colonization justified interventions in nations outside of Europe with appeals to *national* interest, the interwar League of Nations system legitimated such interventions as forms of *international* duty, "in the name of civilization itself." The Treaty of Versailles established the mandate system, understood as a means of enabling mandates (i.e., those nations on the losing side of the First World War) to pass through requisite "stages of development" to become sufficiently modern and independent. The treaty perpetuated older relations between a "'minor' native population and the 'adult' mandatory power" but from this point forward, the "colonial enterprise" would be identified as a universal "sacred trust of civilization," an obligation on the part of developed nations to help the mandates stand on their own two feet. Whatever the outward justification, the late colonial shift to an explicit ideology of developmentalism had clear goals, as Miguel Bandeira Jerónimo points out: the "rejuvenation of empire through schemes of economic development and social engineering; improvements in its political organization; the minimization of sources of internal dissent by focusing more squarely on social welfare; and more systematic efforts to disarm critics at home and abroad."5

Raymond Williams's account of development (in his *Keywords*) argues that English usage of "development" in its current sense of progress was well underway by 1945; what was new in this period was the paired concept of "underdevelopment" and its accompanying argument regarding "economies and societies destined to pass through predictable 'stages of development,' according to a known model." For development to assume its contemporary stature vis-à-vis underdevelopment, another national actor had to enter the stage – the United States. In Rist's estimation, what has come to be known as "Point Four" of US president Harry Truman's 1949 inaugural address ushered in the "development age" by referring to the obligation of the US to make its scientific and industrial progress available for the "improvement and growth of underdeveloped areas." Development further assumed new meaning in the immediate postwar years in texts such as the World Bank's 1948 definition of poverty, which rendered two-thirds of the world's population "poor." Taken up energetically at the United Nations (UN), the concept of development came, by the 1950s, to exemplify what Arturo Escobar identifies as "a growing will to transform drastically two-thirds of the world in pursuit of the goals of material prosperity and economic progress." Rist contends that the new developed/underdeveloped dichotomy proposed equality in theory: in this new paradigm global inequalities were without cause and required courageous and benevolent action on the behalf of wealthy nations to permit underdeveloped nations to "catch up." This is what distinguished it from the older colonialism, which was in turn discredited. The nuances of this discrediting are important, however, because the US "had an evident interest in dismantling the old colonial empires to gain access to new markets."[6]

As the second chapter of this book demonstrates, in the decade following Truman's delivery of Point Four the western development paradigm was strongly shaped by the ideology of high modernism, the belief that scientific and technical progress could, if employed rationally and in a planned fashion, eliminate human need and suffering. By the early 1950s, this paradigm assumed the added imperative of building what Corrina Unger calls a "new, secure global order"; in the context of the Cold War, modernization was understood from within the US development bureaucracy as a guarantor of both economic and political stability in areas of the globe vulnerable to Soviet influence. David Williams and Tom Young contend that the postwar "modernizing elites" of Africa, who were the not necessarily intentional creations of colonial regimes, were largely committed to the high modernist ideals that held sway in the US in these decades. As Rist notes, the desire articulated by the mostly Asian nations at the 1955 Bandung Conference to see the integration of the nations of the global South into the world economy demonstrates their commitment to the promises of modernization; however, Bandung was also a harbinger of the critiques of modernization, some more radical than others, that would emerge by the late 1960s – from the Latin American dependentistas; from the 1967 Arusha Declaration and its promotion of "self-reliance" over foreign aid; and from the non-aligned movement and its calls for a New International Economic Order. Established at the 1964 meeting of the UN Conference on Trade and Development by a group of seventy-seven nations, the non-aligned movement determined to "work urgently for the establishment of a new international economic order based on equity, sovereign equality, interdependence, common interest, and cooperation among all states." As dependency theory and other critiques of modernization exerted pressure on the international development community, international organizations such as the World Bank responded (in 1973) by adopting the principle of "basic needs," a strategy that focuses on reducing poverty by narrowing in on key requirements for life: basic nutrition and the universal provision of health and educational services. The more robust forces that eventually displaced the postwar development paradigm were economic ones: as international Keynesianism was replaced by the monetarism and deregulation of the later 1970s and as western donors confronted the beginnings of the long downturn, Structural Adjustment Programs came to supplant modernization's strategies of foreign aid and technical assistance.[7]

This late twentieth-century reinvention of development, however, exhibited all the tendencies of its progenitor, which, as Sachs points out, was based on "four founding premises" that, by 1990, had lost relevance or had been discredited: the idea that the US "was at the top of the social evolutionary scale"; the idea that the US should lead in a world threatened by the Soviet menace; the idea that development could narrow the wealth gap between rich and poor nations (in fact, it doubled in size between 1960 and 1980); and finally, the idea that development should permit unbridled growth in all nations on earth.[8]

Books for Development

This study understands book development as an instantiation of the broader late twentieth-century development paradigm. It contends that book development carries out a specific function within the paradigm: book development initiatives tend to obfuscate capitalist relations in favour of culture. They suggest that there is no need to change anything about the way that capitalism is shaping things, turning instead to the book and its associated concepts of social mobility and individual improvement as ameliorative measures.

In the larger context of the emergence and elaboration of the development paradigm in the second half of the twentieth century, varying kinds of activities were imagined as suitable to the task of development. The thinking that conjoined *books* and development in these decades was not new. As Joseph Slaughter points out, it drew on a "common assumption about the role of literacy as a link between the material (socioeconomic) and spiritual (cognitive-epistemic) aspects of modernization that reflects a modern-democratic orthodoxy about the benefits and effects of reading and writing that coalesced over the course of the nineteenth and twentieth centuries." Yet in the international institutions that emerged after the Second World War, and particularly within the United Nations Educational, Scientific, and Cultural Organization (UNESCO) and its book- and literacy-oriented work, literacy came to be especially valued "as an essential technology for balancing the asymmetrical geopolitical conditions of an emergent international world system." However, a deep contradiction subtended this conviction, as Slaughter points out: "An analogous asymmetry manifests itself in the unevenness of the international economies" of the book – an unevenness, that, as we will see, emerged as a central concern of newly decolonized nations at UNESCO during the 1960s.[9]

The technical assistance and scholarship programs of development's high modernist period made space for the book. A speech delivered at the National Foreign Trade Convention in New York City in 1964 by Curtis G. Benjamin, then chairman of the board at McGraw-Hill Publishing Company, identified the value of books by invoking both the ideology of high modernism and the spectre of Soviet influence. Books have a "seminal importance that far outruns their small dollar value as a commercial product at home or an export commodity abroad," Benjamin insisted. They are "powerful forces" in "national development and international relations." They can play a "basic role in keeping English as the *lingua franca* of the free world." Because "emerging nations are prepared to import, along with our books, our ideas, our methods, our technology," books serve "in a correlative way as pioneers and conditioners of emerging new markets for U.S. materials, designs, products, and services." In Benjamin's estimation, the US was making a grave miscalculation in lagging behind the book export efforts of the Soviet Union. As Benjamin's words suggest and as the work of book historians such as Greg Barnhisel and Amanda Laugesen has demonstrated, book-related developmental assistance from state and nongovernmental organizations (NGOs) in the US, Britain, the Soviet Union, Germany, and other industrialized nations was an important aspect of the postwar development paradigm. Such schemes were linked to Cold War–era foreign policy goals and to the development of overseas markets for the books of the donor nations. In their 1980 study *Publishing in the Third World*, Philip Altbach and Eva-Maria Rathgeber note that the decline by the 1970s of book donation schemes can be explained by the fact that most western aid programs had by that time "shifted their focus to nonformal education and other areas of concern." This does not mean that western book development ceased but rather that it shifted tactics during the 1960s. Laugesen points out that the United States Agency for International Development (USAID) became a "major source of funding" for American book programs following its establishment in 1961. By the mid-1960s, it aimed not only to secure the distribution of American books abroad, but also to help "establish and expand overseas book industry capabilities through technical assistance grants and loans for writing, printing, publishing, and distributing." Recipients of USAID funding, such as Franklin Book Programs, sought to support the ideological aims of the US government as well as the "commercial interests of book publishers through helping to establish a global culture of modern commercial publishing."[10]

Book-related development was also important to the late twentieth-century work of UNESCO, established in 1945. UNESCO's constitution offers evidence of founding commitments to books, which complemented its efforts to combat illiteracy, initially through the ideal of "fundamental education." Early UNESCO action on the book included the Florence Agreement of 1950, which obliged signatory nations to exempt tariffs on books, and the Universal Copyright Convention of 1952, which introduced shorter copyright terms than the existing Berne Convention (a potential advantage for developing nations). However, according to Julian Behrstock, who directed UNESCO's book development initiatives between 1948 and 1976, it was not until the organization commissioned Robert Barker of the Publishers' Association of Great Britain to conduct a study of publishing in the postwar world that UNESCO's "book development" program became coherent. Barker's *Books for All: A Study of the International Book Trade* (1956) concluded that global book publishing was unevenly concentrated in ten nations. It was followed by more UNESCO-sponsored research on the book trade, including Robert Escarpit's *La Révolution du livre* (1965) and Barker and Escarpit's *The Book Hunger* (1973), as well as by action, including a series of regional conferences (in Asia, Africa, Latin America, and the Arab states) that led, among other things, to the creation of regional book development centres and national book development councils; UNESCO's declaration of 1972 as International Book Year; and the International Book Year's issue of a "Charter of the Book."[11]

Sarah Brouillette contends that the growing influence at UNESCO of the newly independent nations of Africa and other parts of the formerly colonized world during the 1960s and '70s led to newly politicized approaches to the book in this period, when "many people working with and for UNESCO were interested in attempting to translate research about underdeveloped book and media industries into specific strategies for reform." Yet these efforts, focused on remedying the inequalities in the global communications systems (of which the publishing industry was one important element), were ultimately opposed and defeated by the US and Britain and by the western media conglomerates based in those nations. Reflecting in the early 1980s on his *La Révolution du livre*, sociologist Robert Escarpit notes that his study was perhaps misnamed: despite the efforts of organizations like UNESCO, no book revolution occurred in the decades following the Second World War, though the creation of the paperback changed the meaning of the book, permitting it to enter the "mass distribution and consumption system." UNESCO initiatives from the late 1950s to the end of the '70s had certainly aimed to revolutionize book development. Yet despite the increased number of books published in the second half of the twentieth century – world book production, counted by number of titles, increased almost three times between 1950 and 1980 – "the structures of book production and distribution were not fundamentally changed." Escarpit's overview of book development in these years is resigned to the fact that "decolonization often stimulated book production less in the new nations than in the old colonizing countries which had now to meet the new demands from their former colonies for literacy campaigns or educational development."[12]

Much of the book historical scholarship that has accounted for book development has focused on the ideological motivations of the hegemonic donor nation (the US), but recent work on the literary and cultural institutions of the Cold War gauges more finely the ways that African writers negotiated with and responded to American development imperatives. Similarly, if the earliest work on UNESCO's postwar book development and literacy efforts emphasizes the influence of western European and American values on that institution, more recent scholarship points to the important interventions of Third World nations – in the majority at UNESCO during the 1960s and '70s – who insisted on reform of the emergent global communications order. *Books for Development* is deeply anchored in the archives of one donor nation and donor institutions from Canada, an approach that encourages focus on donor ideologies and values; however, I attend at significant moments, particularly in chapters 3 and 5, to the question of how recipients, whether in the Third World or in Canada, imagined the usefulness of what was cast as the axiomatically positive gift of books from Canada. Chapter 4, which analyzes not book donation but rather the importance of development-related experience to the forging of late twentieth-century anglophone settler nationalism, also reconfigures an approach that prioritizes the donor nation as the generative source of cultural and political values, turning its gaze on the ways in which settler Canadians adopted and adapted the ideas of Third World anti-colonialists for their own cultural nationalist ends.[13]

Settler-Colonial Canada and the Late Twentieth-Century Development Paradigm

The focus of this study is on Canadian uses of the book as an instrument of development, whether oriented externally (to South Asia, the Caribbean, Africa, etc.) or internally, to Indigenous communities in Canada. The Canadian history of development assistance has only very recently begun to attract attention, a trend that David Meren suggests is "consistent" with the "marginalizing of the Global South" in Canadian international history. Despite Canadian historians' slow uptake of development assistance, its history is central, as David Morrison contends, to Canada's twentieth-century economic relations with developing countries (trade and private investment in these same countries was minimal in this period). Foreign aid, Morrison claims, constituted "the dominant expression of Canada's North-South relations since the 1960s." There is a longer tradition of analyzing Canadian development assistance in political science and economics, and the work of political scientist Keith Spicer has been important here, influencing much of the historical scholarship. The legacy of the Canadian International Development Agency (CIDA, established in 1968 and dissolved in 2013) is central to debates about Canadian developmental assistance. As historian Kevin Brushett puts it, CIDA has been "variously critiqued for its ineffectiveness, its mixed and often conflicting objectives, and its role in maintaining Canada's economic and political hegemony vis-à-vis the peoples and nations of the Global South." While recent work on the NGO division of CIDA (established 1969) and on the history of Canadian NGOs more generally is complicating some of these critiques, it remains true that Canadian development assistance since the end of the Second World War, like development assistance more generally, has not significantly lessened global inequalities.[14]

Political economy approaches to Canadian development assistance have been especially committed to analyzing its failures, particularly after the neoliberal turn. In their earliest instantiations in the late 1970s, these critiques frame Canadian development assistance as "geared to 'aiding' the Canadian economy in general and corporate accumulation in particular" by providing a market for overproduced wheat and other commodities, by tying aid to the purchase of Canadian goods and services, and by legitimating the maintenance of "relations of global dominance." By the early 1990s, these scholars were analyzing how Department of Finance officials representing Canada at the World Bank and the International Monetary Fund endorsed the shift to Structural Adjustment Programs in the 1980s; this shift trickled down to CIDA, which increasingly tied aid during the latter half of the '80s to Structural Adjustment Program implementation. As Molly Kane points out, many Canadian NGOs were critical of Structural Adjustment Programs, but NGOs also played a "key role" in their implementation. According to Jamie Swift, among others, such an approach did little to improve life in impoverished nations: between 1980 and 1987, there was a net transfer of $287 billion USD from Third World nations to their northern creditors.[15]

Lacking a legislated basis for its development assistance, the Government of Canada (through its External Aid Office and, later, through CIDA) invoked varying justifications for its work in this domain in the late twentieth century. Morrison argues that political and foreign policy objectives were consistently important. Through the 1950s, the anti-communist intent of the Colombo Plan – an aid project for South and Southeast Asian nations developed by Commonwealth countries, including Canada, in the early 1950s – and the nourishment of the "Commonwealth link" guided forays into development. In the 1960s and '70s, aid was used to support France's former African colonies "in order to combat efforts by the government of Quebec to obtain international recognition." Other, more general objectives include "enhancing

Canada's prestige and goodwill," "augmenting its capacity and influence as an 'honest broker,'" and asserting difference from US foreign policy. What Morrison calls "statist" and "dominant-class" approaches to the analysis of Canada's aid performance have tended to bifurcate scholarly discussion; to the latter, which draws on Marxist theory to argue that Official Development Assistance has been "primarily an instrument for supporting the globalization of capitalist relations of production and entrenching the wealth, power, and privilege of dominant classes in both North and South," this book adds the question of settler colonialism. How did Canada's status as a settler-colonial nation shape its engagement of the development paradigm in the last half of the twentieth century? Building on the work of historians like Meren and Will Langford, I attempt to track what Langford calls the "domestic and foreign entanglements of development ideas, practices, and expertise," particularly as these shed light on the constitutive contradictions of settler-colonial ideologies.[16]

Canada's history as a settler colony is in fact crucial to the history of Canadians' implication in the development paradigm, whether in its late colonial, postwar, or later twentieth-century phases. The fact that the nation known as Canada shared some characteristics with the nations it sought to assist through the last half of the twentieth century is important; as we will see, these similarities were frequently cited by proponents of the nation's participation in emergent postwar development efforts. Morrison contends that, like the nations it sought to assist between 1968 and 1998, Canada experienced problems arising from external foreign economic control; a trade profile oriented to the export of primary products and the import of manufactured commodities; a relatively late experience of industrialization; a small population spread across a vast territory; and a tradition of state intervention in the marketplace and in the provision of infrastructure and social welfare. When we turn to the domain of books and publishing in the second half of the twentieth century, there are some parallels to be drawn between Canada and what came to be known as Third World nations: as we will see in chapters 2, 3, and 4, certain conditions were shared, such as the domination of the domestic publishing market by foreign companies (owned by the US and, to a lesser extent, Britain, in the case of Canada, and by former colonial powers in the case of many Third World nations); however, many other conditions experienced in former colonies, such as linguistic erasure and cultural assimilation efforts, did not apply straightforwardly in late twentieth-century Canada, particularly in relation to the dominant settler anglophone population, which shared the language of the former colonial power and the newly hegemonic US.[17]

The similarities are further complicated by the ongoing fact of internal colonization during this same period. Indeed, the emergence of the development paradigm in Canada did not occur in isolation from the operations of internal colonization. In the decades following the Second World War, Canadian foreign aid was fuelled by its prosperity – a prosperity that, as Jill Campbell-Miller points out, depended on its own colonizing forms of domestic resource extraction: "During the 1950s, Canadian industry fuelled the country's own economic growth by using the bountiful natural resources provided by lands taken from Indigenous communities, whether it was through mining, hydroelectric projects, or expanding agricultural production." This then produced "expertise" in "Canadian industries, universities, and governments" that Canadian officials felt was "relevant abroad," under the guise of Colombo Plan projects, for instance. Moreover, as chapters 2 and 5 explore, ideas about development came to shape postwar "Indian" policy, and Indigenous activists who formulated after the mid-1960s a critique of developmentalism did so by engaging the decolonial movements of African and other Third World nations.[18]

Analyzing Canadian involvement in the development paradigm of the second half of the twentieth century – and particularly Canadian involvement in book development – helps us to see contradiction as characteristic of a settler-colonial nation's enmeshment in developmentalism. Such antinomies are especially evident in the context of late twentieth-century book development, which depended on the book as a physical and symbolic manifestation of settler exceptionalism. In the chapters that follow, I track the important relation that emerged in the latter decades of the twentieth century between the book as an instrument of development and settler strategies of exceptionalism and indigenization.

Settler exceptionalism is of course older than the late twentieth century. In her reading of Anglo-Irish writer Anna Brownell Jameson's 1838 account of travelling in Upper Canada, Rachel Bryant locates a "system of thought and inscription" she names "settler exceptionalism":

"the idea of Canada as the place where a chosen and industrious people might take up the iconic mission of the New England Puritans and develop a nobler idea of what a Western nation can or should be." Bryant contends that this exceptionalism emerged in British North America in the decades following American independence, the product of a Loyalist splintering that produced an exceptionalism that differed from its American counterpart insofar as it framed the US as having "failed in its democratic vision." Bryant's analysis of a nineteenth-century British Canadian claim to a "separate and higher moral plane" finds echoes in studies such as Daniel Coleman's study of "white civility" and Margery Fee's tracking of long-standing settler claims to "civility," both of which lay important groundwork for the arguments I develop in the following pages.[19]

Significantly, Bryant sees a direct relationship between this nineteenth-century settler exceptionalism and the "conventional," twentieth-century "image of Canada as a kind of benevolent superpower in the world." This latter image has often been elaborated with reference to Lester B. Pearson's Nobel Peace Prize (given in 1957 for his role in recommending the first large-scale deployment of a UN Peacekeeping Force in the Suez Crisis of 1956) and to Canada's subsequent military and diplomatic support for UN-sponsored peacekeeping missions, which has older echoes in what Paulette Regan calls the "peacemaker myth" – the story of Canada as founded in peaceful treaty-making (as opposed to the violence of American colonization). David Webster analyzes these twentieth-century characteristics of the ideology of settler exceptionalism, demonstrating how foreign policy and international diplomacy in the postwar decades worked to distinguish Canada from both the old colonial powers and the hegemony of the US, emphasizing the nation's lack of a colonial past, its exemplification of a peaceful colony-to-nation transition, and its status as a "friend of the Third World" (via its support for the resolutions of the 1955 Bandung Conference, for instance). As Webster points out, however, this latter friendship had definite limits – as when decolonizing nations turned to revolution or secession.[20]

Historians of Canadian national identity and mythmaking in the decades following the Second World War have interrogated related narratives that were spun out of settler exceptionalism, namely the framing of Canada as a "middle power" and as committed to peacekeeping, international humanitarianism, and international human rights. The recent turn to Canada's international history through what Laura Madokoro and Francine McKenzie call the "prism of race" has been especially important to this work, producing new views of Canadians' entanglements in the late twentieth-century world that probe, among other themes, the "relationship between empire, identity, and liberal internationalism."[21]

Adam Chapnick shows how "middlepowerhood" emerged as a state identity in the context of the new international institutions of the postwar period, noting that this was a concept that Canada's federal government shoehorned onto the international stage by pairing the nation's size, material resources, influence, and stability with its willingness to assume responsibility in areas such as peacekeeping. Especially influential in the 1960s and '70s, Canada's middle power image, as Jamie Swift notes, cast the nation as a "helpful fixer" with "special ties" to the Third World (through its membership in the Commonwealth of Nations and its ties to *la francophonie*). If middlepowerhood rested for much of the late twentieth century on Canada's commitment to peacekeeping, this commitment, though productive of claims of moral superiority, produced a durable narrative that, as scholars such as Massimo Rubboli have pointed out, runs "counter to the actual history of Canadian military operations since the end of the Cold War." Though Canada was one of the largest contributors to peacekeeping in the 1970s and '80s, this commitment had significantly flagged by the early twenty-first century (in 2001, the nation ranked thirty-second among global peacekeepers). Moreover, as the work of Sherene Razack makes clear, Canada's later twentieth-century peacekeeping work in Somalia should be understood as a form of "new imperialism" that repeated colonial structures of power and ideologies of race.[22]

Running parallel to Canada's twentieth-century image as a peacekeeping middle power is what Vin Nguyen and Thy Phu call a narrative of "humanitarian exceptionalism" – a "belief that what sets Canada apart from the U.S. and other nation-states is its distinct benevolence and commitment to human rights." While this narrative has been leveraged in the recent past (in Prime Minister Justin Trudeau's response to President Donald Trump's 2017 ban on refugeed persons from Syria, for instance) and while it sometimes draws on pre-twentieth-century history (such as the narrative of the Underground Railroad that casts Canada as a land of freedom for fugitive slaves), it derives much power from twentieth-century examples, particularly Canada's acceptance of displaced persons in the wake of the Second World War and the Nansen Medal it received from the UN in 1986 for its commitment to alleviating the suffering of refugeed persons. Yet, as Jennifer Tunnicliffe's *Resisting Rights* contends, the mythologizing of Canada's late twentieth-century leadership in the field of international human rights obfuscates the "extent to which Canadian policy makers have historically opposed efforts at the UN to introduce and implement international treaties relating to human rights" – including the development and implementation of the UN's first human rights initiative, the International Bill of Rights – "often relying on arguments of federal jurisdiction to justify their position." Nguyen and Phu are wary of the "humanitarian tradition" because it "obscures exceptionality's varied operations," including the fact that Canada *needs* refugeed persons to "advance its cultural and political interests." Further, they add, "the Canadian settler state's capacity to grant political asylum to refugees – and assert its sovereign power – is contingent on its centuries-long colonial suppression of Indigenous sovereignty over land, natural resources, and people." Exceptionalism can obscure this important contingency, a characteristic that Bryant identifies with exceptionalism's operations in Anna Brownell Jameson's 1838 *Winter Studies and Summer Rambles*. This text, Bryant contends, depends on an opposition between British North American and American settler societies that is "largely illusory," a "construction made, at least in part, to conceal a more fundamental and ongoing struggle between Anglo-American and Indigenous modes of thought." Exceptionalism's power thus lies, at least in part, in what it conceals.[23]

Scholars of postcolonialism have frequently identified the book and print culture more generally as privileged instruments of colonial rule. According to Bryant, nineteenth-century settler exceptionalism in both the US and British North America was premised on the settler disavowal of Indigenous epistemologies, including non-alphabetic literacies, and the concomitant privileging of the written word as a means of mythologizing and canonizing a "chosen relationship to place." Fee argues that "much of the ideological work of colonization has been done by equating the use of writing in the phonetic alphabet with civilization." Fee's recent work dismantles the oral/literate binary upon which the civilized/savage distinction depends, drawing on the work of Indigenous scholars of orality and orature as well as on the

New Literacy Studies, which, in the late twentieth century, began to interrogate the long-standing European privileging of written over oral cultures. Challenging Walter Ong's argument in his influential *Orality and Literacy: The Technologizing of the World* (1982), literacy scholars such as James Paul Gee and Brian Street cast literacy not as an "autonomous" skill that is divorced from its social context (and thus, as Ong would have it, always capable of abstraction, analytical thought, and distancing) but as "ideological," a skill that is bound to what Street calls "'real' social contexts." In her reading of Syilx storyteller Harry Robinson's work, Fee rejects Ong's view of orality and literacy as "starkly conflicting," insisting that they are "intersecting practices that were privileged and used differently by different cultures."[24]

Given the long association of the book and literacy with "civilization" and with higher-order thinking, it is unsurprising that the book became central to the Canadian settler strategies deployed in the context of the late twentieth-century development paradigm. As discussed in chapter 3, James Robbins ("J.R." or "Roby") Kidd was a particularly prominent proponent of the idea that Canada's internationally recognized experiments in adult education, and, by association, its commitments to literacy and the book – its early experimentation with literacy initiatives for frontier workers and immigrants through programs like Frontier College, for instance – had uniquely prepared its citizens to tackle international development. Indeed, Canada's first NGO, also discussed in chapter 3, was a book donation program.

Settler exceptionalism is related to what Emma Battell Lowman and Adam J. Barker identify as one of the three "intertwined goals" of the "trajectory of settler colonialism," indigenization. Supporting "settler claims to the land and obscuring the violence and criminal nature of colonial dispossession," indigenization is the process by which, in the wake of elimination, settler societies render themselves the legitimate occupants of a territory. The strategy of indigenization, at least in its domestic or internal operations, is familiar enough in settler colonial studies. *Books for Development: Canada in the Late Twentieth-Century World* argues that its later twentieth-century *external* operations were intimately linked to this better-known domestic context, and, further, that the book was a key instrument in the external unfolding of the operations of settler exceptionalism and indigenization. While indigenization is often a domestic affair (the use of the phrase "native land" in the anglophone version of the national anthem of Canada, for instance), it is also an international one; settler indigenization can operate internally, via what Lorenzo Veracini calls the "appropriation of indigenous cultural attributes," but it can also function externally, aiming to identify the shared experiences that might be grounds for solidarity between the settler culture and formerly colonized nations. As Swift's comments above make clear, Canada's late twentieth-century middle power image was contingent on its "special ties" to the formerly colonized parts of the globe, ties that late twentieth-century liberal internationalists such as Kidd characterized as birthed by a common colonial experience. In the context of the late 1960s and '70s, a period examined in chapter 4, such indigenization was amplified by the rise of decolonization movements across the globe, movements that many young Anglo Canadians implicated in development work used in key ways – to describe their own experiences of "colonization" and thus to both occlude internal colonization and to cement their own place-claims, and to render their own position-takings vis-à-vis the Third World as forms of solidarity rather than domination.[25]

Whether at the level of the international multilateral organization, the state, or the NGO, settler Canadian participation in the book-related aspects of the development paradigm is important for a number of reasons. Yet, it must be acknowledged, books and printed matter constitute only one minor element of the history of Canadian developmental assistance. Frequently linked to educational or literacy-oriented development schemes, printed texts have never been particularly important in terms of numbers in this history. As chapter 2 demonstrates, the Canadian government's initial forays into book donation schemes in the late 1950s were very small when compared to the massive program being undertaken by the Soviet Union; they remained so. In 1964, Curtis G. Benjamin of McGraw-Hill estimated that the Soviet Union was spending just over $200 million (in US dollars) on its international book program (mostly aimed at nations in Asia and Africa), while the US spent only about $16.5 million for the same purpose in the same year, despite the fact that this was a period of robust experimentation for the United States Information Agency (USIA) and its numerous book export assistance programs. In his later "Benjamin Report" (published in 1984 as *U.S. Books Abroad: Neglected Ambassadors*), Benjamin demonstrates that the Soviet Union continued to dominate globally in the early 1980s in terms of its public support for book assistance programs.[26]

Despite the relatively minor role that books have played in Canadian development initiatives, this study contends that book development is nonetheless crucial to the late twentieth-century elaboration of settler-colonial logic in Canada. There are four main elements to this assertion: the first two examine book development in its outward-facing guise, as international development undertaken by Canadians, and the latter two analyze the inward-facing functions of book development, or rather, the ways that the international development paradigm came to both draw on and influence domestic settler contexts.

The first element of the argument claims that Canada's influence in the second half of the twentieth century on international organizations dedicated to education, literacy, and hence books was significant and, indeed, greater than its size and political power warranted. This influence drew on the robust legacies of settler Canada's pre-1950 voluntary sector, and especially on accomplishments in extension education, adult education, and literacy work. Also important to the strong postwar culture of developmentalism in Canada, as Kevin O'Sullivan contends in his work on the "NGO moment," was a long-standing Protestant missionary and service tradition that was, I contend, particularly bibliocentric. (This influence is analyzed in chapter 1 and returned to throughout; chapter 3, for instance, notes the importance of a Baptist upbringing and exposure to missionary culture for the book-centric work of liberal internationalist Kidd, and chapter 4 discusses the importance of Canada's social gospel–inspired adult literacy tradition to one of the nation's first NGOs, Canadian University Students Overseas.) Second, as I explore in chapters 3 and 4, Canada was in the second half of the twentieth century a global leader in terms of NGO activity, and the nation's first NGO was a book donation program, the Overseas Book Centre (established in 1959 in Toronto). Third, as chapter 4 makes clear, the involvement of Canadians in international development in the late twentieth century significantly shaped the domestic emergence of anglophone settler nationalisms, including cultural nationalisms related to the book. Fourth, as we will see in the final chapter, ideas about books, literacy, and education formed important elements of developmentalism's domestic turn.[27]

From the fledgling, state-led book donation efforts of the immediate postwar period (in the domain of cultural diplomacy and later, in the name of development); to the outsized role played by educationalist Kidd in the international literacy efforts of the postwar decades; to the important role of books in Canada's early NGO movement; to the avid participation of a generation of nationalist authors in development-related work in Africa during the late 1950s and the '60s; to the application of developmentalist logic to book- and literacy-related questions in Indigenous communities – books and the capacity to read and be improved by them have mattered to the elaboration of settler logic both internationally and domestically.

I unfold my arguments across five distinct chapters, each of which considers one or more instances of the book's entanglement in Canadian development initiatives. The first chapter analyzes the uses of the book in the early and mid-twentieth-century liberal missionary culture of the International Committee on Christian Literature for Africa, which was led in the interwar and war years by a Canadian. Focused on the late colonial period, this chapter demonstrates the late colonial genealogy of developmentalist thinking, while considering how the book development efforts of this period anticipated those that followed the Second World War.

The book's subsequent chapters deal with the decades that followed the Second World War, the age of development. Chapter 2 examines two postwar book diplomacy programs developed by the federal Department of External Affairs, the Annual Canadiana Book Presentation program (established in 1948) and Special Book Presentation Programme for Colombo Plan Area Countries (1956–59). While postwar book diplomacy efforts such as the Canadiana program participated in and adopted the rhetoric of the cultural diplomacy practices dominated in this period by the US, these same efforts tendentiously lauded Canada's ostensibly robust domestic publishing industry via an indigenizing cultural nationalism. The subsequent program, developed under the auspices of the Colombo Plan, was oriented more to emerging forms of development aid than to cultural diplomacy, but, like its predecessor, it had to negotiate the contradictions produced by the intersections of international and domestic policy. Promoting liberal internationalism as the identity of the Commonwealth of Nations, the Special Book Presentation Programme silenced the fact of Canada's internal colonization.

Moving away from the state-centric view of chapter 2, chapter 3 turns to the nongovernmental book development efforts of the 1950s, '60s, and '70s, considering civil society involvement in new international organizations like UNESCO and nongovernmental book development programs such as the Overseas Book Centre, Canada's first NGO. These efforts helped settler Canadians distinguish themselves on an international stage from both Europe (whose nations had not recently been colonies) and the US (which, many argued, was recasting the old imperialism) and aided in the elaboration of Canada's identity as a "friend of the Third World." However, this book-centric voluntary internationalism – known by 1950 under the rubric of "development" – did not necessarily redound to the benefit of the nations and peoples it was meant to assist.

Chapter 4 takes a slightly different approach to the study of Canadian book development, examining not book development initiatives per se, as the other chapters do, but rather the ways that involvement in the "NGO moment" shaped the nationalisms of anglophone settler writers – Margaret Laurence, Dorothy Livesay, and Dave Godfrey – who became important to the emergent canon of English Canadian literature.

In the book's final chapter, I track the complex trajectory of developmentalism's domestic turn in the latter decades of the twentieth century. This chapter takes two elements as its focus. First, following the lead of scholars who have studied the mutual implication after 1960 or so of outwardly-oriented development and the work of federal policy aimed at Indigenous Peoples, I examine the settler application, beginning in the late 1950s, of developmentalist thinking to the questions of book and library service provision to Indigenous communities in Ontario. Second, I consider the ways that Indigenous activists and thinkers from across Canada, many of whom were engaged with the ideas of late twentieth-century African decolonization movements, responded to, reframed, and sometimes rejected outright the premises of developmentalist ideology, especially as this was relevant to thinking about books and literacy.

A brief comment on terminology is necessary. Throughout this study, I use terms such as *Third World*, *developing nation*, and *development* without scare quotes, but the study emphasizes at every turn the historical emergence of these terms from material relations of exploitation. As will be discussed in more detail in the chapters (and especially chapters 2 and 3), these are phrases that acquired particular meanings in English after the Second World War and especially in the context of the Cold War and its "three worlds" – the capitalist First World, the communist Second World, and the decolonizing (or developing)

Third World. Michael Denning labels the period between 1945 and 1989 the "age of three worlds," arguing that during these decades "we imagined that the world was divided into three ... as if each were a separate planet involved in an elaborate and dangerous orbit around the others." Jamie Swift observes that the phrase Third World likely came into English from its usage in France in the 1950s (the concept of the "tiers monde" drawing from the older French concept of the "tiers état"). By the early 1950s this distinction of worlds was, according to Arturo Escobar, "firmly in place" in institutions such as the UN. Yet the idea of a Third World in need of development was not naming after 1950 a natural or immutable characteristic of nations like India, but was rather, as Davis (drawing on Alfred Sauvy) puts it, "the outcome of income and ecological differentials – the famous 'development gap' – that were shaped most decisively in the last quarter of the nineteenth century," during the age of imperialism. It is also important to note that this study employs historically specific terminology for development funds: prior to 1970, such funds were referred to as "foreign aid," but, by the early 1970s, the term "development assistance" came to supplant that phrase.[28]

1

"Famine of Books"

Late Colonial Book Development and Margaret Wrong in Africa (1929–48)

The history of the book in Africa has been largely written by non-Africans. David Johnson and Caroline Davis point to the consistent ways the book has signified in this western scholarship: European histories from the colonial period frame the introduction of European books into Africa as a "benevolent deed of spreading light in the darkness," and though the period of political decolonization led more western historians to acknowledge the violence of European colonialism, the book has generally been exonerated. In this narrative, the book is "compensation." As Johnson and Davis write, "the African who has survived military conquest, economic exploitation, political subordination and cultural imperialism gradually seizes the book, first as a means of attaining literacy, and later as a means of writing back to empire." In line with the larger tendency in book historical scholarship to cast, as Margery Fee puts it, the oral as a stage prior to writing and thus "incompatible with literacy and a sense of history," book historical scholarship on Africa has tended to occlude the continent's precolonial manuscript traditions. The late colonial book development initiative that this chapter tracks must be analyzed in relation to such print-centric ideologies.[1]

Christian missionaries began establishing missions throughout Africa in the mid-eighteenth century and soon thereafter began to add modest printing presses to their repertoires. According to Hans Zell, they were the continent's first publishers. Missions on the continent assumed from their earliest days the task of education; by the 1920s, it was estimated that they provided 92 per cent of African education. Missions thus had a practical need for literature to use in classrooms. To this end, they published religious materials (translations of the Bible, hymn books, evangelical tracts, and the like), as well as simple instructional readers, grammars, and vocabularies. Religious and secular works alike were solicited, translated, printed, and distributed through the efforts of the missionary societies (though these stages of production did not always occur in Africa). According to Derek R. Peterson and Emma Hunter, missions also produced more ephemeral kinds of print, such as newsletters, pamphlets, and newspapers, which functioned as "vehicles by which to manage the enlargement of scale in their work, a means also to shape converts' reading habits." Whatever print form they were working in, missionaries in Africa, unlike their European commercial counterparts in the later twentieth century, favoured publishing in African vernaculars, and the first printed texts in many African languages were the products of mission presses. Peterson and Hunter contend that missionaries' "evangelical theology inclined them to regard vernacular language as an essential expression of a people's identity, a vehicle, therefore, for Christian revelation." In most parts of Africa, missions also made the first formal studies of African languages (including word lists, grammar books, and dictionaries, though their newspapers also became sites for the standardization of orthography for African vernaculars). In tandem with the forces of colonization and the field of comparative linguistics, evangelical missionaries of the nineteenth and twentieth centuries exerted what Peterson calls European "definitional authority" over African languages, asserting standards through a dizzying array of print projects that included essay competitions, sponsored translations, funded publications, and dictionaries.[2]

As part of their efforts to create and support print cultures, missionaries in Africa expended considerable effort in both cataloguing what existed and furnishing what did not. In 1923, for instance, a group of British missionary societies formed an African Literature Subcommittee, which published a bibliography of "African Christian Literature." The missionaries from fourteen nations who gathered in 1926 in Le Zoute, Belgium to discuss "educational work in Africa" determined that there was a "great need of literature in Africa, both in the vernaculars and in the languages of various governments." From such early efforts came the International Committee on Christian Literature for Africa (ICCLA), established as a subcommittee of the International Missionary Council in 1929 with a mandate to "promote the preparation, publication and distribution of literature for use in connexion with missionary work in Africa." The ICCLA had two sections at its founding, one in London and the other in New York City. According to Ruth Compton Brouwer, Margaret Wrong, the Canadian-born secretary of the association from 1929 to her death in 1948, interpreted the ICCLA mandate "broadly and creatively," concerned as she was with promoting the "development of written literature by Africans."³

Examining ICCLA documents alongside the work of historians of late colonial development, this chapter builds on Compton Brouwer's claims about the effects of the ICCLA's work in interwar and postwar British Africa, focusing on the book's imbrication in the early and mid-twentieth-century liberal missionary culture of the ICCLA to track how ideas about book development proper to this late colonial period might be related to those that emerged later, in the postwar period, whether at the level of international organizations like UNESCO, the state, or the NGO. This discussion of late colonial book development is elaborated in relation to two claims: first, the chapter argues that the ICCLA was enmeshed in a late colonial vision of education for Africans that failed to acknowledge the inevitability of self-government and the need for structural change – that, in fact, substituted education and the book for actual self-governance; second, it considers the ambivalent legacy of the ICCLA's nourishment of the forms of literature cooperation that eventually became Colonial Literature Bureaus. In both instances, late colonial book development, like its postwar counterpart, instrumentalized the book as part of a vision of development that forestalled discussions about fundamental political and economic change.

The chapters that follow this one examine book development initiatives that are contemporary with the emergence of the postwar development paradigm and associated with governmental and non-governmental organizations in Canada. This chapter is adjacent to these parameters: first, as I have noted, it offers a view of the book's imbrication in late colonial development initiatives rather than those of the postwar period. These were British initiatives in colonial development and welfare that began in the interwar period to take up, among other issues, the question of colonial education. Second, the association that forms the heart of this case study, the ICCLA, was British and American rather than Canadian. Yet its secretary for almost two decades was the Toronto-born Margaret Wrong. Though she lived her adult life in Britain, Wrong maintained very close ties to Canada during her life. Born in 1887 to a prominent settler Canadian family – her father was the Canadian historian George MacKinnon Wrong and her mother, Sophia Hume Blake, was the daughter of Edward Blake, premier of Ontario in the early 1870s and leader of the Liberal Party of Canada during the 1880s – Wrong, known to her family as "Marga," was the eldest of five children. She was educated at Somerville College, Oxford, before going to the University of Toronto to earn a master's degree in history; she remained in Canada (teaching courses in English and history at the University of Toronto and founding a Women's Union at the university) until 1921, when she became travelling secretary for the World Student Christian Federation and, subsequently, secretary of the British Student Christian Movement. As Compton Brouwer notes, Wrong's work with this latter organization took her to sub-Saharan Africa in 1926, a tour that demonstrated her "adaptability and enthusiasm, and liberal tendencies on race questions." "Along with her Canadian identity," Compton Brouwer contends, "these qualities made her a congenial figure for the reform-minded mission bureaucrats within the IMC [International Missionary Council]." As secretary of the ICCLA, Wrong drew on her Canadian connections: when she made her tours of North America, Canadian stops were always included, and Canadian churches were among the ICCLA's regular supporters. Moreover, the Inter Church Council of Canada was the major funder of one of the ICCLA's flagship projects, *Books for Africa*, a journal for educators in Africa.[4]

The ICCLA was British and American, to be sure, but Wrong's leadership demonstrates the closely interwoven relationships of the missionary cultures and institutions of Britain, America, and Canada in the late nineteenth and early twentieth centuries. Such relationships form the backdrop to what Kevin O'Sullivan identifies as the missionary-centric, "broadly Anglophone tradition of aid" in Britain and Canada. Both nations emerged as leaders in voluntary sector developmentalism after the Second World War in what Compton Brouwer has identified as the "missions-to-development trajectory." The "Anglophone tradition of aid" that O'Sullivan traces to nineteenth-century Protestant missionary cultures in both Britain and Canada was a remarkably biblio- and print-centric one, though the book-work of missionary groups leaned in an increasingly secular direction in the twentieth century. In the Canadian context, this tendency is especially apparent in the Canadian Reading Camp Movement (later Frontier College), an adult literacy program that was founded in 1899 by a Presbyterian minister, Alfred Fitzpatrick; in the international context – but one that is nonetheless firmly attached to Canada, as I have argued – it is apparent in the work of the ICCLA. This domestic and international book-work was deeply ideological: as I have argued elsewhere, Frontier College took books to frontier labour camps for the purpose of assimilation to a liberal-capitalist order; the ICCLA under Margaret Wrong's direction took books across British Africa as a means of absorbing emergent critiques of empire and of demonstrating the continued necessity of British tutelage in an era of transition.[5]

Late Colonial Development, the ICCLA, and the Book

Though book development is more commonly associated with the development paradigm of the postwar years and the later twentieth century, the interwar work of the ICCLA anticipated many of its motivating ideas. The development paradigm is premised on what Gilbert Rist calls a "linear reading of world history" in which the "progressive access of every nation to the benefits of development" is possible. As Rist notes, in western European societies, the idea of development ceased toward the end of the seventeenth century to be subject to the idea of a limit – "a kind of optimum level" beyond which growth must move "downward to comply with the laws of 'nature' and God's plan." As part of the more general development paradigm, book development proceeds from a simple premise: given access to the same printed matter available in the West, nations needing development would "catch up" to their more developed counterparts. As it was invoked across the western world in the decades following the Second World War, the concept of book development – especially in the guise of book donation schemes – did not always include assessments of the structural inequalities that keep formerly colonized societies poor, favouring instead the idea that addressing what UNESCO would come to call (in the 1960s) "book hunger" was at the centre of economic and social development.[6]

From its inception in 1929, the ICCLA articulated many of the questions and book-related ideologies that have come to be associated with later twentieth-century book development. The basic line of developmentalist thinking identified by Rist is clear in the report from the 1926 Le Zoute conference (at which the ICCLA was formed), which claims that the future of Africa is associated with "the moral, physical and intellectual development of the African peoples" and that Africans themselves are not yet ready to "carry out that development": "Only by a process of education – which includes work, but much more – can they be fitted to take their share in developing Africa. Physical and moral improvement of the African is a necessary condition of the economic development of the continent." But what did this "physical and moral improvement" entail?[7]

Frederick Cooper tells us that missionary practice in Africa focused on the "individual, shunting aside kinship groups, councils of elders, age groups, and other collectives basic to African life." This line of thinking is evident in ICCLA materials: in chapbook series such as "Little Books for Africa" and the "African Home Library," for example, the ICCLA sought to communicate to individual readers the message that print could be a safe bridge across the chasm separating tradition and modernity. Though not a common feature of these series, the coming-of-age story, with its isolation of a unique individual in the community, suggests that personal development is not a matter of harmonizing with the accepted truths of the community but of exposing irrational precepts. In *King Khama* by Florence Allshorn (the first title in the "Little Books for Africa" series, published in 1927), for instance, a kindly narrator presents the coming-of-age story of the eponymous King, the uniquely brave and good missionary-educated son of a village chief in Bechuanaland who must convince both his people and his father to reject the "fear and tyranny of the old ways" for the "liberty of Christ." Doing this involves not just exposing superstition as false but also imposing limits on white men, whose brandy is destroying his community and whose commercial interests do not consider the people's welfare. Khama's Christian literacy makes it possible for him to discern what is right, to take what is best from contact (the Queen, rationality, principles of Christian justice) and to reject the rest (brandy, money-minded white men). *King Khama* affirms that the kingdom thrives under such leadership.[8]

More common in these chapbook series than the isolation of the individual is an emphasis on the importance of safeguarding community and tradition from the despoiling influence of modernity. As we will see, this theme emerged in the larger context of the ICCLA's promotion

Figure 1.1 Florence Allshorn, *King Khama*, 1927.

of differential (vocational and industrial) education for Africans. In this sense, what late colonial book development shares with its postwar counterpart is the use of books (and education and literacy more broadly) in an ameliorative capacity – as a means of forestalling the possibility of the political change that would be necessary for colonized or decolonizing peoples to alter their own fates.

The larger point here is that late colonial development, which is the context for the birth of the ICCLA, forms a key period in the history of development. Summarizing the work of scholars who, like Cooper and Christophe Bonneuil, emphasize the importance of late colonial development to development's history, Joseph Morgan Hodge notes that "it would take the crisis of the Great Depression before the European powers were prepared to provide metropolitan funding, administrative services, and specialist personnel on a significant and extended scale." This more "*dirigiste* agenda," as Bonneuil describes it, "intervened more directly in the economy, and took steps toward planning and state regulation," inaugurating the modern age of development. British interwar colonial policy, beginning with the 1929 Colonial Development Act, was designed to benefit the struggling metropolitan economy. Bonneuil identifies the shifting relation between the colonial state and rural societies in British Africa as key to this moment; attempting to make agrarian societies legible to the state (and hence subject to new kinds of political control), what Bonneuil call the "emerging developmentalist state" worked through "transportation, irrigation, and agricultural 'modernization,' education, standardization of units, and integration of producers into the market." It was not until the mid-1930s that colonial policy became more focused on attempts to grapple with labour unrest and, in Cooper's words, to "reframe" the problem of strikes as one of "development": "Better social services and economic growth would remove the causes of disorder." This new commitment to "revitalizing empire in Africa" was challenged but also accelerated by the Second World War. The "more expansive definition of development" implemented through the Colonial Development and Welfare Act of 1940 (and beyond) aimed to legitimize imperial rule by ameliorating conditions in the colonies through greater investments and the provision of social welfare services. Monica M. Van Beusekom and Dorothy L. Hodgson argue that "for most Africans," the colonial development programs of the postwar years were not new; rather, the "novel" feature of these programs was their "heightened scale and intensity" – their emphasis on grants instead of loans, for instance, or their faith in large-scale projects guided by a complex bureaucracy that could draw on scientific and technical expertise. The new language of colonial development was also simply a way of defining the problem. As Cooper contends, it allowed the Colonial Office (the department of the British government tasked with overseeing most of Britain's imperial territories) to set aside many other potential definitions, such as class, or wage exploitation, among others.[9]

As what Compton Brouwer calls an "instrument" of the "liberal missionary reformism" of the early twentieth century, the ICCLA offers a particularly telling demonstration of the relations between early twentieth-century missionary work and late colonial development schemes in Africa. Especially important to this relation is the question of education, a feature of the emergent interventionist developmentalist state in Africa after 1930 or so. According to Compton Brouwer, the ICCLA

> came out of a period when leading missionaries and missionary bureaucrats were seeking to improve the standards of their educational work in Africa and to be less ethnocentric in their approach to African cultures. It was also the product of a decade during which the British imperial state undertook to provide increased financial support for missionaries' educational initiatives, both as a practical way of obtaining literate African men for low-echelon positions in colonial service and as a response to pressure from humanitarians like [International Missionary Council member Joseph] Oldham to make schooling more readily available and more directly useful to Africans.

Oldham had been responsible for securing the cooperation of British missionary organizations and the Colonial Office with the two Education Commissions that the American Phelps-Stokes Fund carried out in Africa during the 1920s (1920 and 1924) under the direction of American sociologist Thomas Jesse Jones. Kenneth James King notes that the commissions' recommendations offered a "prescription for cooperation between missions and government which, if heeded by the missions, could secure the place of specifically Christian schools as governments increasingly took control of education in Africa." Indeed, this is the argument that Oldham relayed in publications such as his 1922 *Education in Africa*. The model of education that the commissions recommended – and that Oldham began to associate with mission schools – was vocational (rather than "literary"). It took its inspiration from the differential education for African Americans that had been developed in the southern United States by figures such as Booker T. Washington as a temporary solution to the apparently insoluble problem of racial discrimination. In Sybille Küster's words, this vocational theory was "rooted in notions of African backwardness and racial inferiority," and, as King observes, it appealed to its white proponents on the grounds that it could shelter the "simplicity" of African life from the outside world and help Africans "fulfil better what they naturally were" (a race of peasants). Unsurprisingly, the theory of differentiated education for African Americans and Africans was not uncontested. For instance, as King notes, in the lead-up to the Le Zoute conference, W.E.B. DuBois called out the commissions' dismissal of higher education for Africans, their fear of African independence, and their accommodation to the labour market needs of white settler industry in Africa.[10]

Edward H. Berman points to the influence that the two Phelps-Stokes Commissions had on the Colonial Office, which "needed an African education policy" in the wake of the First World War. According to C.P. Groves, the commissions' reports identified education as an "essential service" that had been provided almost exclusively by missionary groups and pointed to the "meagre expenditure by governments on African education – ranging from four per cent of total revenue to vanishing point," arguments that led colonial governments across British Africa to commit larger proportions of revenues to the education work of missionaries. The fund's Education Commissions also shaped the Colonial Office's common educational policy for Africa, especially its emphasis on the importance of adapting education to the "mentality, aptitudes, and traditions of the various peoples," developed first through an Advisory Committee that was formed in 1923.[11]

The formation of the ICCLA can be traced to this convergence of missionary-led reform and late colonial development initiatives. In the interwar period, many Christian missionaries working in Africa sought new forms of cooperation and reform. Anticipating the interests that would come to seize the Colonial Office in the later interwar period, an unprecedented number of these reform-minded missionaries, along with the Phelps-Stokes commissioners, gathered at a 1926 conference in Le Zoute, Belgium to discuss questions of health, population, land, labour, and education in Africa. The Le Zoute recommendations and resolutions had what Groves calls a "profound" effect on missionary policies and practices in Africa. The creation of the education-centric ICCLA was but one of these effects. Groves's summary of the ICCLA's work indicates the extent to which the reform-minded missionaries of the interwar period sought to attract the notice and support of the Colonial Office and of colonial governments. According to him, Wrong's initiation and direction of a "continent-wide movement for the provision of books for Africa," with its "stimulating visits and well-planned objectives," urged colonial governments to "play their part." While the ICCLA was largely funded through missionary societies, philanthropic organizations, including the Carnegie Corporation and the Phelps-Stokes Fund, assisted with travel grants and funds for special projects. As we will see, by the period of the Second World War, the ICCLA was also receiving direct support for its work from the Colonial Office.[12]

From 1929 to the early 1960s, the ICCLA functioned not as a missionary publisher but rather as a coordinating body that aimed to survey the literature needs of Africans, to increase the production of printed texts for African readers (by both African and non-African authors and in both African and non-African languages), and to improve the distribution of printed material on the continent. As ICCLA secretary, Margaret Wrong toured the continent many times in order to further this work: her first ICCLA trip took her to eastern and central Africa in the first half of 1933; in 1936, she returned to visit British colonies in southern Africa; in 1939, she crossed the continent from Kenya to the Gold Coast; in 1944, she visited West Africa; and in 1948, the year she died (while on tour in Uganda), she was in East Africa (see figure 1.2). Typically, Wrong alternated these tours of Africa with trips to North America, where she kept the missionary and church organizations that funded the ICCLA apprised of literature needs on the continent. In the reports she penned in the wake of her tours, she points to the concerns that animated her work. Wrong's early reports from Africa demonstrate the influence of the major findings of the Phelps-Stokes Education Commissions on the ICCLA, especially the commission's calls to amend educational approaches that bore no relevance to the life of the African communities and to remedy problems resulting from

Figure 1.2 Margaret Wrong, Rev. S. Moore, and three teacher trainees on the border between Sudan and Uganda, 10 April 1948.

a lack of cooperation among missionaries working in education. She observes, for instance, that "school textbooks and religious literature should be far more vitally related than they are at present to the actual life of the communities." The reports also dwell on questions of intermission cooperation, including the need for coordination in selecting African vernaculars to perpetuate in print and in establishing standard orthographies. Clearly anticipating a role for colonial governments, Wrong identifies the need for intermission literature commissions, which could coordinate the regional interests of governments and missions regarding language, education, publishing, and book distribution, and for interterritorial textbook committees, through which governments and missions could establish standard teaching texts. Such cooperating bodies did indeed follow from Wrong's efforts: for instance, the government of Northern Rhodesia agreed during Wrong's 1936 tour to create an African Literature Committee with government, mission, and African members.[13]

Wrong's second and third tours, financed by the Carnegie Corporation, took her in 1936 to the British colonies of southern Africa and in 1939 from Kenya to the Gold Coast (see figure 1.3). These visits involved a greater degree of contact with government officials, particularly those

Figure 1.3   Margaret Wrong at a local market in Nyasaland, 1936.

involved in education, than her 1933 trip. Wrong's report on these tours indicates that they were carried out in concert with missions connected to the ICCLA and with the education departments of the colonies in question. She notes that "for each tour the Colonial Office sent letters of introduction to local governments, and in every case the Departments of Education co-operated actively in providing facilities and in sparing time for consultation about literature needs." Indeed, Wrong's 1939 letters record frequent meetings with directors of education and officials from colonial departments of education across the region. Wrong was also clearly aware that this contact could be made to produce fruit back in England. Her 1939 report reminds her readers that a new department devoted to social services had recently been established in the Colonial Office, a development that the ICCLA could make use of: "General literature should be one of the social services considered in connection with this department."[14]

Not surprisingly, this cooperation with colonial governments in British Africa placed the ICCLA in explicitly politicized contexts. Things could hardly have been otherwise: the period of the later 1930s was characterized by successive strikes across British Africa, a key impetus, Cooper contends, for the 1940 Colonial Development and Welfare Act. Wrong's outline for the second (1936) tour recounts that she will respond to a government commission related to the 1935 workers' strike in the Copperbelt, a centre of mining activity in Northern Rhodesia, by visiting the Rhodesias and Nyasaland to investigate the government's claims that Watchtower literature was largely responsible for the subversion of "civil and spiritual authority" in the area. (Sects of the Watch Tower Bible and Tract Society were just one manifestation of the millenarian and Adventist churches that attracted thousands of African followers during the industrialization of parts of southern Africa in the early twentieth century.) Wrong's tepid assessment of the situation in the mining compound at the Copperbelt indicates that she was unwilling to name causes of discontent as anything more than a need for more "reposeful" social activities than a beerhall. Similarly, colonial authorities failed to name the grievances (including very poorly remunerated labour) of their African subjects, though, as Cooper points out, the commission that studied the strike recognized the problem of falling wages and the gap between wages for African and European workers. Higginson contends that authorities ultimately chose to turn Watchtower sects and their literatures into "specters" and sought to ameliorate the instability of migrant labour through policies of "stabilization." Here is a good demonstration of the ideology of the book that the ICCLA embodied in the interwar years: Wrong's reports tend to focus on the ameliorative capacity of "good literature" (both religious and secular) – the more "reposeful" alternative to the beerhall in mining compounds, for instance – without necessarily identifying specific economic, social, or political problems or their causes. Though her reports occasionally identify specific sources of oppression under colonial rule – the low wages paid to African mineworkers in South Africa, for instance – they more generally frame "literature" as part of a larger Christianization that would be, it is assumed, beneficial to African societies that had, as she contends in *The Land and Life of Africa*, "been swept so suddenly into all the devious currents of modern life."[15]

Wrong's work assessing literature needs and promoting book production for African readers necessarily involved her in questions of selection and curation. She solicited manuscripts (often from missionaries) for series such as "Little Books for Africa" and the "African Home Library," advertised books that could be used in African educational or other settings through the ICCLA periodical *Books for Africa*, and furnished simple periodical literature for Africans in *Listen*. In the 1934 account of her first (1933) African tour for the ICCLA, Wrong indicates her concern with literary quality: "As literacy in European language grows, people will read what they can get – good, bad, or indifferent. The question of general European literature for the African includes helping him to form a sound literary taste while he's in school." Wrong does not identify the elements of this "sound literary taste," but goes on to note that it can only be formed if African readers have access to literature in European languages "written by Africans and Europeans against a background of African life and thought."[16]

In Wrong's other literary curations, this idea is extended into a more explicitly differentiated concept of reading matter for Africans. This differentiation was structured along the lines of the four "simples" that guided the Phelps-Stokes Commissions: health, home life training, industry (including agriculture), and recreation. The inaugural issue of *Books for Africa* called missionary educators' attention to two books that were pillars of differentiated education – Edwin W. Smith's *Aggrey of Africa* (a biography of the Gold Coast–born and missionary-educated James Aggrey, who went on to higher education in the US before taking up employment with the Phelps-Stokes Commissions in Africa) and Booker T. Washington's *Up from Slavery*. Both titles were published in abridged form by G. Harrap & Co. as part of a series of supplementary readers. Because the former abridgement is "better suited for Europeans than for African readers," Wrong notes that the ICCLA is supporting the preparation of a new biography of Aggrey "specially adapted for Africa." A 1943 bibliography of materials for literacy campaigns that Wrong published in *Books for Africa* features pamphlets and books related to Christian living (*Christian Family Life, Studies for Parents on the Christian Home*); agricultural and industrial topics (*A Practicable Poultry Improvement Scheme, Bees and How to Handle Them, Some Industries of Nyasaland and Nigeria*); and health, hygiene, and home life (*The Fight for Health, Health and the Home*). Also included (particularly in the "Little Books for Africa" series) are English translations of African folk tales (*The Leopard and the Goat, Tales of Tortoise*, and so on). Echoing the Phelps-Stokeist impulses to encourage agricultural and village-based pursuits and to preserve traditional African life – often because the "detribalization" of semiskilled Africans posed, in colonies such as Kenya, the risk of politicization and mass protest – such lists avoid political and economic topics almost entirely.[17]

As a curator of literatures for Africa, Wrong was also influenced by Phelps-Stokeist theories regarding African vernaculars. These theories must be distinguished from those of later African promoters of African languages, such as Ngũgĩ wa Thiong'o: the Phelps-Stokes commissioners advocated for the use of vernacular languages because of their particular conception of racial evolution. As the report of the first Phelps-Stokes Commission, *Education in Africa* (1922), concludes, "the processes of education must begin with the characteristics of the people as they are and help them to evolve to the higher levels." While "Native people are as a rule eager to learn an European language," education must begin with African vernaculars, which are suitable to the stage of development in which black Africans find themselves. Wrong's promotion of African vernaculars was both consistent with missionary traditions in Africa and reconciled easily with the Phelps-Stokeist emphasis on education that was adapted to what its proponents identified as the needs of rural African communities and its rejection of "literary" or academic programs in metropolitan languages for rural populations. While the texts that Wrong helped to usher into production in her role as secretary of the ICCLA – the periodicals *Books for Africa* and *Listen* and publishers' series such as "African Home Library" and "Little Books for Africa" – were mostly written in English, her work left a parallel legacy of support for African vernaculars.[18]

For instance, as Compton Brouwer notes, the short texts published in *Listen* were designed to be translated in African languages (or French or Portuguese) and issued in alternative formats. Wrong's reports from her many tours of Africa show that she sought at every turn to cultivate relationships with educated Africans and missionaries fluent in African languages who might produce translations and adaptations of texts; the ICCLA provided subventions for this kind of work. Wrong's ongoing support of literature and translation bureaus, such as the Hausa Translation Bureau in northern Nigeria, was another feature of her commitment to the encouragement of vernacular literature production. As Wrong's address "The Importance of Literatures in African Languages" indicates, her commitment to African languages was embedded in her belief that British colonial policy was superior to French and Portuguese policy in Africa, which had discouraged "the development of African languages" by insisting on French and Portuguese in primary education. A better path, Wrong believed, lay along the route of linguistic diversity, which could be ensured only through primary schooling in African vernaculars and, further, the "encouragement of African authorship," which was crucial to "literature in the true sense of the term, in African languages."[19]

Though the advent of war meant that Wrong was less able to do fieldwork in Africa, it was in other ways a tremendous motor for the work she was attempting to do. The carapace of colonialism in Africa was cracking during the interwar years, as the strike wave of the late 1930s suggests; it split open in the aftermath of the Second World War. Cooper points to the multi-dimensional character of this fracturing. Most obviously, the war brought the contradictions of colonial rule into new visibility: its reliance on ideologies of racial differentiation and its suppression of self-determination could not be squared with the challenge the Allies had posed to Axis powers, particularly not on a continent with a restive population. At the same time, the Colonial Office's attempts to reconcile such contradictions through developmentalism (namely, the Colonial Development and Welfare Act of 1940 and the increased funds channelled through this act in 1945) had the effect of urging Africans to imagine themselves as citizens, even if Africans in the British territories were never given this identity. As difficult labour markets, housing shortages, and inflation in postwar British Africa renewed strike action, the Labour government moved from the long-standing policy of indirect rule to one of local government, a policy that would encourage regional councils to take charge of issues like education. This policy had the effect of hastening the end of colonial rule in places like the Gold Coast, and, Cooper argues, across British Africa, not just because of burgeoning nationalist demands, but also because the British government, like its French counterpart, could "not accept the costs of modernizing colonialism" when the "political and economic benefits were so uncertain."[20]

Like many of her progressive contemporaries, Wrong saw colonial developmentalism as an imperial obligation – or, as the Fabian Colonial Bureau (of which Wrong was a member) had it, a "legacy of responsibility" – rather than as a path to immediate independence. Her wartime letters to ICCLA supporters evince great confidence in the development commitments of the Colonial Office, describing the aims of the Colonial Development and Welfare Act of 1940 as the "protection and advance of the interests and inhabitants in the colonies." This was a moment of opportunity for the ICCLA, which found new sources of connection and support for its work in the Colonial Office. Wrong focused some of her efforts on meeting the increased demand for literacy and literature that the war engendered. Her efforts bore some fruit: by 1939, for instance, the British Council was supporting the ICCLA's magazine *Listen* as a kind of mass subscriber (the Council purchased five hundred copies to be distributed to African schools and clubs), and it was also in the early war years supplying books and magazines to the fledgling libraries in West Africa that Wrong was attempting to get off the ground with funds from the Carnegie Corporation. But it was in the more general area of administrative and economic responsibility for education in Africa that the ICCLA aimed to effect the most significant transformation in the context of the developmental turn at the Colonial Office. To this end, Wrong's 1942 study *Five Points for Africa* asserts that an older arrangement of somewhat ad hoc grants-in-aid to missionary schools would no longer suffice in postwar British Africa: "Africans are beginning to demand compulsory education and, like Europeans, to expect that those who pay taxes to the state should have education provided by the state. Greatly increased support from the state is necessary to meet this need." Actively involved in many of the Colonial Office's wartime assessments of education in British Africa, Wrong saw her efforts realize success after 1945, as missions, which had historically controlled education in the British colonies in Africa, found themselves offered a new opportunity and a new set of challenges. Groves describes how "a harassed secular authority" enjoined missions to make "extended commitments in education and in welfare activities generally." Failing acceptance by the missions, the "State would perforce proceed alone." After the war, a local government system was introduced in British African territories through which local authorities become responsible for education. These had their own revenues for opening schools where required and for continuing grants-in-aid to mission schools where these existed.[21]

According to many of the documents on education that Wrong authored or helped to author during the war, the education that Africans were demanding had to be both culturally relevant and available to children and adults alike. In the emergent language of the period, drawn from communist experiments in the Soviet Union and China, it had to be "mass." In *Five Points for Africa* (as in many other wartime essays she authored), Wrong insists that attending to both children and adults will help to buffer the contradictions between traditional and modern life: "Teaching given to children in school only cannot reconcile these worlds of thought" – the "darkness of ignorance" and the light of knowledge about germs and disease, for instance – "an approach to the grown-up as well as to the child is necessary." With Wrong's assistance, the Colonial Office was also taking up the matter of mass literacy in Africa during the early 1940s. The findings of its subcommittee on mass education (formed in 1941) – understood as community-level campaigns to achieve mass literacy among adults – were published in *Mass Education in African Society* (1944). With frequent reference to experiments in industrial schooling in the "Negro South" of the US, *Mass Education* insists on the centrality of "local industry" to literacy campaigns, framing the revival of local handicrafts alongside a "new type of economic planning" as a means of enabling "people to understand and control the changes which are taking place in their neighbourhood, and to equip them to make fullest use of their own environment." This emphasis on a combination of British "planning" and native craft is one that can be found in the wartime writing of Julian Huxley, who, alongside Wrong and her partner Margaret Read, was a member of the subcommittee that produced *Mass Education*. Huxley's interwar and wartime work for the Colonial Office on education in the British territories in Africa proceeded from his conviction that Britain could retain its colonies in

Africa through what Glenda Sluga calls an "imperially directed economic and political modernization." An evolutionary biologist, Huxley argued that imperial tutelage could help Africans evolve the capacities necessary to participate in a full partnership with Britain. In publications such as *The Future of the Colonies* (coauthored with Phyllis Deane and published in 1944) and "Colonies and Freedom," Huxley calls for the "economic and social development of the colonies," citing Britain's 1940 Colonial Development and Welfare Act as the beginning of a "new phase in British colonial policy" that would help to usher colonies in Africa and other parts of the world into the "modern world" by joining "white man's inventions and techniques" to traditional cultures and economies, such as the making of stoneware in the Gold Coast. As it became increasingly linked to the Colonial Office, this late colonial conception of book development was characterized by both what Sluga calls an "enduring attitude of imperial 'trusteeship' that had shaped the liberal idealism of the League of Nations mandate system" and a conviction that mass education could best be realized in the context of practical, vocational training.[22]

While the Colonial Office's and the ICCLA's wartime turn to the language of "mass education" invoked self-government as its primary aim, this was a self-government that was imagined to be very distant indeed. This is especially evident in the influence of the Phelps-Stokes Fund on the work that Wrong was doing for the ICCLA during the war. Her 1944 tour of West Africa included a leg that served as a kind of follow-up to the earlier Phelps-Stokes Fund Education Commissions (in 1920 and 1924): with Jackson Davis (a white Virginian whose interests in African American and rural education led him to a position with the Rockefeller Foundation's General Education Board) and Thomas Campbell (an African American graduate of the Tuskegee Institute and agent for the Agricultural Extension Service of the US Department of Agriculture), and supported by Davis's General Education Board through the Phelps-Stokes Fund, Wrong embarked on a study of "rural education." The collaborative report that the trio produced, *Africa Advancing*, opens with an apology for British rule in Africa, which American readers are entreated to reconsider in light of the "growing prosperity and improvements in standards of living and economic development" that the Colonial Welfare and Development Act has engendered. The "present system" offers many advantages, the authors contend, including "stability and continuity of relationships within a wide system." Since the British colonies of Africa are not yet able to "hold their own in dealing with the outside world" and could fall prey to "clever and unscrupulous Africans who would like to gain control for selfish advantage," imperial tutelage offers a middle road that will allow African colonies to benefit for as long as required from the "long centuries" of democratic tradition practised by the "liberal colonial powers." While the authors concede that self-government could one day occur, it would be most successful within the context of the British Commonwealth of Nations.[23]

This emphasis on the continued need for imperial guidance in relation to governance is directly connected to the Africa policy promoted by Phelps-Stokeism. Proceeding from the assumption that the concept of "differentiated education" for black Americans in the southern US – an education adapted to that particular rural context and to the supposed capacities of that population – was directly relevant to Africa, Phelps-Stokeism further implied, according to Berman, that both the African American South and Africa would remain rural indefinitely and that "neither the African nor the American Negro would be self-governing, or even have a large say in his welfare for the foreseeable future." The fund's influence, contends Berman, was "greatly augmented" by the cooperation in this period of the Colonial Office's Advisory Committees on Education in Africa and British and North American mission groups, including the ICCLA. While, as we have seen, the educational policy documents and reports that the Colonial Office produced through the interwar and war years, including *Mass Education in African Society* certainly indicate the fund's emphasis on vocational training, colonial policy did not ultimately ignore African calls for higher education. Government commissions to study higher education in East and West Africa led to the establishment during the war of university colleges in the Gold Coast, Ibadan, and East Africa. The Phelps-Stokes Fund's influence on the ICCLA was greater for a longer period of time, as *Africa Advancing* attests.[24]

If the literary materials that Wrong curated for the ICCLA and if her 1942 study *Five Points for Africa* privilege "craft teaching in schools" over schools as "centres for literary movements," *Africa Advancing* builds this point into a larger philosophy of education for rural Africa. The continent's people remain largely rural, assert the authors, and thus African education must proceed from this context. The authors conclude that "in the opinion of many rural people," the school "was not closely related to their lives and occupations." Moreover, "in all the territories there was a realization that with the coming of modern education and trade many of the old African crafts and skills were dying out, with a corresponding impoverishment of the life of the people." *Africa Advancing* samples generously from *Mass Education*, turning that book's arguments about community literacy to rural education – the mode of vocational, agricultural, craft-based education that the authors contend will lead to an improved standard of life among West Africans. Significantly, given Wrong's ties to Canada, *Africa Advancing* also notes that the agriculturally oriented model of community education the authors promote might be compared to Nova Scotia's Antigonish Movement – a rural interwar cooperative movement that sought a "middle way" (the "Antigonish Way") between capitalism and socialism.[25]

The Phelps-Stokeist model that Wrong and her colleagues were promoting in *Africa Advancing* was neither new in 1944 (as the earlier Phelps-Stokes studies that preceded it suggest) nor passively accepted by the Africans it aimed to improve. In British territories like Southern Rhodesia, adapted education had been broadly introduced during the 1920s at such sites as the Government Industrial Schools at Domboshawa and Tjolotjo (examples that are lauded in *Africa Advancing*). According to R.J. Challiss, Thomas Jesse Jones (the American director of the Phelps-Stokes Education Commissions in the 1920s) and Charles T. Loram (a white South African Phelps-Stokeist) shaped the new educational policy devised in 1919 for the Native Affairs Department of the British South Africa Company Administration, which aimed to "divert progress in African education away from possibly subversive regions of more advanced literary work, into directions that concentrated upon a specially simplified form of industrial training." As Küster demonstrates, the settler government turned to this vocational educational policy in the wake of racial segregation and "resettlement" policies that had attempted to neutralize African competition with white settler agriculturalists via the creation of "Native Reserves." The teaching of simple industrial skills and improved agricultural methods was promoted to ensure that these less fertile reserves could be rendered productive. Challiss dates black Zimbabwean "resentment" of differentiated education to its introduction in the 1920s; Küster tracks African opposition in Southern Rhodesia to the Phelps-Stokeist model from the 1930s, noting that this resistance had parallels among Africans in Northern Rhodesia, Nyasaland, and Kenya. Küster attributes the African critique of Phelps-Stokeism in Northern Rhodesia to four factors: the heavy manual labour for students that some missions presented as consonant with the vocational model of education; the policy and legislation that limited the social and economic mobility of Africans engaging in agricultural and industrial work (though literate, educated Africans found attractive labour opportunities as minor civil servants, policemen, interpreters, and so on); the fact that adapted education anachronistically insisted on the separation of African and European communities; and, finally, the emergence of proto-nationalist political organizations that were identifying the vocational educational model as an obstacle to the full participation of Africans in colonial society.[26]

Despite such African critiques, which ultimately influenced the Colonial Office as well as missions and colonial governments in places like Northern Rhodesia, the vocational model promoted by Phelps-Stokeism shaped Wrong's undertakings for the ICCLA until her death in 1948. For instance, as Thomas Campbell notes in a tribute to Wrong written after her death, in addition to visiting Tuskegee in October of 1947 (a visit he suggests was not her first to the school), she facilitated the visits of many African students, missionaries, and government officials to Tuskegee in the wake of their 1944 collaboration, a plan that is promoted in the discussion of teacher training in *Africa Advancing*.[27]

Wrong's posthumous legacy, in the form of the literary prize and medal for African literatures that was established by the Margaret Wrong Memorial Fund in the wake of her death, is similarly associated with Phelps-Stokeist principles. Deliberations regarding the fund's literary prizes, which existed from 1950 to 1962, were entangled in late British colonial development ideology. Those members of the fund's administrative committee who advocated after 1949 and through the 1950s for the inclusion of African vernaculars, such as the Ugandan political leader Eridadi M.K. Mulira and the British educationalist Leonard John Lewis, were appealing to the early twentieth-century ideology of Phelps-Stokeism, and especially to its rationale for legitimizing African languages – a rationale that, as we have seen, was rooted not in a decolonial impulse but rather in a conception of African racial inferiority. In texts such as his 1950 Luganda-language novel *Teefe* or his 1951 booklet *The Vernacular in African Education*, Mulira advocated Phelps-Stokeist ideals of rural life, coeducation (also present in the industrial schools of the American South), and vernacular-language education, including the extended study of grammar and vernacular literatures, written and oral. The British academic Leonard John Lewis had gained experience as an educationalist in colonial Nigeria prior to the Second World War but was appointed lecturer at the Institute of Education of London University in 1944 (and subsequently served from 1959 to 1973 as professor of education with special reference to education in tropical areas). He had been a collaborator of Wrong's just prior to her death: together they organized a 1947 conference jointly sponsored by the ICCLA and the Institute of Education that brought together university teachers, government officers, and missionaries to discuss literacy initiatives, as well as the preparation and distribution of literature in African languages (their coedited report of the proceedings, *Towards a Literate Africa*, was published in the same year). Lewis was a Phelps-Stokes apologist well into the period of decolonization: in essays such as "Anglo-American University Co-Operation in the Changing World" (published in *Education and Political Independence* in 1962 but written earlier), Lewis lauds Phelps-Stokeist ideals of adapted education, noting that "the reports still offer sound guidance about planning educational development." In "The British Contribution to Education in Africa" (also published in *Education and Political Independence*) Lewis offers an apology for continuing British tutelage (and authority) in the period of decolonization and, more particularly, for a postwar model that granted the University of London the power to assess standards at the "new university colleges in Africa." Challiss contends that Lewis's ideologies were not inconsequential in the later twentieth century, as general support for Phelps-Stokeism waned, particularly because of the "special relationship between the Faculty of Education of London University, where the Professor has for long exercised considerable authority, and the education faculties of universities in former British colonies like that of the University of Zimbabwe." As I have argued elsewhere, the extension of Wrong's Phelps-Stokeist thinking in the forms of literary consecration that are a key element of her legacy demonstrates a larger truth about late colonial development: it was deeply invested in an argument for the continued relevance of British presence in and authority over colonies that were becoming nations. Ultimately, it worked to transform a claim of benevolent British tutelage into one of humanitarian interest.[28]

The ICCLA and Publishing in Africa

If Wrong's leadership of the ICCLA was associated with the vocational vision of education for Africans touted by the Phelps-Stokes Fund, her support of publishing in Africa produced similarly complex legacies. In addition to her consistent support for initiatives that aimed to cultivate writing in African languages and African authorship, Wrong was in her role as secretary of the ICCLA also a vocal proponent of publishing in Africa. Yet the publishing infrastructure that her work for the ICCLA built was ultimately more favourable to white settler and British commercial ends than it was to the cultivation of African-operated and African-language publishing in Africa.[29]

When Wrong discussed publishing in Africa, she was referring not to the African publishers that became such a focus of book development conversations in the postindependence period, but rather, as she clarifies in one of her 1933 reports, to a particular set of organizations, most of which were run by white settlers: mission presses in Africa, commercial publishing houses in South Africa, small African commercial printers, and government printers in Africa. "Lack of coordination" among these agents (and with commercial and religious publishing houses in Europe) harms these organizations, Wrong argues. When religious publishing houses in Europe grant the necessary subsidies for publications for Africa, for instance, they have little idea of demand. As we have seen, Wrong believed the solution to this problem was inter-mission language and literature commissions, which would permit regional planning related to languages, education, publishing, and book distribution. Convinced that the ICCLA would "ideally" be working with an "inter-mission literature committee in each area" and that "we cannot hope for effective development until there are effective committees in the field with secretaries in the field who are giving time to literature work," Wrong oversaw ICCLA funding for such secretaries. Her summary of the ICCLA's wartime efforts includes, for example, reference to the organization's support for the training of two Nigerians for "literature work" and funding for a five-year position for a full-time literature worker for the Christian Council of Nigeria.[30]

The coordination of missions and colonial governments around literature work was given a boost by the development-oriented mood of the Colonial Office in the wake of the Second World War. The 1947 conference that Wrong organized with Leonard John Lewis, jointly sponsored by the ICCLA and the Institute of Education in the Colonial Department of the University of London, brought together university teachers, government officers, and missionaries to discuss literacy initiatives, as well as the preparation and distribution of literature in African languages. Colonial governments, with handsome Colonial Development and Welfare funds at their disposal, took action. In northern Nigeria, the government converted its Translation Bureau in 1945 into a grant-aided Literature Bureau, which published a Hausa-language newspaper and literature for Muslims and Christians, among other initiatives. In 1949, the governments of Northern Rhodesia and Nyasaland built on the precedent of the African Literature Committee created at Wrong's urging in 1936 to found a Joint Publications Bureau in Lusaka. In East Africa, the governments of Kenya, Uganda, Tanganyika, and Zanzibar set up in 1948 the East Africa Literature Bureau (EALB), headquartered in Nairobi, to publish periodicals, general literature, and school textbooks for all four territories. In her history of Christian publishing houses in Africa, Modupe Oduyoye (of Daystar Press in Nigeria) credits Wrong's sustained call for missions and colonial officials to work together to create literature bureaus with the establishment of the Northern Rhodesia and Nyasaland Joint Publications Bureau and the EALB. Both, Oduyoye contends, "owe their existence to the work and vision of Margaret Wrong."[31]

The literature bureaus that Wrong's work engendered were important to settler rule in postwar Africa. We have already seen how Wrong was implicated in the colonial administration's efforts, during the 1930s, to combat antigovernment sentiment among African mineworkers in Northern Rhodesia. The Northern Rhodesia and Nyasaland Joint Publications Bureau that the Colonial Office in southern Africa established in 1949 had similar aims. Davis points out that its mission was the "production of literature in Africa to combat subversive movements." To this end, and to ensure the sound financial basis of the scheme, the Colonial Office enlisted the assistance of British commercial publishers, including Oxford University Press, Longmans, and Macmillan. Davis's account of the work that Longmans did for the Joint Publications Bureau demonstrates the ideological quality of the deal. The copublications Longmans produced included an English-language series called "Pathfinder Books," books claiming to "show you the path to a better way of living." The series included how-to titles (*How to Grow Vegetables, How to Run a Society*), as well as what Davis calls "conservative political booklets," such as *African Trade Unions*, an apology for moderate labour reforms, and *African Participation in Government*, which advocated "good government" over "self-government."³²

Wrong's encouragement of literature bureaus also played a crucial role in cultivating the ground for the arrival of British commercial publishers in postindependence African nations. Given the ICCLA's support under Wrong's leadership for the Phelps-Stokeist privileging of African languages, there is irony here; British publishers on the African continent did not ultimately contribute significantly to postindependence African-language publishing efforts. Contending that "each phase of British publishing in East Africa helped create the conditions for the next," Caroline Ritter argues that the interwar Christian Missionary Society (CMS) Bookshop in Kenya laid the groundwork for both the EALB, as well as for the postwar establishment of branches of British publishers, such as Oxford University Press, in East Africa. The CMS was a British organization that had begun its work in East Africa in the 1870s. Like many Christian mission stations in the region in this period, the society used a printing press for the creation of newsletters and pamphlets, and it also opened a bookshop for the sale of Bibles, prayer books, and scripture translated into East African vernaculars. Under the management of Charles Granston Richards, who arrived in East Africa from Britain in 1935, the bookshop became a more ambitious affair. At the outset, Richards took inspiration from Wrong's 1934 report of her first tour for the ICCLA, *Africa and the Making of Books: Being A Survey of Africa's Need of Literature*, which argues that "the few who demand good literature will assuredly multiply. They will need good literature both in the vernaculars and in European languages. If they cannot get good literature they will read bad." Accordingly, Richards expanded the bookshop into the field of publishing (with two imprints, one religious and one secular), including publishing in African vernaculars. Richards's efforts continued through the war years to take instruction from Wrong's work in Africa. As he mentions in a 1944 memo regarding the work of the CMS Bookshop (a copy of which was sent to the ICCLA), he had taken note of *Mass Education in African Society* and was considering a plan to extend the bookshop's mandate to include literacy centres that could be coupled with bookshops and libraries. At the same time, the

CMS Publishers had by the end of the 1930s also become the agent for a handful of British publishing firms that would later set up shop in Africa, notably Oxford University Press.[33]

The EALB, where Richards moved in 1948, was initially financed almost entirely by the Colonial Development and Welfare Fund. Its mandate was to "support" rather than supplant missionary and commercial publishing enterprises in the region (Richards often passed successful titles to private firms for reprinting, for instance). While the publishing of school textbooks and manuals and of other materials related to colonial development initiatives was the mainstay of the EALB and while the EALB published a larger percentage of its books in English than the CMS Publishers had, Richards made some efforts to foster African vernaculars and African authorship, introducing writers like James Ngũgĩ (later Ngũgĩ wa Thiong'o), who won a 1961 EALB writing contest, to British publisher Heinemann. At the same time, like the CMS Publishers, the EALB created an environment in which branches of private British publishing companies could find success. Ritter contends that Oxford University Press, which hired Richards in 1963 to run its new Nairobi branch, benefited (as other British publishers did) from the market assessments that missionary and colonial precedents permitted them to undertake and from the help that the British Colonial Office proffered to private firms looking to export to Africa. Eager to enter the market for English-language school textbooks, Oxford University Press developed its initial *Oxford English Course* (a course package developed in the 1930s) into region-specific coursebooks. As sales of such textbooks increased and as independence arrived in Kenya (ending the mediating role that the British Colonial Office had previously played), Oxford University Press established its eastern Africa branch in Nairobi. If Oxford University Press's predecessors in East Africa had aimed at, in Ritter's words, developing a "reading public" through commitments to publishing in African vernaculars – tepid as these became with the wane of the missionary publishers – Oxford University Press found no commercial viability in such initiatives, focusing instead on the largely English-language educational market that both missionary and colonial publishers had found profitable.[34]

In other words, Margaret Wrong's legacy in the former colonies of British Africa was conducive neither to the emergence of African publishing efforts nor to the development of African-language publishing.

African-owned and African-language publishing ultimately depended not on the print infrastructure engendered through the ICCLA but on a rejection of that infrastructure and its colonial legacies. The Zambian case is instructive. With independence in 1964, educational publishing and distribution in the territory that became Zambia was nationalized (as the National Educational Company of Zambia and the National Educational Distribution Company of Zambia). Although the first of these parastatal companies was established in 1967 in partnership with Macmillan (one of many such time-limited partnerships Macmillan undertook in concert with the governments of independent Africa during the 1960s), which offered the benefit of "professional and technical advice" and the ability to secure financing, Simon D. Allison's 1975 account suggests that the National Educational Company of Zambia was thriving not because of the tutelage of an expatriate publisher but rather because of its role as exclusive publisher for all courses designed by the Zambian Ministry of Education. Given the commitment of the new Zambian government to education in the major Zambian languages and to African educational content (a topic to which we will return in chapter 4), the National Educational Company of Zambia had a mandate to publish primary school readers in each of the seven major Zambian languages. The company's exclusive access to the school market allowed it to publish two or three titles a year in what Allison calls "less dependable fields," such as fiction, history, or cultural affairs in Zambian languages. Given the relatively small market for such titles (the population of newly independent Zambia being only four million) and given the relatively small Zambian population that was in this period reading for pleasure, such publishing would not have been feasible without the publisher's exclusive access to the school trade. This model had other advantages, one being the encouragement of a domestic printing industry. In a presentation also published in 1975 from the same 1973 conference on African publishing that Allison attended, Nigerian publisher G.O. Onibonoje condemns the structures that had, on one hand, permitted non-African publishers to benefit from an emerging African book trade and, on the other, created dependency on NGOs and philanthropic organizations for skills and raw materials, as well as a "feeling of gratitude towards the 'benevolent,' developed countries." Onibonoje saw no future in such an arrangement: "The much-publicized benevolent disposition of the so-called developed countries is a mere smoke-screen to perpetuate their domination over the so-called developing countries." Under such conditions, "development is impossible, at best, only modernisation is likely." Only when Africans "realise that what we originally believe and accept to be our inherent inferiority, our incapacity and helplessness, is, in fact, a result of alienation itself and a demonstration of a condition of domination" will African-owned publishing in Africa be possible.[35]

Conclusion

Through this examination of the interwar and wartime work of the ICCLA, this chapter has argued that late colonial book development, like its postwar counterpart, functioned as a means of forestalling the political and economic change that many Africans were calling for in the first half of the twentieth century. In this broad sense, it tended to serve the population that was disbursing aid more than the population that was the object of development. Important to this claim is the relationship I have tried to establish here between a postwar rhetoric of book development and its late colonial counterpart.

This relationship is visible in a number of examples, and it is with these that I will conclude. One of the strongest sets of links between late colonial and postwar book development can be found in the relation of actors important to the interwar and wartime work of the British Colonial Office to the programs and priorities of postwar UNESCO. Julian Huxley is a key figure here. In the wake of his work for the Colonial Office's Committee on Education in the Colonies, Huxley became the first director-general of UNESCO in 1946 (serving until 1948). Sluga contends that Huxley oversaw a period during which "colonial expertise was highly valued." The organization employed, for instance, the director of the British Colonial Film Unit and British colonial education experts in its own development efforts, and Huxley's particular influence is evident, Sluga argues, in UNESCO's work on "fundamental education" during its first decade. UNESCO's three "fundamental education" pilot projects were created on the model of the British colonial "mass education" ideals that Huxley helped to devise during the war. Among the most notorious (and disastrous) of these, the Tanganyikan groundnut scheme offers, in Sluga's words, "a spectacular measure of how for UNESCO the seeds of the most practical, and even idealistic, aspects of postwar internationalism, including the creation of modernizing cosmopolitan bureaucracies, took root in an imperial setting."[36]

UNESCO's postwar literacy- and book-related work in "fundamental education" had a similarly "imperial" or late colonial genealogy. It took many of its cues from *Mass Education in African Society* and from missionary organizations such as the ICCLA. In a 1946 letter to Wrong, Alfred Moore, the executive secretary of the Foreign Missions Conference of North America, asks for her assistance with UNESCO's request for information regarding mass literacy initiatives and, particularly, reading materials for new and aspiring literates. Ironically, given the complicated relationship of the late colonial concept of "mass education" to the argument for differential education, "fundamental education," and the associated ideas of basic literacy and community development, came, by the late 1950s and especially by the early '60s, to resemble too closely the mass literacy program of communist Cuba. Charles Dorn and Kristen Ghodsee trace how UNESCO, under pressure from the US and the World Bank, formally abandoned "fundamental education" in 1958 in favour of "functional literacy" and similarly vocationally oriented, capitalist-friendly terms. The terminology changed, but, as in the earlier model of differentiated education, the point of book development was to create economies amenable to foreign investment.[37]

Late colonial and postwar book development at UNESCO are also linked by a rhetorical turn. During the war, Wrong developed a new lexicon for what she had earlier termed "literature needs." Gesturing to an emergent concern for colonial "welfare" writ large (education, health, social services, and economic development), Wrong began to refer to the "famine of books" evident across the British territories of Africa. Such phrasing anticipates UNESCO's invocation in the 1960s and '70s of "book hunger," most obviously in Robert Barker and Robert Escarpit's 1973 UNESCO publication, *The Book Hunger*. In interwar publications such as her account of her wartime tour of West Africa, Wrong employs "famine of books" to argue for Britain's responsibility to direct the modernization of its colonies, which would, it is implied, fail utterly without this expertise. By contrast, Barker and Escarpit's study, which formed part of UNESCO's 1972 International Book Year campaign, emphasizes not the dearth of reading matter in the nations of the formerly colonized world, but rather the dearth of book *production* in those nations. The problem of book access cannot be regulated by external aid alone, the authors contend, largely because much of the need is in languages not used in the publishing industries of the biggest producing nations. In these different but related deployments of the concept of "book hunger," we see how, for a brief period during the 1970s, the new Third World majority at UNESCO helped to turn the idea of book development away from the external aid paradigm and toward fundamental questions of production. We return to this brief moment in subsequent chapters.[38]

2

The Department of External Affairs and Postwar Uses of the Book, 1945–59

The popular narrative in the cultural and literary history of English Canada is that literary culture "arrived" in the years between the late 1950s and the mid-'70s, propelled by the economic prosperity of this period; a desire for cultural autonomy from the US; and, as many have claimed, the forms of state support for culture that began to trickle from federal and provincial governments in the wake of the 1951 report of the Royal Commission on Development in the Arts, Letters and Sciences (the Massey Report). What Nick Mount calls the "CanLit boom" can to some extent be assessed using numbers: between 1963 and 1972, the number of Canadian-authored, English-language literary trade books published in Canada (including new titles and new editions of old titles) increased by 259 per cent, from 355 to 1,275 titles. This increase was significantly greater than the worldwide increase in book production, which was 191 per cent for the longer period between 1950 and 1980. While the increase in the number of Canadian-authored, English-language literary trade books in this period is irrefutable, the concept of "arrival" implies a developmental narrative that plots both an origin and an end point. Such a developmental narrative, drawing as it does on the narratives of organic cultural growth that were conjured by the new nation-states of Europe in the eighteenth and nineteenth centuries, has long informed coming-of-age tales of Canadian nationhood.[1]

This chapter complicates the narrative of developmental momentum that frames the concept of CanLit's "arrival" in the period between the late 1950s to the mid-'70s. Moving slightly earlier, to the late 1940s and '50s, it contends that contradiction and disavowal are better analytical terms for understanding the emergence of the institutions that ultimately supported the flourishing of English Canadian writing during the "CanLit boom." Anna Johnston and Alan Lawson theorize such contradiction in relation to the doubled character of the authority and authenticity that the "settler subject is (con)signed to disavow." If the authority of the settler subject is derived from the "imperial enterprise" (in the case of Canada, Britain), this authority is troubled by the distance that separates the settler from the imperium. The settler asserts authority over the "indigene and the land," while "translating desire for the indigene and the land into a desire for native authenticity." This authenticity can only ever be a form of mimicry, even while it helps to render the settler less "like the atavistic inhabitant of the cultural homeland whom he is also reduced to mimicking." As the imperium shifted across the Atlantic in the decade that followed the close of the Second World War, the settler nation struggled to locate itself anew in relation to these "origins of authority and authenticity."[2]

The first case examined here is the Canadian government's attempts to enter the cultural diplomacy field, and the international order more generally, in the wake of the Second World War, just as the Massey Commission was disseminating its findings. Postwar cultural – and especially book – diplomacy efforts, such as the Annual Book Presentation Programme, participated in and adopted the rhetoric of the cultural diplomacy practices dominated in this period by the US. These efforts were thus obliged to emphasize the nation's ostensibly robust domestic book industries, a disingenuous narrative that depended upon a cultural nationalism (settler-imperium difference) that appropriated Indigenous "craft" to its origin story. Seven years after inaugurating its first book diplomacy program, the Department of External Affairs launched its Special Book Presentation Programme for Colombo Plan Area Countries. If this program was oriented more to emerging forms of foreign aid than to cultural diplomacy, it, like its predecessor, was characterized by the contradictions produced by the meeting of international and domestic policy. Using its role in the Commonwealth of Nations to project liberal internationalism through, among other forms of development assistance, books, the Canadian government also in this period found it necessary to defend its record of internal colonization. As the convergences of international development assistance and domestic policy aimed at Indigenous Peoples deepened, so did the antinomies informing the meanings of Canadian books as they circulated among international audiences.

Publishing in Canada at Mid-Century

Despite the common identification of the postwar decades with the "development" of English Canada's national literature, the publishing industry in English Canada was largely controlled from elsewhere well into the period Mount identifies as the "boom." As Paul Litt has shown, the 1951 Massey Report did not lead to any dramatic increases in funding for Canadian-owned publishers, a fact that Litt attributes to the elitist conceptions of "high" art (and the accompanying belief that such art does not require direct state assistance) held by the report's authors. Though the Canada Council (a form of indirect state support for the book recommended by the Massey Report and established in 1957) provided grants to authors and for individual titles, direct state assistance for publishers did not materialize until 1972, when the Canada Council introduced its block grants to publishers who were "actively producing and marketing Canadian books." In this context, and until at least the early 1970s, book publishing in Canada was largely a non-Canadian affair.[3]

The structure that dominated book publishing until the early 1970s was the agency system. George Parker emphasizes the domination of publishing in English Canada for most of the twentieth century by a "distinctive" agency system that was colonial in its structure. In Parker's account, this system emerged around 1900 as British and American publishing companies, now bound by an 1891 agreement to protect one another's copyrights, sought to carve up the expanding Canadian market. Some British publishers actually set up branches in Toronto (Oxford University Press, Macmillan), but others found Canadian publishers to act as agents for their books (as New York's George Doran did with McClelland & Stewart). Decisions regarding contracts, editing, design, production run, and royalties were thus often made elsewhere. Moreover, the whole purpose of agency publishing was to distribute American and British authors and not to develop Canadian publishing. This system prevailed until the early 1970s, when at least two factors coalesced to spell its end. First, a growing Canadian market for textbooks beguiled American companies such as McGraw-Hill to cancel their agencies and set up shop in Canada. Second, anti-American cultural nationalism helped to urge federal support for domestically owned publishers, including the Canada Council block grants and later the Canadian Book Publishing Industry

Development Program (1979). The influence of the agency system meant that in the 1950s, only one-tenth of the books sold in Canada were published in Canada; the majority of book imports came from the US. Moreover, this situation did not immediately change with the advent of funding programs such as the Canada Council's block grants. In 1975, Paul Audley, executive director of what was then called the Independent Publishers' Association, estimated that foreign-owned subsidiaries constituted 84 per cent of the book publishing industry in Canada. Canadian-owned publishers (who have always published the majority of Canadian-authored titles) thus constituted only a small fraction of the total market for domestic book sales during the period that stretched from 1950 to at least the mid-1970s. The "boom" in Canadian-authored, English-language literary trade books published in Canada between 1963 and 1972 that I refer to above must be understood in this context.[4]

Direct state support for domestically owned publishing was thus, to say the least, tepid during the 1950s and '60s and into the early '70s. Indirect sources of support were emerging in this period, however, and a considerable portion of these were directed outward, to the international arena.

"The Free and Earnest Exchange of Ideas": Modernization and the Postwar Rhetoric of the Book

The US State Department established a Division of Cultural Relations in 1938. By 1950, this division had undergone a series of important transformations: the public-private relationships it supported had become instruments of national policy, and its multilateral work, particularly through the newly established UNESCO, was focused on pressuring that organization to carry out American foreign policy. This foreign policy rested, after 1948, on a basic political distinction between the US and the Soviet Union: democracy and the dignity and freedom of the individual versus the police state and the negation of human liberty. Under the leadership of the US-backed director-general Jaime Torres Bodet, UNESCO increasingly stepped out of what Frank Ninkovich calls its "non-political" costume and promoted American values of liberal "freedom" as universal and neutral, condemning, for instance, the North Korean invasion of South Korea as a "menace of aggression."[5]

The book programs overseen by the Cultural Division of the State Department in the late 1940s and early '50s were shaped by these ideologies and policy aims. In the 1950s, as western governments, following the lead of the US, yoked the book to a wide range of overlapping political and economic goals – including the combatting of impressive Soviet book donation schemes, Soviet nuclear aggression, and the development of economies friendly to American capital investment – they described their strategies using a rhetoric that emphasized what Dan Lacy, writing in the mid-1950s in the American periodical *Library Quarterly*, called the "free and earnest exchange of ideas." During the First and Second World Wars, the US developed its government bureaucracies for cultural diplomacy alongside the private partnerships (with groups such as the Ford Foundation) that have always been important to that nation's soft power initiatives. As Greg Barnhisel points out, following the Second World War, the book and a "culturalist" theory of diplomacy – marked by a preference for the "soft" dissemination of messages through reading rooms, exchanges, touring performances, and the like – came to constitute one of the central information technologies of the Cold War of ideas, particularly because US officials were convinced that the book was the most effective medium for reaching European intellectuals hostile to American mass culture and the growing global power associated with it. The USIA and later USAID funded or collaborated with nongovernmental organizations and private industry to create programs that employed books as instruments of cultural diplomacy. These tended to select texts that complemented the "'vital center' argument" favoured within the cultural diplomacy establishment during the 1950s, books that privileged freedom, liberal individualism, and the importance of cooperation between government and industry, for instance, rather than books that espoused the "hard-line anticommunism" that was dominating American domestic politics in the 1950s. Favoured authors from the American book programs of this period include major figures of early American literature (Hawthorne, Irving, Melville), as well as major American writers of the later nineteenth century (Dickinson, Twain, Whitman).[6]

Amanda Laugesen's focus on a particular Cold War book program, Franklin Book Programs (1952–78), offers a good illustration of the importance of an ideology of liberal developmentalism to American book giving, as well as technical assistance linked to the book. Franklin

Book Programs was established with the financial support of the USIA, which after 1953 assumed responsibility for the information work of cultural diplomacy, but it was eventually run by publishers and supported by a mix of public and private funding. The nonprofit agency nurtured a vision of building book industries and book cultures in developing nations, a mission that flowed from the program's commitment to the following ideas: that (US-style) literacy and education were desirable; that US-style modernity should be embraced throughout the world; and that the US book industry offered the best model for developing nations to follow. Laugesen's study provides an important frame for understanding what Sarah Brouillette calls the "developmentalist ethos" of the postwar activities of UNESCO, an organization that, as we have seen, was deeply influenced in the immediate postwar years by American foreign policy goals. If this ethos privileged "literacy, agricultural development, and rational science" as the keys to bringing impoverished nations up to the standard of living enjoyed in western, industrialized economies, these forms of development also offered ways of opening new industries and markets to American influence.[7]

Undergirding these American and multilateral conceptions of development is modernization theory, which provided the motor for the foreign aid programs of the postwar period. Foreign aid and technical assistance – the providing of nonfinancial assistance in the form of experts and expertise – are identified with the immediate end of the Second World War. Both were important to the founding initiatives of the UN and have constituted formal elements of US foreign diplomacy since 1948. As Corrina R. Unger contends, a key moment in the US government's turn to foreign aid as a foreign policy tool was Harry Truman's January 1949 inaugural address, the fourth point of which committed the US to a "bold new program for making the benefits of our scientific advances and industrial progress available for the improvement and growth of underdeveloped areas." Five months later, Truman adapted his concept of development to recognize that such work could also counter the circulation of "false doctrines" in poor nations vulnerable to Soviet influence. While the origins of this postwar idea of development lie in the histories of colonial development and missionary work (and the ideologies of "race" and improvement that attended them), as well as in the interwar efforts of the League of Nations, their concretization in state instruments after 1945 forms part and parcel of the embrace of moderate Keynesianism by western governments in this period.[8]

The US government's involvement in liberal internationalism experienced an élan in the interwar period, but it was the postwar era that saw the US government's self-appointment as a global leader of planned economic development. This would lead to what David Ekbladh calls "the establishment of an integrated global economy based on liberal principles." According to Nick Cullather, this era of "high modernism," which James C. Scott describes as motivated by "self-confidence about scientific and technical progress, the expansion of production, the growing satisfaction of human needs, the mastery of nature (including human nature), and, above all, the rational design of social order commensurate with the scientific understanding of natural laws," began to "systematically" inform US – and Canadian – foreign policy in the years immediately following the Second World War. While the western development programs that issued from modernization theory, such as the Colombo Plan for Co-Operative Development in South and Southeast Asia, tended to favour economic development projects such as Canada's infamous provision in the mid-1950s of a replica of a nuclear research reactor to India, cultural initiatives, including book and print-focused ones, also found a place in the plan: Daniel Oakman shows that, during the 1950s, Australia's Department of External Affairs realized Colombo Plan commitments through Radio Australia, the journal *Hemisphere*, and gifts of books to universities and libraries across Asia. As we will see, this strategy was adopted with limited success in Canada, as well.[9]

As in the US, Canada's development during the Second World War of an information infrastructure – its Wartime Information Board (WIB), led by British filmmaker and National Film Board (NFB) director John Grierson – laid important groundwork for the nation's postwar cultural diplomacy initiatives. L.A.D. Stephens observes that the end of war did not spell the end of the information work initiated by the WIB, though it did mean reorienting that work away from domestic and toward international audiences. The work of the WIB was maintained after 1945 by the Canadian Information Service (CIS) and by the Department of External Affairs, which absorbed the CIS into its own Information Division (created in 1944) in 1947. After the 1947 folding of the CIS into External Affairs, the communications work of the Information Division was wide-ranging, encompassing five area desks (Commonwealth and the Far East, the US, western Europe, central and eastern Europe, and Latin America), as well as eight distinct sections (Inquiries,

Reference, Library, Press, Visitors and Speakers, United Nations and Political Information, Cultural Relations, and Circulation). Although, as Stephens points out, "cultural relations" work was nascent in this period, plagued by some confusion regarding how to separate "cultural" from "information" work, the creation of a specific section devoted to culture in 1947 inaugurated labour that would only expand in subsequent years. According to Stephens, "the decision of the government to place in the bosom of Department of External Affairs responsibility for public information abroad sprang from a realization that programs of information in other countries about Canada were closely related to the implementation of foreign policy and that policy for information abroad must serve foreign policy and be governed by it." More specifically, the work of the new Information Division was meant to support the development and implementation of postwar foreign policy that would, in Stephens's words, "serve Canada's interests as a middle power in international affairs" and its "capacity for mediation." Such positioning was subject to a larger reality, however; John Hilliker and Donald Barry point out that Lester B. Pearson, undersecretary for External Affairs from 1946–49, understood that Canada's effectiveness in the international arena was dependent on its alignment with US and British foreign policy.[10]

If, as Sean Rushton contends, the international cultural relations efforts of various government departments in the wake of the Second World War were uncoordinated and "spasmodic," there was nonetheless, as Maria Tippett documents, a shifting attitude during the late 1940s in Ottawa regarding the role arts and culture could play in international affairs. Wartime information work in Canada, US postwar cultural diplomacy undertakings, and the priorities of the newly formed UNESCO were crucial to the increased enthusiasm in postwar Canada for the idea of state-sponsored culture. Zoë Druick observes that this influence of "internationalism in general and the United Nations in particular" on the Massey Commission has been "left largely neglected." Important to this influence is Druick's assertion that UNESCO's rhetorical and practical combination of education and culture with development and trade allowed nations like Canada, which had experienced some resistance to the idea of state-sponsored culture, to present public spending on culture in a new light; instead of conjuring totalitarian control, such spending could now be cast in UNESCO terms as the necessary overlapping of cultural and economic concerns proper to a modern state.[11]

Drawing on Kevin Dowler's well-known assertion that culture in postwar Canada came to be understood as a form of national defence that could counter both the new hegemony of American cultural and economic power and the very different perceived threat of Soviet communism, Jody Berland argues that the state's increased commitment to the arts during the 1950s and '60s also developed in a context in which "Canada sought to make a place for itself as a modern sovereign nation equal in status to other nations of the postwar world." This pursuit of status within a new international order led by the US – bolstered by Canadian accomplishments during the Second World War, the new independence of its judiciary from the British Privy Council, and its autonomy in foreign policy decisions – was, as Litt observes, deemed appropriate in "internationalist circles," where there was "general agreement" that now that "Canada was rubbing shoulders on the world stage with older nations with venerable cultural traditions it should do something to match their refinement." Though, as I note above, the Massey Report did not lead to significant direct state support for the book, it did contain two recommendations that redounded to the benefit of the literary field: support for the establishment of a National Library and for the idea that diplomatic posts could build their libraries as a means of distributing Canadian books abroad. The Massey commissioners' acknowledgment of the need to make Canada better known to its neighbours via the instrument of the book testifies to the currency in the postwar period of the idea that state support for national culture should be somehow *international* in scope and, indeed, to the idea that the book was an instrument that could be put to work to demonstrate the former settler colony's possession of venerable cultural traditions – that is, as signs of its transition from colony to nation.[12]

Yet such apparently seamless development conceals contradiction: while the Massey commissioners invoked the language of contemporary US models of cultural diplomacy, they simultaneously rejected the hegemony of American cultural (and economic) power. For example, the fifth section of the first part of the Massey Report (entitled "Cultural Relations Abroad") offers numerous and often conflicting justifications for the value (drawing on a metaphor from film) of "the projection of Canada abroad." Among these justifications, one finds the nation's responsibility to make a "reasonable contribution to civilized life" and to benefit from such life in other western democracies, while also increasing "Canadian prestige in other countries"; the need to combat Canada's "too frequent recourse" to American culture and institutions; and the obligation to counter the "false propaganda" of "dictatorships" with the "truth effectively and generously disseminated by every practicable means." Concern regarding excessive American cultural influence was thus paired quite unselfconsciously with the American-defined cultural diplomacy language of the period.[13]

In Canada, a postwar program to disseminate books internationally was developed in 1949, prior to the publication of the Massey Report in 1951. The WIB and the CIS had carried on some book-focused cultural relations work on a very small scale, including a book fair in Mexico, and the Information Division of the Department of External Affairs received in the early postwar years communications from diplomatic missions that indicated the fact that some missions were carrying on or envisioning an expanded scope for this kind of work, but, according to Stephens, a program was not initiated by the Information Division until 1949. In September of that year, the Information Division established a modest book presentation program, which came to be known as the Annual (Canadiana) Book Presentation Programme. Under the auspices of the program, the Information Division was authorized to purchase books "about Canada or by Canadians," as well as subscriptions to Canadian periodicals, to offer as donations to libraries outside the US and Canada. The aim of the program was to "increase the knowledge and understanding of Canada and of Canadian affairs abroad" and to promote "Canada's cultural ties with other countries" through print that represented "all aspects of Canadian life and affairs including history, geography, politics and government, economics, literature and the arts." The program was initially somewhat haphazard but was narrowed by 1954 to the goal of providing three selected libraries (one in Europe, one in Asia, and one elsewhere) with five hundred dollars' worth of books (approximately 130 to 150 volumes) each year.[14]

The Information Division committee tasked with selecting titles had, by early 1950, compiled a list of twenty-eight titles that was, according to Janice Cavell, "evenly balanced between fiction and non-fiction." The list was curated through the decade with the help of the book expertise that was beginning to attract state investment in the 1950s: W.K. Lamb, the first National Librarian, was a frequent correspondent of the Information Division members working on the Canadiana program, and the committee took particular note of titles that received Governor General's Literary Awards (a prizing institution taken over by the Canada Council in 1959). By the end of the 1950s, the list comprised 232 selections in English and French (some selections are multivolume works). Only 32 per cent of titles on this list are in the three arts and letters categories (though some interlopers in other categories, such as Philippe Aubert de Gaspé's 1863 historical romance *Les Anciens canadiens*, could be classified under arts and letters, and many of the periodicals fall into this category). Titles in the social sciences (economics, history, political science) dominate the list (see appendix A). Additional tendencies are evident: histories lean to the national rather than the regional or local; the bilingual character of the list enacts the Massey Report's emphasis on Canada as a nation with two founding cultural traditions, English and French; the presence of Indigenous Peoples is ignored, except in anthropological treatments such as Diamond Jenness's 1932 *Indians of Canada*; national economic development is framed as a matter of resource extraction, as in Harold Innis's "staples thesis"; fiction is dominated by Governor General's Award winners. The poetry is modernist, drawing on the free verse, imagist, and masculinist poetics of Anglo-American modernism that Pierre Berton, in the 1958 edition of *Canada from Sea to Sea* that he penned for the Department of External Affairs, contrasts to the earlier Confederation poets. The moderns – A.M. Klein, Douglas LePan, Earle Birney, P.K. Page, Robert Choquette – says Berton, have "gone further afield and show marked originality and individuality in subject matter and in style."[15]

LePan's 1953 Governor General's Award–winning *The Net and the Sword* is a good instance of the list's literary-aesthetic tilt: well-known in Ottawa by the late 1950s as an External Affairs official who had played a key role in the development of the Colombo Plan; and who had served in Washington as minister-counsellor, as secretary and director of research for the Royal Commission on Canada's Economic Prospects, and, briefly, as assistant undersecretary of state, LePan was a self-professed acolyte of T.S. Eliot. The poems of *The Net and the Sword* spin national mythology out of Canada's experience in the Second World War, drawing on LePan's experiences as a soldier in the Canadian army in the 1943–45 Italian campaign. "An Incident" invites readers to "arrange the scene" set before them slightly differently so that they will see, instead of a soldier examining a map under the punishing Italian sun, a

> ... boy in his own native
> And fern-fronded providence,
> With a map in his hand, searching for a portage overgrown
> With brush. Slim he is as a moccasin-flower
> With his throat open
> To the winds, to the four winds, quivering,
> Who alone by the worm-holed flower of the rose-pink house
> Bears the weight of this many-ringed, foreign noon,
> Shadowless, vast and pitiless.

Native of Canada – and indigenized to it via images associated with the fur trade and with Indigenous Peoples ("portage," "moccasin-flower") – the soldier is splayed "flat on the earth" by a "stray round." The "pink house" that looks on is unperturbed by the death – the "incident" – but the implication is that the death will mean much to those who have been asked to "arrange the scene" differently. As we will see, this indigenizing impulse, this tendency to use Indigenous Peoples or images attached to them as a way of bonding the settler to Canada, is one that permeates the Canadiana list.[16]

In 1956, the Information Division added a second book program to its activities, one that demonstrates the close association between cultural diplomacy and foreign aid in this period. The Special Book Presentation Programme aimed to "combat the present flood of literature of Soviet origin in the Colombo Plan area" and to "build up intellectual resistance to communism and not, except indirectly, to project knowledge of Canada." Through the latter half of the 1950s, this second undertaking complemented and indeed threatened to supplant the Canadiana program; however, the two were merged in 1959 when it became clear that Canada's meagre efforts – approximately 1,800 books in 1957–58 – could do little to counter the influence of "cheaply produced popular books" – some thirty million of which were sent in 1958 alone – that the Soviet Union was sending to Asia and Africa. Moreover, the merging of the two would redound to the benefit of the Canadiana program and thus would be of more obvious benefit to

Canada's soft international diplomacy efforts. Indeed, book donation programs at the Department of External Affairs continued long after the period examined here. McGraw-Hill publisher Curtis G. Benjamin's 1984 survey of American and other national book export assistance efforts notes the work of the Canadian Department of External Affairs, including its purchases of books and periodicals for Overseas Book Centres and Canadian embassies, as well as for schools in developing nations that were designing new curricula in English and French. As Benjamin observes, however, the twentieth-century efforts of External Affairs were minor in comparison to the raft of programs developed in relation to the USIA between 1950 and the end of the 1970s.[17]

According to Stephen Brooks, in contrast to the American and American-influenced book initiatives of the postwar years, the Canadian government's cultural diplomacy efforts were poorly funded and lacked coordination and integration with Canadian foreign policy until well into the 1960s. The initial budget for the Canadiana program was two thousand dollars per year and, during the 1950s, the budget for all book programs combined was never more than ten thousand dollars; in the same period, the USIA was spending about six million dollars to send books to Europe and to nations in what was termed the developing world. Australia, a better nation for comparison due to its size and comparable history, spent fifty thousand dollars in 1959 to distribute books about Australia to schools in Indonesia. Nonetheless, in a period when any effort on the part of the federal government to fund and promote culture was a relative novelty, these dollars mattered.[18]

Cavell suggests that in a period when there was little direct state support for book publishers, the book purchasing undertaken by the Department of External Affairs between 1949 and 1963 likely "made a significant contribution to the economic well-being of the Canadian publishing industry." This is quite likely, given that the department supported many Canadian publishers, such as Éditions Beauchemin, McClelland & Stewart, and Ryerson Press. However, unlike American postwar book programs, Canadian programming did not involve the publishing industry in any significant way. Indeed, some civil servants who ordered books for the Canadiana program prioritized price in cases where a book was available from both a domestically owned and a foreign-owned source. Moreover, according to a 1956 memorandum prepared by the Economic Division of the Department of External Affairs that considers the possibility of shipping plates for Canadian technical publications to printers in Southeast Asia to avoid the cost of shipping printed books, there was some wariness in the department regarding government intervention in the business of "private publishing houses in Canada, particularly where its action might affect the determination of whether or not a book would be published, how many copies printed, and at what price, etc. There must be no possible criticism that the Canadian government is trying to affect the commercial activities of the printing and publishing houses, and certainly 'freedom of the press' must be preserved!" This concern extended to the problem of undermining Canadian publishers, who might find their books, printed more cheaply in Asia, reexported to Canada for sale. Even though a strong domestic publishing industry was implied by Canada's participation in US-dominated postwar cultural diplomacy, support for Canadian-owned publishers was not a formal part of the Canadiana program's initial mission to disseminate books "about Canada or by Canadians," and it certainly did not inform the later Special Book Presentation Programme aimed at nations in the Colombo Plan area.[19]

Settler Contradiction: Promoting Canada's Publishing Culture Abroad Through the Annual Book Presentation Programme

Michael Denning has argued that the "mid-century culture concept" was operative in anglophone nations until about 1950: "The modernist notion of culture thus takes shape as an abstract realm of generalized spirituality or religiosity. Thus, culture, one might say, emerges only under capitalism. Though there appears to be culture in precapitalist societies, the concept is invented by Tylorians and Arnoldians [followers of E.B. Tylor and Matthew Arnold] alike to name those places where the commodity does not yet rule: the arts, leisure, and unproductive luxury consumption of revenues by the accumulators; and the ways of life of so-called primitive peoples. The world dominated by capital – the working day, the labor process, the factory and office, machines and technology, and science itself – is thus outside culture." This "culture concept," split as Denning says it was between literary high modernism and the anthropological "science of culture," influenced the modernists who, as Berland notes, formed an important part of Canada's culture lobby during the Massey years and subsequently came to exert considerable force on Canadian cultural policy. Canada's Massey commissioners possessed what Litt calls a "blend of elitist, liberal, and romantic ideas" about culture. Their thinking, and the thinking of many in the groups that formed a culture lobby around them, also bore what Litt identifies as a strong aversion to mass culture: while they abhorred "purely commercial" (and largely American) mass culture, they saw value in the "folklore, customs, and pastimes that traditionally existed in close relation to a people's social culture." Such "grassroots" culture was "vibrant, participatory, and directly relevant to the community life of the individual"; as such, it could combat the effects of mass culture, which "stultified and then manipulated a gullible public."[20]

While the government of Louis St Laurent was eager to represent Canada as a nation that was assuming a place among its equals on a world stage increasingly directed by US hegemony, Canada's settler-colonial status granted it a flexible position on this stage. The nation could both participate in a postwar international order led by industrialized nations and be associated with the "grassroots" culture privileged by the Massey commissioners. The initial title selection for the Department of External Affairs' Annual Book Presentation Programme, known more commonly as the Canadiana program, offers a telling demonstration of this point. According to Cavell, at the first 1949 meeting of the Information Division committee tasked with overseeing the program, it was agreed that the program would include hardcover books in both English and French on history, economics, cultural subjects, geography, and government. At this meeting, committee member and civil servant Laura Beattie suggested John D. Robins's *A Pocketful of Canada* (1946) and Desmond Pacey's *A Book of Canadian Stories* (1947), both of which remained staples on the Canadiana list through the 1950s. A project of the Canadian Council of Education for Citizenship, an association formed in 1940 with the encouragement of federal government officials that brought together volunteer groups and provincial departments of education concerned about education for newcomers, *A Pocketful of Canada* was more or less tailor-made for the book diplomacy efforts of the postwar period.[21]

H.M. Tory, chair of the Canadian Council of Education for Citizenship (and university administrator), makes the domestic and international aims of the book clear in his introduction; it is meant to "bring to the Canadian at home, and to his friends elsewhere, such an interesting and informative view of the real growing and developing Canada as may be gathered from a study of the written record." The book is a miscellany dominated by short fiction and poetry, some of which is presented in sections with regional themes ("West by North"), but it also includes nonfictional contributions by figures such as Marius Barbeau ("Indian Art and Myth") and Lawren Harris ("Reconstruction Through the Arts"), in addition to political and historical essays and documents, such as Lorne Pierce's "The Underlying Principle of Confederation" and excerpts from the 1763 Treaty of Paris. The importance of *A Pocketful* to the Canadiana program is clear: in his 1952 purchase requisition, an employee in the Information Division observed that the book was in "considerable demand"; and, in a period when the department had a budget of only two thousand dollars per year for the program (about six hundred books), they purchased more copies of *A Pocketful* than any other title – 250 copies in 1952 and a further sixty copies in 1953. By the early 1950s, *A Pocketful* was no stranger to international distribution: as Carole Gerson discusses, it was one of the books selected in 1948 by the Canadian Council for Reconstruction Through UNESCO (CCRU) for inclusion in the twenty thousand boxes of school supplies that were sent to classrooms in war-ravaged parts of Europe; its role in this earlier program may have influenced the Department of External Affairs committee tasked with selecting titles.[22]

The overrepresentation of *A Pocketful of Canada* in the Canadiana program is partly explained by the fact that, unlike most purchases the Department of External Affairs made for cultural diplomacy purposes, this title was primarily ordered as a paperback, which came at the attractive price of fifty cents a copy. The moderately priced hardcover books favoured by the department typically cost three to four dollars. Published by William Collins Sons & Company Canada, a subsidiary of the Glasgow-based company that began operating in Toronto during the 1930s, *A Pocketful* was originally issued in cloth-bound hardcovers, but subsequent editions in 1948 and 1952 were paperbacks, the last of which appeared as a White Circle Pocket Edition (see figure 2.1), a series of cheap reprints of successful British, American, and Canadian titles. Launched in 1942 by Collins's Canadian office, the series was modelled after and competed with American firms, such as Pocket

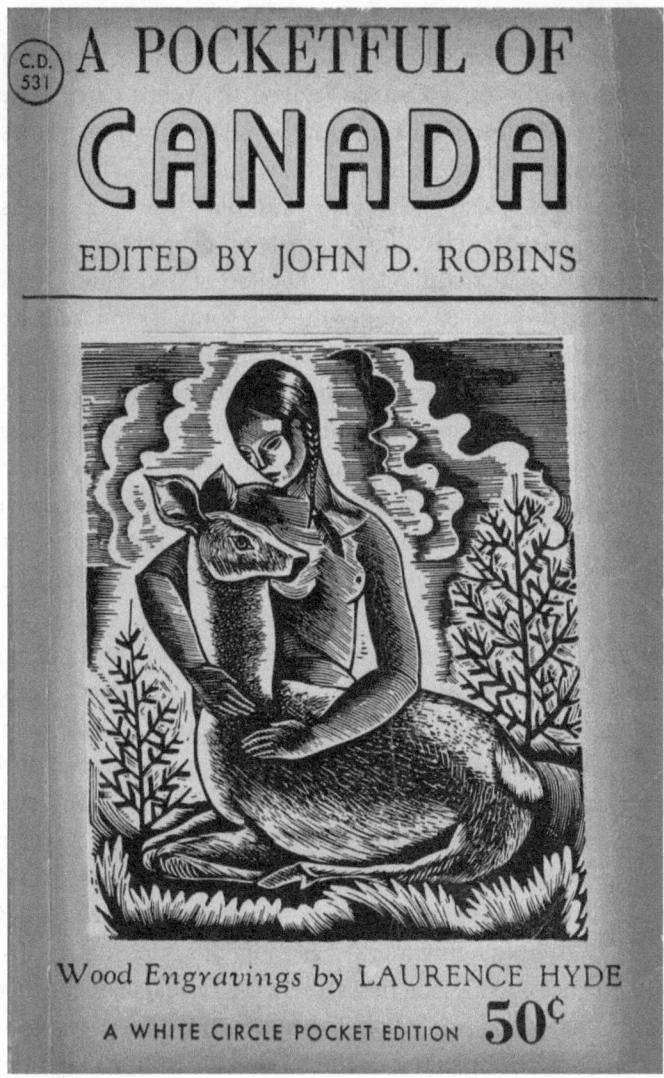

Figure 2.1   The White Circle Pocket Edition of *A Pocketful of Canada*, 1952.

Books and Doubleday, that led the paperback revolution of this period. White Circle Pocket Editions are an early example of mass-market book production – the Toronto branch produced the paperbacks at the rate of eight titles a month – as well as distribution in Canada. According to Grant Campbell and Gerson, the president of Collins's Canadian branch, Franklin Appleton, was an ardent nationalist who used the wartime disruption of the trans-Atlantic book trade to enlarge Collins's Canadian operations, endeavouring through the 1940s to manufacture the majority of the branch's books in Canada. Indeed, the White Circle series was unique for its inclusion of Canadian-authored books – mostly mysteries and romances, though more literary titles, such as Hugh MacLennan's novel *Two Solitudes*, also occasionally found a place. Nonetheless, the White Circle series, which had to compete on drugstore shelves featuring the American and British selections of Pocket Books and Doubleday, was dominated by popular British writers of genre fiction, such as Peter Cheyney and Edwy Searles Brooks. Consequently, although the Canadian branch of Collins became more autonomous during the Second World War and was committed to local manufacturing and to including some Canadian authors in its publishing program, as a subsidiary of a British company that made its money on British and American writers, it was representative of the publishing culture of mid-century English Canada, which was dominated by agency publishers and subsidiaries of foreign companies.[23]

A Pocketful of Canada is an interesting book to read in the context of its use as an instrument of postwar cultural diplomacy because it exemplifies the key operations of settler colonial claims to mature nationhood, which are always premised on an appropriation of Indigenous lifeways as origin. Quite literally enclosing the text's print selections is Laurence Hyde's cover illustration, a wood engraving that features a woman embracing a seated deer. Adorned with simple braids but no clothing and placed in proximity to nature (the deer, the forest background), this is a figure marked as Indigenous for non-Indigenous postwar audiences. As Gerson notes, there is a "visual dialogue" between *A Pocketful*'s woodcuts and its photographs: if Hyde's woodcuts, which pepper the book's endpapers (in the hardcover edition) and mark off each of the book's sections, represent the values of craftsmanship and simplicity of the era's fine-press work, these images contrast with the book's photographic essay by Donald W. Buchanan, which comprises stills from NFB documentaries that narrate the nation's industrial "progress." According to Gerson, this dialogue demonstrates "the differing conceptions of Canada prevalent during the immediate post-war period," but it is also a wonderful material instance of the contradictions that constituted the settler nationalism of this moment. Aligned with an iconography of Indigeneity, the book's woodcuts function as a balm for both the American mass culture the Massey commissioners detested, on one hand, and on the other the modernization and "progress" the book witnesses and, indeed, celebrates. The woodcuts draw on what Lorenzo Veracini describes as "settler indigenization" – settler "appropriation of indigenous cultural attributes" as a means of claiming authenticity for the national project. Like other titles on the Canadiana program list by the end of the 1950s, such as Emily Carr's *Klee Wyck* (1941) and Marius Barbeau's *The Tree of Dreams* (1955; a translation of *L'Arbre des rêves*), the woodcuts function in complex ways. All at once, they critique American models of industrial mass production, while easing the transition to an age characterized in Buchanan's visual essay as the "conquest of space"; they appropriate "traditional" cultures that are not coterminous with settler cultures and thus disavow the foundational violence of the nation; and they value "grassroots" culture, while marking the destruction of the lifeways and knowledges they purport to value.[24]

Layered upon these contradictions is another, one that was produced by English Canada's relation to the concept of "civilization" that was attached to the postwar cultural diplomacy efforts led by the US. As I describe above, Canada's Massey commissioners repeated the language of American cultural diplomacy in their 1951 report; their appeal to the nation's responsibility to make a "reasonable contribution to civilized life," as well as its obligation to counter the "false propaganda" of "dictatorships," refers back to the argument, common in the American-led development establishment of the period, that liberal democracy was contingent on the "free and earnest exchange of ideas," an exchange that rested on the basic assumption that the high literacy rates and modernized book industries of the western democracies were crucial to their freedoms. Yet this language put English Canadians in an uncomfortable position because it implies that the nation had a robust publishing industry. *A Pocketful of Canada* offers an intriguing exemplification of this problem. Its contents suggest that Canada is a nation rich in the preindustrial arts. These arts are associated with both Indigenous and settler cultures, and include totem poles (Barbeau's "Indian Art and Myth"; a photograph of Emily Carr's painting "Blunden Harbour"), the wooden cradle of the *habitant* (Adjutor Rivard's "The Cradle"), and the canoe (one of Hyde's engravings; excerpts from Ralph Connor's *Postscript to Adventure*; John D. Robins's *The Incomplete Anglers*), as well as Hyde's woodcuts. Yet these arts give way to print and publishing, which are cast as handmaidens of the industrial progress the book takes as a sign of the nation's maturity, as H.M. Tory's introduction makes clear in its prizing of the "ever-increasing accumulation of the written word" as the site for the development of the "spirit of a nation." The cultural nationalist argument here emplots a narrative that blithely absorbs the appeal to Indigenous authenticity and preindustrial craft as earlier stages of national development. This nation-story of development is connected to what Johnston and Lawson call the "strategic disavowal of the colonizing act," via which the "'the national' replaces 'the indigenous.'" Such a narrative places Canada among the western leaders of the postwar order, while insisting that its origin is more authentic than crass American mass culture. Moreover, Tory's narration of the nation's print progress contradicts the actual history of publishing conditions in Canada. *A Pocketful of Canada* is a book with small fonts, thin paper, and tiny margins, and as a White Circle paperback – the form in which it most commonly circulated through the Canadiana program – it speaks explicitly to the influence of American mass book production on publishing in Canada and implicitly to the domination of Canadian publishing in this period by British and American companies. In other words, what the book avows in its iconography, its themes, and its arguments, it disavows in its material form.[25]

Desmond Pacey's *A Book of Canadian Stories* (1947), the second book suggested by Laura Beattie at the initial 1949 meeting of the committee tasked with selecting books for the Canadiana program, offers a similar embodiment of the contradictions that Canadian book diplomacy produced in the postwar years. According to Robert Lecker, Pacey's short story anthology was one of the earliest of its kind in Canada. It is thus not surprising that Pacey devotes space in his introduction to a narrative of the "origins" of English Canadian literature, which he locates not in the "Indian tales" that he includes and then passes over, but in Atlantic Canada, and more particularly in the arrival of the printing press in Nova Scotia in the eighteenth century. Looking to the Loyalists who arrived in that region during the American Revolution, Pacey finds the "real beginnings of literary activity in what is now Canada." Key to his narrative are figures such as John Howe (father of Joseph Howe), a Boston editor who arrived in Nova Scotia in 1776 with his printing press. Pacey considers the Howe family significant not merely for their printing and publishing contributions to British North America, but also for Joseph Howe's establishment of "the principle of a free press in

Canada." (*A Pocketful of Canada* similarly privileges this contribution, reprinting "On the Freedom of the Press," an excerpt from Joseph Howe's speech at his libel trial in 1835.)[26]

Yet Pacey's account of "real beginnings" contains a significant error: clearly desiring to link Howe's early *printing* efforts to something closer in identity to *publishing*, Pacey suggests that John Howe was responsible for the establishment of the newspaper the *Novascotian*, and that he passed the newspaper along to his son in 1828, creating the conditions that made the younger Howe a "pioneer in the establishment of a distinctive Canadian culture." Contrary to this account, the paper was actually founded in 1824 by George R. Young, and Joseph Howe assumed control in 1827. This error demonstrates the fact that English Canadian literary history was, in 1947, building narratives out of a scarcity of scholarship; indeed, what scholarship existed did not tend to notice the economic relations that were important in determining the literary field of the former settler colony. Thus the fact that Pacey's critical framing passes over key legal and economic structures – copyright agreements, the agency system – in his tracing of the "inhibiting factors" that have "held back the growth of Canadian short stories" is not surprising. A text that attributes the growth of a national literature to the arrival of the printing press and then does not follow the fate of that press and others like it, favouring instead arguments that attend to aesthetic development, *A Book of Canadian Stories* offered to Canada's postwar cultural diplomacy efforts a narrative that celebrates – but does not examine too closely – a strongly rooted tradition of press freedom, printing, and publishing.[27]

"Human Dignity and Individual Liberty": Books as Colombo Plan Aid

The Canadiana program received a complement in 1956 with the inauguration of the Special Book Presentation Programme. This program differed from the Canadiana program in the sense that its principal task was not to communicate information about Canada to international audiences; instead, it was given the relatively quixotic missions of combatting the influence of print material being sent by the Soviet Union to the Colombo Plan nations of Asia and of building intellectual resistance to communism.

The Colombo Plan was an important element of Canada's postwar foreign policy. The international events of the late 1940s and early '50s marked significant moments in the early Cold War: the 1947 Truman Doctrine, the communist revolution in China during the last half of the 1940s, and the outbreak of the Korean War in June of 1950 brought a new focus to Canadian foreign policy. As Keith Spicer (one of the founders of the Canadian University Service Overseas and author of the first monograph on the topic of Canadian foreign aid) notes in a 1970 assessment of the plan, "after the 1948 coup de Prague had hardened Western resolve to hold the non-communist side of the Iron Curtain through NATO, the focus of imminent communist danger shifted, with Mao's triumph in October 1949, to China's soft, subcontinental underbelly. And however smug and clever Canada's rationalizations for aid became in later years, it is well to recall that the Colombo Plan crystallized essentially to stop the Red and Yellow Perils." Other historians note that, in addition to these Cold War contexts, the plan was at least partly motivated by the need to prevent nations like India, Pakistan, and Ceylon from calling in loans they had made to the British during the Second World War. The plan offered alternative sources of capital for these nations, which in turn meant that Britain's economic difficulties in this period would not be worsened, a fact that was important for Canada, whose second-largest trading partner was Britain. Others note that the genesis of the Colombo Plan must be read as part of the history of decolonization. Corrina R. Unger argues, for instance, that the Colombo Plan "mainly reflected Great Britain's geopolitical interests in Asia"; the United Kingdom sought through the program to preserve "British influence in Asia beyond colonial rule."[28]

Proposed at a 1950 meeting of Commonwealth foreign ministers by Australia, Ceylon (now Sri Lanka), and New Zealand, the Commonwealth Aid Program for the nations of South and Southeast Asia originally comprised member nations India, Pakistan, Ceylon, Malaysia, Canada, Australia, and the United Kingdom. Though the goal of fortifying receiving nations' "capacity to resist communism" was a clear motivation for the initiative, particularly after North Korea's invasion of South Korea in September of 1950, this tended to be framed euphemistically. The stated goal, in the words of the ministers, was to raise living standards and promote social welfare to enable "this area with its vast potential resources to play an increasing part in fostering well-being and furthering world prosperity." Similarly, in the 1950 Colombo Plan Report, Canadian official Douglas LePan wrote: "In a world racked by schism and confusion it is doubtful whether free men can long afford to leave undeveloped and imprisoned in poverty the human resources of the countries of South and South-East Asia which could help us so greatly, not only to restore the world's prosperity, but also to redress its confusion and enrich the lives of all men everywhere."[29]

Canadian officials were important to the design of the plan. LePan, who wore many hats at External Affairs during his 1945–59 tenure, participated in the Canadian delegations to the 1950 meetings of the Commonwealth Consultative Committee and helped to draft the Colombo Plan Report outlining a six-year program of economic development in Asia that would cost $2.8 billion to establish. In early 1951, still waiting for a US commitment, a somewhat reluctant cabinet pledged Canada to twenty-five million for one year (rather than for the full six years that LePan had recommended). Through the 1950s Canada's contributions increased significantly alongside its expanding aid budgets, but US entry into the plan in 1958 injected a contribution that, according to Spicer, nonetheless "dwarfed" those of the Commonwealth nations.[30]

Consistent with a "liberal-capitalist version of modernization," the Colombo Plan at its inception was, as David Meren argues, predicated on a "Eurocentric and linear understanding of societal development from pre-agricultural to consumer society." The roots of postwar foreign aid in colonial regimes and ideologies are important here: as LePan observes in his account of the plan's establishment, there was in 1950 little economic theory and little history of practice in the field of economic development, such that "the principal reservoirs of experience with the problem of underdevelopment still lay with the colonial and ex-colonial powers." Focused on modernization, Canada's Colombo Plan aid favoured economic development projects. Projects under the plan were bilateral, and, during the first decade of the plan, Canadian aid supported hydroelectric and other power projects (including the Canada-India Atomic Reactor), transport, communications, public health, natural resources development, projects linked to agriculture and fisheries, and commodity assistance programs and technical assistance. Receiving nations in this period included India, East and West Pakistan, Ceylon, and Malaya. The economic development impetus of the plan should not conceal the fact that Canada's contributions could and did redound to *Canada's* economic benefit. For example, as Meren points out, the federal government's initial twenty-five-million-dollar contribution to the Colombo Plan was contingent on India's use of ten to fifteen million of these funds to purchase Canadian wheat. Other economic advantages to Canada were more abstract: the incorporation of new economies into the liberal-capitalist world order could serve Canadian economic and political interests.[31]

Complementing the aims of economic development projects were the less frequently studied cultural elements of the plan, which included, during the last half of the 1950s, a book donation program. These "softer" kinds of programs began to emerge after the death of Josef Stalin in 1953, and particularly after the election of John Diefenbaker's Progressive Conservative government in 1957. In this period, the Canadian government became convinced of the need to fight the Cold War by what Cory Scurr calls "other means" – engaging the Soviet Union in trade activities and "exposing Soviet society to Western modalities and cultural life" through cultural diplomacy initiatives, such as an exhibition of Inuit carving that toured Poland, Czechoslovakia, Yugoslavia, and the Soviet Union from 1959 to 1962 under the supervision of the Department of External Affairs. The notes prepared for Jules Léger, the undersecretary of the Department of External Affairs, to speak before a 1956 Standing Committee on External Affairs indicate that although Canada's approach to informational work had been "passive" in the postwar period compared to that of the Soviet Union, this was changing:

> We in Canada have made little or no effort to contest this field believing, as we do, that given access to the truth, normal people will know how to choose. A recent change in Soviet tactics has however made it necessary for us to take stock of the situation. We must consider what new measures should be taken to counteract the new Soviet campaign of culture and education which contains some elements of objectivity. Standard non-political books as well as eminent and equally non-political artists are being sent out from Moscow into many parts of the world. This is a direct challenge to the west as a source of learning, particularly in matters relating to non-materialistic activities. We must, therefore, offer an alternative source of this type of general

information. We know that in many places where books are
scarce large numbers of people are so eager for information that
they will, without discrimination, read whatever is available. It
is in our democratic interest therefore that an attempt should be
made in certain areas to build up collections of standard works of
literature, particularly those works which convey our conception
of human dignity and individual liberty.

The Special Book Presentation Programme was one short-lived manifestation of this shift.[32]

With an initial budget of eight thousand dollars, the Special Book Presentation Programme was concretized in a book list created by the Information Division with the help of National Librarian W.K. Lamb. According to M.Q. Dench of the Information Division, the goal of the program was to "disseminate knowledge and understanding of democracy in the Colombo Plan area" and not to provide "technical education." Donations in the first year of the program went to India, Pakistan, Indonesia, and Ceylon. In 1957–58, the program's budget was scaled back by half as a wait-and-see measure; Lamb continued to consult, but Information Division officials also sought ideas from professors at the University of Toronto and Université de Laval working in the disciplines of political science, economics, sociology, history, and philosophy. Recipient nations in the second year included Malaya, India, Pakistan, and Cambodia. A 1957 draft memorandum on the Special Book Presentation Programme indicates that officials estimated that the program might "be carried out more satisfactorily" if recipient libraries could choose a specified number of books from a predetermined list, which would ideally contain 200 to 250 titles in the categories of history, biography, literature, essays and opinion, politics and government, international relations, economics, and philosophy, as well as the contents of the Canadiana list.[33]

By 1959, the final year of the program, the list comprised 112 selections in English and 98 in French (some selections are multi-volume works). Selections in the areas of economics and politics dominate. Both lists are saturated with economic arguments for welfare state capitalism and for the importance of integrating workers' demands into the capitalist economy, such as those of John Maynard Keynes and of his followers John Kenneth Galbraith and Joan Robinson, or those of André

Marchal and Jean Fourastié in France. The lists offer generous doses of liberal political philosophy (John Locke, Montesquieu), while giving up significant space to apologists for contemporary liberal democracy, from Karl Popper to Arthur R.M. Lower, as well as to texts that tout the new postwar instruments of international governance, such as Stanley Hoffman's *Organisations internationales et pouvoirs politiques des états* (1954), Paul Reuter's *Institutions internationales* (1955), or William Frye's *A United Nations Peace Force* (1957). Books on Canadian history and government in the English-language list – such as Donald Creighton's two-volume biography of John A. Macdonald, Arthur R.M. Lower's *Colony to Nation* (1946), and Lester B. Pearson's *Democracy in World Politics* (1955) – offer a narrative of Canada's desired entry onto the world stage as a mature liberal democracy, but these form only a subplot to the main action, which is dominated by titles dealing with Britain and European nations. The French-language list is populated almost entirely by titles from France (see appendix B). American-authored books constitute a minor presence in the list, an acknowledgment of the fact that American book donation programs were dwarfing Canadian ones in this period. There was no need to donate American books when Americans were doing this very well themselves.

Some titles that are notably absent from the Special Book Presentation Programme list of 1955, such as Igor Gouzenko's *The Fall of a Titan* (1954), demonstrate how American domination of North American publishing and thus book donation shaped the Government of Canada's approach to its earliest book development efforts. Gouzenko, a young cipher clerk for the Soviet Embassy in Ottawa, defected to Canada in 1945 after implicating a number of Canadians in Soviet espionage, but, according to Gary Marcuse and Reginald Whitaker, the Canadian government did not act on his claims for almost half a year, positioned delicately as it was against a US that was looking for reasons to reject an agreement for international control of the atom bomb. Implicating the Soviet Union in international espionage would damage any case for Soviet (and, by extension, British and Canadian) participation in such control. Yet when the Canadian government's hand was finally forced, it was because the Washington journalist Drew Pearson, acting on a leak from inside the US government, broke the story in the US media. Prime Minister Mackenzie King understood the situation: the US, in the thick of its own efforts to expose Soviet spying, wanted Canada to act first. The scandal attracted international attention because it exposed the existence of Soviet spying not just in Canada but also in the US and the United Kingdom and was thus a key event in the inauguration of the Cold War.[34]

The context in which *The Fall of a Titan* was published similarly tells a story in which the US was dictating outcomes. In the context of the agency system that structured Canadian publishing in this decade, another option available to Canadian publishers who wished to finance Canadian-authored titles was a copublication arrangement with a US publisher. This kind of arrangement carried the added bonus of granting US copyright protection to the book, which would otherwise not have had this protection. Given this situation, many Canadian authors went one further and opted for the all-American or American/British route if they could. This is the option that Gouzenko – who had clear designs on the large English-speaking audiences of the US and Britain – chose for his Russian spy novel *The Fall of a Titan*, published in 1954 by W.W. Norton in New York and Cassell in London and Toronto. Translated into English (and possibly ghostwritten) by Mervyn Black, Gouzenko's popular thriller blends anti-communist propaganda with the cachet of the Gouzenko affair. Though the novel was a crucial document in what Richard Cavell identifies as the particular cultural dimensions of Canada's Cold War period – the bestowal of the 1954 Governor General's Award for English-language fiction on the novel was, in Cavell's estimation, "one of the most unambiguously political moves in Canadian cultural history" – it was also thoroughly enmeshed in American Cold War culture: it was a Book-of-the-Month Club selection and received reviews in prominent US publications, such as *The New York Times* and *The Washington Post and Times Herald*, among others, all of which linked the book to the 1945 Gouzenko affair. Cold War cause célèbre, Gouzenko's tale was featured in a series of articles in *Cosmopolitan* magazine in 1947 and formed the basis of the 1948 20th Century-Fox film *The Iron Curtain*, as well as his 1947 memoir *The Iron Curtain: Inside Stalin's Spy Ring* (published in Canada under the much less Hollywood-esque title *This Was My Choice*).[35]

As a novel published in the US and highly identified with the culture of America's Cold War, *The Fall of a Titan* was quite simply snapped up by the USIA before the Canadian government had even put together its first list for the Colombo Plan books program. In February of 1957, less than a year after funding had been announced for the Special Book Presentation Programme, the Canadian embassy in Washington sent to External Affairs information regarding a USIA program "using native methods and facilities" to publish and distribute "low-priced paperbacked books in the under-developed countries," especially nations in Southeast Asia. The list of books includes eighty titles in English as well as sixteen foreign-language titles; among the latter is a Japanese-language translation of *The Fall of a Titan*, a success in the program because it sold eleven thousand copies of a press run of twenty-five thousand in three months.[36]

The Special Book Presentation Programme also avoided contemporary titles that, although they had received significant international attention, had rendered visible some of the domestic contradictions upon which Canada's new postwar forays into foreign aid were based. Farley Mowat's 1952 *The People of the Deer* offers a case in point. As Meren's work shows, the history of Canadian foreign aid, which begins in the immediate postwar years, might be better understood if read in relation to contemporary domestic politics and federal policy aimed at Indigenous Peoples. For Meren, Canada's entanglements in the Colombo Plan reveal "the points of convergence between Canadian aid and Indian policies, highlighting how intersecting notions of 'modernization,' liberal-capitalist preoccupations, and racialized understandings of development informed Canadian efforts in both fields." According to the 1968 Colombo Plan Report, Canada's contributions to the plan had especially drawn on "those fields where Canadian technological experience, gained in many cases through the development of Canada itself, has been of special value." If Canada's involvement was viewed as a product of its experience in domestic resource extraction, itself premised on the dispossession of Indigenous Peoples, Meren's point is that there are still other convergences of domestic and international development to attend to when analyzing the history of the program. Meren's focus is an ill-fated "reciprocal aid" plan that would have seen India send yaks to Ungava in the western Arctic in order to encourage settled lifeways and animal husbandry among the Inuit. Meren's argument is suggestive of a broader set of questions regarding the confluence of development abroad and internal colonization at home during the late 1940s and '50s, while also offering an opportunity to think about the ways that a postwar discourse of development framed development as something that needed to occur elsewhere, as a duty to others to which, as the Department of External Affairs put it in 1962, Canadians could not be "indifferent."[37]

The case presented by Mowat's *The People of the Deer* – a text conspicuously absent from both the Canadiana and the Special Book Presentation Programme lists – is provocatively linked to such questions. Serialized in three issues of *The Atlantic* in 1952 before being published by Little, Brown in the US, Michael Joseph in the United Kingdom, and McClelland & Stewart in Canada, *The People of the Deer* provoked outrage and admiration, as well as considerable skepticism, from readers and reviewers all over the world. Mowat's book presents the inland Inuit of the Keewatin region of the Northwest Territories (living in what is now the Kivalliq region of Nunavut), the Ahiarmiut, as a people suffering from the neglect of a callous federal government. The optics were not favourable: just as the Canadian government was expanding its foreign aid commitments through the Colombo Plan and at the very moment when, as Frank Tester and Peter Kulchyski put it, Canada was trying, "under the tutelage of Lester Pearson and his colleagues," to "play a leading role in world affairs," Mowat was telling the world that Canada did not have its act together at home.[38]

Mowat's pathos-filled account of the two years he spent in the western Arctic narrates the "disintegration and degradation" of a "race" perpetrated by greedy fur traders, who weaned the Inuit of Ennadai Lake from their tradition of caribou hunting, and more recent well-intentioned but misinformed government efforts in the North. Though critical of the federal government's role in the 1950 relocation of this community to Nueltin Lake, for example, Mowat's book at the same time frames its argument in terms that would have readily found an audience in Ottawa, and elsewhere in North America, in the early 1950s. As "guardians and protectors" of the "Eskimos," the federal government is duty bound, Mowat insists, to intervene in the lives of the Ahiarmiut. But this does not mean it should offer handouts; instead, the state must help the Inuit to help themselves by aiding them in the establishment of an effective caribou-raising industry, thus effecting "the transition from primitivism to modernism" and opening "the passageway from the world of the Inuit to our world." The benefits that would redound to settler Canadians would not be simply those of an eased conscience, according to Mowat; such actions would also contribute to arctic defence: "If the Eskimos were our own people instead of being an inferior race, dependent on our charity (and this is the semi-official view of them today), they could assist us in the defence of our common countries as no other ally could." These appeals to both "modernization" and Canada's sovereignty in the North savvily tapped into postwar federal priorities.[39]

The publication of Mowat's book and the furor that ensued dovetailed with the federal government's mounting interest in northern development and increasingly interventionist approach to Inuit affairs during the 1950s. The book was taken up in debates in the House of Commons at least three times in the wake of its publication – in December of 1953, January of 1954, and finally in February of 1954, as Jean Lesage, new minister of Northern Affairs and National Resources, denied the allegations Mowat makes in *The People of the Deer*, that government neglect had led to starvation among the Ahiarmiut. Anxious to avoid further questioning in the House of Commons, the department began to monitor more closely the Inuit who returned to Ennadai Lake in 1955 (after a failed government relocation in 1950) and eventually opted for a second relocation in 1957. Tester and Kulchyski demonstrate that the increasingly interventionist approach favoured by the federal government in the Arctic after 1950 was influenced by a number of interrelated factors, including the strategic importance of the region in the context of the Cold War, a growing awareness of the failure of the private sector to attend to the health and welfare needs of the Inuit population, a sense that this population needed to be "modernized," and a mounting conviction that the North was an important site of potential resource development. Just as the Colombo Plan was at least partly about folding outlier nations in the liberal-capitalist order, so was Ottawa's administration of Inuit affairs during the 1950s.[40]

That *The People of the Deer* did not find a place in the Special Book Presentation Programme is not surprising, but its absence is worth pausing on because it elucidates the ways that the book list, as an external projection of liberal-capitalist values that root Canada in a British economic and political tradition while pointing to its new internationalist commitments, only barely conceals the contradictions of the settler-colonial context. Given the extraordinary international attention Mowat's book received, it would make sense for it to have appeared in the government's postwar book programs, particularly the Canadiana program, which gave up more space to the kind of creative nonfiction that ultimately became Mowat's hallmark. (We recall that after 1957, recipients of the Special Book Presentation Programme titles also received the contents of the Canadiana list.) And yet the book's thematizing of development issues as they pertained in the 1950s not to the nations of Asia but to Canada's own Northwest Territories renders it unspeakable in the context of the dual emergence of the nation's sovereign cultural diplomacy and foreign aid efforts. By the mid-1950s, despite general public support for the federal government's contributions to the Colombo Plan, there was nevertheless sensitivity regarding the question of "underdevelopment" at home, particularly as the nation prepared for the Royal Commission on Canada's Economic Prospects. In October of 1955, for instance, *The Globe and Mail* reported that Newfoundland premier Joey Smallwood was seeking "an all-Canadian Colombo Plan designed to bring help to the underdeveloped parts of our country" – in other words, a plan that would purchase goods from less wealthy provinces. Such sensitivity regarding domestic "underdevelopment" forms part of the larger context in which Mowat's book was received.[41]

What *could* be spoken at mid-century is a narrative of Canadian history that differs significantly from Mowat's. Arthur R.M. Lower's Governor General's Award–winning *Colony to Nation* (1946), for instance, offers a teleological account of a maturing liberal democracy. What Alan Greer calls a "whiggish history" that recounts "a story of the gradual and peaceful development of British liberty within a framework of growing colonial autonomy," Lower's book blithely ignores those for whom British liberty was simply not available. His chapter on the first term of Sir John A. Macdonald, for instance, makes no mention of the 1876 Indian Act, preferring instead to chart the "majestic course" of the "main current of Canadian history." Similarly speakable was the representation of Canada's North found in Pierre Berton's Governor General's Award–winning *The Mysterious North* (1956), which appeared in the Canadiana list and manages to say little about Indigenous Peoples and much about the potential for industrial expansion in the region. Complementing as it did newly elected Prime Minister John Diefenbaker's "northern vision" – a plan to cement Canadian sovereignty in the North and to develop its resources for the ostensible benefit of all Canadians – Berton's book trades in the modernization theory that constituted the bread and butter of the Colombo Plan.[42]

The Special Book Presentation Programme was a short-lived embodiment of the kinds of cultural or "soft" diplomacy efforts that characterized the Cold War in the latter half of the 1950s. Linked as it was to Canada's first significant investment in foreign aid, however, it has also been used to narrate an emergent aspect of what so many settler Canadians referred to in the 1950s as the nation's "character." According to LePan, writing from the vantage point of the late 1970s, Canada's involvement in the Colombo Plan was not primarily a Cold War tactic; the principal motivation of the Canadian government officials involved in the development of the plan, says LePan, was "humanitarian." In LePan's view, it is this motivation that came to shape Canadian society. Canada's involvement after 1950 in the Colombo Plan paved the way for other foreign aid initiatives, which, in addition to the nation's many private and semi-private foreign aid programs, were by 1979 administered by CIDA's annual budget of approximately one million dollars. It is this legacy that LePan connects to his work on the Colombo Plan: "To put it more generally, I believe that the Colombo Plan has lastingly changed Canadian life, has added to it a new and enduring colouring, a tincture, a dye that will not easily disappear, so that year after year external aid will continue to appear on the agenda of Parliament and volunteers will be setting out from Canada to teach – and to learn – in the countries of the developing world." As Ted Cogan observes, a 1951 Department of External Affairs press survey indicates that "humanitarianism" was the public's favoured justification for foreign aid; subsequently, this "humanitarian" narrative came to displace the need to fight communism as the privileged rationale for the Colombo Plan. According to Dan Gorman, settler Canadians' Commonwealth and British-centric identifications gave way in the two decades between 1940 and 1960 to an "ethnically opaque civic nationalism" that could be attached to a "broader, progressive universalist project" of liberal internationalism, sometimes described as "humanitarianism." Yet there is another way of telling this story – one that the Special Book Presentation Programme list (and its notable absences) also tells: modernization theory whether implemented abroad or at home worked to serve the interests of liberal-capitalist development.[43]

Conclusion

In her study of Canada's postwar book diplomacy, Cavell contends that by 1960, "the idea of book presentations as a cornerstone of cultural diplomacy, and especially of Canada's cultural relations with the developing world, was firmly established." After 1959, the state-funded purchase of Canadian-authored books for dissemination abroad became one of the responsibilities of the Canada Council, which disbursed funds for the purchase of Canadian periodicals and books for distribution in Canadian embassies abroad. As a result of a new federal book publishing policy, the Council began after 1972 to manage the federal Book Purchase Program, which acquired Canadian-authored books for distribution to Canadian consulates and libraries around the world.[44]

Canadian postwar book diplomacy offers a rich site for the analysis of the paradoxes that constitute Canada's settler-colonial nationhood, particularly as its myths of origin congealed in the decades following the Second World War. Supported in important ways by Canada's participation in book diplomacy and donation schemes led and defined by the US (a nation that was attempting to counter the emergent efforts of the Soviet Union in this same domain), the dominant narrative of Canada in the 1950–75 period is one of national becoming and of the achievement of cultural and political maturity. Subtending this smooth narrative is a set of bumpy contradictions: Canada's international positioning in these years was dependent on American hegemony but critical of its cultural inauthenticity, a condition countered in the Department of External Affairs' Canadiana program through appeals to Indigenous origins and traditions of preindustrial craft that were in turn subjected to modernizing narratives that drew on the authenticating power of these origins, while erasing their ongoing presence in "modern" Canada. More generally, Canada's participation in the book diplomacy efforts of the postwar years belongs to a larger history of the book in the late twentieth century, a history that is deeply bound up in struggles that eventually pitted American and western European media corporations against the local interests of the world's decolonizing nations. The ambivalent positioning of former settler colonies such as Canada in this struggle is best illuminated not through metaphors of "arrival" but rather through the analysis of contradiction.

3

"Not Even Bread Itself"

Nongovernmental Book Development in Late Twentieth-Century Canada

While Canada's book diplomacy in the late 1940s and '50s played a role in the articulation of what Anna Johnston and Alan Lawson call the "settler-imperium" "vector of difference," and if the previous chapter attended to the ways that this settler cultural nationalism was embedded in the perpetuation of the internal colonization of Indigenous nations in Canada, this chapter turns to nongovernmental book development programs of the 1950s, '60s, and '70s to show how these were imbricated more generally in neocolonial practices beyond Canada's own borders. The contradictions that these practices produced offer another view of the complexity of settler-colonial nation-making during the three and a half decades that followed the close of the Second World War. Nongovernmental book development programs such as the Overseas Book Centre were enmeshed in a voluntary internationalism that depended on rhetorical representations of Canada as unique from European nations because of its recent history as a colony; the implication of such arguments was that Canada was at the same time set apart from the US, which was remaking the old mantle of imperialism for the postwar world. On the new stage provided by the international institutions of the postwar world, Canada could thus be made to seem both exceptional and innocent of ongoing colonization.

At the same time and in concert with what was coming to be called by 1950 "development," this voluntary internationalism perpetuated neocolonial economic systems that failed to nourish – and in some cases even actively undermined – local production capacities, especially as these related to publishing. Premised on the idea that excess books could be redistributed to areas in need, nongovernmental postwar programs such as the Canadian Council for Reconstruction Through UNESCO (CCRU, established 1947) focused on disseminating books to war-ravaged parts of Europe. By the late 1950s and early '60s this same concept of book development as book donation animated the mission of Canada's first NGO, the Overseas Book Centre / Centre du livre pour outre-mer (OBC/CLO, established in 1959). The OBC/CLO book donation model rehearsed in its early decades a practice commonly known as "book dumping": if this practice was decried by Canadian publishers in the nineteenth and early twentieth centuries for its negative effects on local book production, it was recycled under the guise of North-South philanthropy in the mid-twentieth century. Though OBC/CLO founder and internationalist J.R. Kidd actively promulgated Canada's "special mission" as a former colony possessing strong bonds of sympathy with decolonizing nations, book dumping emphasized the disparities between the giver and the receivers.[1]

The primary focus of OBC/CLO's work during its first two decades – the collection of secondhand books for shipment to and distribution in developing countries – speaks to the kind of book development that was possible for a late twentieth-century Canadian NGO. Unlike the much larger Franklin Book Programs in the US, the OBC/CLO could not hope to build domestic book industries from the ground up. As OBC/CLO board member (and program officer for the Canadian Commission for UNESCO) Louise Rohonczy observes in a 1974 discussion paper, few book development programs other than the OBC/CLO existed in Canada, likely due to "our own shaky publishing scene." Though Rohonczy's comment is rare in OBC/CLO records, it indicates an important truth: as we saw in the preceding chapter, there was no significant Canadian-owned publishing industry in Canada at mid-century. Despite policy that began to emerge after the 1951 Massey Report, the situation did not change much until the introduction of federal block grants for Canadian-owned publishers in the early 1970s. The OBC/CLO's book donation scheme, which relied on donations of no-longer-needed books from Canadians rather than the provision of technical know-how about how to build domestic book industries, squared a circle, permitting Canadians to undertake book development while lacking a robust book publishing industry of their own.[2]

The Canadian Council for Reconstruction Through UNESCO: Books for "Hungry Minds"

Quite apart from the book initiatives undertaken by Canada's Department of External Affairs in the immediate postwar years was the work of a variety of semi-governmental and nongovernmental organizations, such as the CCRU, that contributed to postwar reconstruction in Europe, an effort that Ottawa supported to the tune of slightly more than two million dollars. As I argue in the preceding chapter, UNESCO came to exert considerable influence on Canada's postwar discussions about the relation of culture to the state: its mandate shaped the terms and recommendations of the Massey Commission, including the 1951 report's call to establish the Canada Council, which was meant to function, among other things, as a national commission for UNESCO. Moreover, as Zoë Druick points out, each of the five members of the Massey Commission was "actively engaged with international affairs," and most of them were also "directly or indirectly involved with UNESCO." In the context of what Maria Tippett characterizes as civilian postwar enthusiasm in Canada for internationalism – despite some reservations ultimately expressed by the Massey commissioners regarding UNESCO's "catholicity of enterprise" – the CCRU undertook its activities. Alongside institutions like the NFB, which were also in this period linking cultural texts to liberal internationalism and education, the CCRU helped to establish the idea that Canadian culture could be distributed abroad not simply as a tool of cultural diplomacy, but also as an instrument of what was coming to be called "development."[3]

Created in 1947 at the urging of the Department of External Affairs, which did not, according to Linda Goldthorp, desire in the immediate postwar period an active role in UNESCO, the CCRU gathered some thirty voluntary organizations that committed to tackling the UNESCO-mandated work of raising funds for "educational, scientific, and cultural reconstruction in war-devastated countries throughout the world." The CCRU was given financial wings from two sources: the Department of External Affairs, which pledged a two-hundred-thousand-dollar grant; and the Canadian United Allied Relief Fund, which contributed a ten-thousand-dollar grant, as well as office space and administrative assistance from its Sparks Street location in Ottawa. Once established and with a provisional executive committee in place, the CCRU rolled up its fundraising sleeves, joining forces with the Canadian United Nations Appeal for Children in early 1948 to undertake the Canadian Appeal for Children. According to a 1949 CCRU report, this campaign had, by early 1949, raised almost one million dollars for the CCRU (which took 40 per cent of the proceeds).[4]

A central element of the appeal came in the form of *Hungry Minds*, an eleven-minute 1948 NFB film produced in collaboration with the CCRU secretariat and screened across Canada, as well as in the United Kingdom, France, and New Zealand. An estimated five million Canadians viewed the film during the campaign – the most extensive distribution a Canadian film had ever achieved up to that point. The promotional folder that accompanied the film on its tour gives a sense of the rhetoric of development that the CCRU was building in 1948:

> Over half the world hangs the spectre of starvation, not only of the body, but also of the mind. The hunger of minds in war-devastated countries can paralyze effects towards reconstruction, for if young minds are not trained for new leadership, permanent recovery is impossible. Wars begin in the minds of men – and the minds of children too, whose young bodies grow hungry for food and whose young minds grow warped for lack of education. Born under the nightmare of dictatorship, it is hard for them to forget the horror and despair which has surrounded their lives. The objective of the Canadian Council for Reconstruction through UNESCO goes deeper than the giving only of educational supplies to children. Children need teachers: therefore new teachers must be trained to lead young minds. Children need doctors: therefore, medical schools must be helped to increase their output of new doctors. In short, the whole intellectual life of a country – educational, scientific, and cultural – must be restored, if the minds of the children are to be saved.

The need to remedy the mental starvation of children who lack the freedoms of liberal democracy with what is framed as the ideologically neutral instrument of education – this was the dominant UNESCO theme of the late 1940s, and it granted to Canadian voluntary organizations a robust argument for Canada's new importance on the world stage.[5]

During its first two years, the CCRU rolled out numerous programs intended to enable reconstruction, ranging from an initiative to donate used scientific equipment to universities to a program of aid for creative artists. Among these were two book-centric initiatives. The first, a "school-box" project, entailed the creation and dissemination of some twenty thousand boxes of basic school supplies and reading materials to classrooms in "war-devastated areas," offered as gifts from "the children of Canada." Recipients included schools in Austria, Belgium, Ethiopia, France, Greece, Germany, Italy, the Netherlands, Malta, and Poland, as well as one Displaced Persons' Camp. The CCRU estimated in 1949 that through this program it had reached twenty-five thousand teachers and eight hundred thousand students. In addition to *A Pocketful of Canada* (discussed in the previous chapter), each box's reading matter included *Morceaux choisis d'auteurs canadiens* (published by Librairie Beauchemin in 1934); a French- or English-language copy of *Canada from Sea to Sea* (first published by the Canadian Information Service in 1947) (if this could not be procured, a copy of the Dominion Bureau of Statistics' *The Canada Handbook*); and twelve fact-sheets on Canada (in English or French). The solid bilingualism of the selections would be reflected in the 1951 Massey Report's treatment of a "national literature" as a necessary negotiation of "two great literary traditions of the western world."[6]

It is worth pausing for a moment on the inclusion of *Canada from Sea to Sea* in the "school-box" initiative. The book was published by the Canadian Information Service, which from 1945–47 (when it was absorbed by the Information Division of the Department of External Affairs) was responsible for disseminating information about Canada abroad. The book was issued in five editions between 1947 and 1965. The self-identified purpose of the 1947 edition is to affirm Canada's "maturity and status as an independent nation" recognized as such by other sovereign nations. The words and images that form the text of the 1947 edition of *Canada from Sea to Sea* perform this affirmation for an international audience through an appeal to what James C. Scott calls "high modernist ideology": the belief, described in the previous chapter, in scientific progress, the mastery of nature, and the "rational design of the social order" that was so important to the statecraft of the later twentieth century. Here I want to emphasize Scott's insistence on the term "ideology." High modernism is not scientific practice; it is rather, Scott insists, a "faith that borrowed, as it were, the legitimacy of science and technology. It was, accordingly, uncritical, unskeptical, and thus unscientifically optimistic about the possibilities for the comprehensive planning of human settlement and production." While the preceding chapter examines how modernization theory influenced the Colombo Plan and the Government of Canada's approach to the North during the 1950s, here I want to draw attention to the way that *Canada from Sea to Sea* self-consciously plots a history of a "national development" contingent on both institutional (governmental, judicial, educational) and technological progress. As the book's introductory section tells us, "social and cultural development can be measured by the extent to which people master their environment." Invisible in the book is conflict, dispossession, inequality; visible is harmony, production, cooperation. As the illustrated map of Canada that opens the book suggests, the territory claimed by the nation is a veritable cornucopia of natural resources available for the taking; through the twinned forces of governance (figured in a drawing of Ottawa's Peace Tower) and industry (represented, for example, by the pulp and paper smokestacks of Quebec), the state has conjured the fruits of modernization (see figure 3.1). *Canada from Sea to Sea* thus implies that if Canada entered the international arena by leveraging this model, others may do the same.[7]

The second book-focused "hungry minds" initiative was the Joint Canadian Book Project Committee, established in the summer of 1948 by the Canadian Library Association and the CCRU with the goal of helping to refurbish European library collections destroyed during the war. With the support of national and local media; the Boy Scouts of Canada and local Lions Clubs, who collected donations from homes; local firehalls, which accepted donations; and messaging that framed lost libraries as victims of Nazi aggression that threatened, as the *Toronto Daily Star* had it, the "free exchange of knowledge and ideas," the committee undertook a 1949 nationwide book collection campaign. The campaign, "March of Books / En avant les livres," amassed forty-seven thousand books in the first three months of 1949 (see figure 3.2). Donated books found their way to the Joint Committee's Canadian Book Centre, located in Halifax, which then prepared them for shipment to Europe. Not just any book was solicited and shipped overseas: the Canadian Library Association instructed Canadians on the question of which books to donate, and using an application form developed by UNESCO, European libraries were encouraged to request specific titles. Asking Canadians

Figure 3.1   Pages from *Canada from Sea to Sea*, 1947.

particularly for "standard works and classics in all subjects; reference books, dictionaries, Government publications, publications of learned and scientific societies, dating from 1935; encyclopedias published since 1918, and recognized texts on science, medicine, law, art, economics, agriculture, history, music, literature, philosophy, religion, and related subjects," the committee rejected "slick paper magazines," Canadiana, light fiction, and humour. Though subject to some criticism at home, the efforts of the joint committee, and of the CCRU more generally, redounded to the benefit of Canada's image on the world stage. Acknowledging the committee's gift of six thousand books to French libraries in the spring of 1950, UNESCO director-general Jaime Torres Bodet noted that the donation was a practical demonstration of Canadians' "will to share efficiently in the educational reconstruction of Europe." By April 1950, the Canadian Book Centre had shipped 98,426 books to Europe (West Germany received the most – 19,189 books).[8]

The CCRU also engaged in minor undertakings linked to books and print. In consultation with the head of the library division of UNESCO, it worked on a project to reprint in-demand but out-of-print periodicals.

Figure 3.2 "Canada's March of Books for War-Devastated Libraries," promotional material for the 1949 "March of Books" campaign led by the Joint Canadian Book Project Committee.

The executive committee's 1950 report notes that the CCRU spent $2,250 to reprint *Nature* and *The Economist* on "condition that in the reproduction process due credit were given for CCRU assistance." Also noted in this report is the fact that the CCRU offered three-year subscriptions to "certain selected publications of learned and educational organizations" to 109 institutions in twenty countries.[9]

The postwar initiatives of the CCRU were rooted in a particular conviction. As *The Globe and Mail* phrased it in a promotion of the 1949 "March of Books" campaign, the CCRU aimed to "revive learning in Europe, the continent to which Western civilization owes most." Subsequent undertakings that would follow the CCRU in using books as instruments to support international education and development, would not, like the CCRU, aim at Europe; they set their sights instead on the nations of what was coming to be known in Canada as the developing world.[10]

The Overseas Book Centre / Centre du livres pour outre-mer: Book Donation for Development

Many of those Canadians promoting liberal internationalist ideals in the 1940s could be found in the country's robust education movement. Two individuals – Robert Wallace and Vincent Massey – amply demonstrate this fact. Founder of Canada's National Film Society, adult educator, founding member of the Canadian Association for Adult Education (CAAE), and president of the University of Alberta, Wallace participated, along with Massey, in the Canadian delegation to the 1945 meeting at which UNESCO's constitution was formulated. Massey, the Oxford-educated heir to the fortune of Massey-Harris, a farm-equipment manufacturer, was similarly a promoter of educational and cultural initiatives, especially as these intersected with Canada's place in international affairs. President of the National Council of Education and, like Wallace, founding member of the CAAE and participant in the National Film Society, Massey was also high commissioner in London during the Second World War. He returned to Canada in 1949 to chair the Royal Commission that takes his name.[11]

Another liberal internationalist affiliated with the adult education movement in the postwar years was James Robbins ("J.R." or "Roby") Kidd (1915–1982), director from 1950 to 1960 of the CAAE and promoter of adult education in a wide array of the era's national and international cultural organizations. During the late 1950s, while president of the CAAE, Kidd began to agitate for a greater formal Canadian commitment to international bodies such as UNESCO. Goldthorp contends that "reluctant internationalism" characterized the federal government's approach to UNESCO through the second half of the twentieth century; however, the involvement of individuals such as Kidd (and others in Canada's adult education movement) offers an alternative history of Canadian support for UNESCO. Kidd's "Canada's Stake at UNESCO" (1956), for instance, predicts that the debate at the 1957 General Conference at New Delhi "will be about fundamental education and community development, two subjects on which Canada can contribute and in which Canada has an enviable international reputation."[12]

In the same half-decade, Kidd became involved in a project called the Overseas Book Centre / Centre du livre pour outre-mer (OBC/CLO) – a manifestation of his belief that Canada had particular international contributions to make to "fundamental education and community development." Cofounded in 1959 by Kidd, fellow CAAE member Marion McFarland, Harry Campbell (director of the Toronto Public Library), and Kurt Swinton (president of Encyclopedia Britannica Canada), the OBC/CLO aimed to "mobilize Canadian efforts in educational and technical assistance to developing countries, particularly those within the Commonwealth and those where the first language is French." The OBC/CLO had Canadian precedents in nongovernmental undertakings like the CCRU and other book donation campaigns that responded in the wake of the Second World War to the call of reconstruction, such as a 1956 collaboration between Harry Campbell and Helen Tucker, president of Voice of Women Canada, that led to the shipment of 250 books to the Peace Library in Hiroshima, Japan. The OBC/CLO's flagship program, "Books for Developing Countries," had, according to Campbell, a second purpose: to provide a use for surplus books from Toronto libraries and Britannica that would otherwise have been "burned or shredded" (though the OBC/CLO also received donated books from publishers, schools, colleges, professional groups, and individuals). Initially the OBC/CLO operated from space supplied by Swinton in an Encyclopedia Britannica warehouse in Toronto where volunteers collected and packed books for shipment. The Saguenay Shipping Company agreed to transport books free of charge to the Caribbean, and other shipping companies later contributed free or low-cost transport.[13]

In addition to his work with the CAAE and the OBC/CLO, Kidd was involved in the two decades between 1950 and 1970 in a dizzying array of national and international philanthropic and later development-related groups and projects, including the Canadian Film Institute; the Canadian Citizenship Council; Frontier College; the Bon Echo Foundation (a nonprofit devoted to arts and culture that he founded in 1955); the Overseas Institute of Canada (which was founded in 1962 to promote Canadian involvement in international development projects); Canada's UN-affiliated International Co-operation Year program; a CAAE-sponsored project to study adult education in the British West Indies; UNESCO's Adult Education Committee; the Adult Education Committee of the World Conference of the Organization of the Teaching Profession; and an initiative to establish a Department of Adult Education at the University of Rajasthan in partnership with the University of British Columbia (conducted under the auspices of the Colombo Plan). Raised a Baptist in both British Columbia and Saskatchewan, Kidd observes in his memoir that the many talks given by returned missionaries he listened to as a young person "programmed" him for life in international development work. As one of the first Canadians to earn a doctorate in adult education (from Columbia University), Kidd was uniquely prepared to lead the postwar organizations that placed adult education at the centre of emergent ideas about development.[14]

Other OBC/CLO cofounders were similarly implicated in mid-century philanthropic and developmental organizations. Remembered in the obituary created for Harry Campbell by the Canadian Organization for Development Through Education (CODE, the name for the OBC/CLO since 1982) as a cofounder of the OBC/CLO (though W.A. Teager's history casts her an employee, a CAAE member hired by Kidd to be secretary-manager of the OBC/CLO), Marion McFarland was a CAAE member and a member of the United Nations Association.[15]

The career of librarian Henry ("Harry") Cummings Campbell (1919–2009) was similarly embedded in the era's emergent internationalism: he was producer at the NFB from 1941 to 1946; archivist for the UN in New York from 1946 to 1949; director of the Library of Congress Survey of World Bibliographical Services for UNESCO and the UNESCO Clearing House for Libraries from 1949 to 1956; and chief librarian of the Toronto Public Library from 1956 to 1978. After his retirement, Campbell participated in UNESCO's Developing Public Library Systems and Services initiative. His 2009 obituary in *Feliciter*, the periodical of the Canadian Library Association, celebrates him as an individual who "believed in the access of people in all countries to the knowledge and information that would help them in their social development." President of the Canadian Library Association (1973–74) and executive member of the International Federation of Library Associations (1972–79), Campbell was committed to the latter's role as a nongovernmental body "supporting library development in post-colonial and developing nations."[16]

Kurt Swinton (1914–87) was an Austrian-born radio engineer who served in the Royal Canadian Signal Corps during the Second World War and who later led companies such as RCA Victor Canada, the Thomas A. Edison Company, and, during the late 1950s and early '60s, Encyclopedia Britannica Canada. An opponent of Nazism who fled Nazi-occupied Austria in the late 1930s, Swinton was committed to both adult education and liberal internationalism: he was chair of International Council for Adult Education (ICAE); an executive member of the Canadian Institute for International Affairs; a member of the United Nations Association; president of the Couchiching Institute of Public Affairs; and an adviser to CIDA.[17]

The Postwar Development Paradigm, the NGO, and the Book

As historians of NGOs have argued, the NGO emerged hand-in-hand with development – the concept that, along with the Third World, modernization, and related ideas, was so important to the US-dominated postwar decades. Although NGOs were in existence prior to the 1950s, and although historians of development, as we have seen, identify the modern age of development as emerging in the interwar period, the UN's designation of the first Development Decade in 1960 added further urgency to the development idea, making the 1960s, in Ruth Compton Brouwer's words, "a decisive decade for the expansion, transplanting, and creation of development-focused NGOs." Canada saw the emergence in this decade of groups such as the Mennonite Central Committee, Oxfam Canada, and Canadian University Service Overseas (CUSO), this last established in the same year, 1961, as the Peace Corps in the US. While Compton Brouwer argues that CUSO was the first Canadian NGO to undertake development work from a "secular stance and in a context of rapid decolonization," the OBC/CLO could similarly qualify under this definition, and it was founded two years earlier.[18]

Though the OBC/CLO was unique in Canada at its inception, it was part of the broader emergence during the late 1950s and early '60s of book development initiatives undertaken by the US, Britain, the Soviet Union, Germany, and other industrialized nations and that included state as well as nongovernmental organizations and private foundations, such as America's Ford Foundation and Franklin Book Programs. As Joseph Slaughter points out, the thinking that conjoined books and development in these decades drew on an older set of western ideas about the role of literacy and its relation to material and spiritual development. According to Slaughter, in the postwar years, "the technology of literacy," particularly in "the artifactual form of the book," "became something of a fetish within certain humanitarian strands of development discourse." Slaughter locates these "strands" in the US-backed modernization imperatives of the decades following the Second World War, which influenced American foreign aid initiatives such as USAID (established in 1961). Yet Slaughter's analysis does not tell the whole story: as American publisher Curtis G. Benjamin acknowledged in a 1964 speech at the National Foreign Trade Convention in New York City, developing nations were clamouring for print materials, but, more importantly, "these emerging nations are prepared to import, along with our books, our ideas, our methods, our technology. Thus do books serve in the vanguard of international trade. Thus do they serve in a correlative way as pioneers and conditioners of emerging markets for US materials, designs, products and services." In other words, books could also serve as levers to open markets. In his 1983 "Benjamin Report," Benjamin laments the decline of US public support for book donation and other book export assistance programs, noting their multiple advantages – they "condition overseas markets and increase exports of US products and services," while smoothing "the path for the pursuit of our foreign policies." Benjamin's comments clarify the proximity of the book development initiatives of the postwar decades and US economic and foreign policy objectives.[19]

The relation of the OBC/CLO and of the people centrally involved in its genesis, particularly Kidd, to this culture of book developmentalism is complex. The many Canadians who came to take up roles at UNESCO in the 1960s and '70s did not side unthinkingly with the US political establishment and the global institutions it backed – the World Bank, in particular. On the contrary, Canadians such as Kidd were attempting to materialize a philosophy of development through education that would draw on and benefit from Canada's traditions of rural adult education and its experiences as a former colony of Britain. The contradictions embedded in this position eventually became apparent to NGOs like the OBC/CLO as they engaged in the self-assessment exercises encouraged in the second wave of development thinking that emerged with the decolonization movements of the late 1960s.

The OBC/CLO and the First Development Decade

In the early 1960s, Kidd's involvement in the international development efforts of the era ramped up. Kidd's work through the 1950s had been principally domestic in scope: as director of the CAAE, Kidd oversaw domestically focused adult education and community development work, such as the Farm Forum and, later, Citizens' Forum programs. By the later 1950s, this work was clearly influenced by the emergent postwar international development paradigm. By 1957, the CAAE had launched its international development program with a project related to adult education in the Caribbean. In 1958, at the prompting of CAAE member Father André Renaud, the CAAE established a National Commission on the Indian Canadian (later the Indian-Eskimo Association of Canada), which aimed to address the specific educational and vocational training challenges facing Indigenous adults. Kidd left his post at the CAAE in 1960; his paid and volunteer commitments during the subsequent decade were almost exclusively focused on international development. In 1962, the OBC/CLO was brought under the aegis of the Overseas Institute of Canada (OIC) – an organization Kidd founded in the same year. In *An International Development Program for Canada*, authored in 1961, Kidd argues that a nonprofit organization like his Bon Echo Foundation could tackle what he saw as priorities for Canada in the field: the establishment of an information program; support and encouragement of Canadian organizations; the recruitment of Canadians for service abroad; and study and research. What eventually became the OIC benefited, like so many Canadian organizations before it, from the deep pockets of the Ford Foundation, which provided both a founding grant of $60,000 and a 1965 grant worth $150,000. Through the 1960s, the OIC sponsored or cosponsored a number of events that, according to W.A. Teager, "did much to give impetus to Canada's efforts in international development," including a "Conference on Overseas Aid" (May 1962); a "Conference on Mass Media in International Development" (November 1962); a workshop dedicated to Canada's participation in social development abroad (June 1963); and the Second National Workshop on Canada's Participation in International Development (November 1965). Additionally, the OIC published booklets, directories, film lists, and reports, including a quarterly bulletin that was distributed to both its domestic members and to Canadians engaged in international development efforts abroad, and it made grants of its own to organizations such as CUSO.[20]

The work of the OBC/CLO (and, more broadly, the OIC) during the 1960s occurred in the context of a more general expansion of federal commitments to foreign aid. At the time of his election in 1963, Prime Minister Lester B. Pearson was strongly identified with the foreign aid file – because of his work on the Colombo Plan and his tenure as both undersecretary and secretary of state for External Affairs – and with liberal internationalism, more generally. During the Pearson years (1963–68), when Paul Martin was secretary of state for External Affairs, Canada's foreign aid tripled in terms of dollar amounts and expanded its geographic reach (to the Caribbean, French Africa, and Latin America), but it also experienced significant reorganization as the External Aid Office in External Affairs was granted the capacity to develop policy and engage in analysis, advocacy, and outreach. With the creation of CIDA in 1968, the importance of the foreign aid file was further confirmed.[21]

Also important to the work of the OBC/CLO in the 1960s is the larger context of the UN's first Development Decade campaign (1960–70), which the Pearson government engaged in multiple ways. According to Ted Cogan, the federal government committed in 1966 to meet a new foreign aid target of one per cent of gross national product as recommended by the 1964 United Nations Conference on Trade and Development. The UN's first Development Decade was most dramatically marked by that organization's designation of 1965 as International Co-operation Year, and the Government of Canada's commitment to the International Co-operation Year campaign was considerable. Paul Martin endorsed the campaign, and his department subsequently orchestrated and funded a Canadian conference of more than one hundred organizations, which sponsored some four hundred projects.

Kidd was a key mediating figure: as president of the conference, Kidd brought OIC administrative services along with him, as well as connections to projects needing funding.[22]

In these years, Kidd urged Canadian audiences, such as the one gathered at the opening of the Don Mills Public Library in November 1964, to view books not simply as aids to development but as *the most important* development tool available: "We have much to share with our brothers overseas but nothing, not even bread itself, is more needed by them than books. It is a sobering experience to see, as I have seen, a class of men and women learning to read and write without any paper and forced to write with a pointed stick on sand. Think about that as you look at our disposal cans full of discarded newsprint on a Monday morning. It is almost unbearable to watch, as I have seen, a library van pull into a village in the Caribbean, or Africa, or Asia, to observe every book taken down from the shelves and yet some of the eager children or adults still go without." As Kidd noted to this audience, the OBC/CLO had sent about a million books to approximately forty countries during 1964 and, with "planning, and some assistance with money and time," could send another million during International Co-operation Year. Books, Kidd told the assembled, are a defence against political and technological tyranny, as well as a bulwark against a third tyranny – that of "things, goods, possessions, against the shrill blast to buy, own, display, consume ... till we are not possessors but the possessed." The work of the OBC/CLO was thus a perfect fit for the emphasis on education as a tool for international cooperation that characterized Canada's International Co-operation Year campaign. While other projects funded by the conference enabled scholarships for students from the Caribbean to study at Canada's Coady Institute and general financial support for schools in developing nations, the OBC/CLO set and then met its goal of sending one million books to schools, libraries, universities, and community groups in developing nations.[23]

In other speeches from the early 1960s, Kidd revised previous arguments that had been made by English Canadian elites, such as Vincent Massey, regarding Canada's role in postwar development. Massey's *On Being Canadian* (1948), for instance, calls on Canadians to rally behind the colonial reforms the British had been devising since the late 1920s. According to Massey, this "contemporary Commonwealth" was a far cry from the old imperialism, and Canada had a unique role to play in this "contemporary Commonwealth," which would lead the colonies in their "march to self-government." Similarly emphasizing the unique role that Canada could play in the UN's Development Decade, and, more particularly, in the continuing education that he saw as basic to development, Kidd cast Canada's historical relationship to the British Empire in a slightly different light than Massey had. In his memoir of the 1960 UNESCO World Conference on Adult Education (which he served as conference president), Kidd represents Canada as an ideal broker for Cold War tensions. In his account, Kidd contends that what some Europeans and Americans view as "traditional Canadian naivete" enabled him to win over the Russian delegation and to achieve the Montreal Declaration on adult education. Kidd follows this same line of thinking in a 1961 address: Canada, as a nation dependent on its international associations, was poised to lead the new "creative crusade."[24]

The nation's technological and scientific capacities are key to Kidd's argument, but more important is his emphasis on the nation's political status. Canada, he argues, is not "perceived as a threat": "Other people can accept aid from us without feeling demeaned or becoming fearful that this is the beginning of a new imperialism. Moreover, we ourselves have recently passed out of colonialism and are even now going through rapid industrialization. We seem to be nearer in our own development to what others want to do." Here is the heart of what I describe in this book's introduction as Kidd's settler exceptionalism – what Rachel Bryant has analyzed as "the set of beliefs through which Settler Canadians have continuously consolidated themselves against their perceived rivals (particularly 'the Americans'), articulating themselves onto a separate and higher moral plane." This 1961 address echoes some of the rhetoric of Kidd's 1961 report, *An International Development Program for Canada*, which insists that "Canada has successfully emerged from a colonial position. It is even now going through rapid industrialization of the kind that other nations wish to emulate. The stage in national and economic development that we have reached gives assurance to new nations that they may be able to learn from us. Likewise, the size and scale of our life does not seem so overwhelming as does that of such nations as the United States or Soviet Union." Such a moderate "size and scale" means that "Canada is not perceived as a threat to anyone. Association with us, or aid received from Canada will not be looked upon as a prelude to some economic form of imperialism or as an act in the cold war." Such settler exceptionalism undergirds Kidd's idea of the nation's "special mission": "If there is anything in the doctrine of leadership by a middle power, if Canada does have a special mission among the nations, it is in international development that it will be best shown." Though Kidd, like Massey, depends on Canada's history as a settler colony to imagine its future in the postwar world, his concept of "special mission" is not British-centric; it depends on older imperial ties, but it also suggests that the breaking of some of those ties has created a kind of natural sympathy between settler Canadians and newly decolonizing peoples.[25]

An important geopolitical context for Kidd's framing of Canada's "special mission" can be found in Amanda Laugesen's work on US book donation schemes of the Cold War era – USIA efforts and private-public or private agencies, such as Bookshelf USA, Books USA, and Franklin Book Programs. Laugesen demonstrates that these programs sought to combat recipients' resistance to American "cultural imperialism" and to address the challenge of convincing developing and decolonizing nations "that American goodwill was sincere (or that America was the ideal to emulate) when images of racial violence in the American South appeared in the international press." As we saw in chapter 2, Farley Mowat's *The People of the Deer* raised the thorny problem of contradiction for the Government of Canada's new postwar forays into cultural diplomacy and book donation. Such problems similarly plagued public and private American book programs after 1950, prompting, at least in part, Kidd's insistence on Canada's distinction from the US.[26]

As his comments make clear, Kidd's view of Canada in the early 1960s was shaped by the settler-colonial conviction that the nation was not itself complicit in perpetuating colonizing practices. Such an assertion depends not only on a disavowal of ongoing colonial practices within 1960s Canada, such as the residential school system, but also of the fact that the Commonwealth idea was based on a racialized hierarchy. Canada's status in the postwar world was less a sign of its successful "development" than a symptom of this hierarchy. As Dan Freeman-Maloy contends, self-governing settler states such as Canada, Australia, and South Africa were imagined by the British to be "operating on a different constitutional plane" than Britain's colonial dependencies through most of the first half of the twentieth century, a distinction that persisted after the Second World War in the rhetoric of the "old" and "new" Commonwealths (despite the fact that many "new" Commonwealth members, such as India, were among the "oldest" members of the British Empire). Freeman-Maloy attributes this differential status to racialization, with white settler states experiencing different trajectories than brown and black colonial dependencies, even when the white settler population, as in the case of Southern Rhodesia, was a small minority. Yet in Kidd's framing, Canada is the equal of other Commonwealth nations; having recently set down the yoke of colonialism, Canada could aid fellow decolonizing nations in the march to modernity. This line of argument could also serve domestic interests well: Kidd predicts in "The Creative Crusade" that the newly independent francophone nations of Africa would prefer the assistance of the Government of Quebec over aid from the former colonizers of Europe; the Pearson government simultaneously saw its expansion of aid to French Africa as an opportunity to associate an increasingly sovereigntist Quebec with Canada's foreign policy and, as Robin Gendron observes, to "deflect Quebec's interest in pursuing its own foreign relations."[27]

If the liberal internationalism of Kidd's "creative crusade" was built on a conception of Canada as innocent of colonizing practices and on a retrospective image of the British Empire as undifferentiated, it also drew on an earlier Indigenous internationalism without acknowledging the conflictual relation of that diplomacy to the global institutions that emerged in the wake of the First World War. Kidd notes in his 1962 address "Continuing – Not Fundamental Education Only" that the new international organizations – the UN, UNESCO, and so on – could find inspiration for their collaborative work on educational development in the "shared purposes" of the Six Nations Confederacy, forged in the late seventeenth century. Turning to this example in his address of an audience gathered for a seminar on international development in Syracuse, New York, Kidd was self-consciously enacting his own conviction regarding the importance of local knowledges in adapting European and North American educational systems. For instance, Kidd insists that "the finest product for any culture is developed in that culture," meaning that the new institutions of higher learning in Africa and Asia might well adopt "the spirit" of European and North American educational models, but they would need to adapt them. At the same time, however, he frames Indigenous diplomacy as a historical rather than a present practice. The complex relation of the Six Nations Confederacy to the liberal internationalism of the League of Nations or to its successor, the UN – evident in the 1923 attempt of the Haudenosaunee, led by Cayuga Hoyaneh Levi General (Deskaheh), to bring the treaty status of Indigenous nations to the attention of the League of Nations, for instance – falls out of view. Framing the multilateral collaboration that he viewed as crucial to the success of the UN's first Development Decade through the Six Nations Confederacy analogy, Kidd's speech acknowledges but then ossifies this latter group as a political force, absorbing its model of "shared purposes" into the development projects of the postwar world.[28]

Kidd's speeches from the early 1960s pinpointed education, and particularly continuing education, as the building block of development, amplifying his conception of Canada's "special mission" by suggesting that the nation's increasingly internationally recognized experiments in adult education – and, by association, its commitments to literacy and the book – had uniquely prepared its citizens to tackle international development. Kidd was deeply involved in these experiments, including the Canadian Film Institute, the Canadian Citizenship Council, Frontier College, the CAAE, and the OIC. Building on these experiences, Kidd was increasingly involved from the 1960s forward in international adult education initiatives, including the 1960 UNESCO World Conference on Adult Education (he was conference president); UNESCO's Experimental World Literacy Programme (EWLP), which he chaired from 1967–73; and, eventually, the ICAE (founded 1973). In 1966, Kidd undertook for the OIC a two-year study that examined how Canada might assist with the global campaign to eradicate illiteracy – the EWLP – that UNESCO spearheaded at its 1965 World Conference of Ministers on the Eradication of Illiteracy (held in Tehran). *Functional Literacy and International Development* (1968) was the result.[29]

This report demonstrates that Kidd's rhetoric regarding Canada's proximity to and understanding of decolonizing nations was translated into action in this period, leading him to query US-supported concepts of development that he did not feel were in the best interest of those nations. Kidd and his Canadian research team were conducting their work in the particular contexts that were shaping UNESCO through the 1960s. The period of René Maheu's leadership as director-general (1962–74) saw an increased commitment to education as a means of economic development. The US government- and World Bank-backed concept of "functional literacy" that proceeded from this ideology was the motor for UNESCO's EWLP (1966–74), which delivered short-term vocational training to the vast majority of adult learners it engaged. Though Kidd and his team also employ the phrase "functional literacy," they clearly mean something different from the skills training promoted by Americans at UNESCO in this period: pressing for an expanded conception of the adjective in the phrase, they dismiss out of hand the idea that these programs will amount to nothing more than the rapid acquisition of a "few elementary skills" and instead outline a three-stage program that would culminate in the lifelong pursuit of continuing education. In this sense, and as we will see, Kidd and his coauthors were anticipating the UNESCO critique of "functional literacy" that developed in the mid-1970s during the director-generalship of Amadou-Mahtar M'Bow.[30]

In short, Kidd was negotiating significant tensions in the development work he undertook and promoted through the 1960s. A consideration of his wider philosophy of adult education in this period illustrates the antinomies that subtended the work of the OBC/CLO during the 1960s and into the '70s. In his writings from the 1960s, Kidd was adamant that adult education programs in the developing world had to be built on local foundations: departing from respect for the "facility in verbal communication" that many illiterate populations possess (rather than from an attitude that would dismiss such knowledge as a skill), such programs, even when assisted by foreigners and partly inspired by foreign models, needed to have local expertise and experience at their core. In making such arguments, Kidd frequently drew on the literatures of decolonizing nations, allowing writers from Caribbean or African nations to make the case for him and thus instantiating the practice he was recommending. For instance, in a 1962 address, Kidd warns that men and women in developing countries were sometimes "demeaned, rather than uplifted" by literacy classes. He makes his point with relation to Jamaican author V.S. Reid's 1958 novel *The Leopard*, a sensitive depiction of the Kenyan Mau Mau Rebellion that privileges the point of view of a half-Kikuyu, half-Masai man, Nebu, who has lost both his young wife and his village in a settler raid. Kidd zeroes in on a scene near the beginning of the novel, in which Nebu ponders the humiliation he and his people have been made to feel by the British:

Nebu had been (only once) to an Adult Education class at
Kiambu and had seen some tribal elders stuttering over the words
in the white man's book while a couple of young white overseers
outside the hut grinned in at the window. And when Nebu had
remembered the wine-skin of words which would pour from the
mouths of those elders at a tribal council, words whose whispers
were the winds combing the heads of the taller pines, or thunder
at the commencement of the seasons, or the sweet poetry of his
people singing at the spring ngoma, he had turned to look at the
young overseers, the wish to torture bright in his eyes.[31]

Kidd first became familiar with the Caribbean during the early 1950s, when he met Philip Sherlock, director of extramural studies at the University College of the West Indies. It is likely through Sherlock, who was, according to Kidd's memoir, "searching out the artists of his own country to ensure that adult education would be warm and deeply penetrating," that Kidd came to know writers such as Reid. Kidd's acquaintance with Sherlock led to his 1958 study of adult education in the British West Indies, *Adult Education in the Caribbean*, which argues that "the best model was being constructed in the West Indies by West Indians, not in London or Chicago or Montreal." Other evaluations that Kidd went on to write in the 1960s echo this line of thinking. His 1962 report on adult education in Alaska (commissioned by the University of Alaska and summarized in his memoir) offers a vision of the "Open University" that is based in the "development of human resources in situ instead of the continual importation of visitors." The 1968 report discussed above, *Functional Literacy*, insists that the projects of the EWLP should be at once locally relevant and resourced: "Texts and classes should be about local adult practices in farming, and food, and marketing, and elections, and home-life; they should not be based on middle-class experiences and foreign textbooks or readers." Similarly, "teaching aids of all kinds for a literacy campaign must be developed close to the communities in which instruction will be offered."[32]

As the examples above demonstrate, Kidd's account of adult education as development acknowledges production narratives – the importance of local production capacity; yet his accounts often skim over such narratives in favour of emphasizing Canada's ability to provide the necessary expertise and materials. While *Functional Literacy* notes that Canada is well-positioned to supply developing nations with the technical assistance needed to create local teaching aids (duplicating technologies such as hand-operated printing presses, for example), it also contends, somewhat contradictorily, that organizations like the OBC were offering valuable donations of discarded textbooks and could do more of this work in the context of the EWLP.[33]

This contradiction is particularly germane to the work of the OBC/CLO. Kidd recounts in his memoir that the OBC shipped nearly twenty million books to fifty countries between 1960 and 1975. As noted above, Kidd felt that books were at the heart of the projects he was proposing – "not even bread itself" was more important to the success of adult education initiatives. For Kidd, libraries, librarians, and books were neutral and axiomatically positive tools, and, quite at odds with his promotion of local knowledges and materials, he often suggested that any book from any place could lead to development in a poor nation. In his 1964 speech for the opening of the Don Mills Public Library, Kidd quotes from South African writer Peter Abrahams's 1954 memoir, *Tell Freedom*, to make just this point. In Kidd's framing, Abrahams's narration of his youthful encounter with a white librarian leads him to school and then to a life of letters: "Who ever knows what a book will do, or a librarian?" Yet Kidd gets some of the crucial details wrong here: in the scene he quotes from, Abrahams is not in a library but rather in the office of the smithy where he is employed as a "coloured" child labourer. The office assistant, whom Abrahams identifies as a "shortsighted Jewish girl," reads him "Othello" from Charles and Mary Lamb's *Tales from Shakespeare* (an English children's book first published in 1807). The story enchants Abrahams and helps him resolve to attend school, despite the fact that education was not compulsory for black or "coloured" children like Abrahams during the 1930s, and regardless of the more pressing fact that he is a fatherless child whose mother and aunt depend on his wages from the smithy. *Tell Freedom* is about the problem of education in South Africa: most of the primary education offered to black and "coloured" students in the interwar period was provided by Anglican missionaries, and though Abrahams offers a positive account of his encounter with this culture of schooling, he notes its disconnection from the society around it; it is figured as a "peaceful valley" that does not correspond with, or engage, the "big world" of a newly independent South Africa. The tools it offers are not ones that will allow Abrahams to change the racist and fundamentally unjust structure of South African society. His solution is to leave South Africa for London at the end of the 1930s. *Tell Freedom* is not a story about the universally liberating power of books; it is about the misery that follows from an education system that is not an organic part of its society – what Kidd and the coauthors of a 1976 report on the EWLP call the schoolhouse as "outpost of civilization," cut off from the reality around it. In this sense, *Tell Freedom* is about the limits of developmentalist ideology that does not seek to alter economic and social structures. It is telling that this is not how Kidd read the book.[34]

The OBC/CLO and Development's Second Wave

The political turmoil and radicalism of the late 1960s brought new energy and conflict to the field of foreign aid. In 1968, as the operations of the OIC expanded, the OIC and OBC/CLO were separated to become, on the one hand, a council, and on the other, a practical program of overseas aid. The OIC subsequently became the Canadian Council for International Cooperation, the first umbrella organization for NGOs in Canada. In the same year, CIDA was born, and with it a division that assumed the work of overseeing Canadian NGOs. In this period, the Council was attempting to challenge the federal policy narrative of foreign aid with a position that was, in Cogan's words, "progressive in orientation, often calling for dramatic changes in the global economic system." Aligned with the second wave of development thinking, Canada's NGOs were by the early 1970s shifting the narrative of development "from portrayals of Western nations as benevolent, all-knowing, civilizing benefactors to a focus on co-operation with the developing world." This second wave was influenced by the era's anticolonial nationalist movements, the anti–Vietnam War movement, dependency theory, and texts such as Paulo Freire's *Pedagogy of the Oppressed* (1968). According to Compton Brouwer, there were by the mid-1970s "plenty of CUSO activists who deplored the sending of any teachers to promulgate Western-style education. Like Western-style medicine with its alien values, impossible requirements, and lack of cultural fit, formal education was doing more harm than good, the politicized activists argued."[35]

Not surprisingly, second-wave thinking created some tensions between NGOs and CIDA. Indeed, Cogan argues that the federal government in this period failed to leverage the "growing influence and power of youth to grow support for international development in Canadian society." Cogan's account argues that, from the latter half of the 1960s, Canadian nongovernmental foreign aid organizations, many of which, like CUSO, were associated with student radicalism and commitments to social change, clashed increasingly with CIDA, whose mandate was economic and not political development. Yet Compton Brouwer's history of CUSO suggests that the NGO division at CIDA was fairly restrained in terms of its handling of CUSO radicalism in the late 1960s and '70s – CUSO's condemnation of Canadian foreign policy in South Africa in 1970, for instance, or the support of its eastern, central, and southern African arms of the liberation movements in southern Africa during the 1970s. However, as Compton Brouwer demonstrates, an NGO could be starved if CIDA withdrew support because of such activities, as it did to CUSO's francophone wing after 1979. Despite the political tensions and the federal budget cuts that were in this decade responding to the global economic crisis, aid dollars continued to grow through the mid-1970s, before the Liberal government's cuts to foreign aid in 1978 and its more general shift to what Cogan calls "commercial and economically-motivated foreign aid policy" in the wake of the global economic downturn after 1975.[36]

From its creation in 1968, CIDA's contributions to the OBC expanded to become its single most important source of annual funding. The OBC/CLO received its first grant from the External Aid Office of the federal government in 1967, and, by the mid-1970s, the OBC/CLO was almost entirely dependent for its funding on the NGO division of CIDA: in 1969–70, a CIDA grant of $35,240 comprised less than half of the OBC's total revenue; in 1975–76, CIDA grants amounted to $304,997.73 or 74 per cent of the organization's total revenue, dwarfing other sources (other grants, donations, memberships, an annual "Miles for Millions" fundraiser, interest earned, and sale of surplus materials).[37]

The OBC/CLO was not impervious to the shifting politics of development that characterized the period after 1965, even if, as an organization distanced from youth radicalism, it was somewhat slow to respond to this second wave. As part of the 1968 reorganization of the OIC, W.A. Teager became the executive director of the OBC/CLO, the organization incorporated, and both an executive committee and a board of directors were created. By the 1970s, the OBC/CLO was headquartered in Ottawa (first at 75 Sparks Street and later, at 323 Chapel Street) and was encouraging the growth of mostly volunteer-run local committees in Vancouver, Edmonton, Calgary, Regina, Winnipeg, Hamilton, Kitchener-Waterloo, Toronto, Montreal, and Halifax. The book donation program remained its central activity: a 1969 pamphlet describes the NGO's work as focused on collecting "new and used educational books" for distribution in "schools, libraries, universities, hospitals and community centres in developing countries"; a promotional poster from the late 1960s or early '70s bears the same message (figure 3.3). However, as Teager notes in his 1986 overview of OBC/CLO activities, the program "expanded steadily" after 1968 "to include provision of all kinds of educational aids, from paper to mechanical equipment as well as books." The minutes from a 1974 meeting of the board of directors confirms this: a list of special projects (costing more than five hundred dollars) includes funds for a loudspeaker, projector, and duplicator for a seminary in Cameroon; audio-visual aids for Côte d'Ivoire; an adding machine and a truck for an education project in Haiti; an IBM Selectric Composer and spheres for existing offset printing machinery at a printing company in Lesotho; and duplicating equipment for a YMCA in Sri Lanka.[38]

More to the point, an increasing sensitivity to questions about the appropriateness of donations emerged in the mid-1970s that is indicative of the fact that OBC/CLO was beginning to apprehend the importance of distinguishing between the colonial histories of Canada and the nations that were receiving book donations. Teager's elevennation tour of Africa in 1971 may have been important in this regard: noting the skepticism of "one prominent educator" "about the value of books from outside the country," Teager's report touches on specificities in each nation that the OBC/CLO must acknowledge, such as the exclusive use of Swahili in Tanzanian primary schools, the efforts of newly independent governments to publish their own school textbooks, or the inapplicability of Canadian arithmetic textbooks in nations that use a monetary system not based in dollars.[39]

In the early 1970s, the OBC/CLO began to collaborate with other Canadian NGOs such as CUSO, seeking to benefit from the local overseas contacts that the latter established with its volunteer service model.

Figure 3.3   "You Can Help," Overseas Book Centre promotional poster.

The OBC/CLO sought from CUSO volunteers book-related information about the countries they served in, including detailed information about educational systems, textbook needs for education, and the usefulness of "surplus" books from Canada. By 1974, the OBC/CLO was identifying its book donation program as "responsive." An executive newsletter from early 1974 notes that this "responsive" approach is key to the effectiveness of the program and, further, that some nations are willing to accept anything the OBC can supply but others, especially those with well-organized ministries of education, have more "sophisticated" preferences. This latter group "do not want textbooks unless these fit the curriculum"; moreover, if "the countries are former British colonies, as most of those where English is widely used, happen to be, the curriculum is based on the English system and Canadian books are not very suitable." An OBC/CLO pamphlet from the mid-1970s (figure 3.4) specifies that the organization seeks "new and nearly-new books as well as educational aids and equipment to send *on request* to schools, universities, libraries and medical centres in developing countries." Recipient feedback in annual reports, which is uniformly positive and must be read as information curated by the OBC/CLO, also signals that some attention was being given by the mid-1970s to the value of complementing donations of already purchased or used books with money for the purchase of local books. A 1976 newsletter records the response of the Schools Library Service in Grenada to a "modest grant" given to assist them in "securing some books locally": "We can't adequately convey how grateful we are for having this opportunity to buy West Indian materials. We have very few books in these categories, and our need is critical. We are so delighted to be able to BUY."[40]

Related to the struggles in the field of foreign aid after 1965 was UNESCO's embrace, following the 1973 oil crisis and ensuing economic fallout in the western world, of efforts to support the poorest nations in the world. Under the leadership of M'Bow of Senegal (1974–87), UNESCO was moving into a newly radical phase that was at odds with the concepts of modernization and functional literacy dominant at UNESCO from the late 1940s through the '60s. Influenced by Latin American dependency theory, dozens of recently decolonized nations – newly identified by the UN in 1971 as the globe's "least developed countries" – came to insist that the World Bank's economic development programs were consolidating First World wealth. They formed a voting block in the General Assembly, demanding the establishment of a New International Economic Order. The period of M'Bow's leadership of UNESCO must be identified, Sarah Brouillette contends, with policies, programs, and research explicitly supportive of developing nations' attempts to use their new power within international organizations to call for change in the global communications order.[41]

Figure 3.4   "Books and Educational Aids for Developing Countries," Overseas Book Centre pamphlet.

Charles Dorn and Kristen Ghodsee contend that these new "internal politics" at UNESCO shaped the 1974–75 evaluation of the EWLP undertaken by members from Canada, Vietnam, Algeria, Brazil, and India. Kidd chaired the Expert Group tasked with the evaluation. The report questions the "view prevalent in United Nations and Western academic circles at the beginning of the First Development Decade that development was first and foremost a question of economic growth, stressing capital-intensive development and high-level technical skills. From this point of view, education in general and literacy in particular were considered as means of 'developing' the 'undeveloped' people in terms of giving them the knowledge and skills necessary to expend their 'potential capital in the services of society.'" A human being, Kidd and his coauthors argue, cannot be "underdeveloped"; moreover, "the relative underdevelopment of certain economies is a partial result of the iniquities of the prevailing world economic system." The report is not fundamentally opposed to economic development, noting that its authors do not wish to "discredit economically functional literacy in general," but rather "to question narrowly productivity-centered functionality." Broadly "economic literacy," which the authors define as "critical awareness of the producer-learner's problems and roles in society," would "support rather than contradict the humanism" of UNESCO's critique of functionality. The report also repeats convictions that Kidd, as we have seen, had long been promoting, particularly claims about material resources. The eleven EWLP projects too infrequently realized the ideal of locally sourced and produced educational materials, relying instead on "the routine kinds of classical technical assistance": "Curiously, in a programme that publicly stressed its adaptability to diverse conditions, EWLP was not notable for stimulating the imaginative use of locally available materials and facilities, or the equally creative local generation of import substitutes when materials were not available." In sum, the report offers scathing criticism of the functionality of the EWLP (often placed in the mouths of vocal critics of the EWLP, such as N. Salamé), while attempting to recuperate the possibility that UN agencies like UNESCO and the United Nations Development Agency would undertake, in the future, literacy campaigns that would make fuller use of antifunctionalist mass literacy campaigns such as Cuba's.[42]

The line of critique apparent in the EWLP report coauthored by Kidd had begun to emerge at UNESCO during the 1960s. UNESCO discussions of book-related programming in this decade and the subsequent one turned to problems ensuing from "lack of indigenous cultural production." UNESCO-sponsored research on the book from the 1960s and '70s attests to this shift: Ronald Barker and Robert Escarpit's *The Book Hunger* (1973), for instance, offers a frank assessment of the fact that book donations from the world's book "producing" nations could not solve acute book shortages in Africa because the greatest need was for books in languages not published in the producing nations; Philip Altbach and Eva-Maria Rathgeber's *Publishing in the Third World* (1980) critiques the tendency of book donation schemes to undermine fragile local publishing industries by flooding markets with subsidized books; Philip Altbach and Saravanan Gopinathan's research on textbook publishing in the Third World makes it clear that the textbook donation schemes of Britain, the US, the Soviet Union, and West Germany did nothing to "develop local publishing industries or help build capabilities for indigenous textbook development." The 1968 report of the Meeting of Experts on Book Development in Africa, part of a series of UNESCO-sponsored regional meetings on book development in the same period, insists on domestic book production as the key element in any book development program. In the latter part of this same period, the New World Information and Communications Order, a concept first raised at UNESCO in 1970 as part of the larger debates regarding the New International Economic Order, flagged what Richard Hoggart (assistant director-general of UNESCO, 1969–75) calls "the imbalance in media resources and output as between the developed and developing world."[43]

This thinking reached the OBC/CLO. Referring to the report issued from a 1973 UNESCO meeting that convened experts on "Book Promotion and Development" (one of a series of meetings related to book development that UNESCO had been hosting since the mid-1960s), OBC/CLO board member Louise Rohonczy notes the report's dismissal of secondhand book donation schemes as "ineffective and consequently not worthwhile." She proposes some "possible new directions" for the OBC/CLO, including the training of local personnel in the book trade, while noting that the organization is not equipped to undertake the kind of structural development of the book trade associated with private foundations like Franklin Book Programs. Following from this prompt, the annual report for 1976–77 notes that the "support of indigenous publishing" – mostly in the form of helping developing nations produce "pamphlets and books with an easy vocabulary and a high level of local interest" – is a "significant trend" in the NGO's operations, but that its "traditional program" (its book donation program) is of "continuing importance." Indeed, in 1976–77, OBC/CLO shipped just under four hundred tonnes of books and supplies to eighty-three countries; however, it also gave seventy-five project grants, a fact which suggests the new orientation toward supporting recipient-generated projects. A 1976 executive newsletter tracks this increasing interest in projects "that will have a significant impact on educational problems in a developing country," including the provision of thirty-five tonnes of paper to a rural educational program in Ivory Coast, West Africa.[44]

This reorientation of OBC/CLO activities intensified in the wake of a 1979 evaluation of the organization undertaken by the ICAE (a body founded in 1972 by Kidd and which he served as secretary-general through the 1970s). The report, "The Overseas Book Centre in the Near Future," begins with an assessment of the decade's global economic crisis. The downturn increased the cost of imports and decreased the value of exports for developing nations that were not part of the Organization of Petroleum Exporting Countries; it consequently widened the gap between affluent and impoverished nations. This larger context for development is one that OBC/CLO did not fail to register during the 1970s. A 1976 newsletter opens with an assessment of the situation, which further notes that "the inability of the developing countries to progress on the basis of their own earnings has meant that they have had to borrow substantially. Three years ago the poor countries of the world owed about sixty billion dollars [in US dollars]. This figure has already doubled. No doubt it will continue to rise because the poor countries must have food, technology, and oil. Without more help from the developed world, in the form of direct aid and particularly in the form of more equitable international trade, the outlook for the Third World remains gloomy." The report's list of recommendations issues from this context, focusing as it does on growing local production capacity. The assessors suggest that OBC/CLO should, among other things, focus on the world's forty poorest nations, continue its commitment to formal as well as nonformal education, and pursue the local production of low-cost education materials. Responding to recipients who noted that, for instance, "Canadian examples cannot be understood and are indeed culturally irrelevant to Botswana," the assessors conclude that the OBC/CLO should place a "high priority" on "indigenous publishing": "In considering support of publishing the OBC must decide how far it wants to go in this area. Should it gradually become an organization dedicated to assisting book publishing, something like the Franklin Book Programs in the USA?" The cost of books was increasing, the assessors point out, so the OBC/CLO could likely make its "most valuable contribution by supporting low-cost printing."[45]

Tony Richards's brief history of the organization (written from his perspective as then–communications officer for CODE) characterizes this as a shift from "giving to helping," arguing that the 1979 evaluation engendered a shift from a supply-led to a recipient-led philosophy, moving away from the provision of books and toward the development of both domestic publishing and educational infrastructure in the nations where OBC/CLO focused its efforts. The renaming of OBC/CLO as the Canadian Organization for Development in Education / L'Organisation canadienne pour l'éducation au service du développement (CODE/OCED) in 1982 was meant to reflect a new mode of operation, as the June 1980 issue of NGOMA – the organization's newsletter in this period – indicates: "Maybe it's time that the name should evolve along with our programs and become something which denotes education in a broader sense rather than focusing only on books. The book programme is an important part of our activities but OBC's support to indigenous printing and literacy projects is increasing each year." Indeed, the name of the newsletter itself, Swahili for "talking drum," invokes a mode of nonwritten communication proper to the societies of West Africa and thus a concept of "literacy" that is local to these societies rather than to Europe or North America. The movement away from book shipments is evident in the annual reports: if almost four hundred tonnes of books (and equipment) were shipped overseas in 1976–77, less than two hundred were shipped in 1984. New methods for encouraging a recipient-led book donation program probably encouraged some of this slimming. The 1980–81 annual report observes that "a greater involvement in the selection of books by overseas schools," via a new request form and postdonation evaluation procedure, provided the OBC/CLO with "feedback which allows us to more accurately meet the needs of those we serve."[46]

Yet evidence that CODE moved in the early 1980s in the direction of support for local publishing initiatives is somewhat thin. Perhaps the most important new initiative of the period was one that applied itself to the problem of paper: proposed in 1981 and brought to fruition with CIDA assistance, the OBC/CLO paper program was designed to address domestic paper supply challenges in newly independent nations that had designed curricula and learning materials to meet "local needs." The program favoured "specific publishing projects" rather than "nonspecific paper requests," and privileged projects that maximized local contributions and demonstrated "tangible local commitment." As is clear from the essays collected in the 1985 study *Publishing in the Third World*, paper supply was a consistent problem for many Third World nations that were attempting through the 1970s to increase their domestic publishing efforts. In her study of the African book industry, for instance, Eva-Maria Rathgeber cites a UNESCO estimate that only 42 per cent of the paper needs of the African book industry could be met locally in 1976. As a result, paper had to be purchased on the international market and at high prices. The OBC/CLO paper program attempted to address this problem, but efforts to supply the technology necessary for printing were somewhat less robust. OBC/CLO correspondence from this period indicates that a group in Chile applied for funds to purchase an offset printer for a rural adult education program but was denied a second request for the same purpose, "to avoid creating a dependence on us as a funding source." Archival records show that by 1984, CODE was coming slightly closer to its goal of encouraging local publishing efforts: that year, the organization sent thirty-five typewriters to Bunumbu Press in Sierre Leone, a nonprofit organization that had received previous CODE funding to purchase a silkscreen press for rural literacy classes. As this evidence suggests, and as Richards acknowledges, local book publishing was, in the late 1970s and early '80s, a "utopia" for which the organization could aim, but "in the short term, donated books would continue to play a role in supporting literacy."[47]

By the early 1990s, when Richards authored his history of the NGO, CODE was continuing its donation programs with fifteen countries, "where rural schools and libraries receive a steady flow of books they have specifically requested." Book publishing, meanwhile, remained a field in which CODE could "do more." By 1990–91, CODE was allocating almost three million dollars per year to local publishing projects, ranging from the donation of Canadian newsprint to Jamaica for use in the printing of primary-level textbooks to the provision of an offset press and ancillary equipment to a small publishing cooperative in Bamako, Mali. Yet Richards couches his examples with caution, pointing to the "shortcomings in this type of assistance": "Supplying free paper to a printing project does not contribute to its future prospects as an independent, self-reliant operation. Rather, it inhibits those prospects by creating a dependence on a subsidy. Withdraw the subsidy and you have a printing project doomed to fail. The alternative is to find means of building the capacity of existing publishers or helping new publishers get started without creating unrealistic and unhealthy competition. CODE has learned to avoid projects which stifle local initiative."[48]

While shifting conditions in the Canadian publishing industry after 1972 might have permitted book development NGOs like the OBC/CLO to close down book donation schemes in favour of sharing the insights and strategies of those Canadians who were attempting to build a robust Canadian-owned publishing sector, this is not what transpired. Indeed, the NGO seems to have operated in relative isolation from the transformations in Canadian publishing that occurred during the 1970s. CODE continued its book donation work into the late twentieth century and was an important international actor in the field, drafting in 1991 (together with UNESCO and the Baltimore, Maryland-based International Book Bank) a policy of "correct giving," and in 2005 (with UNESCO), a set of guidelines for the "hundreds" of organizations in the global North that were continuing to send books to the global South. This latter, *Book Donations for Development*, emphasizes that the most effective means of donation are "largely works published locally, often written by local authors and bought at local bookshops, then delivered free of charge to those libraries which request them." Acknowledging that book "transfers" from the North to the South tend to increase disparities, the guidelines recommend that donating organizations have an integrated concept of the "book chain" in the receiving nation and that their work must strengthen rather than diminish the chain. While CODE continued its North-South book transfer in this period, this is presented as a recipient-led process, by which recipients choose books from a select list. Moreover, the profile of CODE in *Book Donations for Development* emphasizes the complementary activities CODE was undertaking in this period in concert with local partners: the purchase of books from local publishers; the establishment of school libraries and resource centres; and the training of teachers and community leaders to support "the development of a reading habit."[49]

Conclusion

Why did CODE remain a book donation program for so long, given that UNESCO research from the 1960s and '70s pointed clearly to the limitations of this model? In the closing decades of the twentieth century, the work of an NGO like CODE was tied to two related transformations: shifting North-South relations (embodied most forcefully in the 1974 UN Declaration on the New International Economic Order), and the economic downturn of the 1970s. The common experience of colonialism that Kidd had evoked in speeches during the 1960s disappeared from his rhetoric as the complexities of Third World decolonization came into full view during the global economic crisis of the 1970s. Moreover, Kidd seems to have become increasingly disenchanted after 1970 with UNESCO as a site for organizing globally around issues related to adult education. In the mid-1960s, as he organized in educational journals for the possibility of a world council on adult education, he observed that "it was never considered possible by the secretariat or anyone else connected with UNESCO that all things affecting the education of men and women could be fully looked after by UNESCO." In Kidd's view, UNESCO was simply too "broad" to "focus on any single field or respond quickly to demands, requests, and urgencies." As Kidd wrote in 1966, a world council for adult education would need to avoid domination by "those of Anglo-Saxon origin, or by Western Europe and North America"; that he deemed such domination a constant and unavoidable threat at UNESCO is clear enough. The ties that Kidd retained to UNESCO through the 1970s suggest his escalating frustration with the US- and World Bank-backed concept of "functional literacy." As noted above, Kidd's evaluation of the EWLP makes his criticisms clear, as do his comments regarding Canada's response to the 1976 UNESCO Recommendation on Development of Adult Education, which he viewed as promoting the "standpoint of traditionalist theoreticians rather than that of educators involved in adult education" and a definition of education that "placed too much emphasis on the training of the individual and on the benefits accruing to the employers and to the state from training." With the formation of the ICAE in 1973, Kidd redirected his energies away from what his partner Margaret Kidd describes as his "perception of the increasingly bureaucratic leadership being provided by UNESCO" and toward the "more spontaneous practitioner-centered exchange" of the ICAE.[50]

Dependency theory and its critique of modernization theory confronted the resistance of both the US and Britain in bodies such as UNESCO in the years that followed 1975. The New World Information and Communications Order generated policy that aimed to transform a global communications environment in which, as Richard Hoggart's 1978 commentary puts it, "the flow of materials and opinions is massively one-way." The eventual withdrawal of both Britain and the US (along with other nations) from UNESCO in the 1980s was a response to this politicization of media policy – a politicization that might have combatted what Graham Huggan calls the "larger patterns of structural underdevelopment governing a global knowledge industry." In this same period, Canada neither withheld monetary support from UNESCO (as Britain and the US did in the 1970s) nor withdrew its membership, but in the end this did not matter much. As Greg Donaghy demonstrates, the governments of Pierre Trudeau (1968–79 and 1980–84) played important leadership roles in the North-South dialogue that dominated international relations during the 1970s and early '80s, though Trudeau's desire to respond to discussions of the New International Economic Order at the UN General Assembly was hampered by a variety of domestic and international pressures (the slumping domestic economy; the separatist movement in Quebec; negative domestic media coverage of CIDA; and US recalcitrance, particularly after the election of Ronald Reagan in 1980). That CODE, in this context, found itself unable to launch a program that would transform the means of production of print materials in developing nations is hardly surprising.[51]

Indeed, as Hans Zell documented in 2015, book donation programs based in the global North continue to ship millions of books per year to nations in Africa. In moving away from this model, CODE has distinguished itself. CODE continues its operations today from Ottawa and focuses on two branches of activity: literacy projects and research. The first of these is most closely connected to the original OBC/CLO book donation program: projects partner with local civil society organizations in Africa to support teacher training and to provide high quality and culturally relevant reading materials. The "Teaching and Learning in Fragile Contexts" (2022–26) program, for instance, is a collaborative initiative in Liberia and Sierre Leone that supports teacher training (with a focus on "active learning, gender-responsive pedagogy, and foundational literacy") and the development of locally authored and illustrated reading anthologies. (It is not clear from the website if these materials are published in Africa.) Research grants constitute the second branch of contemporary CODE programming: "Context Matters" research grants fund literacy research "initiated, designed, and undertaken by African researchers." A third branch of CODE activity, the CODE Burt Literary Awards, existed until very recently. Between 2009 and 2019, the prize was awarded to young adult literature from Africa and the Caribbean. In 2013, an additional award for First Nations, Inuit, and Métis Young Adult Literature was added to recognize "excellence in Indigenous-authored literature for young adults"; this second award was offered in partnership with the Assembly of First Nations, the Métis National Council, Inuit Tapiriit Kanatami, the National Association of Friendship Centres, the Association of Canadian Publishers, and Frontier College. Although this second prize was originally for English-language titles only, an Indigenous-language category was added in 2019.[52]

The CODE Burt Award for First Nations, Inuit, and Métis, Young Adult Literature suggests that CODE was seeking in the early twenty-first century to redress the problem of an externally oriented literacy program that fails to address literacy challenges at home. (The domestic award program was also less expensive to run than its African counterpart, a significant factor in the period between 2012 and 2015, when CODE saw its federal funding decline precipitously.) While the award offered prestige and payment to authors, its guaranteed purchase element (CODE purchased "up to" 2,500 copies of each winning title and distributed these to schools, libraries, and friendship centres across the country) was an important and distinguishing feature of the award. Mainstream Canadian book prizes, such as the Giller Prize, have been criticized for their support of the multinational publishing companies that have long dominated publishing in Canada. The Burt Award for First Nations, Inuit, and Métis Young Adult Literature has not been immune to such criticism, but it is misplaced. Awards under this prize were given to twenty titles, of which five were published by Indigenous-owned and -operated small presses (Theytus Books, Kegedonce Press, and Inhabit Media); thirteen by small presses; five by medium-sized, Canadian-owned publishers; and only two by a multinational publisher (Penguin Random House Canada). In this context, the "guaranteed purchase" element of the program was significant because, although the maximum number of titles purchased was small (2,500 titles), it represented an important source of financial support for small presses that typically sell fewer than 250,000 titles per year. Scholars have questioned the fact that CODE's description of the Burt Award for First Nations, Inuit, and Métis Young Adult Literature does not name the historical or ongoing colonialist and neocolonial policies and laws that have kept literacy rates lower in Indigenous communities than in non-Indigenous ones and are skeptical that the provision of reading material or increased literacy might serve as solutions in this context, or in the contexts of impoverishment and structural dispossession that persist throughout Africa; however, the support for small publishers and particularly for Indigenous-owned and -operated publishers (and, briefly, Indigenous-language publishing) in the second iteration of the Burt Awards was an important if short-lived response to the legacy of residential schooling in Canada and its devastating effects on Indigenous cultures and languages.[53]

Many of the chapters of this book suggest that book development experiments abroad, whether state-orchestrated or issuing from civil society, blithely ignored colonialism at home. The chronology in CODE's case suggests that instruments and ideologies of development that were first tested externally returned to Canada when state support for development assistance tapered off and CIDA was shuttered in 2013. However, as we will see, book development work aimed at Indigenous Peoples in Canada runs parallel to the history of organizations like CODE. The question of their mutual relation is one that I will unpack in chapter 5.

4

Developing Africa and Late Twentieth-Century Anglophone Settler Nationalism

Just as the paperback revolution and the larger international expansion of the book trade in the decades following the Second World War formed part of the global substrate of what Nick Mount calls the "CanLit boom" of the late twentieth century, so this period's conjoining of books to the new concept of international development constitutes part of the story one might tell about the "boom." More broadly, this chapter contends that the development paradigm, whether in its late colonial or NGO phase, is an important and yet underexamined influence on late twentieth-century English Canadian settler-colonial cultural nationalism and the national literature and publishing infrastructure it sought to generate.[1]

Margaret Laurence's African writing from the 1960s builds allegories for international development schemes, using books to reflect on the problem of foreign tools to fix domestic problems. Narratives such as Laurence's *The Prophet's Camel Bell* (1963) offer a counter to initiatives like the Overseas Book Centre. At the same time, the comparisons of settler-colonial and colonized cultures in the African oeuvres of settler writers who, like Laurence, Dorothy Livesay, and Dave Godfrey, spent time on the continent during the burgeoning of the Canadian NGO movement there, intensify the analogies we encountered in J.R. Kidd's mid-century rhetoric of Canada's "special mission." Such parallels came to assume particular importance in the settler nationalisms of the centennial period – in, for example, the argument that Canada's artists and its book industries were "colonized." The disavowal on which such nationalisms are premised has been well documented, largely by the generation of scholars who brought the tools and insights of postcolonial theory to bear on the study of literatures in Canada from the 1990s forward. This chapter aims to draw particular attention to a context that postcolonial approaches to literary cultures in Canada have not explored, the development paradigm of the latter half of the twentieth century. In what follows, I demonstrate how this paradigm shaped late twentieth-century settler nationalism and the literary aesthetics and politics of the influential anglophone settler authors who came to define the period's emergent canon of national literature.[2]

Anglophone Settler Nationalism and the Colonized Mind

The conflation of colonized and settler-colonial cultures came to be important to the settler nationalisms of Canada's centennial period, including the cultural nationalisms that centred on the book; however, as we saw in the preceding chapter, this line of argument was not original to the settler writers of the 1960s and '70s. It had since the early postwar years offered settler Canadians a comfortable position that was not Britain's, as well as a justification for Canadian leadership of the emerging international development paradigm. In this sense, the conflation was key to Canadians' international elaboration of settler exceptionalism – an insistence that the nation did not, like Britain, need to atone for the sins of colonialism, as well as the related implication that it was innocent of the new forms of political power attached to the US – after the Second World War. Yet by the mid-1960s, something new was happening to settler exceptionalism: as youth cultures multiplied in the friendly medium of Canadian universities, which were expanding rapidly as a result of the postwar baby boom, and as hundreds of young Canadians set off for developing nations as part of a burgeoning NGO movement committed to ideals of social justice and equality, the settler-nationalist argument that casts English Canadian culture as "colonized" was drawing on a deepening awareness of and direct engagement with the post-independence politics of the globe's former colonies.

The heady nationalism of English Canada's 1960s and '70s was accompanied by a growing literary culture that was being nourished by an emergent system of institutions: public funding bodies for the arts at all levels of government, which issued grants for literary authors, individual titles, and, eventually, publishers; and growing postsecondary institutions, with their literature departments, university libraries, archival collections, writer-in-residence programs, and academic journals are just two examples of the field-altering institutions of this period. While what Paul Litt calls an elite "high-culture nationalism" informed postwar state initiatives vis-à-vis the arts, writers' arguments for public support for the arts in English Canada and for a more general cultivation of a national literary idiom turned increasingly by the early 1970s to assertions that are best understood as settler-nationalist: they were anti-American and characterized by a sense of the need for settler indigenization, or, as Ryan Edwardson puts it in his history of cultural policy in Canada, a "means by which to reclaim Canadian sovereignty from forces of imperialism."[3]

Settler-nationalist arguments were broadly embedded in the late twentieth-century writing of English Canada, which tended to cast settler identity in terms of experiences of colonization, whether as the colonization of England or the more diffuse cultural and economic domination of the US. During the 1950s, '60s, and '70s, anglophone settler writers consistently lamented the compromised environment for the Canadian artist, often linking the artist's failures to historical and ongoing experiences of colonialism: the frustrated painter in Sinclair Ross's *As for Me and My House* (1947); A.M. Klein's poet, "incognito, lost, lacunal" ("A Portrait of the Poet as Landscape," 1948); James Reaney's writer, who figures himself via the geese who float in the pond where he was born, "In continual circles / and never get out" ("The Upper Canadian," 1949); Ernest Buckler's tragic David Canaan (*The Mountain and the Valley*, 1952); and Graeme Gibson's culturally and spiritually oppressed professor and student in *Five Legs* (1960). By the 1970s, such arguments coalesced in widely influential texts like Margaret Atwood's *Survival* (1972), which draws on Northrop Frye's "garrison mentality" archetype to identify the "paralyzed artist" in English Canadian writing. In his 1974 essay "Cadence, Country, Silence: Writing In Colonial Space," the poet Dennis Lee captures a generation of artistic angst with his desire to "explore how, in a colony, the simple act of writing becomes a problem to itself." As Cynthia Sugars notes, political and cultural commentators of the late 1960s and '70s similarly treated settler societies as "colonized" and appealed to indigenizing rhetoric to make their arguments. George Grant's *Lament for a Nation* (1965), for instance, speaks of the need to create an "indigenous society" in Canada, and, in a 1975 editorial, John Moss called for a "native or indigenous vocabulary."[4]

The book that Stephen Azzi describes as "one of the best-known nationalist tracts" of the late 1960s, Al Purdy's 1968 bestselling collection *The New Romans: Candid Canadian Opinions of the U.S.*, gathers many of the era's settler nationalists between two covers, while also demonstrating what Azzi and others identify as the diversity of political views that animated these nationalisms. The project was the brainchild of Purdy and Edmonton-based nationalist publisher Mel Hurtig. Both were members of the steering committee for the Committee for an Independent Canada, an organization founded in 1970 to promote government regulation to protect Canada's cultural and economic independence. Associated with former Liberal finance minister and promoter of increased Canadian economic independence, Walter Gordon, the committee was the avowedly nonpartisan alternative to the social-democratic Waffle movement within the New Democratic Party, which espoused, through figures like Robin Mathews, a resolutely leftist nationalism.[5]

Purdy's purpose in *The New Romans* is to instantiate a dialogue about "Canadian sovereignty" – about the "fair and adequate taxation of American branch plants," for instance – and to "register a sullen protest, a belated yap from a captive dog" against those "big real estate dealers in Ottawa who have sold this country down the river to Americans for the last thirty years." Drawing on but not identifying what James W. St G. Walker has called the "North Star myth" – the enduring portrayal of racism and white supremacy as American and not Canadian qualities – Purdy acknowledges that in Canada there is "an Indian problem of growing seriousness," as well as "poverty and underdevelopment in many areas," but Canada's problems "do not affect the rest of the world" as does the "interracial violence" in America. Contributors include the three writers whose involvement in the late twentieth-century development paradigm this chapter will explore. In brief contributions, Laurence, Livesay (also a member of the steering committee of the Committee for an Independent Canada), and Godfrey articulate anti-American positions. Godfrey's short story "The Generation of Hunters" was first published in 1966 in *Saturday Night*, part of a suite of hunting stories that, as we will see, Godfrey used to elaborate his settler nationalism. The story, a dialogue between a Canadian and an American Marine from Minnesota, casts America as a masculine, aggressive hunter, full of "driving rages." Laurence's "Open Letter to the Mother of Joe Bass" and Livesay's poem "New Jersey: 1935" zero in on the same American racism that Purdy isolates. Both begin by establishing their own intimacy with racialized women (Laurence with the Ghanaian midwife who delivered her son in 1956 and Livesay with an African American social worker whom she encountered in her field work in New Jersey in the 1930s) before proceeding to identify racism as a specifically American disease.[6]

While writers like Atwood and Lee focused on the internal, psychological effects of the colonial condition and the Committee for an Independent Canada called for modest reforms to a capitalist system, other activists and intellectuals who identified with the social-democratic and socialist New Left connected the colonized mind to the American capitalism that was enabled by Canada's business elite. A vigorous spokesperson for this point of view was another contributor to Purdy's *The New Romans*, Robin Mathews, poet, political activist, professor in the Department of English at Carleton University, and member of the Waffle. Decrying American hegemony over cultural and intellectual life in Canada, Mathews sought to establish the institutional supports for "basic scholarship" in Canadian literary studies in both English and French, and his publications, including *The Struggle for Canadian Universities* (with James Steele, 1969) and *Canadian Literature: Surrender or Revolution* (1978), participated in a larger left-nationalist critique of the nation's failure to teach its own history and culture in schools, while calling for the nation's "native inhabitants" to embrace their common inclination to collectivity and "spiritual, material, and social participation" as alternatives to American-style capitalism.[7]

The anglophone New Left was galvanized by a critique of racial injustice in the US and American imperialism abroad. As Philip Resnick notes, English Canadian sentiment during the 1960s shifted away from support for continentalism as a response to the weakening of American imperialism on the global stage, opening the way for anti-imperialist attitudes. Somewhat paradoxically, the New Left anglophone student movement of Canada's 1960s built this critique from European and American sources, including, in Bryan Palmer's words, "Aldermaston peace marches and the idea of nuclear disarmament; Fabian socialism and the British Labour Party; the existentialism, Marxism, and anti-colonialism of Albert Camus, Jean-Paul Sartre, and Frantz Fanon – all jostled with the iconic personages, places, and powderkegs of the US movement: Selma and Newark, Tom Hayden and Malcolm X, Students for a Democratic Society and the League of Revolutionary Black Workers, Eldridge Cleaver and Stokely Carmichael." However, this anti-imperialist critique as it was elaborated by nonracialized settler anglophones did not tend to grapple with the ongoing colonization of Indigenous Peoples in Canada. Books like Mathews's *Canadian Literature*, for instance, make no appeal to the fact of internal colonization; Mathews's "native inhabitants" are not Indigenous Peoples.[8]

In the context of the sovereignty movement in Quebec, settler nationalism was differently motivated but drew on analogous references to oppression and colonization, as the infamous title of Pierre Vallières's *Les n— blancs d'amérique* (1968) indicates. Settler New Left cultures in Quebec in this period turned to the decolonizing cultures of Africa and other nations to understand their own colonial predicament, and scholars such as Sean Mills have begun to document these complex networks of solidarity and influence. As David Austin's work demonstrates, it was not just white settler Quebeckers who were taking inspiration from the global decolonization movement in this period. Fuelled by new immigration from the Caribbean, in particular, Montreal's black population grew through the 1960s; powered like the sovereignty movement by the era's language of decolonization, a movement of black students and activists was fed by visits from and relationships with writers and activists like George Lamming, C.L.R. James, and Walter Rodney, and nourished print forms, such as the Montreal movement paper UHURU (Swahili for "freedom"), that took clear inspiration from African decolonization movements. As Peter Graham and Ian McKay point out, the organizations of black New Left activists in Toronto through the late 1960s and particularly in the '70s were similarly "fundamentally transnational." Like "their counterparts in Montreal, many of them were intensely studying movements for decolonization and taking their cues from Third World leaders." As we will see in the subsequent chapter, the same kind of transnational connection to global decolonization movements shaped the activism of the Red Power movement of the late 1960s and '70s.[9]

Although these kinds of transnational networks and solidarities have typically been viewed as less important to the nonracialized New Left in the rest of Canada, this chapter aims to show how African nations, their political fates, and their relations to the development paradigm occupy an important but overlooked site in the articulation of late twentieth-century anglophone settler nationalisms. The impulse to indigenization that is so omnipresent in the anglophone settler literatures of the later 1960s and '70s – driven by what Lorenzo Veracini calls the "crucial need to transform an historical tie ('we came here') into a natural one ('the land made us')" – has the ongoing presence of Indigenous Peoples in Canada as its primary motivating force. As the development paradigm created new opportunities for young settler writers to go to Africa, they began to imagine their cultural and political predicaments via the anticolonial politics of new nations such as Ghana. Such forms of intellectual solidarity permitted them to move beyond the thorny question of ongoing forms of settler colonization at home, while cementing their claims to "native" space.[10]

Though African connections have been emphasized less in the study of anglophone settler nationalisms, the English Canadian canonizing initiatives of the later twentieth century noticed the significant presence of Africa in the writing of the generation of authors who came of age in the 1960s, many of whom came to be identified with elements of the New Left and its cultural nationalisms. In her 1994 study of Audrey Thomas, Barbara Godard observes that "in the late 1960s, travelling to Africa became a new twist in the Canadian myth of the noble savage." Also writing in the 1990s, Kerry Vincent points out that the same year Northrop Frye's now-canonical *The Bush Garden: Essays on the Canadian Imagination* was published (1971), no fewer than three novels by Canadian-born writers took African nations as their settings: Dave Godfrey's *The New Ancestors* (actually published in 1970, though it won the 1971 Governor General's Award for English-Language Fiction), David Knight's *Farquarson's Physique and What It Did to His Mind*, and Hugh Hood's *You Can't Get There from Here*. Audrey Thomas's novel *Mrs. Blood* was published in 1970; her earlier collection of African stories, *Ten Green Bottles*, was published in 1967; and her first published story, also set in Africa, "In Ten Green Bottles," appeared in *The Atlantic* in 1965. Margaret Laurence's African titles were all published in the 1950s and early '60s. The poet Dorothy Livesay, whose influence on English Canadian poetry was significant during the centennial era, also published poems beginning in the 1960s that explored her experiences in Northern Rhodesia earlier in that decade. As Vincent points out, this presence of Africa in the period's settler writing "did not go unnoticed by Canadian critics."[11]

For instance, contributors to the tenth-anniversary issue of the field-defining journal *Canadian Literature* – founded in 1959 by George Woodcock at the University of British Columbia – reflect on the state of the emergent field of Canadian literature, and two of the eight writers featured emphasize the importance of an African sojourn to their writing. Alongside essays by authors now synonymous with the coalescing of the field of English Canadian writing in this period (P.K. Page, Mordecai Richler, Hugh MacLennan, Norman Levine, James Reaney, and Al Purdy), Laurence's and Livesay's essays point to the ways that their experiences in the decolonizing territories of Somaliland, the Gold Coast, and Northern Rhodesia shaped what Laurence calls the previous "ten years' sentences."[12]

Important figures associated with the late twentieth-century canonization and institutionalization of Canadian literature in English also observed across the 1970s the influence of African experiences on this national literature. Settler scholar W.H. New, an early proponent of the "Commonwealth" frame for understanding literary culture in settler Canada, was a keen observer of the uses of Africa in English Canadian writing. In "Africanadiana" (1971), he notes the sheer number of well-known Canadian writers who, in the decades following the Second World War, had spent time on the continent: Laurence in Somaliland and the Gold Coast, Knight in Nigeria; Livesay in Northern Rhodesia; and Thomas and Godfrey in Ghana. In "Canadian Literature and Commonwealth Responses" (1975), New focuses on this same group of writers but expands his view to consider all manner of Commonwealth connections in Canadian writing, emphasizing how the "responses" of Canadian-born writers to experiences in African and other Commonwealth nations "stirred [their] artistry into being." In a 1971 essay for *Maclean's*, settler critic Donald Cameron invokes colonial tropes in his querying of the "mysterious literary fondness for darkest Africa" present in the Canadian fiction of the period. It is not uncommon for a "developing literature" like English Canada's to "ransack the world for molds, models and definitions," but why, Cameron wonders, does Africa hold such "fascination" for novelists such as Laurence, Knight, Thomas, and Godfrey? He concludes: "Conceivably the attempt to understand so various and exotic a society helps to define experiences for novelists from a society which has never really defined itself." Deane E.D. Downey's analysis of Godfrey's, Knight's, and

Hood's novels about Africa concludes that their shared "pessimism" about independence might be attributed to "these writers' awareness of analogous difficulties" in Canada of "economic and cultural if not outright political domination."[13]

As was typical of anglophone settler criticism in the 1970s, these arguments tend, with some exceptions (such as New's observation that writers such as Godfrey had actually worked in Africa), to avoid materialist analyses of what Cameron calls setter "fondness" for Africa. Many rely on analogies that compare the "domination" experienced by Africans and settler Canadians or refer to African settings as important to archetypes that are linked to colonized cultures. In what follows, I make a different argument: the engagement with Africa that one finds in the late twentieth-century work of anglophone settler writers like Laurence, Livesay, and Godfrey must be primarily understood in the context of the emergent development paradigm, whether in its late colonial phase (Laurence) or its slightly later UNESCO-led/NGO phase (Livesay and Godfrey). This paradigm was an important influence on the settler indigenization that came to characterize the anglophone nationalist ideologies and literary aesthetics of the late twentieth century.[14]

"Imported Paints" and Aspirin: Margaret Laurence and Late Colonial Development in Somaliland and the Gold Coast, 1950–57

When the Neepawa, Manitoba-born woman who would become the most widely heralded Canadian novelist of her generation, Margaret Laurence, arrived in the British Protectorate of Somaliland in 1950, she found a colony that was being prepared for nationhood. The British claim to what became the Protectorate lay in the Anglo-Egyptian condominium of the early 1880s. The Protectorate's Horn-of-Africa coastline, which faces what was then the British port of Aden, granted the British a strategic position in a region where European powers such as France and Italy had designs, an effective choking-off point in the Gulf of Aden for traffic issuing from the newly constructed Suez Canal. Despite these advantages, this was a notoriously difficult region to administer because its largely nomadic population lived in the deserts of the Haud and the Ogaden, beyond the reach of the coastal settlements and the inland city of Hargeisa, where the Protectorate government was headquartered; moreover, until the rebel Islamic forces that fought under Abdullah Hassan were subdued by aerial bombing after the First World War, it was impossible for the British to administer the interior because of the constant threat of attack. In the wake of the Second World War and the political changes that ensued, such as the independence of Ethiopia and the placement of the colony of Somaliland that lay to the south of the British Protectorate under UN trusteeship, the writing was on the wall: if what had formerly been Italian Somaliland was set to declare independence in 1960, the British Protectorate would likely follow.[15]

As Myles Osborne and Susan Kingsley Kent point out, the British desired a transition to independence that would not leave it with egg on its face at a time when the US, the Soviet Union, and those in the colonies with western education tended to view British "overrule" in Africa as "anachronistic." Through legislation such as the Colonial Development and Welfare Acts of 1940 and 1945 or the postwar annual reviews of the Development Plan in British Somaliland, "development" and "welfare" became the new dispensation, as the British acknowledged the importance of their African colonies to their own postwar economic recovery. British efforts of the 1950s to prepare the Protectorate for home rule were, in the words of historian Brock Millman, "frenzied." Through the decade, the Protectorate government focused not only on the "Somalization" of the civil service, but also on what it called "development": it concentrated its brief efforts on natural resources (it sought and failed to identify oil and other resources that could be exploited for the economic benefit of the impoverished population, which was largely nomadic and pastoral); infrastructure; and education. British colonial administrators imagined that Somaliland would need to shed its childish impracticality and backwardness to become an adult nation in the new global order, sentiments that were very much in keeping with what Millman calls the "despotic paternalism" of the Protectorate's political structure.[16]

Laurence travelled to Somaliland because her husband, Jack Laurence, a Canadian-trained civil engineer, took a position with Her Majesty's Colonial Service in the Somaliland Protectorate. Anxious to establish some agriculture and sedentary animal husbandry as an alternative to pastoralism, the Protectorate undertook exploratory drilling for underground water sources in 1949. When no water was found, Britain's National Agricultural Advisory Service, which was devoting significant resources to developing self-sufficiency in British Somaliland, began to promote containment as a solution. The building of "ballehs" – "small dams which would control rainy season run-off for irrigation and thus avoid excessive concentrations around the very few existing wells" – commenced; by 1954, two years after Jack Laurence left the Protectorate, nineteen ballehs had been constructed, mainly along the Protectorate's arid southern border.[17]

Between 1954 and 1957, Jack Laurence continued his work for the Colonial Service in the Gold Coast – the territory that became Ghana in 1957 – as second-in-command of building a new port at Tema. Laurence's earliest published writing is set in British Somalia and the Gold Coast, though most of this was completed and published after she returned to Vancouver in 1957: the story "Uncertain Flowering" and her English translation of Somali poetry, *A Tree for Poverty*, were published in 1953 and 1954; her first story set in what became Ghana, "The Drummer of All the World," was published in the Canadian periodical *Queen's Quarterly* while she was still living in the Gold Coast; the stories that were eventually collected in *The Tomorrow-Tamer and Other Stories* (1963) were published in Canadian, British, and American periodicals between 1959 and 1963; "Mask of Beaten Gold" appeared in *The Tamarack Review* in 1963; *This Side Jordan*, her first novel and a national allegory set in the Gold Coast on the eve of its independence, was published in 1960; and her memoir of British Somaliland, *The Prophet's Camel Bell*, was published in 1963. As many critics have observed and as Laurence herself avowed, this body of writing is anti-imperialist, but less frequently noticed is the fact that her writing about Somaliland, in particular, dwells on the perils of the late colonial development paradigm. *A Tree for Poverty* and *The Prophet's Camel Bell* counter initiatives like the Overseas Book Centre and postwar developmentalism more generally.[18]

Though associated with the work of her husband, Jack, the balleh project was attached to a development paradigm that Laurence understood to be fundamentally compromised. *The Prophet's Camel Bell* uses parables to illustrate the perils of development generally. The first of these is unfolded when Laurence hosts in her home Zahara and Hawa, the wives of two of the local elders, who are intrigued by the "bold and simple designs" of Laurence's handmade, block-printed cotton curtains. She offers to show them how to create this effect, easier to execute than their own traditional embroidery, with potatoes, cotton, and textile paints she had brought from England. Shortly after this meeting, Laurence encounters the wife of the director of education, who has worked for "several years in convincing the local elders that some kind of education was desirable for Somali women, but not the highly theoretical education which at this stage of the country's development would inevitably separate a woman from her people and turn her into a prostitute." Her class of Somali girls, the first in the country to be educated in a secular school, was premised on her understanding that the students needed to know how to manage their homes in the new settled communities, contexts that required skills that had not been necessary to nomadic life. "In her class," Laurence tells us, "the girls worked with materials they would find available to them when they left school and got married." This knowledge prompts Laurence to return home to "put away my imported paints."[19]

Laurence's second parable of development is less anodyne. She represents her time in the Haud with Jack, who was testing sites for ballehs. She was living in a temporary camp that was guarded during the day by "Illaloes," nomadic Somalis who were working for the Protectorate to enforce British law and order in the desert. They come to know that she is the guardian of the tin first-aid kit provided by the colonial service and begin to seek out her medical care; she is aghast, but also complimented, and soon she has a "regular sick-parade." As her patients and their maladies come to teach her, however, she knows little of this place: "What had I known of life here at all? I recalled the faith-healing of the Illalo's ear, and the simple boracic treatment of Abdi's eyes. It seemed to me that I had been like a child, playing doctor with candy pills, not knowing – not really knowing – that the people I was treating were not dolls. Had I wanted to help them for their sake or my own? Had I needed their gratitude so much?" Laurence puts her tin box of aspirins and Dettol away but soon sees that "this, too, was an exaggeration" – "would I do nothing simply because I could not do everything?" Shortly thereafter she is approached by a group of nomadic Somali women, who ask if Laurence has "anything to relieve their menstrual pain." Laurence suspects that this pain is linked to female circumcision, but this is a practice she knows very little about, "partly because in our early days every Somali to whom I put this question gave me a different answer, and partly because I no longer questioned people in this glib fashion." She decides to tell the women that she has nothing to give them: "This was the only undeceptive [sic] reply I could make." In this parable, Laurence offers what seems to be her strongest condemnation of the development paradigm: as her sheepish awareness of the self-importance that the first-aid kit afforded her suggests, development is always necessarily self-interested. And indeed, British colonial development and welfare schemes epitomized self-interest: the resources and raw materials of Africa, properly "developed" and managed "scientifically" were understood by the British to offer a solution to its dire postwar financial situation and food and fuel shortages.[20]

Laurence's evident unease with the emergent development paradigm can be read alongside her own development initiative, a project she undertook while in Somalia. The project, an effort to translate oral poems and stories in Somali into English, germinated throughout her time in Somaliland. As she told Adele Wiseman in a 1951 letter, she found in Somali poetry "much that is fresh and imaginative and original," and she endeavoured in her limited Somali to understand some of the literature in its original language. Most of her translation work was aided by others more fluent in Somali than her, particularly the Polish linguist and poet B.W. Andrzejewski of the School of Oriental and African Studies in London, who had a Colonial Office research grant to study Somali language and literature and whom Laurence befriended. Laurence's project was brought to fruition when she discovered she was pregnant with her first child and was obliged to retreat from Jack's field team in the Haud to Hargeisa, where she went to work for the Protectorate government as secretary for Chief Secretary Philip Shirley. Shirley was an apparently dispassionate man who was overseeing the "gradual transfer of power"; Laurence recalls in *The Prophet's Camel Bell* that he seemed unmoved by the people whom he governed, but that she "discovered one day that this was not true at all." When he discovered her work on translations of Somali poetry and prose, Shirley responded with "unexpected intensity," insisting that he would pursue "an allocation of money from the government for the purposes of publication." Laurence's translations of oral Somali poetry into English were published in 1954 (after her departure from Somaliland) by the British colonial government of the Somaliland Protectorate.[21]

The book, *A Tree for Poverty*, has a complex relation to the late colonial development paradigm that clearly made Laurence so uneasy.

It must be partly understood as her anti-imperialist critique of developmentalism. This critique was targeted at colonial administrators and not at Somalis. As her introduction to *A Tree for Poverty* explains, "the purpose of this work is not to arouse interest in the national literature among the Somalis, since this already exists." Though Protectorate educators and literate Somalis faced the constant challenge of procuring reading materials through the decade that followed Laurence's sojourn – the Protectorate did not open its first library until 1949 and the first commercial bookstore was established in Hargeisa in 1954 – this lack of materials does not seem to have been the most important spur to Laurence's work. Similarly, though her African oeuvre is clearly aware of the problem of using culturally irrelevant British materials in African classrooms, the provision of culturally meaningful materials in English for Somali classrooms does not seem to have been Laurence's aim. Indeed, very few Somalis were in the 1950s literate in English *or* Somali (Somali was in the '50s a language without a standard orthography). Protectorate administrators estimated in 1958 that only one per cent of Somalis were literate in English and two per cent in Arabic.[22]

Valorizing Somali culture and literature, *A Tree for Poverty* instead attempts to render a "nation of poets" with an "unwritten literature" visible to Protectorate administrators, a group whom she characterizes in *The Prophet's Camel Bell* as "so desperately uncertain of their own worth and their ability to cope within their own societies that they were forced to seek some kind of mastery in a place where all the cards were stacked in their favour and where they could live in a self-generated glory by transferring all evils, all weaknesses, on to another people." *A Tree for Poverty* also turns the mid-century language of development on its head: "in their own terms," Laurence insists, the literary tastes of Somalis "are highly developed." She notes in her introduction that "owing to the extreme difficulty of the Somali literary language," the "greatest poems in the language, for example some of Mohamed Abdullah Hassan's gabei, are as yet completely unknown to us." It is important that she chooses the gabei – complex, long-lined poems on topics such as love, war, philosophy, and politics – of Mohamed Abdullah Hassan. Hassan, also known as "the Sayyid" (follower of the Prophet), was consistently demonized in British representations, such as Douglas Jardine's *The Mad Mullah of Somaliland* (1923), for his rebellious early twentieth-century rejection of British rule in the Haud. While drawing attention to the great body of oral Somali literature her book cannot hope to represent, Laurence curated her selection of poems for British readers, accentuating what David Richards calls their "proximity to western literary criteria" and their "universal archetypal forms." Fiona Sparrow contrasts the translation work in *A Tree for Poverty* to the translations that Andrzejewski ultimately produced (with I.M. Lewis) in 1964, arguing that Laurence's "aim was to construct independent poems, faithful to but detached from the original" that would "ma[ke] sense to a western reader." Appropriately, then, in her account of her translation project in *The Prophet's Camel Bell*, which was drafted and published almost a decade after the 1954 publication of *A Tree for Poverty*, Laurence casts her translation work as intended for a British audience – as a rejoinder to the Protectorate administration rather than a contribution to its development efforts. She notes that her initial idea for a book of translations met with displeasure when she suggested it to Musa H.I. Galal, the Somali poet and education department employee who worked as Andrzejewski's assistant: he claimed that Somali poems "would be wasted on the cold and unemotional English." But Laurence insists, "[T]hink of all the English here who had no idea that the Somalis had ever composed poems – think of showing them some of the epic *gabei*, the lyrical *belwo*. This was my line of persuasion."[23]

At the same time, there are elements of *A Tree for Poverty* that suggest it might be read as a participant in the late colonial rhetoric of development. The Protectorate's development plans for Somaliland through the 1950s emphasized the development of natural resources, the creation of infrastructure, and education. To accomplish work in any of these fields required references – maps, geological surveys, dictionaries, anthropological studies – because, as Millman observes, it would have been difficult to proceed with development "without some knowledge of what there was to develop." Work on the transliteration of the Somali language had begun in the prewar period under the Protectorate's director of education, and in 1951, the British Colonial Office brought Andrzejewski to Somaliland to continue this undertaking. Andrzejewski and Galal collaborated on research related to Somali dialects, phonetics, and tonal structures, work they completed in 1953 (a Somali orthography in the form of a print dictionary was not published in the Protectorate until 1960). Laurence met this pair soon after her arrival in Somaliland in 1950, and they spent evenings together, discussing, as she tells us in *The Prophet's Camel Bell*, "Somali customs, language, poetry." These poet scholars provided Laurence with the "literal translations" of the poems collected in *A Tree for Poverty*, and Laurence used Galal's paraphrasing to render two of the stories in the collection (the others are paraphrased from Hersi and Arabetto, Somalis hired to assist Jack Laurence in his work). Laurence evinces in the introduction to *A Tree for Poverty* the desire to "record poems which otherwise will be lost in another fifty years," a nod to the rhetoric of cultural documentation that was part of the Protectorate development agenda that brought Andrzejewski to Somaliland. The statement seems influenced by the Protectorate officials, particularly Shirley, who encouraged Laurence's translation efforts and helped her to obtain official funds for her book's publication.[24]

Moreover, the contexts for the initial publication and dissemination of the book suggest its proximity to the late colonial development paradigm. The first edition of *A Tree for Poverty* indicates on its title page that the Somaliland Protectorate had the book published by The Eagle Press in Kampala, Nairobi, and Dar Es Salaam in 1954 (see figure 4.1). This identifies the book as the product of the Eagle Press imprint of the EALB, a service that, as we saw in chapter 1, was established in 1948 under the new regional government, the East African High Commission, a colonial structure that administered the territories of Kenya, Uganda, Tanganyika, and Zanzibar in the wake of the Second World War. According to Caroline Ritter, the postwar EALB reflected both its "missionary publishing roots" (its first director was the former manager of the Christian Missionary Society Bookshop, headquartered in Kenya) and the British "government's new interest in colonial development and welfare" (the EALB was funded almost entirely in its first decade by money from the Colonial Development and Welfare Fund, and its list through the 1950s was dominated by education titles, followed by books that addressed other fields targeted by British development projects in the region). The publication of *A Tree for Poverty* in this late colonial development context alters its meanings significantly; Laurence may have intended a rejoinder to colonial administrators, but her book became part of a print culture committed to the "uplifting and modernizing" of Africans' lives. Moreover, as we saw in chapter 1, the publishing legacy of the EALB extends well into the twentieth century: as Ritter argues, the EALB and the involvement of the British Colonial

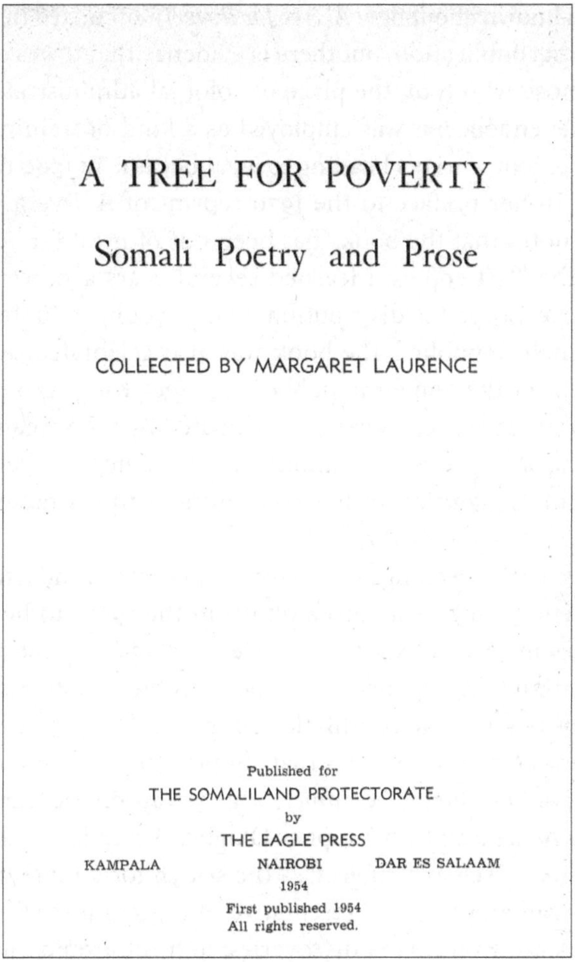

> A TREE FOR POVERTY
>
> Somali Poetry and Prose
>
> COLLECTED BY MARGARET LAURENCE
>
> Published for
> THE SOMALILAND PROTECTORATE
> by
> THE EAGLE PRESS
> KAMPALA   NAIROBI   DAR ES SALAAM
> 1954
> First published 1954
> All rights reserved.

Figure 4.1 Title page of first edition of *A Tree for Poverty: Somali Poetry and Prose*, published under the Eagle Press imprint by the East African Literature Bureau, 1954.

Office in late colonial publishing initiatives functioned as a kind of free market research and development for British publishers, which began to reap the rewards of this gift in the postindependence era when Oxford University Press, for instance, set up an eastern Africa branch in Nairobi, concentrating on lucrative English-language publishing for the education market.[25]

Little is known about how *A Tree for Poverty* circulated in the initial years after its publication, but there is evidence that it was eventually used by those who took the place of colonial administrators in the era of independence: it was employed as a kind of training manual for development workers heading to what became in 1960 the Somali Republic. In her preface to the 1970 reprint of *A Tree for Poverty*, Laurence notes that the book "has been out of print for years now" and that the "last copies, I learned several years ago, were bought by the Peace Corps for distribution among young volunteers going to the Somali Republic." The book was also celebrated by the new government of the Somali Republic. As James King recounts in his biography of Laurence, Laurence was invited by the Somali minister of information to attend his nation's Independence Day celebrations in 1966, "in recognition of her commitment to his nation as evidenced in *A Tree for Poverty*."[26]

Whatever the meanings of *A Tree for Poverty* in the late colonial development context, Laurence's return in the 1960s to her postwar experiences in the Protectorate was clearly shaped by the politics of decolonization that were becoming more visible in both French- and English-speaking Canada in this decade, particularly, as we have seen, among New Leftists. New notes that, despite the successful realism of the stories of *The Tomorrow-Tamer*, which draw on the "sensibilities" of Chinua Achebe and Christopher Okigbo, Africa is simultaneously a "metaphor as well as a subject": "The search for a route to survival is not African alone but representative of a general search; the wry discoveries are Everyman's discoveries; and the ironic mode is the twentieth century's." New's contention that Laurence was aware of her own interest in the "African motif" as a tool for self-discovery seems accurate. In *The Prophet's Camel Bell*, she acknowledges that "the last thing in the world" that would have occurred to her younger self was that "the strangest glimpses you may have of any creature in the distant lands will be those you catch of yourself." In the decades after 1960, Laurence modified this idea, emphasizing Africa as analogy rather than as a site of self-discovery. A year after the publication of *The Prophet's Camel Bell* (and following her completion of *The Stone Angel*), Laurence drafted an essay that returns to the topic of Somaliland. Drawing extensively on Andrzejewski and Lewis's translations of Mohamed Abdullah Hassan's poetry as well as on Octave Mannoni's *The Psychology of*

Colonization (1956), it compares Hassan's resistance to the Highlanders at Culloden and the Métis at the Red River. The essay, "The Poem and the Spear," remained unpublished until 1974, when it was included in *Heart of a Stranger*; in this book's headnote to the essay, Laurence writes: "It seems to me now a rather curious piece of work, because I was making some attempt not only to tell the Sayyid's story but also to understand the plight of a tribal people faced with imperialist opponents who do not possess superior values, but who have greater material resources and more efficient weapons of killing. A long time later, this same theme came into my novel, *The Diviners*, in the portions which deal with the Highland clans and with the prairie Métis." As Laurence built her critique of colonialism (including colonial development), her ideas about nationalism, and her commitment to social democracy across the decades that closed the twentieth century, she increasingly elaborated comparisons among Africans, Scottish-Canadian settlers, and Indigenous Peoples in Canada.[27]

Laurence's African writing offers an influential and widely read example of how the instrumentalization of the term "colonized" played out in the context of the anglophone settler nationalism of the 1960s and '70s. On one hand, Laurence explicitly complicates analogies between Canada and Africa in her African writing. In *The Prophet's Camel Bell*, for instance, she acknowledges her role as a colonizer, a Prospero in an "island place." Quoting Mannoni, whose 1956 study *Prospero and Caliban* she read after returning to Canada in 1957, Laurence admits that she may have "started out in righteous disapproval of the empire-builders" but that she, too, "had been of that company." On the other hand, Laurence indulges these same analogies, noting her exceptional subjectivity as a "colonial," for instance:

> Every traveller sets foot on shore with some bias. Not being a scholar in Arabic literature or anything else, I had no specific pre-conceived ideas of what the Somalis would be like, or ought to be like. My bias lay in another direction. I believed that the overwhelming majority of Englishmen in colonies could be properly classified as imperialists, and my feeling about imperialism was very simple – I was against it. I had been born and had grown up in a country that once was a colony, a country which many people believed still to be suffering from a colonial

outlook, and like most Canadians I took umbrage swiftly at a certain type of English who felt they had a divinely bestowed superiority over the lesser breeds without the law.

The positioning of these two statements matters: since the former is placed at the conclusion of the memoir, it seems to represent Laurence's changed thinking from her first arrival in Somaliland in 1950 to her completion of the manuscript in the early 1960s, when she was reading Mannoni. At the same time, it is the second assertion – the desire to be a "colonial" – that permeates the fiction and nonfiction that Laurence went on to write through the 1970s. We might think here of the way *The Diviners* (1974) conflates settler women's oppression under patriarchy as well as the disenfranchisement of the Scottish Highlanders with the lot of the Métis, or of the many analogies Laurence drew between African and settler Canadian writers in essays such as "The Poem and the Spear," discussed above, and "Ivory Tower or Grassroots" (1978). In the latter, Laurence elaborates a comparison of settler Canadian and Nigerian writers as "Third World writers" who share the experience of finding their "own voices" and writing "in the face of an overwhelming cultural imperialism" and describes the influence of Achebe's work on her own attempts to "write out of my own cultural background." Following Laurence's lead, the "Commonwealth"-oriented Laurence criticism of the closing decades of the twentieth century tends to conflate the experiences of colonization in African nations with those of anglophone settlers in Canada.[28]

It is important to note that Laurence's comparisons were not untutored: as the extensive library (over one hundred volumes) of African literature, history, sociology, and anthropology that she built after her return to Canada in 1957 and as her 1968 study of Nigerian drama and fiction, *Long Drums and Cannons*, demonstrate, she was a careful student of African literatures in English and an early important contributor to its study. Like her sovereigntist contemporaries in francophone Quebec, she was an avid reader of the cultural texts of decolonizing Africa, though she was more attuned to the continent's literary output than to its political cultures. As the subsequent case studies will show, Laurence's experiences of Africa in the 1950s, her 1968 critical evaluation of Nigerian writing, and her literary successes in the '60s and '70s positioned her as an important commentator on the role and function of Africa in late twentieth-century settler Canadian writing.[29]

"No Literature of Their Own?":
Dorothy Livesay in Northern Rhodesia, 1960–63

In 1958, when Dorothy Livesay arrived in Paris to work as a programme assistant for UNESCO's Department of Education, she was an established Canadian poet with two Governor General's Awards for English-language poetry (for *Day and Night* in 1944 and *Poems for People* in 1947); her long-time publisher, Ryerson Press, had just released her *Selected Poems* (in 1957). Despite the accolades she had already received for her work, Livesay was on the cusp of an experience – a three-year stint in what was then Northern Rhodesia as a teacher training expert for UNESCO – that she would later characterize as transformative. In the autobiographical writing that she published after 1965, she attributed her contact with the cultures of this region of Africa with the renewal of her poetics. Indeed, the commencement of this second phase of her writing career would render her one of the best-known anglophone Canadian poets of the twentieth century, identified with both second-wave feminism and the New Left through late twentieth-century publications such as *The Unquiet Bed* (1967) and *Right Hand Left Hand: A True Life of the Thirties* (1977). However, there are interesting contradictions at play here: although Livesay credited southern African traditions of music and dance with her renewal, the time she spent in the nation that was soon to become Zambia was devoted to the teaching of canonical British texts.[30]

Educated in the 1930s as part of Canada's first generation of social workers, Livesay had spent the 1940s raising her two children, writing, and teaching in various capacities, including a stint teaching creative writing with the University of British Columbia's Extension Department. In 1958, propelled by an interest in teaching adults and a failed experiment teaching high school students in Vancouver, Livesay applied for and won one of the first Canada Council grants (the Council was established in 1957), which permitted her to study methods for the teaching of English at the University of London's School of Education. This experience, coupled with her husband's death in 1959 and a desire to "experience the lot of young people in the third world, a world headed for independence from colonial domination," encouraged her to seek a position at UNESCO. In this she was likely aided by the friendly words of J.R. Kidd, who wrote her a letter of introduction that identified her as "one of our finest and most sensitive poets." At UNESCO, Livesay focused on the study of women's education in Africa, reading widely

Figure 4.2   Dorothy Livesay's Federation of Rhodesia and Nyasaland residence permit, 1961–62.

Figure 4.3   Dorothy Livesay at her residence at Kitwe Training College, c. 1960.

to "determine the conditions under which African girls and women can best adapt themselves to the requirements of the new social and economic situation." Her Paris notebook from 1959–60 indicates that she was immersed in the book-centric UNESCO literature of the era that we encountered in the previous chapter, including *World Illiteracy at Mid-Century* (1957), *Facilities for Education in Rural Areas* (1958), and the UNESCO *Bulletin*. During her tenure in Paris, Livesay prepared two working papers on the topic of adult education and the education of girls in Africa, and in August of 1960 she was hired as a teacher training expert for Northern Rhodesia under the auspices of UNESCO's Technical Assistance Program. In November of 1960 she arrived by plane in Lusaka, Northern Rhodesia. Her first appointment was to Kitwe Training College in the Copperbelt region, where she worked teaching English to teacher trainees and as a librarian; after seven months, she obtained a transfer to Chalimbana Training College near Lusaka, a school that was, as Livesay explains in her memoir, for the training of "higher-level teachers" and thus more suited to her work of "explaining methods of teaching English for secondary-school pupils." Livesay remained at Chalimbana until the spring of 1963, when she returned to Vancouver.[31]

What was the UNESCO environment that Livesay engaged with in these years? From its inception in 1945, UNESCO members from the global South, due to their numbers, were able to exert significant influence on the organization's direction, most notably shaping its concern with "equalization" and, ultimately, literacy and education. The new two-thirds majority at UNESCO during the 1960s constituted by newly decolonized nations meant that the influence of nations from the global South increased, resulting in book development initiatives, such as the book-related research critical of an uneven global communications order and the concept of a New World Information and Communications Order that we encountered in the previous chapter. It was not until the mid-1960s that pressure from the US (among other major funders of UNESCO initiatives) led to a shift away from mass literacy campaigns and toward a concept of functional literacy linked to economic development.[32]

In its founding decade, UNESCO was building its capacity to collect and standardize global data on literacy and education and thus to formulate quantitative assessments of educational needs; in doing this, the organization was able to render visible – for the first time – the inequalities in education between North and South. This "scientific" and empirically grounded demonstration of inequality in education was congruent with the UNESCO-backed argument that underdevelopment could be addressed through investments in education (an argument advanced in UNESCO's 1957 publication, *World Illiteracy at Mid-Century: A Statistical Study*). In 1951, UNESCO officially launched a worldwide educational campaign aimed at globalizing the right to education and promoting the ideal of free, compulsory education for all. By the late 1950s, when Livesay arrived at UNESCO, this approach was dominant. According to Damiano Matasci, UNESCO's "normative efforts" related to education were accompanied by its "increasing investment in providing material assistance to developing countries" to build educational infrastructure and to train administrators and teachers. Between 1947 and 1968, thousands of "field missions," funded by the organization's ordinary program or by the UN's Expanded Programme of Technical Assistance, sent UNESCO experts to nations where such needs existed; more than 60 per cent of these (or 614 missions) concerned education. A dramatic rise in the number of such missions in sub-Saharan Africa occurred between 1960 and 1963 – the years that Livesay was in Northern Rhodesia.[33]

The Northern Rhodesia that Livesay visited in the early 1960s was transitioning to independence. Formerly British South Africa Company territories that were merged in 1911 to become Northern Rhodesia, it was administered first by the British South Africa Company and, after 1924, as a protectorate by the British Colonial Office. According to Miles Larmer, the rapid development in the interwar years of the copper mining industry by multinational mining corporations was an "important spur to African self-organisation and political radicalisation" because the towns in the new Copperbelt where African workers migrated created new sites for political organization and new routes of communication between the central regions and the Northern Province, where many of the African mine workers originated. The British territories of Southern and Northern Rhodesia and Nyasaland were brought into a semi-autonomous political union, the Central African Federation, in 1953. Osborne and Kingsley Kent's history of the British in Africa describes the Federation as designed for the economic and political benefit of white settlers – an extension of the settler dominance that had been achieved in postwar Southern Rhodesia to other parts of the Federation and a means of exploiting natural resources, such as Northern Rhodesian copper, for settler benefit. The Federation was driven by a rapidly expanding settler population in Southern Rhodesia, which hoped that it could ultimately become a British dominion like South Africa. According to David C. Mulford, the "vast majority of Africans" rejected the Federation, which included only very limited forms of African enfranchisement and representation (only four Africans sat on the twenty-six-seat legislative council in 1953). Opposing the Federation during the 1950s in both Southern and Northern Rhodesia was the African National Congress (later the Zimbabwe African People's Union and the Zambian African People's Union). In Northern Rhodesia, where the settler population was smaller and politically weaker, the United National Independence Party (UNIP), led by Kenneth Kaunda after January 1960, also attacked the Federation, decried the colour bar, and called for independence.[34]

In the period of Livesay's visit, the UNIP was a young party (it was established in 1959 in the aftermath of the breakaway of the Zambian African National Congress from Harry Nkumbla's African National Congress), and its support was concentrated in the Bemba-speaking Northern and Luapula Provinces, as well as the Copperbelt. Livesay's presence between 1960 and 1963 as a UNESCO teacher and expert in the Copperbelt and Central regions was thus under the oversight of the settler government of the Federation, which was in these years grappling with the rising challenge being mounted by independence activists. The situation in the northern areas of Northern Rhodesia was especially tense in the first half of 1960 (Livesay arrived in November) and in July and August of 1961: murders of settlers, school burnings, and other UNIP acts of protest, concentrated in the "Cha Cha Cha," led to the government's invocation of emergency powers and mass arrests of UNIP members and sympathizers. According to Larmer, Kaunda's willingness to negotiate with colonial authorities – a willingness not widely supported by UNIP members – led to a proposed constitution and elections that produced black majority rule by the end of 1962 and, ultimately, in October of 1964 (about a year and half after Livesay had returned to Vancouver), independence.[35]

Livesay occasionally mentions this unrest in her journal and in her UNESCO reports, observing in December 1960, for instance, that her work is dependent on the "political situation." Her papers from her African sojourn include an undated CUSO primer on Northern Rhodesia written in the voice of the "President of the UNIP" that warns development workers that independence is nigh and that expatriates in the country who choose to stay "must recognize that they are the guests of our people. The days have gone when they could impose their way of life and pattern of society upon us." Livesay clearly imagined herself as different from white settlers in Northern Rhodesia, whose prejudice she abhorred, but she also tends to cast herself as somewhat separate from most white expatriates teaching in Northern Rhodesia. In a 1961 letter to her sister she reports that "the students regard me as being different – i.e., as from UNESCO, which came out last November for 'freedom from colonialism.'" Nevertheless, she was aware that "as the passions are aroused and the violence starts no white skin will be immune."[36]

As her journals from Africa and her later African poetry indicate, Livesay knew about and was sympathetic to the UNIP and its organizing in and around the Copperbelt and Lusaka. Her account of Kaunda's visit to Chalimbana in July of 1962 emphasizes her admiration for his "reasonable and quiet" leadership style. Her Zambian poetry, written after her return to Vancouver in 1963, devotes much space to Kaunda and offers evidence of her admiration of what she perceived as his power and dignity. If Livesay's earliest attempts to create poetry from her experiences in Africa are lyrics focused on her subjectivity as a foreigner observing daily life, the poems she was drafting by the mid-1960s are explicitly focused on Zambia's independence and its African leaders. "The Leader," a poem best known because of its appearance in Livesay's *The Unquiet Bed* (1967) and her *Collected Poems* (1972), had many lives before it appeared in these publications: its first section was initially titled "U.N.I.P. Meeting" and was published as part of the cycle "Zambia" in the Montreal literary magazine *Cyclic* in 1965; its second section was first a poem titled "Prophet" that Livesay published in *Canadian Forum* in 1962 and in the "Zambia" cycle published in *Cyclic* in 1965. In her 1964 chapbook *The Colour of God's Face*, she brought the two poems together as "The Leader"; she placed "The Leader" at the end of the chapbook, following "The Prophetess," a poem dedicated to spiritual leader Alice Lenchina that offers a sympathetic view of the place of women in the emergent political leadership of Northern Rhodesia. The various iterations of "The Leader" show that Livesay was attempting to remove her subjective first-person voice from her portrayal of Kaunda. While Kaunda is named in "U.N.I.P. Meeting" as he who is "shouting from the Anthill, my countrymen!," the revised stanzas that comprise the first section of "The Leader" in *The Colour of God's Face*, *The Unquiet Bed*, and the *Collected Poems* identify Kaunda in the third person as "the man on the anthill / crying out 'Kwatcha!'" (Bemba for "freedom"). The second section of "The Leader," originally "Prophet," shifts to the first person, but the speaker is not a persona for Livesay but rather for Kaunda himself:

> Heaven lets down a rope
> whereon I swing
> the clapper of a bell
> on sounding sky
>
> and all below
> they cluster with uplifted faces
> black on white
> and sway like flowers
> to my wild clanging

At the same time, Livesay's writing clearly demonstrates that she felt uncertain about how to express her solidarity: in a 1961 letter to her sister, she refers to political gatherings to which she was not invited, such as Kaunda's visit to Chalimbana in August of 1961; in her 1991 memoir, she recalls that police were surveilling her in 1962 because she had given a "lift" to an African who was attending a UNIP meeting; in her correspondence she points out that, unlike other development workers in the region, she, a "U.N. civil servant," was not free to join the UNIP.[37]

Livesay's work in Northern Rhodesia in the early 1960s focused on promoting the then-dominant UNESCO ideal of free, compulsory education for all and, more specifically, on the training of high school teachers in methods of English literature instruction and pedagogy. Enabled by increasing financial backing provided by UN funds for technical assistance (particularly from the Expanded Program of Technical Assistance) during the 1950s, UNESCO was able to carry out a wider program than would have otherwise been possible. By the late 1950s, however, new challenges to the concept of technical assistance were arising from within the UN and UNESCO. As Phillip W. Jones reminds us, technical assistance can be defined as "the provision of skilled or experienced persons for the exercising, demonstrating, or teaching of particular skills or equipment, or the provision of the equipment itself for such purposes"; it is "designed as an instrument for promoting development not as a source of capital but as a source of the skills that can make capital work." As the multilateral system was opened to "scores of new nations" from the late 1950s onward, newly decolonized nations began to articulate a critique of technical assistance that questioned the "role and function of western expertise in settings which were not western and no longer colonial."[38]

The politicized question of education's purpose and function in a decolonizing territory unsurprisingly put pressure on Livesay's work in Northern Rhodesia. The view of education that she was enacting at Chalimbana was one that the first government of independent Zambia ultimately came to reject. Just after her arrival in late 1960, a Four-Year Capital Plan (1961–65) for Northern Rhodesia was introduced; aimed at a "rapid expansion of secondary education," this development plan was inherited by the Zambian government when it assumed power in 1964. As Zambia's first Minister of Education J.M. Mwanakatwe recounts in his history of education in postindependence Zambia, the UNIP government immediately set to work on the universal provision of primary education (a commitment that was of a piece with the contemporary UNESCO focus on universality of access) but was obliged at the same time to address the dearth of trained African teachers and suitable buildings for schools, as well as the problem of "largely foreign" content in both primary and secondary schools. The development of secondary schooling presented special challenges to the new nation, and Mwanakatwe despairs that "the cost of improving the secondary school system to allow more than one-third of grade VII school leavers to enter Form I is prohibitive." The government's education plan turned therefore by the end of the 1960s to an agriculturally oriented curricula for both primary and secondary schooling. Inspired by Julius Nyerere's promotion of "education for self-reliance" in newly independent Tanzania, the UNIP government of the later 1960s diversified primary and secondary curricula to emphasize "agricultural education"; vigorously promoted a "back to the land" policy (that framed, in Mwanakatwe's words, the "gradual disintegration of rural life" as "one of the disastrous influences of colonialism"); and sought to retrain teachers in rural science. Although the Final Report of the 1961 UNESCO-sponsored Meeting of Ministers of Education of African Countries requests UNESCO support for educational development in African nations, noting the importance of technical assistance programs for the provision of administrative and teaching expertise, Mwanatakwe's history rarely mentions UNESCO and does not promote foreign-trained experts as part of the solution to Zambia's education-related challenges.[39]

In newly independent Zambia, the secondary teacher training program known as "s3" that Livesay was participating in at Chalimbana was associated, on one hand, with the vision of "rapid expansion of secondary education" found in the colonial development plan of 1961–65 and, on the other hand, with what Mwanakatwe terms the "politically unacceptable" University College of Rhodesia in Salisbury – an institution that in the mid-1960s remained under the authority of the white settler minority that governed Rhodesia. With a genealogy connected to colonial powers like the British South Africa Company (and its founder Alfred Beit) and foreign donors like the Carnegie Corporation, Chalimbana's teacher training program was between 1961 and 1965 under the administrative control of the University College of

Rhodesia, which determined its syllabus. In 1965, the UNIP government suspended Chalimbana's program; training for the nation's secondary teachers was subsequently established in 1967 at the new University of Zambia.[40]

Moreover, the curriculum that Livesay devised for the training of secondary school teachers of English was decidedly British, despite the fact that the published work of African writers – albeit in English and issued by British publishers – was becoming increasingly available in this period. The 1952 publication of Amos Tutuola's novel *The Palm Wine Drinkard* by Faber and Faber marked the beginning of what Gail Ching-Liang Low calls the "metropolitan scramble" for African titles that could be published in English, largely as a means of granting British publishers, which were in the early 1960s establishing branches across Africa, access to the emerging educational markets of postindependence African nations. Oxford University Press and Heinemann both introduced series devoted to African writing in English in the early 1960s. In 1962, while Livesay was still teaching in Northern Rhodesia, Heinemann published four titles in its new African Writers Series: Chinua Achebe's *Things Fall Apart* and *No Longer at Ease* (first published by Heinemann in 1958 and 1960, respectively), Cyprian Ekwensi's *Burning Grass*, and Kenneth Kaunda's *Zambia Shall Be Free*. By the later 1960s, educational materials in Zambia had been transformed. While English remained the language of government and education in postindependence Zambia, the UNIP subjected the questions of educational content and purpose, as well as the issue of provision of educational materials, to new scrutiny. Via the establishment in 1967 of the National Educational Company of Zambia, a state publisher run by the parastatal Kenneth Kaunda Foundation and (for its first five years) British publisher Macmillan, the Zambian government, unlike other newly independent nations such as Kenya, was able to furnish its own school textbooks (and by the early 1970s, almost 13 per cent of the company's list was devoted to African-language publishing).[41]

Yet as a trainer of secondary school teachers in the early 1960s, Livesay was firmly committed to the teaching of a British literary canon, while also being critical of the way that English was being taught in Northern Rhodesian classrooms. In "The Teaching of English in the Junior Secondary School," an undated report Livesay drafted for UNESCO, she laments that "English is taught in Central Africa as if passing exams were the sole aim" and calls for "a new emphasis" that will "stress the value of English as a skill in the use of communication; as a social asset which may enlarge the pupil's circle of friendship, travel, and vocation; and as a means for developing the pupil's emotional and intellectual capacities." To be able to identify oneself with the protagonist of *Great Expectations* or *Julius Caesar* is "to take a step, sometimes a leap forward, in emotional and psychological work." Her recommended reading for junior secondary school students in Central Africa includes classics in abridged form, detective stories, science fiction, adventure stories, fables, and Greek legends. Because "African students respond remarkedly to the rhythm and music of words in poetry; and to all dramatic situations," English classes should make ample use of ballads, narrative poems, and "free dramatizations" that may lead to the study of scripted plays, such as the abbreviated works of Shakespeare. She does note that the new writing in English by African authors being published by Cambridge University Press and Heinemann (she lists titles such as Ekwensi's *The Drummer Boy* and *Burning Grass* and Achebe's *Things Fall Apart*) is "worth investing in," yet there is no evidence that Livesay took her own advice about using African writing in English in her classrooms – except for her use of the white South African novelist Alan Paton's anti-apartheid novel *Cry, the Beloved Country* (1948).[42]

Like the British government in the same period, which was expanding what Ritter calls the "cultural project of the late British Empire" to Africa through the medium of "imperial institutions" such as the BBC, private publishing firms such as Oxford University Press, and the British Council and its sponsorship of travelling theatre troupes, Livesay turned as a teacher trainer to canonical standards such as Shakespeare as she developed a "communication and literature"-centric (rather than "grammar and methods"-centric) curriculum at Kitwe and then Chalimbaba. At Kitwe she directed a performance of Shakespeare's *The Merchant of Venice*, and at Chalimbaba, George Bernard Shaw's *Androcles and the Lion* (see figures 4.4a and 4.4b). Livesay's correspondence with her former Kitwe student Joe Mulenga offers some evidence of the former production; thanking Livesay for her gift of W.A. Illsley's *A Shakespeare Manual for Schools* (1957), Mulenga goes on to note that his participation in the play "really breathed a lot of confidence in me." Livesay quotes Mulenga in further correspondence with UNESCO: "I can now read 'The Merchant of Venice' with understanding and it

Figure 4.4a Play program for *Androcles and the Lion* (undated), cover.

will help me to understand his other plays. My friends in Luanyasha [about fifty kilometres south of Kitwe] say that they will not forget the play because it is so real to them. Most of them have read the play but the performance startled them ... In fact it has so inspired me in drama more than any other plays I have seen or read, or acted." Alongside such performances, Livesay developed an ambitious program of literary study. From January to October 1962, for instance, her Chalimbana students studied George Bernard Shaw's *Saint Joan*, followed by a "brief history of English literature up to Chaucer," considering "examples of

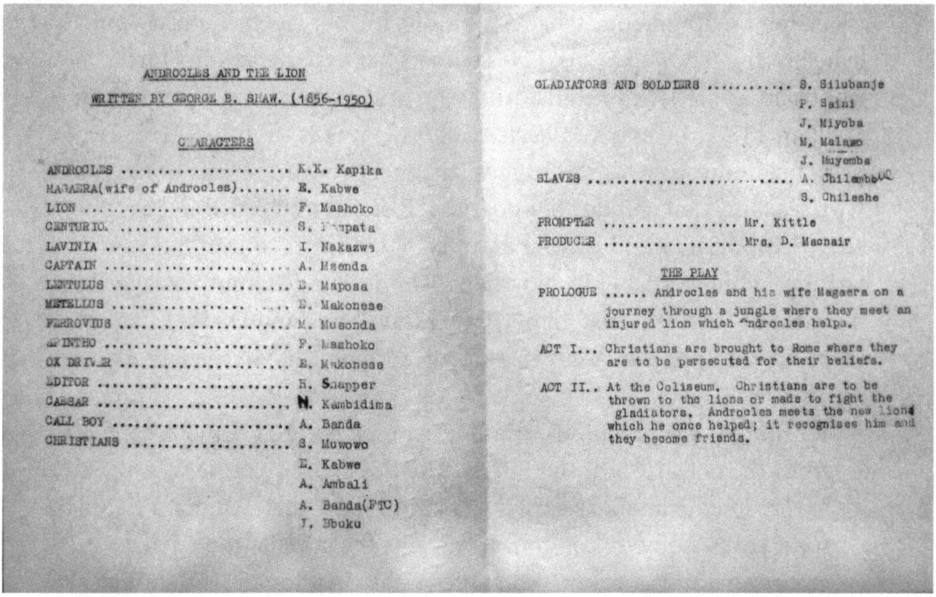
ANDROCLES AND THE LION
WRITTEN BY GEORGE B. SHAW. (1856-1950)

CHARACTERS

ANDROCLES .... K.K. Kapika
MAGAERA(wife of Androcles)....... E. Kabwe
LION .... F. Mashoko
CENTURION .... S. [illegible]upata
LAVINIA .... I. Nakazwe
CAPTAIN .... A. Msenda
LENTULUS .... E. Maposa
METELLUS .... E. Makonese
FERROVIUS .... M. Musonda
SPINTHO .... F. Mashoko
OX DRIVER .... E. Makonese
EDITOR .... H. Snapper
CAESAR .... N. Kambidima
CALL BOY .... A. Banda
CHRISTIANS .... S. Muwowo
E. Kabwe
A. Ambali
A. Banda(FTC)
J. Mbuku

GLADIATORS AND SOLDIERS .... S. Silubanje
P. Saini
J. Miyoba
M. Malawo
J. Muyemba
SLAVES .... A. Chilambo
S. Chileshe

PROMPTER .... Mr. Kittle
PRODUCER .... Mrs. D. Macnair

THE PLAY

PROLOGUE ...... Androcles and his wife Magaera on a journey through a jungle where they meet an injured lion which Androcles helps.

ACT I... Christians are brought to Rome where they are to be persecuted for their beliefs.

ACT II.. At the Coliseum. Christians are to be thrown to the lions or made to fight the gladiators. Androcles meets the new lions which he once helped; it recognises him and they become friends.

Figure 4.4b Play program for *Androcles and the Lion* (undated), interior pages.

old English writing – medieval poems and ballads, carols; and read a bit of Beowulf's Prologue in translation, and the Nonne Preest's [Chaucer's Nun's Priest's] Tale." While Livesay was attempting to promote a method of teaching that embraced a living language over rote memorization and while her selection of literary texts demonstrates a desire to introduce themes of cultural and religious conflict and racism, she was also committed to an idea of "literary" education that was, as her choice of plays and records of her teaching attest, centred on the British canon.[43]

Ironically, given that Livesay was teaching her students a British tradition of drama, poetry, and prose, she found in Northern Rhodesia a means of renewing her own poetic practice that was anything but British. While in Africa, Livesay did not publish poems about her experiences; however, upon her return to Vancouver in 1963, she published a number of poems set in what is now Zambia in periodicals, chapbooks, and eventually the full-length book collections *The Unquiet Bed* (1967), *Collected Poems: The Two Seasons* (1972), and *The Self-Completing Tree* (1986). As she says in her 1991 memoir, *Journey with My Selves*, her post-Africa poetry "freely expressed the pent-up passion within me"; the origin of that passion "had been the Zambian experience."[44]

In her writing about what Africa did for her poetry, mostly published in the 1960s and '70s, Livesay casts her experiences in Northern Rhodesia as renewing, transformative, and enchanting. Drawing on William Blake, Livesay's *Collected Poems* (1972) is subtitled "The Two Seasons," indicating, as she suggests in the foreword to this book, the "two seasons" that animate her poetics – Blakean innocence and experience, "community and private identity," "town and country." Livesay's writing about her time in Northern Rhodesia adds another layer to this idea of "two seasons." In her 1969 essay "Song and Dance," Livesay identifies an important shift that occurred in her life in the late 1950s:

> It required a tremendous, traumatic break before I could escape from the defeatism of the Fifties. The opportunity came when I won an educational fellowship from the Canada Council, for a year's study in London. Ironically, the stimulation of that environment was countered by deep personal loss ... the sudden death of my husband and the growing independence of my children – one working, one away at boarding school. Yet, for the first time in some twenty years, I was a free woman. I took off for Paris, where a former professor of mine, Felix Walter, was stationed at Unesco. He helped me get a job there, and from that vantage point I applied and was accepted for a teaching post in Northern Rhodesia. The experience of three years in Africa was so intense and fascinating it cannot be set down in a few words. It needs a book. Lacking the time to write that, I made jottings for poems. And when I returned to British Columbia at the end of my Unesco tour, in July 1963, I was a changed person.

This change, Livesay recalls, was rooted in her disappointment with the Canada that greeted her upon her return ("the great developments I had hoped to see in Canada towards a just society had not materialized") and, more fundamentally, in her enchantment with the people of the nation becoming Zambia: "I had participated in a sudden and dramatic changeover from a tribal society (in which there was much of goodness and beauty) to an industrial society in which the people were to a large extent participating intensely. All the evils of capitalism and automation were rearing their heads in the new Zambia; but opposed to these destructive forces were human beings who commanded my deepest respect. Such a one was Kenneth Kaunda, the new president." As we have seen, Livesay translated this "respect" for humans like Kaunda into the poem that is now best known as "The Leader."[45]

Livesay's comments from a 1978 interview expand on her thoughts in "Song and Dance" about what she perceived to be the relation between Canada and Northern Rhodesia in the early 1960s:

> The impressive experience for me was the fact that we had fought all through the thirties for a changed society – we thought the War would bring an entirely new social world into Canada; soldiers would come back and would refuse to be treated as they had been before and we would change society – then it all collapsed. Nothing happened except the Korean War – a terribly dark victory. So we felt we had lost on all those fronts. The thing about Rhodesia for me was the fact that I was living through a complete change in society which succeeded; of course it didn't succeed in being socialist, but it took the first step of being nationalist and free from colonial chains and we had been very much under colonial chains in Canada. So it was a great psychic release for me to be close to these people who were changing their society.

Drawing, as Laurence was doing in the same period, a parallel between African and Canadian experiences of "colonial chains," Livesay locates her generation's disappearing youth and its political idealism, as well as the possibility of social and political transformation, in what became Zambia. For Livesay, this renewal was also creative.[46]

In "Song and Dance," Livesay links her enchantment with Zambia to her rediscovery of dance, of rhythm, and of the musicality of life that she associates with her earliest memories of her mother at the piano attempting to replicate the Ukrainian ballads sung by their housekeepers. The parallel is not anodyne: as Livesay recounts in a 1978 interview, her mother, Florence Randal Livesay, had in the period prior to the First World War asked a Ukrainian Baptist minister in Winnipeg to translate the folk songs of her Ukrainian and Polish housekeepers into English. Randal Livesay in turn rendered these songs in English verse and published them in *Poetry* (the Chicago-based little magazine that was a centre for Anglo-modernist verse) before collecting them as *Songs of Ukraina*, which was published by J.M. Dent in 1916. Just as Randal Livesay's modernist primitivism had enabled her entry into an elite high modernist sphere, so the younger Livesay's self-renewal through contact with a "tribal society" in the throes of change created an opening for the rebirth of her career as a Canadian poet:

> And so Africa set me dancing again! My students, I discovered, woke up singing; no sooner was their breakfast of "mealie-meal" over when they would cluster in a common room, turn on the record player, and dance. Most of their dances were unsophisticated, jive and jitterbug; it was easy for my feet to catch the beat. Best of all, you didn't need a partner. You could dance opposite a girl student as easily as opposite a youth. Not a dance of touch, but one where the rhythm itself created an unseen wire holding two people together in the leap of movement. I had never been happier!

Livesay resumes this theme in her 1991 memoir, recalling that "just the way they lived their music was fascinating to me ... For me, life had become part of the music." Her fascination with the music of southern Africa, and with drumming, in particular, is demonstrated in the recordings she captured while in Northern Rhodesia. In "Song and Dance," she attributes this experience of the body in rhythm with a "confidence" that allowed her, in the poems published immediately after her return to Vancouver in the early 1960s, to "speak out of immediate experience."[47]

Livesay's solution to the problem of returning to Vancouver in the early 1960s, where "nobody knew me or my work in that crowd and I thought I was done for as a writer," was at least partly a matter of shaping her experience of Africa into a narrative that was consonant with the spontaneous, body-centric poetics of the North American West Coast of the 1960s – the "projective verse" of the Black Mountain poets and the aurally-oriented poets of the Vancouver TISH group. Lee Briscoe Thompson reads this consonance as happy coincidence:

> Gradually put at ease by attending outdoor readings, teaching creative writing at UBC [the University of British Columbia], and coming to know the major faces and trends on the Canadian literary scene, Livesay found herself perfectly in tune with many

elements of the 1960s. The hippie celebration of love, peace, and self-expression, the interest in artifacts of native peoples and natural lifestyles, and the experiments in expansion of consciousness and of language were all intensely compatible with the new openness to life that she felt and wished to embody in her art.

Whether a coincidence or a self-conscious representation crafted by a poet uncertain of her place in 1960s-era Canada, or both, Livesay's experience of Africa was clearly central to what critics widely recognize as the more sensual, voice- and body-centric poetics of Livesay's second "season," a poetic renewal that granted her a central place in the emergent canon of English Canadian literature that was congealing in the decades after 1960.[48]

Those literary critics who have engaged Livesay's African poetry tend to both reiterate and intensify her narration of the effect of her Zambian experience on her work, often employing primitivist ideologies and accepting what Antje M. Rauwerda, discussing the "Zambia" section of *The Unquiet Bed*, calls the "derogatory sexualizing of blackness." Briscoe Thompson, for instance, associates the drums that fascinated Livesay with "the blood-pumping beat of our hearts, the lunar and solar cycles, the pleasure of patterned movement, the throb and thrust of sex." Fiona Sparrow argues that Livesay's time in Zambia led to the "rich poetic harvest of her second season": "Africa was intense and fascinating in many ways. It was dramatically different from Canada and forced the poet to reexamine her own language, its sounds as well as its vocabulary and imagery. Africa remained sufficiently primitive to make the magical possible." According to Sparrow, a "newly-born" person returned to Vancouver in 1963: "A remarkably resilient and responsive woman, Dorothy Livesay stood upright beneath the African sun and rains, and like the wild fig tree she felt herself grow young and fertile again." This wild fig tree trope is in fact Livesay's own. In her African journal, she describes one of the first walks she took in Kitwe in 1960, through the "wild country surrounding the copper silt dump" in the wake of heavy rains: "Suddenly I notice a strange sight: a huge tree, the left half abloom and leafy, the right with branches stripped, sere and autumnal. This must be the mythical fig tree! So even in this flat countryside the ancient reverberations emerge: colour for the eye, music for the ear." The fig tree as figure for "two seasons" also made its way into her African poetry (as the third section of "The Land" in *The Colour of God's Face*;

as "The Wild Fig Tree," published as part of the "Zambia" sequence in *Cyclic* in 1965; and as the third section of "Zambia: The Land" in *The Self-Completing Tree*) and her 1991 memoir, in which she quotes her 1960 account of witnessing the fig tree verbatim.[49]

Despite the tendency to cast her experience in Northern Rhodesia in the modernist terms of spiritual and sexual renewal via contact with a "tribal" other, Livesay was a dialectical thinker, and many of the African poems first drafted in the 1960s attempt to deconstruct the binary terms of colonialism. While in Northern Rhodesia, Livesay experienced what she refers to in her memoir as a "deep psychic relationship" with some of her African colleagues and students. One of these was Raphael (Ralph) Chbota, a young, married teacher who appears as "Raphael" in the poem "Politics" and to whom she dedicated "The Second Language" (both of these poems were written in the 1960s but not published until 1972, as parts of the suite entitled "The Second Language" in *Collected Poems*). In the latter poem, the speaker figures the relation of "I" and "you," "white" and "black" as a shared discovery of a common "second language":

> We walk between words
> as if they were trees
> touching rough bark
> exploring origins.
> Linked, in this green shade
> a tree's name shadows us
> I share its history
> with you
> who came
> a first man to this forest.
> And you find roots
> your look uncurls each leaf
> till every word we speak
> thrusts upwards from its mother dark
> and sparks our eyes with light.

This "second language," thrusting upward from "its mother dark" and producing "light," is a common tongue that supplants the initial binary of "I" and "you" (and the implied binary of the white speaker and the Raphael figure, "a first man"). Yet this language has limits; a shared intimacy that exceeds "our words" is figured as sexual:

> If in the dark
> I stumbled against your mouth
> would my arms stay pinned
> at my back –
>> or shiver forward
>> white flowering
>> into black?

Livesay describes this desire for spiritual, physical, and psychic communion with Africans in her memoir. She recounts a scene in which she is made to feel her difference as a "European lady," which is followed by a casual and friendly encounter with the son of one of the African teachers that leads her to reflect: "Like the Japanese riddle of the man who dreamed he was a butterfly: was he a human or was he a butterfly dreaming he was a human? Am I that Canadian lady? Or am I a young black boy hugging his baby sister, asking to be frozen in a photograph?"[50]

At the same time, and as she frankly acknowledges in her 1972 unpublished text "Zambia," her thinking during her time in Northern Rhodesia was often more dichotomous than dialectical. The autobiographical text narrates Livesay's exit from Africa in the third person. It opens with an admission of what she had come to understand as her failures in the territory becoming Zambia:

> The feeling of guilt was foremost: that she was somehow being turned out of this loved land because of her own failures. Failures to override there white-black distances: to be utterly friend to those men and women who had so completely trusted her: who were warmer, more open, than anyone she had known in her own cold country. Failures because she had succumbed to the british [sic] educational hierarchy and acted as their tool; rather than free-wheeling; rather even, then stressing continually the greater loyalty she had at the beginning of her sojourn, a loyalty to the world and its intricate organization, UNESCO.

The tone of the text is full of self-mockery and contrition, an older Livesay's understanding that her Eurocentric values had limited her work at Kitwe and Chalimbana:

> It was only a pretence that she had, in youth, sloughed off
> Christianity; for its accoutrements, its raphaels, Titians,
> Velasqueths [Velázquezs]; stone builded streets, vision of Dante
> in the cobbles of Florence – these she valued above all else. These
> she unconsciously forced her students to learn. Thinking of that
> painting of the House of Lords in session, that she had given to
> 12-year-olds to test their vocabulary! Think of her acceptance of
> the secondary school curriculum, geared only to the Cambridge
> examinations. Think how she had struggled with Emma and The
> Mill on the Floss (Oh some of them liked that one because it dealt
> with family relationships, but how much must have been obscure
> to them). No literature of their own? She had sought for such; but
> had not really made the effort to introduce Achebe to her college
> of ed syllabus.

The force of the text, however, lies in its concluding insistence that "soon-to-be Zambia (or say Northern Rhodesia?)," with its "black epople [sic] drumming up the sun at dawn and dancing, dancing all day," was a "country she belonged to, even in exile, her frantic exit had its meaning if she could have time to serach [sic] for it." Livesay's desire to be claimed by Zambia, to "belong" to its ancient cultures of drumming and dancing and, by extension, its difference from British- and US-dominated modernity, speaks to the complex ways that the development paradigm shaped the settler literatures that came to constitute English Canada's literary canon.[51]

The "NGO Moment": CUSO and Settler Literatures of the 1960s and '70s

While Laurence's experience of development was of the late colonial variety and Livesay's was attached to UNESCO's postwar vision of universal access to free, compulsory education, writers who were important to a burgeoning national literature in English Canada during the 1960s and '70s were also shaped by what Kevin O'Sullivan calls the "NGO moment." As O'Sullivan describes it, this "moment," which occurred from the 1960s to the mid-'80s, was a period of "profound change for the West's relationship with the Third World," as "humanitarian aid and development NGOs became the primary conduits of Western compassion for the global poor." This transformation was not without struggle; if, in the decades following the Second World War, a "Westernised, NGO-led model of compassion became the dominant global expression of solidarity with the Third World," this model had to compete "for primacy with alternative projects of compassion that emerged from the communist world and within the wider anti-colonial movement." O'Sullivan focuses his study on Britain, Ireland, and Canada, arguing that the NGOs of these nations "were to the forefront of the new global aid industry that emerged in this period." Although differently motivated – British NGOs by "post-imperial benevolence," Irish NGOs by anticolonialism, and Canadian NGOs by the nation's "self-defined role as 'humane internationalist'" – the nongovernmental aid sector in each of these places (with the exception of Quebec) "shared in a broadly Anglophone tradition of aid" that recast missionary and colonial connections as "public morality" and, later, as "popular movement." Given Canada's importance to this global transformation, it should not be surprising that the NGO moment shaped cultural expression and cultural debates among settler Canadians in the last decades of the twentieth century.[52]

Two settler Canadian writers volunteered with CUSO in its early years: Audrey Thomas's and Dave Godfrey's involvement with CUSO took them both to Ghana, Thomas from 1964 to 1966 and Godfrey from 1963 to 1965. In the previous chapter, we encountered CUSO as an important organization in the "NGO moment" – the first NGO in Canada to receive government assistance for development work; the motivating force behind the establishment of an NGO division within CIDA in 1968; and the NGO that received the most money from CIDA during the period that spanned from the early 1960s to the late '80s. Although, as I point out in the previous chapter, CUSO (like the western NGO movement more generally) was transformed by an increasingly radical self-critique after 1968 or so, Thomas's and Godfrey's experiences of CUSO coincided with the organization's idealistic earlier years.[53]

Ruth Compton Brouwer notes that most of the English Canadian student volunteers who participated in CUSO service abroad during the 1960s were born in Canada and possessed middle- or skilled working-class, urban or suburban, Anglo-Saxon or Anglo-Celtic backgrounds. The vast majority were under twenty-four years of age, had a Bachelor of Arts general degree, and lacked work experience. Those who had grown up on farms or who, like Godfrey and Ross Kidd (son of J.R. Kidd), had volunteered with Frontier College, the adult literacy program we have already encountered and that was in the 1960s still sending university students to remote work camps as labourer-teachers, could draw on those experiences. Like Frontier College labourer-teachers, CUSO volunteers were volunteering in a nominal sense: according to the minutes of a 1965 meeting of CUSO's Executive Committee, CUSO volunteers were agreeing to work in "basically comparable conditions of service to those of [their] indigenous colleagues." In its first decade, CUSO placed Canadian volunteers at the request of agencies in the host nations; because the newly independent nations of Africa were clamouring for teachers from the West during the 1960s, most CUSO volunteers, including Godfrey, Kidd, and Thomas, took up teaching. The teaching-centric focus of the organization is evident in the images that adorn the cover a 1965 pamphlet, issued in French and English, "SUCO et Vous" ("CUSO and You") (see figure 4.5). Of the volunteers who went to Ghana before 1965, almost all of them went to teach (in 1963–64, for instance, seventeen teachers and one engineer were sent to Ghana).[54]

The preponderance of former Frontier College volunteers in the first generation of CUSO volunteers – the group included not only Godfrey and Kidd but also John R. Wood, Tom Schatzky, Steve Woollcombe, and Jim Morrison – is suggestive of the genealogical links between CUSO and its voluntary sector predecessors in Canada, organizations that had emerged from the social gospel movement of the early twentieth century. Unsurprisingly, CUSO, according to Compton Brouwer, was keen to detach itself from the more explicitly Christian aspects of this genealogy, particularly mission work, with which its overseas placements shared many structural similarities. CUSO volunteers with Frontier College experience were perhaps especially prickly about this connection. In his 1963 account of his "extra-gang days," Godfrey treats the Frontier College mission of "staunch Canadianism" with trenchant irony, putting much distance between himself and the concept of "aid and uplift." Yet in its first decade CUSO was obliged to rely on teacher educators with mission experience or connections, including Margaret Wrong's partner Margaret Read, to train its recruits, most of whom lacked teaching experience. Indeed, as Compton Brouwer points out, "missions were the only Canadian organizations with extensive experience in preparing personnel for such overseas service." While many CUSO volunteers

Figure 4.5   "SUCO et Vous," CUSO/SUCO pamphlet, 1965.

in the 1960s were uncomfortable with the connection of CUSO work to "traditional missionary activity," the cultural backgrounds of most recruits from English-speaking Canada meant that many would have had exposure to Christianity as children in the 1940s and '50s. Indeed, as Doug Owram and others have argued, Anglo-Protestant and Anglo-Catholic values were important to the student activism of Canada in the 1960s, which depended in the first instance on a "belief in service, duty, and commitment."[55]

The Ghana that Thomas and Godfrey encountered in the mid-1960s was newly independent. CUSO had established itself in West Africa with two home economists in 1961; by 1968, the organization had sent over three hundred volunteers to English-speaking West Africa (Ghana and Nigeria), mainly as secondary school teachers. Independence from Britain came quickly in Ghana, the first colony to achieve independence in West Africa. The British colony of the Gold Coast provides what Osborne and Kingsley Kent call a "prime example" of the fact that the British had to work differently in Africa after the Second World War: no longer able to rule through the cooperation of traditional chiefs but envisaging the need to anticipate home rule in the African colonies, the British had to contend with educated African elites, which also meant acceding to their inevitable demands for reform. The governor of the Gold Coast adopted in 1946 a new constitution for the colony that made elective eighteen of the thirty seats on the legislative council. Change was slow, however, and Africans who desired a quicker transition of power flocked to leaders such as Joseph Danquah and his United Gold Coast Convention or Kwame Nkrumah's Convention People's Party. The strikes and riots led by these leaders, particularly Nkrumah, provoked change: when the Party took thirty-five of thirty-eight seats in the 1950 legislative council elections, Nkrumah, who was in jail for leading a general strike, was released and permitted to take a role in government. By 1952, colonial officials had granted him the title of prime minister. When the transition to independence occurred in March 1957 – a uniting of the former British colonies of the Gold Coast, Ashanti, the Northern Territories, and British Togoland to form the nation of Ghana – Laurence and her young family had just left, departing so that Laurence could see her "Mum," who was dying in Canada.[56]

In the wake of Laurence's departure, the UN's declaration of the 1960s as the first "Development Decade," and the ramping up of the "NGO moment," young Canadians like Thomas and Godfrey arrived in post-independence Ghana to take up work as teachers. The Ghana of the immediate postindependence period that they experienced was shaped by Nkrumah's vision of African socialism, which included marketing boards, rapid industrialization (of which the massive Volta River Project, the subject of Laurence's short story "The Tomorrow-Tamer," was a key element), and a system of free education. Nkrumah's approach, his choice to align with neither the western capitalist states nor the Soviet Union, was shaped by his keen apprehension of the threat that neocolonialism posed to Ghanaian autonomy in the context of the global Cold War, as his 1965 evisceration of this threat as "the worst form of imperialism" makes clear. Yet Nkrumah's vision was beleaguered by inherited colonial structures that affected trade, economic organization, infrastructure, and the culture of governance, which was rife with corruption and graft. Though Marxists such as C.L.R. James were initially deeply sympathetic to Nkrumah's leadership, James ultimately condemned Nkrumah's government, warning in a 1960 speech given in Accra, for instance, that government corruption could only be brought to account by the people. According to Osborne and Kingsley Kent, many rural Ghanaians and poor city dwellers came to "feel that their president spent so much time playing the role of international statesman that he forgot about his people at home." A sham referendum in 1964 led to the establishment of a one-party state, and in 1966, while Nkrumah was travelling in Beijing, he was overthrown in a military coup.[57]

Thomas arrived in Kumasi, Ghana with her sculptor husband, Ian Thomas, in 1964. Unlike Godfrey, she returned twice (in 1971 and 1991), both times with the intention of writing more fiction set in Africa; like Godfrey, she was becoming a writer in the first years she spent there, publishing her work in North American periodicals. Because Thomas was less involved in the public articulation of 1960s-era settler nationalism, I will focus the discussion on Godfrey, but Thomas's African oeuvre certainly merits further analysis in the present, not least because the fiction she wrote with Ghana as a setting, many of her stories, *Mrs. Blood* (1970), and *Blown Figures* (1974) (the respective bookends of her "Isobel Cleary" trilogy) – played a role in the elaboration of second-wave settler feminism after 1970.[58]

Godfrey set off for his CUSO placement in Ghana in 1963. He was twenty-five years old, a settler Canadian from Winnipeg who had grown up west of Toronto. He had two English degrees (a bachelor's degree from the University of Iowa, a master's degree from Stanford University), a Master of Fine Arts degree from what is now the Iowa Writers' Workshop, and years of experience working summers as a "gandy dancer" – repairing railway tracks – alongside the men he taught for Frontier College in the work camps of northern Ontario. Compton Brouwer points out that although Godfrey's "day job" with CUSO in Cape Coast, Ghana was "teaching literature in an elite high school" - Adisadel College - "under an Oxford-educated headmaster who valued his Stanford MA" in English, "Godfrey had his Frontier College experience to draw upon when he started a night-school class for working men in a nearby town." He was also newly married to Ellen Swartz, whom he had met at Stanford in 1960; Ellen, who would become a writer of mystery novels, accompanied Godfrey to Ghana, where she also worked as a teacher for CUSO. When the couple left Ghana in 1965, they returned to the US where Godfrey began a doctoral program in American Literature, but, disenchanted with what he later described as the "catastrophe" of American life in the mid-1960s and buoyed by the emergent settler nationalism of this period, they moved with their young son to Toronto, where Godfrey took up a position at Trinity College (University of Toronto).[59]

In the University of Toronto Book Room in 1966, Godfrey had what Roy MacSkimming calls a "startling realization": "Canada was invisible." A young writer who had, prior to, during, and after his African sojourn, published short fiction in *Canadian Forum* (1920–2000), Robert Weaver's *The Tamarack Review* (1956–82), one of the only magazines publishing Canadian writing in this period, as well as in *Saturday Night* (1887–2005), Godfrey resented American dominance of literary cultures in Canada. He had refused an invitation to appear in an annual anthology of best American stories when the publisher would not change the name to reflect his Canadian nationality, and he recoiled at the idea that Canadian writing was still not taught as a subject of its own in the University of Toronto's Department of English. His solution was to found, alongside poet and University of Toronto colleague Dennis Lee, his own publishing company, House of Anansi Press. In his history of Canadian publishing, MacSkimming rehearses a conversation he once had with Godfrey about the founding of Anansi: "In Cape Coast, Ghana, Godfrey had visited a man of very limited means who printed his own books and bound them himself by hand. If that guy could be a publisher, Godfrey insisted, we all could." In naming the company as they did - after the West African trickster associated with stories and knowledge - Lee and Godfrey materialized their debt to the example of the resourceful Ghanaian publisher.[60]

Propped up by a modest Canada Council grant of $2,500, Godfrey and Lee published two new books in the fall of 1967, Godfrey's story collection *Death Goes Better with Coca-Cola* and George Jonas's poetry collection *The Absolute Smile*, and reprinted two others, Lee's poetry collection *Kingdom of Absence* (which they had already published in a more limited way in the spring of 1967) and Margaret Atwood's out-of-print first collection of poetry *The Circle Game*. Anansi became a leading small-press publisher in the anglophone national literature of this period, publishing literary and nonfiction titles that were central to the articulation of the era's settler nationalisms, such as Northrop Frye's *The Bush Garden* (1971), Lee's *Civil Elegies* (1972), and Margaret Atwood's *Survival: A Thematic Guide to Canadian Literature* (1972). Godfrey's Ghanaian publisher-inspired House of Anansi Press was just the first in a series of publishing ventures that came to be important to the era's cultural nationalism. At New Press, he, Jim Bacque, and MacSkimming published books that were central to the political culture of the anglophone New Left. Titles such as *The Struggle for Canadian Universities* and *Gordon to Watkins to You, A Documentary: The Battle for Control of Our Economy* (1970) aimed, as Godfrey commented in a 1973 interview, to create "awareness in Canadians about a variety of problems: what's happening in schools, what's happening in the military, what's happening in the economy, what's happening in the oil industry." Later, at Press Porcépic, Godfrey, Ellen (Swartz) Godfrey, and Tim Inkster continued to nourish and disseminate the settler-nationalist ideologies of the 1960s and '70s through literary publishing that included the 1973 reprinting of *Death Goes Better with Coca-Cola*.[61]

The context of Anansi and its African inspiration is crucial to the many roles Godfrey came to play in late twentieth-century publishing in Canada. In addition to founding three presses, serving as editor of McClelland & Stewart's Canadian Writers' Series (1968–72), and writing the anonymous literary review feature, "Piquefort's Column," in *Canadian Forum*, he became an advocate for independent, Canadian-owned publishers as an officer of the Independent Publishers' Association (IPA, later, the Association of Canadian Publishers), authoring arguments that drew on his experiences in Ghana to condemn the colonized state of the book in Canada. Established in 1970 in response to the impending sale of Ryerson Press to the American firm McGraw-Hill (in addition to other American acquisitions in the field of publishing in this period), the IPA issued recommendations to the Ontario Royal Commission on Book Publishing that followed from American threats to the domestic industry. Many of the IPA recommendations draw directly on the language of contemporary African book development efforts. For instance, the IPA call for a federal "loan fund for book publishers" – a program for the provision of "long-term, low-interest development loans at 2% under prime interest rates" to help small Canadian-owned publishers meet the costs of advances to authors, new projects, hiring of skilled staff, and marketing – echoes the primary demand of the landmark 1968 Accra Conference, a UNESCO-convened meeting that formed part of that organization's comprehensive book development program for African, Asian, Latin American, and Arab states.[62]

This (and other) IPA recommendations bore fruit: the final report of the Royal Commission (issued in 1972, UNESCO's International Year of the Book) in turn recommended the creation of a program of government-backed loans for Canadian-owned, Ontario-based book publishers, as well as public grants based on the number of titles published in a qualifying period, resulting in the 1972 Ontario Book Publishers' Assistance Program and, at the federal level, the Canada Council's system of block grants to publishers (established in 1972), and, later, the Book Publishing Industry Development Program (established in 1979).[63]

The concept of a colonized book industry is implicit in the 1971 IPA recommendations. In a 1972 study of Canadian publishing he coauthored with James Lorimer, Godfrey is more explicit, characterizing Canada as "colonized and deprived of its own sense of itself" and drawing on an NGO-linked rhetoric of development to make a case for the sad state of the nation's publishing industry: "The present gross underdevelopment of our branch-plant-dominated publishing industry connects directly to the gross underdevelopment of our national cultural life at every level, from books on gardening and travel to poetry and philosophy." As Godfrey and Lorimer suggest, the effects of former colonial ties on publishing in late twentieth-century Canada shared some similarities with publishing in postindependence African nations. Principal among these was the dominance of large publishing companies from former colonial powers, namely Britain and France. In Canada, this had material effect: the Ontario Royal Commission on Book Publishing found that 65 per cent of all books sold in Canada in 1969 were imported from abroad.

Also shared was the obstacle of copyright regulations, which, in Third World nations, limited the ability to translate and publish materials originally published in industrialized nations and, in Canada, according to Eli MacLaren and Josée Vincent, prevented the growth of original Canadian publishing until the 1960s.[64]

However, the publishing conditions experienced by African nations in the late twentieth century can be more meaningfully compared to those experienced by Indigenous communities in Canada in the same period. The vast literature produced on conditions in the book trades in Africa, Asia, and Latin America during the 1960s, '70s, and '80s makes it clear that the nations of this part of the world were themselves far from homogenous – India, Egypt, and Argentina all possessed large and sophisticated publishing industries compared to other nations in these regions – but they also shared certain challenges. Central among these were problems linked to colonial legacies: the atrophying of what Philip Altbach calls "traditional intellectual institutions" and native languages under colonial rule; small book markets created by the confluence of low literacy rates, low per capita purchasing power, and a diversity of languages; book distribution problems caused by factors such as poor transportation; and, as we have seen, foreign aid programs that sometimes had the effect of undermining local publishing efforts. The situation confronted by Indigenous Peoples in Canada offers a better parallel for these conditions than that faced by settler anglophones in Canada in the same period. The IPA's 1971 recommendations indicate some sensitivity to the pressing needs of Indigenous communities in Canada vis-à-vis book publishing but treat these needs as part of a larger national picture and do not identify any of the unique challenges that Indigenous writers and would-be publishers were confronting in the early 1970s. If Indigenous nations began to produce periodicals in the mid-1940s – supported after the mid-'70s by the federally funded Native Communications Program – Indigenous-owned book publishing did not emerge in earnest until 1980 with the founding of Pemmican Publications (owned by the Manitoba Métis Federation) and Theytus Books (located on Syilx Territory in British Columbia). Many more of the conditions applying to Third World nations and identified by Altbach are relevant in this latter case, particularly the problems ensuing from linguistic erasure and assimilation efforts.[65]

Godfrey's invocation as a publisher of the rhetoric of settler Canada's "colonized" identity can also be found in his creative writing from the 1960s and early '70s, the period that coincides with his time in Ghana. Godfrey is best known for his Governor General's Award–winning 1970 novel *The New Ancestors*. Set in "Lost Coast," a thinly disguised Ghana, this experimental narrative departs from the then-dominant preference in English Canada for realism. Given their shared experiences of Ghana, it is not surprising that an important interlocutor for Godfrey in this period was Laurence: she read drafts of *The New Ancestors* (parts of which he published after 1966 in various Canadian periodicals) and was, according to Godfrey, "really the only one who saw the whole thing as it was coming down the stretch." She also enthusiastically reviewed the novel, isolating themes that struck her as universal and highly relevant to settler Canadians, namely "man's eternal search for and fight against the hated and loved father, the ancestors who are mythical and yet whose blood flows in ours, the gods who will neither let us go nor answer us when we beseech them." The novel's influence on Laurence's own thinking is evident in her 1978 essay "Ivory Tower or Grassroots," in which she compares Achebe's writing to her own, arguing that, in the context of an "overwhelming cultural imperialism," Nigerian and settler Canadian writers "stand in need of our gods, and we need links with our ancestors, partly in order to determine who and what we are, to decide what we hope to become, and to know what sort of society we will try to form."[66]

Yet no sustained attention has been paid to how settler indigenization functions via Africa in Godfrey's oeuvre from this period. Focusing on Godfrey's lesser-known writing from the period contemporary with and immediately following his sojourn in Ghana, we can trace the characteristics of the settler-nationalist toolkit he was assembling from the beginning to the end of the 1960s, just prior to the 1970 publication of *The New Ancestors*. The stories and essays that Godfrey published in the Canadian periodicals *The Tamarack Review* and *Saturday Night* in this period, many of which he later collected in *Death Goes Better with Coca-Cola*, elaborate a fantasy of indigenization that draws implicit analogies between settler Canada and newly independent Ghana. This body of work seeks to identify what Godfrey called, in a 1973 interview with Graeme Gibson, the "natural form" of Canadian speech – "reticence" – while also yearning after what he identified in an interview from the same year with Donald Cameron as "true Canadianism," a Canadianism that draws its "primal power" from being "burnt into the land."[67]

Beginning in 1962, Godfrey published regularly in *The Tamarack Review*, contributing short stories, essays, and reviews on an annual basis until the autumn issue of 1966. Though his first contributions all take Canada as their setting, his final story, "The First Encountering of Mr. Basa-Basa and His Excellency, Ling Huo," is set in "Lost Coast" (Ghana). Godfrey was functioning as a kind of Africa correspondent for *The Tamarack Review* in these years, as his spring 1964 omnibus fiction review suggests in its positive assessment of Laurence's *The Tomorrow-Tamer*: "I am myself perhaps her ideal reader, since I can not only appreciate her prose and her command of the story form, but I am here in Africa to be properly amazed by the accuracy of her perceptions and conclusions." The initial stories in *The Tamarack Review* inaugurate early attempts to formulate the themes of hunting that are central to *Death Goes Better with Coca-Cola*. "River Two Blind Jacks" (1961) and "Gossip: The Birds That Flew, the Birds That Fell" (1964) both attend to failed settler attempts to indigenize. In the former story, two feuding loggers, the English-born Albert Godspeed and the "Frenchie" Reginald Couteau, are consumed by a bear when they fail to realize their conflict should not be with one another but with the "Yankee hunter" who "couldn't catch the buttons on his breeches." The latter story gives us Mr Courtney, a history teacher living on the edge of a tangled bush that is being bulldozed to create "two huge apartment houses." Disturbed by the destruction and yet immobilized by his alienation from his own community and family, Mr Courtney takes up the "shotgun his father had taken during the Boer War from a South African who, supposedly, had used it to kill running negroes from his horse, and whom, supposedly, his father had frightened near to death with a similar chase" and indulges in a petulant mockery of hunting for need, shooting two pheasants who would have "died anyhow" in the bulldozing. Alluding to the hopes of turn-of-the-century Canadian imperialism, the story suggests the failure of this legacy to mark contemporary life and community in Canada, leaving its readers with the birds "turning slowly" on an "electric spit which revolved like clockwork at whatever speed you desired."[68]

In 1966, following his return to Canada, Godfrey's three final contributions to *The Tamarack Review* appeared. At least one of these was written while he was still in Ghana: his "Letter from Africa, To an American Negro," published in the winter 1966 issue, identifies its writing context as prior to the January 1964 referendum that led to the establishment of a one-party state in Ghana. The best-known of these three pieces is "The Hard-Headed Collector." It was published in the summer 1966 issue of *The Tamarack Review* (it later appeared as the last story in *Death Goes Better with Coca-Cola* and, as Godfrey acknowledged in a 1973 interview with Graeme Gibson, was written in 1966 after Godfrey's return to North America). It turns the hunting motif of the earlier stories into the more abstract quest, but the quest is ironic because, like the hunting expeditions, it fails.[69]

In a series of barely narrated and vaguely mythical vignettes, we follow a band of artists of diverse settler ethnicities as they trek from the Queen Charlotte Islands to Bay of Chaleur to carve a tree, "Eggsdrull." The artists fall out of the quest one by one and only the leader, Piet Catogas, arrives at the bay, but he is too late. Due to the damming of a creek into the bay, the trees have all been flooded and none is "fit for a trip back to the coast. Hollow rotten." This story has attracted the most critical attention of any of Godfrey's stories, perhaps because it, as Margaret Atwood observes in *Survival*, names "real causes of victimization." Godfrey accomplishes this naming with the insertion of journalistic prose he adapted from *The New York Times*, fragments from the obituary of an American businessman, Mr Hirshhorn. In "The Hard-Headed Collector," Hirshhorn's wealth, made from mining investments in Canada, has enabled him to acquire art and to donate it the Smithsonian in Washington. Unlike the ragtag band of artists, Hirshhorn, according to the testimony of President Lyndon B. Johnson, has "sought the great art of our time – those expressions of man's will to make sense of his experience on earth, to find order and meaning in the physical world about him, to render what is familiar in a new way." What the extant criticism of the story has not acknowledged is the extent to which its failure depends, as in the earlier stories, on an attempt at indigenization: intending to carry out an art form, totem carving, traditionally associated with the Haida Nation (their origin in Haida Gwaii/the Queen Charlotte Islands implies this) while reversing the trajectory of European exploration, the artists encounter groups that are clearly Indigenous, though with mythical and slightly comical names (the Narnians, the Sasarians, and blue-robed figures who are associated with the Anishinaabe of Amik Ziibii [French River, Ontario]). Yet if the art of the people of Amik Ziibii, a mashkinonje sculpture known as "God's fish," signifies the kind of "order and meaning" to which President Johnson refers, "Eggsdrull" fails to conjure such a society-ordering myth. Godfrey's use of laconic speech and threadbare narration attempt to capture what he called in his interview with Gibson the "natural form" of settler Canadian society – a "tight-lipped" "reticence," but he ironizes, at the same time, the failure of this form to become truly native to the land.[70]

Godfrey's first story with an African setting in *The Tamarack Review*, "The First Encountering of Mr. Basa-Basa and His Excellency, Ling Huo," would later form part of the first section of *The New Ancestors*. The story comments cynically though comically on Nkrumah's one-party state through the perspective of First Samuels, "Party thug." Similarly, in "Letter From Africa," Godfrey observes that the people of Ghana, having achieved independence, were now being betrayed by Nkrumah's government and tricked by "a baggage of bourgeois wish-promises which would gladden the hearts of the American Council of Advertisers." Such "wish-promises" bear a remarkable similarity to the American mail-order advertisements that were added to the 1973 Press Porcépic edition of *Death Goes Better with Coca-Cola* (figure 4.6). Like Hirshhorn's art, which, as New observes, is linked to capitalism, institutionalizing, "political motives," and military (hence potentially destructive) strength, the advertisements, like the Convention People's Party's "wish-promises," pervert what Godfrey understood to be creative potential. That Nkrumah's rhetoric is linked to socialism and Hirshhorn's and the mail-order advertisements' to American-style capitalism matters little to Godfrey: both, Godfrey's writing from this period implies and as he explained in his interview with Cameron, are "new ancestors." They represent values that are foreign to the societies in which they have taken hold and prevent individuals "from moving back toward the gods." For Godfrey, this moving "back into the past" in the settler Canadian context involved indigenization, a process of becoming native that he, like many of his contemporaries, understood as necessary to the survival of settler culture in Canada. This conception of indigenization makes little room for Indigenous Peoples or

Figure 4.6   Pages from Dave Godfrey's *Death Goes Better with Coca-Cola*, 1973.

their continued existence in late twentieth-century Canada. Ghana thus makes a convenient analogy for Canada in Godfrey's 1960s-era settler-colonial toolkit: "moving back toward the gods" in Ghana would not involve a settler-Indigenous dynamic.[71]

Of the eight hunting stories and essays that Godfrey published in the "Outdoors" section of *Saturday Night* between 1966 and 1967 – "The Generation of Hunters" (December 1966), "Of Bucks and Death" (January 1967), "Elephant He Go Come Here Plenty" (February 1967), "Escape from My Winter Pent House" (April 1967), "The Big Game Fisherman in Florida" (May 1967), "Pheasants in the Corn" (August 1967), and "Up in the Rainforest" (November 1967) – six eventually appeared in *Death Goes Better with Coca-Cola*, though with some minor changes (including new titles). This suite of ironic hunting-themed texts includes two stories with African settings (the remaining six have American or

Canadian settings). If "Up in the Rainforest" ironizes the masculinist and imperialist ideologies that propel European fantasies of possession, "Elephant He Go Come Here Plenty" (retitled "Fulfilling our Foray" in *Death Goes Better*) takes this irony elsewhere, exploring the desire of African drummer Gamaliel Harding (a character who reappears in *The New Ancestors*) for a "true African xylophone." Like Theophile Karamm, who descends from Lebanese traders but was "reared in Britain away from the trade" and who seeks an "African elephant," Harding is "hunting" for something that has little relevance in contemporary Accra, where "the young people all followed the Avengers, whose electric guitars had been purchased by the Ministry of Defence." This irony gains much of its power from the many texts in the "Outdoors" suite and *Death Goes Better* that feature rapacious American hunters alongside settler Canadians who fail, like the Godfrey persona and would-be wilderness guide in "Of Bucks and Death," to understand the land. In the "Outdoors" suite, this failure and the desire to overcome it is sometimes observed by Godfrey himself, in personal essays such as "Escape from My Winter Pent House." In this essay, Godfrey seeks respite from his urban existence on Spadina Avenue by reading *Life and Sport on the North Shore*, the 1909 memoir of Napoleon A. Comeau, son of a North West Company trapper. Godfrey admires the book because Comeau "writes out of the land and it gives him more stark form than one man needs." As he reads, Godfrey can "go with him, do what he did." This vicarious experience includes sitting alongside Comeau as he "feast[s] on bear with the Montagnais hunters," and "finally smearing my hair with grease from the cooled bowl of fat." The pronoun shift from third to first person demonstrates a more general desire articulated in the "Outdoors" suite: to claim, as the Godfrey persona of "Of Bucks and Death" can do only tentatively, the "old Indian" or "true ancestor" who "really lives here."[72]

Conclusion

In his contribution to Al Purdy's 1968 nationalist collection *The New Romans*, anglophone New Leftist Cy Gonick identifies the untenability of the American-led concept of development, lambasting its capitalist assumptions and urging Canadians to ally themselves instead with the "collectivist-type solution" that could materially improve quality of life in the global South. By the late 1970s, the Toronto-based New Left was arguably more conscious of the implication of Canadians in American-led global processes of exploitation and underdevelopment. In a jointly authored 1977 essay, for instance, the Toronto-based Development Education Centre and the Latin American Working Group argue that "Canada's place in the complex of imperial relations is not simply one of domination by foreign capital. Canadian-owned and Canadian-based capital, particularly banking capital, have been able to take advantage of relations of unequal exchange with Third World countries to drain economic surplus particularly from the Caribbean and Latin America." Such "relations of unequal exchange" extend to Canadian development assistance, which, despite "a great fog of humanitarian legitimation," functions to absorb surpluses of capitalist overproduction and to benefit Canadian producers through mechanisms such as tied aid. Typical of the arguments crafted in such New Left contexts in this period, however, the essay does not develop its analysis of a double imperialism in the direction of internal colonialism. Rejecting, on the one hand, the kinds of assertions of Canada's colonized status that were common to the anglophone New Left of the late 1960s, the essay's authors call for the building of a socialist movement that is attentive to, among other things, the "rights of native peoples," but they do not build a critique of internal colonialism as primitive accumulation.[73]

The writers examined in this chapter share three experiences: all were directly implicated in the development paradigm and its late twentieth-century labours; all were important to the emergence and elaboration after 1965 of a canon of English-language literature in Canada; and all were involved in the expression of the New Left settler nationalisms of the late 1960s and '70s. There are other ways of approaching this history. The focus could be placed exclusively on the cultural and educational labour that young settler Canadians undertook in their host nations, so that one could compare the motivations, ideologies, and goals of these settler volunteers. Narrowing the topic in this way would have the advantage of permitting more actors to come into view.

The work of cuso volunteer Ross Kidd, son of J.R. Kidd, in the emergent field of nonformal education and the performing arts would contribute a fascinating narrative here. He is barely visible in the history I have narrated not least because he did not return to Canada in the wake of his CUSO service in the mid-1960s and did not participate in the elaboration of the literary or cultural nationalisms of the late twentieth century. Instead, Kidd married a Zambian and became a citizen of Botswana, where he established himself as a training and community development specialist. Working with the concept of the performing arts as popular "two-way" forms of education and communication that could not only "put across information" but also "make people more aware of their situation and committed to doing something about it," Kidd was important to Laedza Batanani ("Community Awakening"), a community action movement he helped to found in northern Botswana in 1974. Through the 1970s and '80s, he initiated a series of workshops on the theatre of development in Africa (Botswana, Zambia, Zimbabwe) and Bangladesh. Kidd's critique of the cooptation during the 1970s of radical concepts "for the continued domestication of Third World peasants and workers in the interests of foreign capital," as well as his interest in using popular theatre to push Paulo Freire's ideas beyond "conscientization" toward "organization," demonstrate his importance as an activist and a theorist of radical alternatives to the western development paradigm that emerged in the global South in the 1970s.[74]

Yet by focusing in this chapter on Laurence, Livesay, Godfrey, I have emphasized how, during the 1960s and '70s, development abroad and settler nationalism at home were mutually implicated. In the cases analyzed in this chapter, we see how the African rhetorics of decolonization that settler Canadians encountered in the context of their development work came to shape their conceptions of domestic politics and culture. The influence could work in the other direction, too: Ross Kidd's theory and praxis of theatre for development, for instance, drew on the practices of labour organizers in Canada, whose collaborations with the Mummers Troupe of Newfoundland generated documentary-style performances that were more intimately connected to the "actual words and memories of people in the community" than the initial experiments of Laedza Batanani had been. The enactment of the development paradigm from within Canada in the 1960s and '70s was clearly not unidirectional; it did not only work in the direction of those being "developed." The concepts, motivations, and political sympathies of development, whether in its late colonial or its NGO phase, in turn shaped the anglophone settler nationalisms and literary culture of the period.[75]

If Indigenous Peoples and their claims for justice in the 1960s and beyond are rendered invisible in this chapter's account of settler indigenization, the subsequent and final chapter will demonstrate how ideas about development also played an important role in domestic settler-Indigenous relationships and in the day-to-day lives of Indigenous Peoples in this same period and beyond.

5

The Fourth World Challenge to Developmentalism

As the editors of a special issue of the *Journal of African History* published at the beginning of this century point out, much of the influential literature on development "has focussed on dissecting development discourse emanating from international institutions and Western governments." It is equally important, they contend, to problematize the "relationship between the discourses and the practices of development": "In considering the local configurations within which experts and officials sought to implement their ambitious master plans, these papers show that few if any plans remained uninfluenced by local struggles over land, labor or agricultural and environmental expertise." In other words, developmentalism was not only an ideology imposed; it was at the same time an ideology received, adapted, and transformed in local contexts. In this final chapter, I attempt to explore this receiving, adapting, and transforming of late twentieth-century developmentalist ideology.[1]

This shift of focus is paralleled by a second shift, one that demonstrates the complex multidirectionality of an ideology that, as we saw in the introduction, initially functioned by neatly dividing the globe into developed and undeveloped halves. As chapter 3 discusses, with the emergence in the later 1960s of development's second wave – the various critiques of developmentalism that focused on its failure to effect structural change – came an opportunity to reconsider the binary structure on which the ideology was based. Fuelling development's second wave was, as we have seen, the global decolonization movements of the period, which in turn powered the critiques of the dependency theorists, subsequently taken up in decolonial manifestos such as Walter Rodney's 1972 *How Europe Underdeveloped Africa*. Such thinking lit fires in Canada, too, as the previous chapter demonstrates; what that chapter leaves out are the ways that the thinking and practice of global decolonization movements were adopted and adapted by Indigenous thinkers and activists in Canada. As Indigenous leaders such as Harold Cardinal (Cree) contended, settler Canadians were avid devotees of the voluntary sector and its walkathons for development-oriented activities but were much less interested in the problems faced by Indigenous Peoples in Canada. In issuing this critique in his widely read manifesto, *The Unjust Society* (1969), Cardinal invited the application of developmentalist thinking to the domestic settler-colonial context.[2]

This chapter tracks the complex trajectory of developmentalism's domestic turn in the latter decades of the twentieth century. It takes two elements as its focus: first, following the lead of scholars who have documented the mutual implication in this period of outward-oriented development and the work of federal policy aimed at Indigenous Peoples, I examine the settler application, beginning in Ontario in the late 1950s, of developmentalist thinking to the question of book and library service provision to Indigenous communities; second, I consider the ways that Indigenous communities from across Canada responded to, reframed, and sometimes rejected outright the premises of developmentalist ideology, especially as it related to literacy, books, and education.

Books for the Moose Factory Reserve: Integration as Development

As early as 1901, Indigenous Peoples in Canada were asking the Department of Indian Affairs to establish school and public libraries in their communities. In 1904, Charles Angus Cooke (Kanien'kehá:ka), who had been working for the records branch of Indian Affairs since 1893, proposed a scheme by which the department could turn the collection of books relating to Indigenous Peoples he had amassed into an "Indian National Library of literature," part of which could circulate to reserves. In response, officials at Indian Affairs cited prohibitive cost and the conviction that Indigenous Peoples had little interest in books; the department's accountant, Duncan Campbell Scott (later deputy superintendent), dismissed the library scheme on the grounds of cost, but also rejected the premise that Indian Affairs should be collecting materials authored by Indigenous Peoples and the suggestion that any such materials should circulate. Though some books were provided to Indigenous students in day, industrial, and residential schools beginning in the late nineteenth century, Brendan Edwards's survey of such collections for the period after 1930 (the years for which there is documentation) suggests that they were poorly funded and in disrepair. Like their school textbook counterparts, those books issued from Indian Affairs lists were selected from similar lists for non-Indigenous children and were meant to serve the purpose of assimilation. A 1943 survey of library materials in Canada's 253 Indian Day Schools counted 140 schools with a library collection and observed that most of these collections were not actually furnished by Indian Affairs but by haphazard collection, often from donations of discarded books. Edwards concludes that officials at Indian Affairs were up to the 1960s "reluctant to support the establishment of collections outside of the schools," desiring to "maintain a certain level of control over the reading materials available to First Peoples, which effectively limited the degree to which the people could educate themselves and articulate Western practices on their own terms."[3]

In 1959, the same year that Canada's first NGO, the international book donation program of the Overseas Book Centre (discussed in chapter 3), was established in Toronto, the first public library on a reserve – at Moose Factory, Ontario – opened its doors. Inspired by texts that applied the postwar language of developmentalism to Indigenous Peoples in Canada, Angus McGill Mowat, director of Provincial Library Service in Ontario from 1948 to his retirement in 1960, pursued throughout the late 1950s and early '60s not only the Moose Factory project but a greater vision of public library service for Indigenous communities throughout the province. His work and the ideologies informing it offer an important mid-twentieth-century example of how developmentalist thinking turned inward to domestic contexts in this period.

As we saw in chapter 2, the emergence of a postwar development paradigm and its high modernist ideology influenced not only Canada's externally oriented aid initiatives but also policy related to Indigenous Peoples. David Meren urges historians of international development in Canada to draw on scholarship that interrogates "the divide between the 'domestic' and the 'foreign' spheres of this transnational phenomenon."

His own work on the intersections of the Colombo Plan and high modernist development in the western Arctic, and on figures such as Cyril Belshaw, who authored studies that applied developmentalist thinking to Indigenous Peoples and later worked as director of the UN Regional Training Centre in Vancouver (a centre for international technical assistance training that operated between 1959 and 1962), demonstrates the mutual implication of developmentalism and Indian Affairs' policy in the decades that followed the Second World War. Dominique Marshall and Julia Sterparn have tracked a similar set of entanglements between the work of one of Canada's earliest NGOs, Oxfam Canada, and Indigenous communities in Canada, beginning with Oxfam's 1962 attempt to mitigate starvation among families of the Nisichawayasihk Cree Nation of northern Manitoba.[4]

Angus Mowat, a veteran of the First and Second World Wars, was by the 1950s keenly attuned to the problem of federal policy and social attitudes that assumed the racial and cultural inferiority of Indigenous Peoples. By the late 1950s, the federal government was slowly acknowledging the problems that ensued from such attitudes. According to Hugh Shewell, in the decade and a half after 1948, the Indian Affairs Branch "concentrated on improving its methods of welfare provision," as well as on coaxing the provinces to extend their welfare services to Indigenous communities. In 1959, Prime Minister John Diefenbaker struck a Joint Committee of Senate and the House of Commons – the second in a little more than a decade – to investigate and advise on the administration of what was then known as Indian Affairs. In Sally Weaver's estimation, the committee's 1961 report was "largely incremental, recommending various measures to accelerate the process of Indian integration" – the term favoured after the late 1950s for what Indian Affairs had previously called "assimilation." A more robust examination of Indian Affairs did not occur until the later 1960s, when public sentiment, fuelled by the Civil Rights and urban antipoverty movements of that decade, encouraged what Weaver calls a "general awakening" to what was then framed as the "Indian problem." Mowat was part of an earlier settler apprehension of the fact that the treatment of Indigenous Peoples in Canada sat uncomfortably close to the racist logics that had informed Nazi ideology, and of the fact that their status within Canada was not easily reconciled with the UN's postwar commitments to decolonization and human rights. In a 1959 letter to the editors of major Toronto papers, for instance, Mowat decried a March

1959 RCMP raid on proponents of traditional government at Six Nations, asking readers if they "remember Nazi Germany," or "pictures of the Gestapo in action?" While his letter does not endorse the protestors' challenge to the Six Nations Band Council – "that is the Indians' business and only an Indian has the right to speak of that" – it condemns unequivocally the use of "violence" and "downright savagery" in the arrest of four Kanien'kehá:ka men: "Great God! Have the Indians not suffered enough at our pious, thieving hands these past two hundred years? Are our consciences not yet black enough? Shall we sit by and see yet another outrage inflicted upon these unarmed, honourable people by our servants (servants?) the RCMP?"[5]

As a champion of public library service in the first part of the twentieth century, Mowat was also an unselfconscious and ardent proponent of literacy and of literary cultures, both implicitly premised on the denigration of nontextual ways of knowing, such as orature and testimonial. Though Mowat was not especially attuned to the explosion of interest in literacy questions in the new international institutions of the 1940s and '50s, his thinking was very much aligned with what Joseph Slaughter calls the "international problematization of illiteracy" that emerged in the international development sphere, and particularly within UNESCO, in the decade or so after the Second World War. As Slaughter's phrasing suggests, this "international institutional transformation of anthropological orality into sociological illiteracy" drew on a broader hierarchized distinction in classical anthropology between "traditional" oral cultures and "modern" literate ones to present literacy as a key to development and modernization. What Harvey Graff calls the "literacy myth" – an association of literacy with progress that informed the utilitarian thought of the nineteenth century (though the association is older than this, as James Paul Gee points out) – was thus recycled in the context of developmentalist ideology to identify the ostensibly bridgeable gulf between the reading and the nonreading worlds. Though Mowat was committed to the principle of Indigenous-run services for Indigenous Peoples and believed that "the responsibility for management" of publicly provided library collections belonged to Indigenous Peoples, his assumptions about the book as the primary tool of "self-enlightenment" (as he describes it in a 1959 letter to anthropologist J.J. Honigmann) shaped his underestimation of the complexity of existing communications systems in the Indigenous communities he visited.[6]

Mowat's career in the Ontario library system, which began with a post as chief librarian in Trenton, Ontario, in 1922, was marked by a commitment to the ideal of public library provision for all communities in the province. Though, as Mowat's colleague W.A. Roedde recalled in the late 1970s, Mowat was initially warned by the deputy minister of Indian Affairs to avoid indicating publicly that there was "anything wrong with education for native people," he saw that the provision of books in schools for Indigenous children was poor and sought to do something about it. As he wrote in 1958 to Ethel Brant Monture (Kanien'kehá:ka), a writer originally from the New Credit Reserve (now Mississaugas of the Credit First Nation) and great-great granddaughter of Joseph Brant, "books supplied by that damned department [Indian Affairs] look to me as if they had been bought at Woolworth's." His strategy involved tapping the resources of both the provincial and federal governments, neither of which was especially keen in the late 1950s to assume responsibility for providing library service to reserves. Beginning in the winter of 1958, Mowat began visiting reserves in the Thunder Bay region, hoping to find an Indigenous person who would be willing to serve as a board member for the newly formed Northwestern Regional Library Cooperative. The man he befriended and convinced to take on the position, Fred Greene (Anishinaabe), chief of the Shoal Lake Reserve (now Shoal Lake 40 First Nation), remained a correspondent for the rest of Mowat's life. That same winter, Mowat's visit to the Moose Factory Reserve (now Moose Cree First Nation) resulted in a plan to open a community library. With 2,500 books provided by the Government of Ontario and selected with care by Mowat; librarian training for a community member, Nellie Faries (Mōsonī), provided by Orillia librarian Grace Crooks; rent-free space in an Indian Affairs-owned community centre; and a sign that welcomed borrowers in both English and Cree, the Moose Factory library opened its doors in the fall of 1958. By the winter of 1959, Mowat had accomplished a similar arrangement on the Shoal Lake Reserve, with Fred Greene's sister, Ella Greene, serving as librarian (though Greene was not remunerated for her labours as Nellie Faries was). Using the books furnished by the Ontario Department of Education to rural areas (but not, before Mowat, to reserves) in the form of travelling libraries, Mowat attempted to set up more modest arrangements at other reserves, often encouraging communities to establish boards so that they could gain the status of Association Libraries for the purposes of an annual provincial grant. Upon retirement in 1960, Mowat wanted to continue his work on reserves and sought the support of the Ontario Department of Education and Indian Affairs. Though there was considerable debate about jurisdiction, a deal struck in 1961 saw Indian Affairs pay his annual travel expenses and the Ministry of Education agree to provide travelling libraries for reserves. This arrangement continued until the mid-1960s, when Mowat, by his own admission, "petered out."[7]

Mowat's opinions in this period about library service for Indigenous communities were clearly influenced by two aspects of his later life: with his wife, Helen, he adopted two Indigenous children in the 1950s (an Anishinaabe boy, John, and a Kanien'kehá:ka girl, Mary), and in this period he read avidly about Indigenous history and Indigenous relations with federal and provincial governments. As he began the work in 1958 of extending library service to reserves, he established friendships and correspondence with a handful of Indigenous people who had some interest in his work, and these letters discuss his reading and his attempts to locate materials that could give him more information about the history and contemporary circumstances of Indigenous Peoples in Canada. Four texts particularly influenced his thinking. In addition to *Traditional History and Characteristic Sketches of the Ojibway Nation* by George Copway (Kahgegagahbowh) (Anishinaabe), a book that was difficult to obtain in mid-twentieth-century Ontario, even for the director of public libraries, and anthropologist Diamond Jenness's *The Indians of Canada* (1932), Mowat was deeply impressed by his son Farley's *The People of the Deer* (1952) and Harry Hawthorn, C.S. Belshaw, and S.M. Jamieson's *The Indians of British Columbia* (1958). He studied these carefully and shared them with Indigenous friends, including Fred Greene; Ethel Brant Monture; and Nellie and Gilbert Faries (Mōsonī), the latter a former chief of the Moose Factory Reserve. *The People of the Deer* and *The Indians of British Columbia* are of particular interest here because both draw upon the postwar ideology of developmentalism.[8]

In a 1958 letter to Ethel Brant Monture, Mowat refers to the copy of *The People of the Deer* he has enclosed, admiringly noting that the book "was in some measure responsible for a thoroughgoing revolution in the Department of Northern Affairs." He also shared copies with Gilbert Faries and Sarah Cowley (Anishinaabe) of Whitefish Lake Reserve (now Atikameksheng Anishnawbek). Chapter 2 discusses *The People of the Deer*'s representation of the inland Inuit of the Keewatin region of the Northwest Territories (the Ahiarmiut, living in what is now the Kivalliq region of Nunavut), who were relocated (unsuccessfully) from Ennadai Lake to Nueltin Lake in 1950, as a people suffering from the neglect of a callous federal government. There, I note (Farley) Mowat's call for the federal government, as "guardians and protectors" of the "Eskimos," to encourage self-sufficiency through programs such as a caribou-raising scheme, which could help the Inuit effect the "final stage of the transition from primitivism to modernism," and the role of Mowat's book in encouraging increased government attention to and surveillance of the Inuit who had been relocated in 1955 back to Ennadai Lake. In that discussion, I am interested in the book's omission from the federal government's Special Book Presentation Programme, but here it is worth pausing on how Mowat's framing of the problems experienced in the late 1940s and '50s by the Ahiarmiut is not distinct from the high modernist ideologies of development that the federal government began to apply in the Arctic after the Second World War; rather, it is a call for the government to apply this thinking *correctly*. To implement high modernist planning – defined by James C. Scott as the postwar approach that sought to apply "rational engineering to all aspects of social life in order to improve the human condition" – would be to restore the Inuit of Ennadai Lake with a food source rather than a handout, and further, it would realize the assimilation of this population to liberal-capitalist modernity: "Freed of the incubus of malnutrition and its hand-maiden, disease, our Eskimos are capable of quick and sane adjustment to the conditions of the white man's world, as the Aklavik people have abundantly demonstrated."[9]

The second title that fascinated Angus Mowat, *The Indians of British Columbia*, was important to the larger postwar effort to review Canada's policy regarding Indigenous Peoples. The book, commissioned by the Department of Citizenship and Immigration (which housed the Indian Affairs branch during the 1950s), was coauthored by a team from the University of British Columbia that included Cyril Belshaw, Harry Hawthorn, and Stuart M. Jamieson. The latter was an economist, and the former two were anthropologists. As Meren points out, Belshaw, a settler New Zealander, had experience in the Colonial Service in the British Solomon Islands Protectorate, which informed his later research on postwar administration and reconstruction in South Pacific Islands territories. A one-time member of the Fabian Colonial Bureau, he was a proponent of developmentalism as a progressive element of late colonial administration. Belshaw turned his colonial development experience to Indigenous Peoples in Canada after his hiring at the University of British Columbia in 1953, first through his coauthored book and later, as author of a report for the National Film Board on the use of film as an instrument of "social development" among Indigenous Peoples. Hawthorn, also a settler New Zealander, had studied the Maori for his doctoral fieldwork. He went on in the 1960s to lead an extensive survey of Indigenous Peoples in Canada, again commissioned by the federal government, known as the Hawthorn Report.[10]

The Indians of British Columbia "takes as axiomatic that the acculturative change of the Indian is irreversible and is going to continue," while also insisting that "further deliberate pressure or planning directed towards the changing of custom, attitude or belief" should "be a matter for the Indian's own decision." Mowat echoed this sentiment almost exactly in his correspondence, insisting in a June 1958 letter to Fred Greene that "integration may be, and in many cases I have seen, is a good thing. But *only* where your People want it that way." Mowat believed that wanting could be encouraged if whites treated Indigenous Peoples as humans deserving of dignity and respect. *The Indians of British Columbia* assesses the "rapid industrial expansion, including new resource development projects and larger-scale, more mechanized operations" occurring in the province, noting that the Indigenous population was both expanding and concentrated in the declining primary industry sector of the economy. The authors offer administrative, economic, and social policy suggestions meant to ease the integration that they view as an inevitable result of this capitalist expansion. For instance, they suggest that education for children should aim to soften the "discontinuities" produced by a system that "can transmit elements of White culture only" by incorporating Indigenous lifeways, such as "Indian arts and crafts." By the early 1960s, Mowat was thinking about how library materials with cultural relevance to the communities could be incorporated into larger collections. Though the original Moose Factory collection for children was chosen by the children's librarian for the Ontario Department of Education and was not directed "particularly to the taste and requirements of the Indians," it was, Mowat felt, "a good cross section, though a small one, of the best children's literature in English." By 1962, he was observing in his reports to Indian Affairs that his first selections for children were inadequate: children on reserves "want material dealing with child life among their own people." Like the authors of *The Indians of British Columbia*, Mowat saw that settler cultural institutions such as the library would be more likely to serve the purpose of integration if they could incorporate some elements of Indigenous culture.[11]

Mowat's initiative dwindled by the early 1960s, but by that time much in Ontario had changed since he began his first efforts in Moose Factory. According to Shewell, much to the delight of Indian Affairs, which had been attempting since the end of the Second World War to persuade provincial governments to extend their welfare services to Indigenous Peoples, the Government of Ontario amended its General Welfare Assistance Act in 1959 to give bands quasi-municipal status. This enabled the province to administer social assistance on reserves. More possibilities for the provision of library services to reserves were thus created and, by the late 1960s, Ontario's Public Library Act recognized Band Councils as equivalent to municipal governments for the purpose of receiving library grants. As Mowat was withdrawing from his work with reserve libraries in the mid-1960s, he suggested to R.F. Davey (then–chief of the education division of the Indian Affairs branch in the Department of Citizenship and Immigration) that the travelling library service could be extended to more reserves in Ontario with an Indigenous person at the head of the program. Davey indicated interest in pursuing this and asked Mowat to find a suitable candidate. Unable to do so by the spring of 1965, Mowat left matters in the hands of Indian Affairs. Consequently, Indian Affairs created the position of library consultant in its education division in 1966, hiring Edith Adamson, a settler librarian who had trained at McGill University. Under a new program, Indian Affairs encouraged Band Councils to join in existing public library services under provincial and municipal governments with a dollar per capita grant and a cost-sharing agreement with provincial public library authorities (an arrangement facilitated in Ontario by the kinds of changes discussed above). According to Adamson, this plan was deemed "consistent with current Departmental policy which is to enable Indians of Canada to enter the mainstream of Canadian life and take their place alongside their non-Indian fellow citizens with equal rights and privileges." In other words, the plan was consistent with privileging of integration that informed Indian Affairs in the years leading up to the White Paper.[12]

Whatever the intentions of Indian Affairs, it is important to remember that some Indigenous communities organized library services in the later twentieth century for their own purposes and needs and did so with no more than meagre support from any level of government. In its coverage of the opening of the Six Nations Public Library in June 1969, the Six Nations newspaper *Tekawennake News* patiently reports the praise of R.F. Davey, director of education for Indian Affairs: Davey lauded both the fine work of the district superintendent of Indian schools, J.C. Hill, who had gone "far beyond the call of duty" in the name of reserve education, as well as the Band Council's wise use of band funds for educational purposes, such as the appointment of a school inspector, T.W. Standing, in 1907, and the establishment of "one of the first night schools in the Dominion in 1910." Davey laments that he has visited many reserves to help solve educational problems but notes that visits to Six Nations were always for the purpose of participating in "a progressive event." In a style typical of *Tekawennake News*, the reporter speaks back to Davey: "We're flattered but there's no reflection on other Reserves who are progressive according to opportunity." Moreover, the reporter corrects the record: the library is not primarily the result of efforts from Indian Affairs but of the women of the reserve, including Bernice Loft Winslow, a former teacher at Six Nations, who originated the idea for the library "over thirty years ago," and the local Women's Institute, which doggedly raised funds in the community over a period of two years. Davey, like his employee, the library consultant Edith Adamson, was eager to credit Indian Affairs for its support of the Six Nations Library; Richard Pilant of the Institute for Iroquoian Studies was eager to credit Mowat, who began taking travelling library boxes to the reserve in 1958 and encouraged in the early 1960s the establishment of a local library committee. Yet, according to the testimony of Six Nations' community members in the pages of *Tekawennake News*, *The Globe and Mail*, and the *New Credit Reporter*, the library was very much a Six Nations effort, involving euchre parties, bake sales, and community meals. The library's space, a brick home that had once belonged to a doctor on the reserve, was donated by the Band Council.[13]

Development's "Discovery" of Indigenous Peoples

Leader of the Indian Association of Alberta Harold Cardinal's 1969 critical response to the "new Indian policy" proposed by the federal government in June of 1969 – better known as the White Paper – begins by observing settler Canadian fervour for developmental issues: "We have watched the justifiably indignant reaction of fellow Canadians to the horrors of starvation in Biafra ... The Unitarian Service committee reminds us of the starving conditions of hundreds of thousands of Asians. Canadian urbanites have walked blisters on their feet and fat off their rumps to raise money for underdeveloped countries outside of Canada." Cardinal then acidly observes that Indigenous Peoples "do not question the concern of Canadians about such problems," but they do "question how sincere or how deep such concern may be when Canadians ignore the plight of the Indian or Métis or Eskimo in their own country." With development's second wave in the late 1960s – a turn shaped by decolonial activism in the global South and the emergence of dependency theory, among other forces – and with the establishment of political organizations on the national stage, such as the National Indian Brotherhood (NIB) in 1970, the question of the relevance of developmentalism to Indigenous Peoples in Canada came to assume greater visibility. In encouraging non-Indigenous Peoples to understand Indigenous experiences through the lens of developmentalism, activists like Cardinal were calling attention to difficulties faced in their communities, but they were also inviting the application of developmentalist logics to their communities. By 1970, many Canadian NGOs were either involved in some form of development work with Indigenous communities in Canada, or, like CUSO, they were learning to develop rationales for limiting their efforts to overseas contexts.[14]

As we have seen, Mowat conducted his efforts to implement libraries on reserves in relative isolation from the instrumentalization of literacy within international development that was occurring in the postwar decades. Nonetheless, with the unfolding of literacy as a key paradigm within UNESCO, attempts to apply developmentalist thinking about literacy to Indigenous Peoples living in Canada emerged. J.R. Kidd, whose domestic and international work in adult literacy and book development we encountered in chapter 3, makes room in his 1968 UNESCO-commissioned *Functional Literacy and International Development* for the question of literacy rates among Indigenous Peoples in Canada. *Functional Literacy* cites Edith Adamson's report on the National Seminar on Adult Basic Education, which took place in Toronto in the mid-1960s and which observes that the percentage of the population aged fifteen and older with no schooling or with no schooling beyond grade 4 was much higher among Indigenous Peoples (43.7 per cent versus 9.3 per cent in the total population). According to Adamson, the same figure for the Inuit was 90 per cent. While such statistics did not significantly alter the work of Canadian book development NGOs like the OBC/CLO, this organization did include by the late 1960s reference to Indigenous communities in Canada in the description of its work, noting in 1969–70 that its policy was to "send to developing countries ... those countries which have an annual per capita gross national product of $750.00 or less" but that this did not "exclude developing areas of Canada," such as the Northwest Territories, where books had been sent to "embryo libraries." According to Marshall and Sterparn, Oxfam Canada's 1971 grant to the Indian-Eskimo Association of Canada – which marked that NGO's turn to domestic development issues under the leadership of Jack Shea – enabled the Yukon Native Brotherhood to establish a radio and television programming initiative, an information dissemination program that speaks to the changing media environment of the later twentieth century. With the grant, the Brotherhood hired Métis journalist Wally Firth to fly a Cessna 185 aircraft – known as the "talking bird" – as a means of fostering information exchange across Indigenous communities in the North and between northern and southern Canada.[15]

The orientation of Canada's longest-running adult literacy program, Frontier College, toward Indigenous Peoples began in earnest at the end of the 1960s, when the organization experimented with two initiatives. The first of these mimicked the work of NGOs like the OBC/CLO: by 1969, Frontier College was shipping 155 boxes of magazines per month to schools run by the Department of Indian Affairs and Northern Development (the department covered the cost of shipping). In a 1969 letter to Indian Affairs Minister Jean Chrétien, Frontier College principal Eric Robinson framed the program in terms palatable to the integration-forward policy of the department, noting that it "assist[s] Reserve Indians to important information about the Canadian way of life." However, by 1970, unable to secure what Program Coordinator

Ian Morrison called "secure adequate financial return to cover even our direct postal and shipping costs," Frontier College had wound down the magazine donation program.[16]

The second initiative emerged from Frontier College's experimentation in the late 1960s with what it called "community education," programs through which it sent out "skilled community educators" to "respond to local educational and cultural needs" with the "overall aim" of assisting "individuals and groups toward greater influence over their situation." As Morrison explained in a 1971 letter to regional directors for Indian Affairs, Frontier College was actively seeking to offer its programs, both its traditional labourer-teacher program and its newer community education program, to Indigenous communities. Frontier College hoped to offer the latter program through contracts with the Department of Indian Affairs and Northern Development, an arrangement it had by then already tested in multiple Indigenous communities: Eabametoong First Nation in Ontario (referred to as Fort Hope); Lennox Island First Nation on Prince Edward Island; and five communities in the Northwest Territories (two projects at Frobisher Bay [now Iqualuit], and one each at Smith's Landing First Nation and Deninu Kųę́ First Nation). The phrase "community educator" recalls the nonhierarchical and community-led language of the community development movement that constituted an important element of development's second wave (I discuss this movement at more length in the section that follows). In the iterations of the community education program that emerged in largely settler communities, Frontier College educators attempted to combine what educator Drew Lamont called "formal or informal adult education and community development." However, the version of the program that was created in concert with the Department of Indian Affairs and Northern Development did not support community-led change but rather provided classes for adults in subjects like English and mathematics, with some additional offerings in areas like history and the sciences for more advanced students. The contracts for these programs, offered in conjunction with vocational counselors for Indian Affairs or with support from Canada Manpower, indicate that their main purpose was to present programs of upgrading with a view to bettering employment opportunities.[17]

Unsurprisingly, there was some personnel traffic during the late 1960s and '70s between Indian Affairs and Frontier College and between Frontier College and externally oriented NGOs like CUSO. Bob Homes, a Frontier College veteran, was hired by the Department of Indian Affairs and Northern Development in 1970 to be acting superintendent of Adult Education for Arctic Quebec. As Ruth Compton Brouwer points out, Jack Pearpoint extended his initial experiences with developmentalism in Africa to tackle Frontier College's literacy efforts in Indigenous communities. Pearpoint worked as a CUSO volunteer in the early 1970s on an educational rehabilitation project in postwar Biafra. Subsequently, he was appointed head of CUSO's new Projects Division. In 1975, Pearpoint assumed the role of president of Frontier College, where he attempted to help the organization through its period of transition from literacy instruction in remote work camps to other kinds of settings, including Indigenous communities in Alberta, Saskatchewan, and the Northwest Territories. Under Pearpoint's leadership, Frontier College moved beyond working through Indian Affairs, assuming partnerships with Indigenous-led organizations such as the Inuit Tapirisat of Canada (now Inuit Tapiriit Kanatami), for whom it created, in anticipation of a settlement with the federal government in the wake of its land claims negotiations, an Inuit Management Training Project. This project, run under the direction of the Inuit Tapirisat of Canada, was rooted in significant local consultation with Inuit with the goal of creating a training series "based on Inuit experience."[18]

The Fourth World Challenge to Developmentalism

As developmentalist thinking was "discovering" Indigenous People in the late 1960s and '70s, Indigenous leaders and activists brought their own views to bear on developmentalist ideology and its relevance to Indigenous communities. If, as we saw in the preceding chapter, Third World anti-imperialism broadly influenced the anglophone New Left in Canada, its reverberations within the Red Power movement of the late 1960s and early '70s have been less frequently acknowledged. Like settlers who were rethinking the postwar development paradigm after 1965 or so, Indigenous activists tended to interrogate developmentalist precepts by engaging with the struggles of Third World decolonization movements, adapting the ideas of Third World thinkers to the context of what they perceived (though many of their settler counterparts in this period did not) as a settler-colonial state.[19]

Glen Sean Coulthard (Yellowknives Dene) has documented the fact that Red Power activists in Vancouver "drew profound inspiration from the decolonisation struggles of the Third World and, like many radicalised communities of colour during this period, molded and adapted the insights they gleaned from these struggles abroad into their own critiques of capitalism, patriarchy, and internal colonialism at home." Coulthard contends that the adaptation of the thinking of Mao Zedong was especially important for Indigenous activists in Vancouver-based Red Power organizations such as the Native Alliance for Red Power (NARP) and the Native Study Group, particularly his shifting of the geographical location of "classic accounts of revolutionary struggle from the cities to the countryside, or in this case, *the land*." Stó:lō and Métis writer Lee Maracle's 1975 memoir recounts how her own emergence as an "Indian rebel" and early member of NARP was shaped by her struggle to relate the anti-imperialist and Marxist texts – Frantz Fanon's *Black Skin, White Masks* and *The Wretched of the Earth*; *Malcolm X Speaks*; Leon Trotsky's *Permanent Revolution*; and the writings of Mao Zedong – that she encountered in both Toronto and Vancouver in the late 1960s to her own situation as an Indigenous woman in North America. Critical of the "racism and national chauvinism" that provided the white leftists she knew in Vancouver through the Progressive Workers' Movement (which printed the NARP newsletter and shared space in an office on Hastings Street) with a "distorted view of Marx," Maracle participated in the Native People's Friendship Delegation to the People's Republic of China in June 1975, prior to which she engaged (as part of NARP's Native Study Group) in careful study of the work of Mao Zedong.[20]

As the work of Coulthard and Jonathan Crossen has shown, the internationalism of Indigenous activists and organizers in the late 1960s and '70s also reveals the deep influence of pan-African liberation movements. In *Red Skin, White Masks*, Coulthard focuses on the political organization of the Dene in the mid-1970s as the Indian Brotherhood of the Northwest Territories (renamed the Dene Nation in 1978) and the role that postindependence African socialism played in their formulation of the 1975 Dene Declaration, a response to the proposed Mackenzie Valley Pipeline project and the federal Royal Commission struck in 1974 to examine the potential impact of a natural gas pipeline in the Mackenzie Valley (from Alaska through the Yukon, the Northwest Territories, and Alberta). The draft manifesto included an appendix entitled "declaration on development," which proposes an economic model for the Dene that took its inspiration, Coulthard argues, from socialist development as it was unfolding in Julius Nyerere's Tanzania in the wake of that nation's 1967 Arusha Declaration (which promoted self-reliance over foreign aid). Crossen's work on internationalists such as Marie Smallface (Kanai) and George Manuel (Secwépemc) reveals a similar set of influences.[21]

The importance of African decolonization movements to Indigenous critiques of development is especially evident in the life and work of Smallface. After studying sociology and anthropology at the University of Alberta in the mid-1960s, where she encountered African students who, according to Crossen, introduced her to the "politics of imperialism and decolonization," and active participation in political organizations, including the National Indian Council, Smallface became one of the first Indigenous Peoples to volunteer for CUSO. As an overseas CUSO volunteer from 1966 to 1970, Smallface served in northern Zambia at a girls' camp and, subsequently, as a senior officer in Lusaka with the government's adult literacy program. Both of these roles gave her an opportunity to explore community development that was markedly different from the work that many CUSO volunteers in Zambia were undertaking in this period – described in a 1968 CUSO program review as government work in Lusaka among white expatriates who had little sympathy with the aims of decolonization. In a 1980 interview for *Kanai News*, Smallface recalled that her experience at the girls' camp exposed her to "people finding pride in" their "tribal cultures through dances, songs, and languages" and that the latter position, which involved radio programming for adults, was based in "concepts of self-reliance and self-help for communities." As a *CUSO/SUCO Bulletin* from 1968 indicates, Smallface had some reading ability in two of the major Zambian languages and hoped to expand the radio programming "to include radio lessons" in these languages during 1969 (figure 5.1). As we saw in the previous chapter, Zambia gained its independence from Britain in 1964. The UNIP, led by Kenneth Kaunda, was deeply influenced by the African socialism of neighbouring Tanzania and was supportive of African liberation movements in the region, as well as the international decolonial non-aligned movement. As Crossen notes, Smallface found easy sympathy with the politics of African socialism. She travelled to Tanzania during her CUSO sojourn and "became particularly intrigued

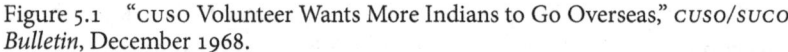

CUSO VOLUNTEER WANTS MORE INDIANS TO GO OVERSEAS

Marie Smallface, 24-year-old Blackfoot Indian now in her third year with CUSO in Zambia, said on a recent visit to Canada that she is interested in seeing more Indian people going overseas. "It's an invaluable, intense education." An education she feels will be of great help to her upon returning to Canada and hopefully, a job with the Indian Affairs Department.

Born on a reservation at Cardston, Alberta, Marie is one of seven children and a member of the Blood Tribe, Blackfoot Nation. When she decided to join CUSO while attending the University of Alberta in Edmonton, Marie said that many Indians criticized her but "I didn't want to become stunted in my ideas as a 'professional' Indian. At university I was cast as an Indian spokesman. In Zambia my being an Indian is irrelevant."

Employed in the Zambian capital of Lusaka as a senior officer with the government's adult literacy programme, Marie produces programmes for radio communication in community development. "In January, I hope to expand the project to include radio lessons in one or two of the major Zambian languages with others to be added on a quarterly basis." Marie, a bilingual Canadian whose two main languages are Blackfoot and English, understands two of the Zambian languages well enough to read but uses Lusaka translators for the broadcasts.

Interested in African political and social development even before going overseas, Marie now says, "as a result of my work in Zambia, I have become particularly interested in the use of mass communications in education. When I return home I intend to use my African experience to help bring Canada out of its racial dark ages."

Figure 5.1   "CUSO Volunteer Wants More Indians to Go Overseas," *CUSO/SUCO Bulletin*, December 1968.

by Nyerere's ideas." In a 2011 interview with Crossen, she recalled that Nyerere's vision of pan-Africanism gave her hope that Indigenous cultures could be a source of strength from which groups could build "from the communities upwards."[22]

In the late 1960s, the pages of the *CUSO/SUCO Bulletin* featured voices from a range of the more than sixty CUSO volunteers who were in or had recently been in Zambia. Veteran David Beer, who spent three years in Zambia as a youth service worker, reflects in a 1967–68 *Bulletin* on the racism that plagued the nations of southern Africa, particularly in contexts such as Rhodesia (to the south of Zambia, now Zimbabwe), where a settler minority had taken the reigns of political rule in the period of independence after 1965. "CUSO has a very special role to play in bridging the gap of understanding" in these countries, Beer notes:

> I do not think that Canadians are any more enlightened nor holier-than-thou but the fact that we can have young people in such a country as Zambia on the forefront of the battle of freedom in Southern Africa is a contribution in itself. Because of the fact that we are naïve and have not been tainted by the brush

of colonialism and imperialism means that we have a chance to contribute. Because of our membership in the Commonwealth and our own history of development from a colony to an independent state among nations we have a chance to contribute. Because CUSO has drawn many young Canadians who are motivated by ideas of service and the betterment of mankind in general (I do not want to sound too idealistic because in Central Africa this kind of motivation is all too rare) we have a chance.

Beer's deployment of an ideology of settler exceptionalism as a structuring element of the involvement of Canadians in developmentalism is one we have encountered already. Smallface did not accept this ideology. As she reports in the 1968 CUSO/SUCO Bulletin, she found it "liberating" not to be "an Indian spokesman" in her CUSO role, but notes that "when I return home, I intend to use my African experience to help bring Canada out of its racial dark ages." In the *Kanai News* interview from 1980, Marule recalled that her experience in Africa helped her to a "new understanding of what racism is" and "clarified my own identity as an aboriginal person." "By observing the African colonial experience," Marule claimed that she "understood the Indian experience in Canada as colonial" and "saw the structures of Imperialism, neo-colonialism and the limitations of 'paper' independence."[23]

In Zambia, Smallface married Jacob Marule, an exiled black South African who was actively organizing for the African National Congress. When Smallface-Marule returned to Canada in 1970, she became secretary and subsequently executive director of the NIB, where she influenced the thinking of that organization's elected leader George Manuel, who writes in his book *The Fourth World: An Indian Reality* (1974) that she was "the first person to be able to show me, from direct and personal experience, the close relationship and common bonds between our own condition as Indian people, and the struggles of other Aboriginal people and the nations of the Third World." Crossen's account of this relationship demonstrates the instrumental role that Smallface-Marule played in facilitating Manuel's contact with Tanzanian and other African politicians, students, and diplomats. Smallface-Marule eventually helped found the World Council of Indigenous Peoples and was involved in many other political and educational activities related to Indigenous Peoples until her death in 2014. Particularly notable in relation to her

CUSO experience is the fact that she dedicated much of her later career to the building of educational institutions exclusively with and for Indigenous Peoples – first in the new Native American Studies Department at the University of Lethbridge and later at Red Crow Community College on the Kanai reserve (now Mi'kai'stow Community College).[24]

Manuel's engagement with Smallface-Marule's thinking about the relevance of African decolonial thought, and especially of Tanzanian socialism, to the Indigenous Peoples of North America is evident in *The Fourth World*. Of Manuel's *The Fourth World*, Coulthard notes that it is "productive to read the book as a crucial Indigenous intervention into the ideological influence that the decolonization struggles of the 'Third World' had on the North American left's critique of racial capitalism and imperialism in the 1960s and early 1970s," but he also insists that activists and thinkers such as Manuel "fundamentally adapted and transformed" the "inherited conceptual apparatus" of global decolonization movements "through a critical engagement with their own local, land-informed situations." I would add that Manuel's particular critique and adaptation of developmentalism deserves more attention.[25]

Manuel's "fourth world" concept emerged not only from his interaction with Smallface-Marule, but also from his firsthand contact, in the early 1970s, with both Indigenous groups and Third World decolonization movements, opportunities that helped him to see not only the common struggles of these peoples but also the unique challenges faced by Indigenous Peoples of the globe. As leader of the NIB, he travelled to Australia and Aotearoa/New Zealand in 1971; in the same year, he led a Canadian delegation to Tanzania on the occasion of that nation's celebration of the tenth anniversary of its independence; in 1972, he participated in the UN Conference on the Human Environment in Sweden, where he made contact with Tanzanian and Chinese diplomats, as well as the International Working Group for Indigenous Affairs, who helped him make contact with the Sámi community at Rensjön; in 1974 and 1975, he helped to organize meetings in Georgetown, Guyana and Port Alberni, British Columbia that led to formation in 1975 of the World Council of Indigenous Peoples. From a Tanzanian diplomat he met through the Marules in 1971, he took the phrase "fourth world" to refer to the Indigenous Peoples of the world who were formally excluded from recognition as colonized peoples by the postwar international institutions, particularly the UN. As Manuel stated in his 1974 testimony to the Mackenzie Valley Pipeline Inquiry, "While we identify in many respects with the third world community, we are not of their world. We are of the fourth world, a forgotten world, the world of aboriginal peoples locked into independent states but without an adequate voice or say in the decisions which affect our lives."[26]

Like Maracle and Smallface-Marule, Manuel sought to adapt the emerging Third World critique of the development paradigm, which he encountered in texts such as Julius Nyerere's *Uhuru Na Ujamaa* (Freedom and Socialism), to what he understood to be the unique needs of Indigenous Peoples in North America. Central to Manuel's discomfort with developmentalism is the ideology's tendency to skirt the central demand of bodies such as the NIB – that the "custodian-child" relationship must be terminated and that Indigenous Peoples must "take our place at the table with all the rest of the adults" as equal partners in Confederation. As neither "an ethnic group" nor a "province of Canada," Indigenous Peoples in Canada require, Manuel insists, the "*conditions for the different groups to become equal partners*," and the "right to design our own model" for "home rule." In both *The Fourth World* and in his Mackenzie Valley Pipeline testimony, Manuel points to the guaranteed participation of the Maori in the Parliament of New Zealand as elected cabinet ministers as a model for what might occur in Canada, arguing that the "degree of Maori development – culturally, economically and politically – can be measured exactly by the amount of participation they enjoy in the political institutions of New Zealand." There can be no "development," Manuel posits, without this participation. Manuel's adaptation of African socialist principles to his settler-colonial context is crucial here: in place of the economic self-sufficiency of the socialist state that was so important to documents like the 1967 Arusha Declaration, Manuel privileged political representation and self-governance within the settler state. At the same time, Manuel's thinking shares a crucial feature with Nyerere's insofar as it links economic development – and thus "home rule" – to the land.[27]

As Manuel observed at an economic development conference in 1972, the usurpation of the basis of traditional Indigenous economies – land – was an obstacle to contemporary economic development. African nations were in the early 1970s attempting to "recover their land base" to "discover how it can be used to lift up the common standard of the community"; Indigenous communities in Canada would need to do the same. In *The Fourth World*, Manuel spells out clearly the fact that he understood this land-dependent economic development to be at the core of any possible political sovereignty: "Self-government, even on its grandest level, without an economic base simply creates the economic colonialism we are witnessing throughout much of Asia and Africa today." Just as, according to Coulthard, contemporary Indigenous groups such as NARP and the Native Study Group were drawn to Maoist adaptations of orthodox Marxism, so Manuel found in the thinking of Nyerere, and in African socialism more generally, a means of shifting the logic of orthodox Marxism away from long-term industrialization and an urban proletariat to rural contexts and a peasant revolutionary vanguard. Nyerere's philosophy of *ujamaa* was, according to Manuel's account in *The Fourth World*, "the closest example to my understanding of the way that Indian people want to develop." *Ujamaa* relied on a strategy of villagization that, as Priya Lal points out, has a complex genealogy. Rooted in the "tribal socialism" of postwar pan-Africanism and shaped by colonial policy that had fixated on the village as a "liminal stage" in the transition to modernity, villagization also drew on the Chinese socialist model, which became increasingly important to Tanzanian political discourse during the 1960s. Linked as it was to the concept of land as a source of liberation, *ujamaa* held potent appeal for Manuel.[28]

The Fourth World's challenge to developmentalist ideologies is also rooted in Manuel's firsthand experience of development's second wave as a community development worker in the late 1960s. In 1964, he took a job as a community development worker with the Department of Indian Affairs. The concept of community development became central to developmentalist ideology during the 1950s: the UN's study *Social Progress Through Community Development* (1955) sought to address the problem of rural communities' poor response to modernization efforts with a call to "create conditions of economic and social progress for the whole community with its active participation and the fullest possible reliance on the community's initiative." While "local leadership" was a keystone of community development, financial and technical assistance (assistance in the form of experts and expertise) from government was equally so. The phrase was taken up in Canada by the authors of the 1958 study *The Indians of British Columbia*, who call for a continued role for the Indian Affairs branch while cautioning that administration must be transformed: "It is better, we would say, at this stage of Indian development, to leave people with substandard housing, or without roads or bridges or irrigation systems, if the only way of getting them is for the superintendent or his agent to move into the community and lay down the law." While they concede that "this kind of direct administration, by far the most common in the Province, has certain immediate results in dealing with specific limited problems of a material kind," it "does nothing whatsoever to develop initiative and responsibility." As Rob Cunningham's study of the emergence of the Community Development program at Indian Affairs indicates, the concept served a convenient end for those at Indian Affairs who were committed in this period to reducing what Weaver calls the "dependency aspect" of the "patron-client relationship." One of many programs developed by the Indian Affairs Branch to deal with a growing public critique of its perceived paternalism (prior to the attempts to revise the Indian Act beginning in 1967), the Community Development program was the first state endeavour of its kind at the federal level in Canada (preceding the better-known Company of Young Canadians experiment unveiled in 1966). In the cabinet document that announced the program in July 1964, the public was informed that the initiative aimed to "accelerate transfer to Indian communities of responsibility and authority for the management of their affairs, with concurrent limitations in government controls."[29]

As Manuel's account in *The Fourth World* of his hiring and training attests, the program signalled what Cunningham describes as a "radical departure" from Indian Affairs practices, even if the departure was short-lived. Community development was taken up in many second-wave contexts as a means of empowering grassroots collectives to call for radical change, but Indian Affairs could not tolerate much of this kind of activity. University-educated Community Development Officers were paired with Indigenous "junior colleagues"; both were given training in Quebec City by University of Toronto psychologist Farrell Toombs, whose unconventional methods aimed to encourage collective decision-making. Once his training was complete, Manuel was placed among the Hul'q'umi'num of Cowichan Reserve (the program deliberately placed Indigenous assistants in communities that were not their own). He soon realized that his training in Quebec had provided a "scientific basis" for a theory of human community that his grandfather had taught him as a child. With Tony Karch, the

Community Development Officer at Cowichan, Manuel participated in a successful community-led housing project and cultivated leadership skills and adult education efforts; however, he resigned when Indian Affairs issued a "directive, telling us of the need to be more versatile and responsive to direction from the [Indian] agent in the future." Manuel's evaluation of the program lays bare the "implicit threat to the traditional civil-servant-Indian relationship" it posed, as well as its limits, given the fact that Indian Affairs' Economic Development Fund loans were offered on terms much less favourable than those offered by CIDA to developing nations. Assessing the reasons for the program's transformation into something much more insipid after 1968, Weaver notes that branch officials did not initially apprehend that Indigenous self-sufficiency "would probably bring with it a vehement rejection of the branch and its representatives at the local level." Though Manuel left the program, he took what he learned to the Indian Association of Alberta, which hired him as a community development worker. The lesson he gleaned from his experience working with Indian Affairs – that "economic development without full local control is only another form of imperial conquest" – clearly shaped his later response to questions of development in contexts such as the Mackenzie Valley Pipeline Inquiry. His presentation to that inquiry emphasizes that some kinds of "development," those that do not assure Indigenous Peoples "economic, political, and cultural self-reliance," have no futurity. The James Bay Agreement, in his view, offered this short-sighted kind of development because it included clauses that surrendered title to the land, leading to "inevitable" destruction, recovery from which "becomes the burden of the Indian people."[30]

Manuel's critique of developmentalism in *The Fourth World* thus draws on both his exposure to and adaptation of Third Worldist critiques of the paradigm and his firsthand experience of the Indian Affairs community development experiment. His thinking about education offers a particularly important site for analyzing his interrogation of the development paradigm. It both draws on developmental expertise and challenges the basic assumptions of international organizations like UNESCO, which was so deeply imbricated in question of global education and literacy in this period. In *The Fourth World*, Manuel makes use of the global educational and literacy statistics that UNESCO had been generating since the end of the Second World War to point out the discrepancy between secondary school graduation rates for non-Indigenous Canadians (which compared favourably to most European nations in the mid-1970s) and Indigenous Peoples in Canada, which compared to rates in this period for Botswana or Guatemala and were "below the average for Africa and Latin America in general." As we saw in chapter 3, the US government- and World Bank-promoted concept of "functional literacy" shaped UNESCO's literacy work in the later 1960s. Its Experimental World Literacy Programme (1966–71), for instance, cast education as a means of shifting the rural, tradition-bound populations of the Third World into modernity and readying them to contribute to capitalist economies. Manuel's argument, by contrast, insists that control of land and economic development will be the basis from which any meaningful attempt to create local education will grow, not the other way around. The argument he makes in *The Fourth World* thus anticipates and is in concert with the critique of functional literacy that emerged at UNESCO after 1974 under the director-generalship of Amadou-Mahtar M'Bow, as formerly colonized and anticolonial nations formed a voting block, pushing regulatory measures to curtail imbalances in the emergent global communications order of the later twentieth century.[31]

First published in 1974, it is not surprising that *The Fourth World* pays particular attention to education, which became in the late 1960s what Helen Buckley calls a "leading item on the list of [Indigenous] demands nationwide." From the mid-1950s, Indian Affairs had begun to favour the integration of Indigenous children into existing provincial schools over the separate residential school system. Though this arrangement was greeted favourably by the provinces, which received new funds from Indian Affairs for the purposes of Indigenous education, it created new problems for Indigenous students, who dealt with long bus rides, curriculum and materials that had no relevance to their lives, and the challenges of racism in the classroom. In the late 1950s, Manuel had been involved in community consultations that led to a submission to the Diefenbaker government's Joint Committee of Senate and the House of Commons. The Aboriginal Native Rights Committee of the Interior Tribes of British Columbia's submission emphasized, among other issues, the importance of granting Indigenous parents a "voice in the education of their children, through a local school authority." Unsurprisingly, then, education, alongside economic development, was a key focus of the NIB under Manuel's leadership (from 1970 to 1976). Encouraged by both the Indian Association of Alberta's 1970 response to the White Paper, which called on the federal government to direct its educational funding for Indigenous students to local Band Councils, and a 1971 Indian Affairs Standing Committee that had called for a new partnership between Indigenous Peoples and the government to develop curriculum and to create new roles for Indigenous parents in the running of schools for Indigenous students, the NIB both recommended a moratorium on the transfer of Indigenous schools to the provinces and presented a policy paper to the Minister of Indian Affairs and Northern Development in 1972. This paper, *Indian Control of Indian Education*, was an important salvo, as Manuel acknowledges in *The Fourth World*: it was the "first time that the Indian people of Canada, through their own organization, had presented to the government a single document stating their position on a matter vital to our daily lives."[32]

Authored by the NIB's Education Committee, which comprised members of eight provincial and two territorial Indigenous organizations, the paper elaborates an "Indian philosophy of education" and tackles the question of responsibility. As Manuel indicates in *The Fourth World*, the paper took inspiration from Nyerere's philosophy of "education for self-reliance," articulating what Manuel understood to be that philosophy's privileging of a curriculum "designed in harmony with the local economy and the goals and aspirations of the people." While the document insists that the federal government should remain responsible for the funds needed for the provision of education, it also demands "local control of education," or local "Education Authorities" that would assume responsibility for budgeting, spending, decisions about school infrastructure, hiring and direction of staff, curriculum development and evaluation, and negotiation with provinces for special arrangements. Lamenting the fact that the present school system is "culturally alien to native students," the policy paper also identifies the importance of Indigenous teachers; the teaching of and in Indigenous languages; and programs that are continuous with the "attitudes and habits which are based on experiences in the family" (self-reliance, respect for personal freedom, generosity, respect for nature, and wisdom).[33]

The Fourth World elaborates the argument of *Indian Control of Indian Education* while also making it clear that Manuel understood change at the level of education would not be sufficient because education is fundamentally tied to the question of economic development: "Education at any level is only possible when the economic potential of the community is being developed. Otherwise, the learning of the individual is either wasted or drives him away from the community to which he should be contributing." And, as we have seen, Manuel understood this economic development as contingent on a land base. In the concluding chapter of *The Fourth World*, he cites education as the field in which authentic community development might be most likely to succeed in the present, but, rejecting the assimilationist ideology of the White Paper and the paternalism of the Community Development program, Manuel insists that the "fastest way to bring about change among an oppressed people is to put the decision-making authority, and the economic resources that go with it, into their own hands." In early 1973, the NIB's policy paper was accepted as the policy of Indian Affairs, though the question of Indigenous control of education and federal funding per Indigenous student on reserve have remained consistent policy concerns for the Assembly of First Nations (the organization that succeeded the NIB in the early 1980s) and Indigenous education activists and scholars up to the present.[34]

Anti-Developmentalism and "Grounded Normativity" in Jeannette Armstrong's *Slash*

An early and frequently referenced text in the emergence of Indigenous writing in English, Jeannette Armstrong's (Syilx Okanagan) novel *Slash* (1985) has nonetheless garnered little sustained critical analysis. Its publishing history alone warrants more attention. As part of her work for the En'owkin Centre, a cultural and educational initiative of the Syilx Okanagan Nation Alliance located on the land of the Snpink'tn Indian Band (Penticton Indian Band), Armstrong was involved from 1979 in the Okanagan Indian Curriculum Project. The project, funded by the Department of Indian Affairs and Northern Development and the provincial government of British Columbia, assumed the task of presenting Okanagan history and culture in an appropriate way. (In the context of the kinds of pressures on Indigenous education that were being exerted in the late 1960s, the federal government introduced a project in 1968 to develop curriculum for federal and band-controlled schools on reserves, which had previously followed provincial curricula. While the formal curriculum project of the Department of Indian Affairs and Northern Development ended in 1978, the Education Department of Indian Affairs remained involved because curriculum was a budget item in the funding formula for schools on reserve. Indian Affairs' support for the Okanagan Indian Curriculum Project was an instance of what Kenneth and Vinita Watson call its "indirect" efforts after 1979.) Among other new materials, the project commissioned a text that could be used in grade 11 classrooms as part of the study of the contemporary history of Indigenous Peoples in North America. Though, as Armstrong recounted in interviews in the early 1990s, non-Indigenous consultants on the project urged the involvement of non-Indigenous writers in the creation of new texts (because there were so few published Indigenous writers at the time), Armstrong and others fought for the principle of Indigenous control. Armstrong thus found herself responsible for the grade 11 text. Though she held a degree in creative writing from the University of Victoria, Armstrong had never written a novel. After researching for two years the history of late twentieth-century Indigenous activism and political organizing, better known as the Red Power movement, Armstrong began to write in 1982. The result, *Slash*, was published in 1985 by Theytus Books, another initiative of the Okanagan Curriculum Project, established in 1980 as the first publisher in Canada under Indigenous ownership and control.[35]

The production of the novel, and of the larger commitment to training Indigenous People for the cultural work undertaken at En'owkin, is evidence of what Armstrong, in conversation with Hartmut Lutz in 1991, affirmed as "development from the bottom up." Insofar as it depended on Syilx Okanagan creative vision and material production, the publishing history of Armstrong's novel enacts Manuel's vision of authentic community development, as well as the calls of *Indian Control of Indian Education* (a document the novel alludes to directly). The text of *Slash* parallels this enactment. The novel's representation of the Red Power movement shows clearly that the Indigenous activism of the later 1960s and '70s drew, as we have seen, important sustenance from Third World decolonization movements. For instance, like the fictionalized Lee Maracle in *Bobbi Lee: Indian Rebel* (1975), the novel's protagonist, Tommy ("Slash") Kelasket, observes the influence of the iconography and idiom of the Black Power movement – itself deeply influenced by the African liberation movements of the 1950s and '60s – on the activists he meets at the Red Power Centre in Vancouver. Yet the novel's revision of developmentalist thinking comes not so much from these Third World sources as it does from Syilx Okanagan thinking about education and the individual's enmeshment in social relations of community. The novel thematizes the kind of local, from-the-ground-up development that Armstrong was involved in via the Okanagan Indian Curriculum Project, drawing on Syilx philosophy to pose a radical challenge to the progress-oriented ideology of much developmental thinking.[36]

While there are no Indian Affairs community development workers in Armstrong's novel, its initial chapters are filled with settler characters who are implicated in development's "discovery" of Indigenous Peoples after 1965 or so. While *Slash* treats these characters quite gently, the solutions they have to offer are represented as having little use to Tommy Kelasket and his community, the Syilx Okanagan of the Snpink'tn Reserves. Tommy and, by extension, his community, must identify their own problems and formulate their own strategies for addressing them. The first two chapters of the novel focus on Tommy's life as an adolescent in his community at a time, the early to mid-1960s, when Indigenous Peoples were dealing with the introduction of integrated schooling and other integration-forward initiatives in the lead-up to the White Paper. The community is increasingly divided between traditionalists, who have less education in settler schools and favour traditional modes of governance and living, and assimilationists, who tend to be educated in settler schools, to prefer modern homes and lifestyles, and to favour "opening up our lands to development." Into this mix arrive development-minded individuals from outside – a new priest, who is generally liked because he "played ball, sang and played guitar, drank beer, told jokes and talked serious politics with the men," and Dave, "from some university," who "came to study our ways." The reform-minded priest is bent on doing things differently: he respects Tommy's choice to "pray Indian"; he initiates a Youth Club with "Current Affairs Discussions" that cover the Civil Rights Movement and nuclear testing; and he organizes a leadership meeting with "men and women from other reserves." Dave the anthropologist is less activist, but the magazines and books he brings into the community introduce Tommy and his adolescent friends to 1960s-era new age culture – marijuana, "self-hypnosis and the occult." The narrative links marijuana, especially, to the settler "hippie" culture that lures Tommy out of his community and toward an activist politics that the novel ultimately rejects.[37]

At the same time, the novel views the organization of groups like the American Indian Movement (AIM) with skepticism (Armstrong stated in a 1992 interview that she was frustrated with the tendency of AIM activists to centre the "male ego" in a way that she found unfaithful to Indigenous values), and the more moderate organizing of groups like the NIB and the Union of British Columbia Indian Chiefs with what can only be called ambivalence (Tommy's partner Maeg dies after choosing, against Tommy's wishes, to commit herself to the cause of the Constitution Express). Against this backdrop, the novel unequivocally privileges Tommy's choice to return to his reserve, to reject the heavy shame and dependency imposed by colonization, to "depend on my own resources and what I could gather around me to do things," and to become "a teacher," to "work with people the way they were, not condemn them." This is Armstrong's version of Manuel's authentic community development. Tommy calls this "decolonization," recognizing that "our solutions to some of those social problems are in progress already," even if the "D.I.A." and "D.I.A.-orientated leadership" disagree.[38]

The novel also poses a radical challenge to the progressivist logic of developmentalist thinking; it is fundamentally anti-developmentalist. Post-development theorist Gilbert Rist contends that such logic is sutured into developmentalism, an entirely ideological concept whose "distinctive practices" have little relation to the "unverifiable (and indubitable) feelings" it evokes. The postwar alternative to the colony-metropole hierarchy, development offers a "linear reading of world history" that emerged in the West in the eighteenth century and is rooted in a myth of the "progressive access of every nation to the benefits of 'development'" and thus to an ideal of equality among nations. However, this "truth," as Rist points out, "is actually based on the way in which Western society – to the exclusion of all others – has conceptualized its relationship to the past and the future." Moreover, Rist tells us, it is a "truth" dependent on a lie: the promise of "endless growth" inherent in the development narrative is not an "achievable objective." Thomas McCarthy's analysis of developmentalism emphasizes how the progressivist telos of the ideology speaks to the ideological continuity of imperialism and developmentalism. McCarthy observes that postcolonial theory has called for the displacement of such progressivist historicist ideology, "according to which non-Western modernities will merely replicate the Western model, albeit at more or less retarded rates of development."[39]

Armstrong's *Slash* might seem related to the coming-of-age novel, a western European genre that is identified in its classic nineteenth-century form as the bildungsroman. The bildungsroman plots the linear progression of its ostensibly universal (though usually white, male) citizen-subject from youth to maturity, from what liberal philosophy frames as the private realm of home and family to the public realm of the nation and the world. Crucial to the bildungsroman, Jed Esty argues, is the "symbolic function of nationhood, which gives finished form to modern societies in the same way that adulthood gives finished form to the modern subject." The closure of the nineteenth-century bildungsroman therefore depends on the arrival of both individual adulthood and collective nationhood. The form's progressivist logic thus closely tracks twentieth-century developmentalism, which draws in turn, as Rist's account makes clear, on the earlier imperialist ideology of social evolutionism and its central premise that all societies must pass through stages of development but "that all do not advance at the same speed as Western society." However, while the structure and plot of *Slash* allude to the generic conventions of the bildungsroman, they bend and deform them. As scholars such as Pheng Cheah, Esty, and Slaughter have pointed out, twentieth-century revisions of the bildungsroman form are linked, first, to the Age of Empire and its supplanting of the bildungsroman's developmental nation-time with the uneven temporalities and economies of the global, and second, to postcolonial writers' translations of the form to "narrate affirmative claims for inclusion in the franchise of the nation-state" (as Slaughter would have it), or to grapple with the lack of a "preexisting community for the individual to be reconciled to" in decolonizing contexts (as Cheah would have it). Such translation, however critical it may be of colonial logics of oppression, neocolonial failures to ensure global equality, or idealist closure, is not Armstrong's project.[40]

Instead, *Slash* invokes the bildungsroman form of progressive individual development – presenting us with a first-person narrator-protagonist between the ages of about twelve and thirty-one – but deforms it, bending it into a shape that casts coming of age as neither smooth, linear development (as the classic bildungsroman would have it), nor fragmented, nonteleological development (as the postcolonial bildungsroman might have it), nor the impossibility of development (as the anti-bildungsroman would have it), but rather as a confidently recursive process. *Slash* thus offers what Simon Hay calls a "genuine alternative" to the bildungsroman, one that might be compared to Ngũgĩ wa Thiong'o's *Caitaani mũtharaba-Inĩ* (1980, translated in 1982 as *Devil on the Cross*) insofar as it "rejects the conventional developmental narrative of the subject," describing instead the "coming of age of a collective protagonist." Referring in a 1991 interview to the negative criticism she received from non-Indigenous reviewers of *Slash*, who found Tommy's character development weak, Armstrong described the process of creating the novel: "In the writing process I couldn't isolate the character and keep the character in isolation from the development of events in the community, and the whole of the people." She had been trained in the creative writing program at the University of Victoria, which had taught her "what I should have been doing," but, as she told Lutz, "I know what I couldn't do and make the story for my people."[41]

Though Armstrong employs a protagonist who is also a first-person narrator, the novel works against his individuation at every turn. For instance, the prologue and epilogue, which frame the text, function as meta-devices that encourage the reader to understand Tommy as linked to Armstrong, the writer, who, along with him, begins "to write this story." This parallelism is furthered by the fact that Tommy's community is Armstrong's, even if she did not have the same experience of the Red Power movement that Tommy does. This doubling effect continues in the novel's chapters with characters such as Jimmy, who functions less as a foil (despite his differences from Tommy) than as a source of alternative thinking that Tommy must negotiate and incorporate into his own. When Tommy considers his own situation, he is always also analyzing that of his people, a tendency that is actuated in the novel's privileging of dialogue and scenes of listening. In the final chapter of the novel, as Tommy overcomes his addictions and learns to set aside the anger and shame that have been fuelling his participation in the events of the Red Power movement, he acknowledges that "being an Indian, I could never be a person only to myself. I was part of all the rest of the people. I was responsible to that. Everything I did affected that. What I was would affect everyone around me, both then and far into the future, through me and my descendants. They would carry whatever I left them. I was important as one person but more important as a part of everything else. That being so, I realized, I carried the weight of all my people as we each did." Moreover, the recursive structures of the narrative undermine the bildungsroman's teleology, consistently sending Tommy back to his community, where the novel concludes. While Ngũgĩ's collective protagonist is an "anticolonial class" forged in opposition to colonialism, Armstrong's collective protagonist is forged by forces broader than anticolonialism, including the "good feelings" that are attached across the narrative to the ceremony, song, story, language, and natural environment of the Syilx Okanagan.[42]

Slash deviates from, and offers an alternative to, the bildungsroman form in other crucial ways. Slaughter's study of the mutual implication of the bildungsroman and the postwar developmentalist framing of literacy as the cornerstone of the "free and full development of the human personality" demonstrates that the form depends on "stratification (or classification) of the world into non-readers and readers for its teleology of human personality development." The typical protagonist of the form moves from orality to writing, while the form more broadly replays "the grand civilizational transition to modernity as the personalizing process of literary socialization that must be repeated in the life narrative of every modern individual." This identification of literacy and development is so ubiquitous in western cultures that their conflation in the bildungsroman "rarely receives notice" in scholarship on the form. While *Slash* teasingly invokes the kind of "literacy apprenticeship" that is, according to Slaughter, so central to the form, it abandons it after the first chapter. Twelve-year-old Tommy "liked reading a lot" – "I could imagine all those places and things just like I was there" – but this same reading (in English) is associated with the space of the integrated school, which is a site of racist paternalism and physical confinement, and it "stank something awful, too." Tommy explicitly compares this space to the land "high up near Flint Mountain where the fir and pine smells mixed with the sage" and contrasts his school learning with the learning he does on the land with his Uncle Joe. This latter kind of education, featured in the novel's first chapter, belies the binary (savage/civilized, oral/literate) ideology on which the bildungsroman depends, acknowledging, as Cherokee scholar Christopher Teuton does, that oral literacies are complex and not "lesser" than alphabetic ones, and that they play a crucial role in nurturing "strong relationships with the other-than-human world," as well as one's understanding of the "negotiated moral universe." Tommy's education on the land and through story is rooted in principles that Armstrong, in a 1987 essay on the subject of traditional Indigenous education, identifies as key: generational transfer of traditional knowledge; pedagogical methods that are "natural to the lifestyle" and synced to the rhythms of the day and year; and a concept of learning as based on "experience of the environment" and the "sources of sustenance" it may provide if approached in sustainable ways.[43]

However, despite this apparent opposition of settler and Indigenous modes of learning and knowing, *Slash* fundamentally rejects the neat orality-literacy dichotomy that Slaughter identifies with the developmental structure of the bildungsroman. As Manina Jones points out, *Slash* refuses priority to either speech or writing. For instance, the "informal, spoken quality" of Tommy's English must be understood in relation to the prologue's staging of a scene of writing ("As I begin to write this story …"). Armstrong's interview with Lutz further clarifies her understanding of the novel's handling of the orality-literacy relation. In response to Lutz's query – did Armstrong "design the novel to stand" in the oral tradition? – Armstrong answered: while an "oral tradition *will* be there" because it "is remaining and it is intact," a "written piece like a novel can reach further than that." The modes coexist and intersect throughout the narrative; neither is figured as a developmental stage that must be passed through en route to adulthood. As Margery Fee argues, such a nonbinary approach to the relation of orality and literacy is one that can disrupt the colonial emplotment of orality as a stage prior to literacy, or of orality as "incompatible with literacy and a sense of history, advanced thought, science, and modernity." Germaine Warkentin further claims that the imperialist hierarchization of orality and literacy occludes the continuities between early oral and non-alphabetic literatures and contemporary Indigenous writings – continuities that Indigenous scholars such as Lee Maracle regularly point to in their theorizations of oratory.[44]

Armstrong's novel offers not so much a modified bildungsroman, but a collectivist *alternative* to this form and its progressivist, individualist, binary ideologies. Coulthard's "grounded normativity" helps to identify what exactly constitutes the basis of difference between the various iterations of the bildungsroman form and Armstrong's coming-of-age novel. The phrase is rooted in Coulthard's adaptation of Marx's theory of primitive accumulation as a process not of proletarianization but rather of dispossession, and his related claim that "the theory and practice of Indigenous anticolonialism, including Indigenous anticapitalism, is best understood as a struggle not only for land in the material sense, but also deeply informed by what the land as a system of reciprocal relations and obligations can teach us about living our lives in relation to one another and the natural world in nondominating and nonexploitative terms." In other words, "grounded normativity" is meant to capture the fact that the central site of struggle for Indigenous Peoples is not simply the land itself but also the ontological framework that has emerged from a particular relation to the land.[45]

A theory of the "land as a system of reciprocal relations and obligations" is central to Syilx Okanagan thought. As Armstrong's scholarly work demonstrates, the nsyilxcen words "Syilx" and "tmxwulaxw" (land) are related, such that the people themselves are understood in nsyilxcen to be one strand in the continuous coil of the larger "life force" of the land. The people are *not understood to coexist with the land* but are rather "one of the many strands which are continuously being bound with others to form one strong thread coiling year after year into the future as the life force of the land." There is no "people" without this coil, without this life force of the land. Syilx literature, Armstrong adds, is "an expression of a long-term immersed-in-nature relationship between a people and a land." Such an ontology has an obvious place in the alternative coming-of-age form that *Slash* unfolds. Because "grounded normativity" privileges "respectful, nondominating, and nonexploitative" relations, it also necessarily privileges the collective over the individual and characterization as a matter of relations rather than a set of attributes to be discarded or acquired. In *Slash*, Tommy's return to his community in the final chapter involves a marriage and the birth of a child, but these individual events in his life are merely elements of a larger collective future being forged on the land. They could be cast as individual triumphs; instead they are narrated as strands in a "strong thread": as Maeg, Tommy's partner, is about to give birth to their child, she speaks to Tommy in nsyilxcen, and he says "we flowed into all the things around us. We had no clear edges that set us apart as different from everything." The near-breaking of the coil is the subject of the book, but its rebinding into the future is the subject of its concluding chapter.[46]

Conclusion

The need for quality library services on reserves has not diminished since Mowat's day, and the response to this need from well-meaning donors is generally an outpouring of used books. A well-known story illustrates the point, but there are countless similar examples: in 2001, thirteen-year-old Skawenniio Barnes from Kahnawà:ke wrote to her Chief and Band Council asking for the establishment of a public library in her community. "We do not have any place to go to obtain books, both for leisure reading and for research," she wrote. Barnes then forwarded her letter to her local newspaper, *Eastern Door*, and it was soon picked up by Montreal newspapers, including *The Gazette* and *Le Devoir*. The story went international when an essay that she wrote about her desire for a community library was published in the American magazine *Cosmo Girl* (which also awarded her a ten-thousand-dollar scholarship). Donations from all over the world arrived, ultimately resulting in a collection of more than thirty thousand books, many more than could be used in the space that was eventually secured to serve as a community library. Media coverage of the story identifies some of the larger donations: *The Gazette* announced in September of 2002 that St George's, a private school in Westmount, Quebec, had donated "many boxes of books" and twenty years' worth of old *National Geographic* magazines, for instance.[47]

Book drives for Indigenous communities have continued in the early twenty-first century to function as responses to the social and economic inequalities that characterize Indigenous experience in Canada. Another well-known example is the Lieutenant-Governor's Book Program, established by then–Ontario Lieutenant-Governor James Bartelman (Chippewas of Mnjikaning First Nation) in 2004. The program had by 2018 collected more than two million books to create libraries and summer reading camps in Indigenous communities in the north of the province, northern Quebec, Nunavut, and the Northwest Territories. On many occasions, Bartelman described his conviction that reading could offer an escape from the kinds of injustices that produced disproportionate rates of depression and suicide among Indigenous youth. As Roy McGregor reported in *The Globe and Mail* in 2005, for instance, Bartelman claimed that his childhood reading at the Port Carling, Ontario public library allowed him to "escape from the discrimination and the world which was around me." While Bartelman's campaign does not deserve derision, it does present interesting problems that this chapter has tried to parse.[48]

The difficult-to-challenge assertion that literacy initiatives, including book drive campaigns, can only ever be good things deserves critical examination. In his 1972 excoriation of the development paradigm, Walter Rodney – a historian who, like Smallface-Marule and Manuel, had meaningful contact with Tanzanian socialism in the late 1960s and early '70s – punctured the developmentalist axiom that low literacy rates in Africa were the result of what had come to be known as "book famine." The problem was not a lack of books, Rodney insisted, but rather colonial regimes that appropriated the wealth of Africans "to develop all aspects of European capitalist society, including its educational institutions." As developmentalism was turned on Indigenous communities in Canada during the latter decades of the twentieth century, its basic premises were similarly turned on their heads. Manuel, for instance, insisted that there could be no development without meaningful Indigenous sovereignty over land and governance, without, in other words, meaningful transformation of the structures that had determined Indigenous-settler relations up to that point. In Manuel's view, articulated clearly in *The Fourth World*, anything less, even if it involved new schools equipped with new educational materials, was simply a handout designed to perpetuate a paternalistic relation. The larger ideology of developmentalism, premised in its broadest sense on a progressivist telos according to which the so-called undeveloped had only to catch up and in a slightly narrower sense on the assertion that the world has premodern, nonliterate and modern, literate populations, is one that Indigenous writers such as Jeanette Armstrong have both rejected and recast in relation to their own knowledges.[49]

Conclusion

Developmentalism's End

Developmentalism as it is characterized in the pages of this book was not an enduring paradigm. By 1970, the forces shaping development were already shifting. As we have seen, the high modernist ideology of the postwar years found itself subject to vigorous critique from the various parties that comprised development's second wave, as well as from those who simply rejected its premises. Though, as Gilbert Rist contends, the early 1970s saw the near "triumph" of Third Worldist attempts to challenge the very premises of postwar developmentalist ideology, as the 1970s wore on, governments in the industrialized world contended with the energy crisis, new austerity measures, and an emergent neoliberal agenda, all of which combined to put new pressures on the development paradigm. In his account of development theory, Colin Leys observes that the events of the 1970s – notably the deregulation of global financial markets, the rise of international currency speculation, and, by the end of the decade, the abandonment of Keynesian economic policy by wealthy nations – combined to gut the price for many of the primary commodities produced in Third World nations, resulting in a dramatic decrease in their share of global trade and a concomitant increase in their borrowing. The language of development experienced a related shift, from the postwar concepts of "equity, redistribution, and growth" to the World Bank's concept of "basic needs," a development strategy that, as Leys points out, acknowledges that, under capitalism, the "poor will always be with us." By the 1980s, the policies of the global North toward the global South coalesced around "structural adjustment," a strategy meant to restore so-called equilibrium in a global financial system that had been unbalanced by Third World borrowing. As Rist notes, Third World nations were blamed by the world's wealthy nations for their apparent "bloated administrative apparatuses," the "low productivity of nationalized corporations," the tax evasion endemic to their informal economies, and their subsidization of basic needs like food. In Rist's estimation, the end of the twentieth century thus marked the end of the "huge enterprise" of development.[1]

The shifting ground under late twentieth-century developmentalism similarly affected the book- and literacy-related elements of the paradigm. International cultural organizations such as UNESCO weathered the storms of the long downturn by adapting. What Rist terms the near "triumph" of Third Worldist claims resulted, at UNESCO, in the New World Information and Communications Order concept, which aimed for democratic global access to information. However, as Sarah Brouillette's account makes clear, this language of "direct advocacy of state regulation of a balanced media system" met from the late 1970s with deep resistance from the US and Britain (the nations where the emergent media conglomerates of the late twentieth century were located), both of which exited UNESCO in protest in the 1980s. They were lured back in the early years of the twenty-first century by what Brouillette terms the "third era" of UNESCO's cultural policy making, characterized by "market-facing rationales for cultural programming" and "assurances that it is committed to working in the service of capitalist democracy, with freedom of speech and individual human rights trumpeted above anything like collectivization or state control of media and cultural industries."[2]

Alongside this history, one can track the ways that Canada's identification with the postwar literacy and book development paradigm has shifted. The central claim of *Books for Development* is that, between 1945 and the end of the 1970s, the book came to function as a key representative of settler exceptionalism. It was used within the context of the development paradigm to express solidarity with newly decolonized nations; to argue for the importance of Canadian leadership in the new international order; and to consolidate settler liberal rule at home. Relatedly, I argue that Canada's influence in the second half of the twentieth century on international organizations dedicated to education, literacy, and hence books was significant, and in fact greater than its global political, economic, and cultural influence warrants. In the first chapter, I show how this late twentieth-century influence built on and amplified the legacies of Canada's pre-1950 voluntary sector, itself rooted in a strong Protestant missionary and service tradition. The internationally recognized experiments in extension education, adult education, and literacy initiatives that were established in the late nineteenth and early twentieth centuries built the expertise that led to Canada's outsized influence on UNESCO's postwar literacy work and on domestic efforts linked to postwar developmentalism, such as the nation's first NGO, a book donation program. By the later twentieth century, Canada had established an international reputation as a world leader in literacy; in 1977, for instance, Frontier College, Canada's longest-running adult literacy program, was awarded a UNESCO Medal.

However, since the early years of the twenty-first century, the Government of Canada has been increasingly aligned with the instrumentalization of books and literacy that has occurred in international bodies such as UNESCO. For instance, in 2006, Canada's federal government shuttered its National Literacy Secretariat and moved its work to what is now the Literacy and Essential Skills Program within Employment and Social Development Canada, a reorganization that, as I have argued elsewhere, "clearly indicates the new functionality that characterizes the state definition of literacy." This instrumentalist ideology of literacy is in turn shaped by a larger global shift, exemplified by the international literacy surveys of the Organisation for Economic Co-Operation and Development (OECD), which tend to reduce literacy to a question of economic productivity. In her 2019 study of these surveys and their effects on policy in Ontario since their introduction in 1994, Tannis Atkinson contends that the "normative literacy" established by these surveys identifies a "calculable capacity that corresponds to an individual's value as a unit of human capital" and operates as a mechanism "through which subjects are responsibilized and enjoined to relate to themselves as primarily economic actors." The final report of the first OECD survey, intended to "inform labour market and other social policies to address structural changes in labour markets resulting from globalization and the emerging knowledge economy," identified a "literacy skills deficit" in Canada (among other OECD countries). While this led to increased funding for adult literacy initiatives in Canada, Atkinson notes that funding for adult basic education remains inadequate because government support tends to be directed at "programming for those who can progress most quickly," leaving behind those who "have the least education and face the greatest barriers."[3]

In this context, a new literacy myth has supplanted the earlier one identified by Harvey J. Graff. Graff's 1979 study *The Literacy Myth*, a key text in the field of New Literacy Studies that unfolded in its wake, examines the longstanding association of literacy with social and economic progress, identifying the roots of what he terms the "literacy myth" in the utilitarian and idealist thought of nineteenth-century England. Focusing on the societies of nineteenth-century Hamilton, London, and Kingston, all of which had very high literacy rates, Graff contends that literacy in these locations "was neither neutral, unambiguous, nor radically advantageous or liberatory." Its value "depended heavily on other factors" – ascribed social characteristics like ethnicity and sex but also institutional, economic, and cultural contexts, such that the "role of literacy in the life of the individual and society is contradictory and complex." With the platform capitalism of the twenty-first century, a newer myth has emerged. Focusing on the US in the early twenty-first century, Evan Watkins describes the new literacy myth as follows: if we provide low-income learners with a chance to master technologies associated with the new literacies (and particularly the new "adjectival literacies," such as digital literacy), they will realize economic gains that will narrow the growing income gap in the US. Watkins punctures this myth as Graff did the older one. It is a mistake, Watkins insists, to assume that the "benefits available from a range of new literacy skills" – from using an ATM to interacting on social media – "naturally remain in the hands of the users who do the literacy work involving new technologies." Instead, the "literacy work" performed regularly by people in everyday life (and not merely in the workplace) is rendered as "just-in-time human capital" that "minimizes reserves as much as possible," making workers "redundant in much the same way as excess material inventory." Nonetheless, the new literacy myth, which urges North Americans to ensure that elementary and secondary schools are equipping students for the knowledge economy, has proven as durable as the old one.[4]

Performing Canadian Book Culture in the Twenty-First Century

Interestingly, however, neither the reigning instrumentalist ideology of literacy nor the new myth associated with it is especially visible in the book culture that has been circulating as "Canadian" in the global literary market since the last decade of the twentieth century. (As Gillian Roberts, among others, has pointed out, anglophone Canadian literature went "global" in the early 1990s, a process most dramatically kickstarted by Michael Ondaatje's 1992 Booker Prize for *The English Patient*.) In the introduction, I argue that Canadian book culture – not simply the tendencies of theme and plot in literary titles authored by those living in Canada, but more specifically the nation's biblio-performances, its globally circulating performances of book consumption and consecration – has since the late twentieth century been associated with a moralizing rhetoric that associates reading with an enlightened liberal tolerance for difference. Scholarship on the various instruments that perform Canadian book culture for domestic and international audiences – namely mass reading events like CBC's Canada Reads and literary prizes like the Giller Prize – tends to focus on two elements: first, the fact that such instruments reinforce what Danielle Fuller and DeNel Rehberg Sedo call the "blockbuster culture" of contemporary literary publishing, and second, their tendency to perform the nation's cultural differences in depoliticized, neutralizing terms that seek to maintain rather than disrupt the racialized hierarchies of power that are a legacy of settler-colonial rule.[5]

The role of what Vin Nguyen and Thy Phu call "humanitarian exceptionalism" in performances of Canadian book culture has been especially in evidence in the last decade or so, particularly after the issue of refugeed persons returned to public consciousness in the wake of the global media attention that followed from the 2015 death of Alan Kurdi, a Syrian-born toddler who perished by drowning as his family sought to leave Turkey by boat. A photo of Kurdi's drowned body received heightened public attention in Canada because the family had been attempting to join relatives in British Columbia. The photo erupted in global news media in the middle of the 2015 federal election campaign, a campaign that brought the Liberal Party to power with a promise to accept twenty-five thousand refugeed persons from Syria. In her analysis of the 2019 Canada Reads competition, which featured two nonfictional accounts of refugeed persons finding a safe haven in Canada (Abu Bakr Rabeeah's *Homes* and Max Eisen's *By Chance Alone*), Orly Lael Netzer argues that the celebrity panelists (each of whom champions a particular book) understood themselves as "humanitarian and multicultural subjects" "empathically recognizing justice claims and strongly advocating for their recognition by others." At the same time, Lael Netzer contends, the debates from this season show how the books' calls for justice are "partially fulfilled at best, or left unanswered at worst" because the panelists' "forms of recognition preserve Canada's humanitarian myth and celebrate its multicultural brand."[6]

Critics have attended to the ways that the consecration of Indigenous writing from Canada has tended to function along similar lines, as a means of affirming the liberal politics of reconciliation and thus the transcendence of settler colonialism. Anouk Lang reads the reception of Joseph Boyden's 2006 novel *Three Day Road* (then positioned, by Boyden's conglomerate publisher Penguin Random House and by Canada Reads, as "an exemplar of multicultural hybridity" by a "legitimate interpreter of First Nations life and literature to other Canadians") in the 2006 Canada Reads debates as a depoliticizing process that performs reconciliation as a means of what Deena Rymhs calls "reconstructing national imaginaries." Lael Netzer draws on Pauline Wakeham's theorization of the "cunning of reconciliation" – a practice that grounds settler-Indigenous reconciliation in a state-dominated process of political recognition that does not disturb the economic or political status quo in Canada – to show how mass reading events like Canada Reads were by the late 2010s demonstrating a liberal politics of reconciliation. In my work with Sarah Pelletier on the Government of Canada's Guest-of-Honour campaign for the 2021 Frankfurt Book Fair, we draw on such insights, as well as Glen Sean Coulthard's critique of the "politics of recognition," to demonstrate the centrality of such "cunning" to the settler strategies of transcendence that typify Canada's cultural branding in the era of the global cultural industries.[7]

As Canada's prominence in Fuller and Rehberg Sedo's *Reading Beyond the Book: The Social Practices of Contemporary Literary Culture* suggests, what Jim Collins calls the "exuberantly social activity" of global public book consumption is alive and well in early twenty-first-century Canada. Such staged book consumption is not unique to Canada; what *is* unique to Canada in the context of this wider contemporary global performance of book culture is what I would like to call its bibliocultural morality claim, proffered via the repeated emphasis in performances of book culture on a liberal tolerance of difference, humanitarian benevolence, and reconciliation – understood in this context in the limited sense of recognition of past wrongs as a means of accommodating Indigenous assertions of nationhood within the settler state. *Books for Development* contends that this bibliocultural morality claim does not emerge ex nihilo in the 1990s but rather that it is bound to an older concept of the book that emerged within the settler cultures in Canada in the context of the late twentieth-century global development paradigm. Though developmentalism has seen an end, returning to it permits us to see this earlier elaboration on a global stage of settler exceptionalism via the book.[8]

Appendix A

Selections for the Canadiana Program (1948–59), by Category

Table A.1 Publications selected for the Annual "Canadiana" Book Presentation Program (1948–59), by category and year of first publication

ARTS, LETTERS AND EDUCATION

Béraud, Jean	350 ans de théâtre au Canada français	1958
Buchanan, Donald, ed.	Canadian Painters from Paul Kane to the Group of Seven	1945
Canada	A Selection of Essays Prepared for the Royal Commission on the Arts, Letters and Sciences	1951
Duval, Paul	Canadian Drawings and Prints	1952
Duval, Paul	Canadian Water Colour Painting	1954
Eggleston, Wilfrid	The Frontier and Canadian Letters	1957
Fowke, Edith, and Richard Johnston	Folk Songs of Canada	1954
Gowans, Alan	Looking at Architecture in Canada	1958
Gustafson, Ralph	The Penguin Book of Canadian Verse	1958
Hubbard, Robert	European Paintings in Canadian Collections, 2 vols	1956–62
Katz, Joseph, ed.	Canadian Education Today: A Symposium	1956
Klinck, Carl F., and Reginald E. Watters	Canadian Anthology	1955
MacMillan, Ernest	Music in Canada	1955
McInnes, Graham	Canadian Art	1950
Morisset, Gérard	Coup d'oeil sur les arts en Nouvelle-France	1941
O'Leary, Dostaler	Le roman canadien-français	1954
Pacey, Desmond	Creative Writing in Canada: A Short History of English-Canadian Literature	1952
Park, Julian, ed.	The Culture of Contemporary Canada	1957
Phelps, Arthur L.	Canadian Writers	1953

Phillips, Charles	*Development of Education in Canada*	1957
Rièse, Laura	*L'âme de la poésie canadienne française*	1955
Ross, Malcolm, ed.	*The Arts in Canada: A Stock-Taking at Mid-Century*	1958
Smith, Arthur James Marshall	*The Book of Canadian Poetry: A Critical and Historical Anthology*	1943
Sylvestre, Guy	*Anthologie de la poésie canadienne d'expression française*	1942
Whittaker, Herbert	*The Stratford Festival, 1953–57: A Record in Pictures and Text of the Shakespearean Festival in Canada*	1958

Total, Arts, Letters and Education: 25

CANADA IN WORLD AFFAIRS SERIES

Harrison, William Eric Craven	*Canada in World Affairs: 1949 to 1950*	1957
Keirstead, Burton Seely	*Canada in World Affairs: September 1951 to October 1953*	1956
Lingard, Charles Cecil, and Reginald George Trotter	*Canada in World Affairs: September 1941 to May 1944*	1950
Masters, Donald C.	*Canada in World Affairs: 1953 to 1955*	1959
Soward, Frederick H.	*Canada in World Affairs: From Normandy to Paris, 1944–1946*	1950
Spencer, Robert A.	*Canada in World Affairs: From UN to NATO, 1946–1949*	1959

Total, Canada in World Affairs Series: 6

CANADIAN ECONOMICS SERIES, UNIVERSITY OF TORONTO

Blake, Gordon	*Customs Administration in Canada*	1957
Brecher, Irving	*Monetary and Fiscal Thought and Policy in Canada, 1919–1939*	1957
Buckley, Kenneth	*Capital Formation in Canada, 1896–1930*	1955
Logan, Harold Amos	*State Intervention and Assistance in Collective Bargaining: The Canadian Experience, 1943–1954*	1956
Malach, Vernon Walter	*International Cycles and Canada's Balance of Payments, 1921–1933*	1954
Neufeld, Edward Peter	*Bank of Canada Operations, 1935–54*	1958
Phillips, William Gregory	*The Agricultural Implement Industry in Canada: A Study in Competition*	1956
Safarian, Albert Edward	*The Canadian Economy in the Great Depression*	1959
Scott, Anthony	*Natural Resources: The Economics of Conservation*	1955

Total, Canadian Economics Series, University of Toronto: 9

COUNTRY AND PEOPLE

Berton, Pierre	*The Mysterious North**	1956
Bolus, Malvina	*Image of Canada*	1829
Brown, George W., ed.	*Canada*	1950
Bruchési, Jean	*Le Canada*	1948
Brunet, Michel	*Canadians et Canadiens*	1954
Chapin, Miriam	*Atlantic Canada*	1956
Chapin, Miriam	*Contemporary Canada*	1959
Clark, Samuel Delbert	*Church and Sect in Canada*	1948
Clark, Samuel Delbert	*The Social Development of Canada: An Introductory Study with Select Documents*	1942
Falardeau, Jean-Charles	*Essais sur le Québec contemporain*	1953
Gérin, Léon	*Le type économique et social des Canadiens: milieux agricoles de traditions françaises*	1937
Gilmour, George Peel, ed.	*Canada's Tomorrow: Papers and Discussion, Canada's Tomorrow Conference, Quebec City, November 1953*	1954
Harrington, Richard	*Face of the Arctic: A Cameraman's Story in Words and Pictures of Five Journeys into the Far North*	1952
Hutchison, Bruce	*Canada: Tomorrow's Giant*	1957
Jenness, Diamond	*The Indians of Canada*	1932
Putnam, Donald F.	*Canadian Regions: A Geography of Canada*	1952
Ross, Malcolm, ed.	*Our Sense of Identity: A Book of Canadian Essays*	1945
Tanghe, Raymond	*Géographie économique du Canada*	1944
Taylor, Thomas Griffith	*Canada: A Study of Cool Continental Environments and Their Effect on British and French Settlement*	1947
Walsh, Henry Horace	*The Christian Church in Canada*	1956
Watters, Reginald Eyre	*British Columbia: A Centennial Anthology*	1958
	Total, Country and People:	21

ECONOMICS

Ashley, Charles, and James Everit Smith	*Corporation Finance in Canada*	1956
Buck, Arthur Eugene	*Financing Canadian Government*	1949
Corbett, David Charles	*Canada's Immigration Policy: A Critique*	1957
Currie, Archibald William	*Economics of Canadian Transportation*	1954
Currie, Archibald William	*The Grand Trunk Railway of Canada*	1957

Easterbrook, William Thomas, and Hugh Aitken	*Canadian Economic History*	1956
Firestone, O.J.	*Canadian Economic Development, 1867–1953*	1958
Fowke, Vernon	*The National Policy and the Wheat Economy*	1957
Gordon, Walter L.	*Final Report of the Royal Commission on Canada's Economic Prospects*	1957
Innis, Harold	*Essays in Canadian Economic History*	1956
Innis, Harold	*The Fur Trade in Canada: An Introduction to Canadian Economic History*	1927
Jamieson, Archibald Black	*Chartered Banking in Canada*	1953
Jamieson, Stuart	*Industrial Relations in Canada*	1957
LeBourdais, Donat Marc	*Metals and Men: The Story of Canadian Mining*	1957
Logan, Harold Amos	*Trade Unions in Canada: Their Development and Functioning*	1948
McDiarmid, Orville John	*Commercial Policy in the Canadian Economy*	1946
McIvor, Russell Craig	*Canadian Monetary, Banking and Fiscal Development*	1958
Perry, John Harvey	*Taxation in Canada*	1951
	Total, Economics:	18

EXTERNAL RELATIONS

Angus, Henry Forbes	*Canada and the Far East, 1940–1953*	1953
Brebner, John B.	*North Atlantic Triangle: The Interplay of Canada, the United States and Great Britain*	1945
Glazebrook, George Parkin de Twenebrokes	*A History of Canadian External Relations*	1950
Keenleyside, Hugh, and Gerald S. Brown	*Canada and the United States: Some Aspects of Their Historical Relations*	1929
Lower, Arthur Reginald Marsden	*Canada and the Far East: 1940*	1940
Lower, Arthur Reginald Marsden	*Canada: Nation and Neighbour*	1952
Skilling, Harold Gordon	*Canadian Representation Abroad: From Agency to Embassy*	1945
Soward, Frederick H., and Edgar McInnis	*Canada and the United Nations*	1956
Underhill, Frank H.	*The British Commonwealth: An Experiment in Co-operation Among Nations*	1956
	Total, External Relations:	9

GENERAL REFERENCE WORKS

	Encyclopedia Canadiana, 10 vols	1957–58
Census and Statistics Office	*The Canada Year Book 1957–58*	1958
Dept. of Mines and Tech. Surveys Geographical Branch	*Atlas of Canada*	1957
Wallace, W.J.	*Dictionary of Canadian Biography*, 2 vols	1926
	Total, General Reference Works:	4

GOVERNMENT AND POLITICS

Beck, James Murray	*The Government of Nova Scotia*	1957
Bonenfant, Jean-Charles	*Les institutions politiques canadiennes*	1954
Corry, James Alexander	*Democratic Government and Politics*	1946
Crawford, Kenneth Grant	*Canadian Municipal Government*	1954
Dawson, Robert MacGregor	*Democratic Government in Canada**	1949
Dawson, Robert MacGregor	*The Government of Canada**	1947
Gérin-Lajoie, Paul	*Constitutional Amendment in Canada*	1950
Information Canada	*Organization of the Government of Canada* (1st ed.)	1958
Lamontagne, Maurice	*Le fédéralisme canadien: évolution et problèmes*	1954
Lower, Arthur Reginald Marsden	*This Most Famous Stream: The Liberal Democratic Way of Life**	1954
Lower, Arthur Reginald Marsden, Francis Reginald Scott, et al.	*Evolving Canadian Federalism*	1958
Macpherson, Crawford Brough	*Democracy in Alberta: The Theory and Practice of a Quasi-Party System*	1953
Mallory, James Russell	*Social Credit and the Federal Power in Canada*	1954
Olivier, Maurice	*Problems of Canadian Sovereignty from the British North American Act, 1867, to the Statute of Westminster, 1931*	1945
Saywell, John Tupper	*The Office of Lieutenant-Governor: A Study in Canadian Government and Politics*	1957
Sirois, Joseph, and Newton Wesley Rowell	*Report of the Royal Commission on Dominion Provincial Relations*	1940
Ward, Norman	*The Canadian House of Commons: Representation*	1950
	Total, Government and Politics:	17

HISTORY

Brebner, John B.	*The Explorers of North America*	1933
Brown, George W.	*Canada in the Making*	1943
Bruchési, Jean	*Canada: réalités d'hier et d'aujourd'hui*	1948
Bruchési, Jean	*L'histoire du Canada*	1954
Campbell, Marjorie W.	*The North West Company*	1957
Careless, James Maurice Stockford	*Canada: A Story of Challenge**	1953
Creighton, Donald	*Dominion of the North: A History of Canada*	1944
Creighton, Donald	*The Commercial Empire of the St. Lawrence, 1760–1850*	1937
de Gaspé, Philippe Aubert	*Les anciens Canadiens*	1863
Frégault, Guy	*La guerre de la conquête, 1754–1760*	1955
Groulx, Lionel	*Histoire du Canada français depuis la découverte**	1950
Groulx, Lionel	*Notre grande aventure: l'empire français en Amérique du Nord*	1958
Hutchison, Bruce	*The Struggle for the Border*	1955
Lanctôt, Gustave	*L'oeuvre de la France en Amérique du Nord*	1950
Lower, Arthur Reginald Marsden	*Canadians in the Making: A Social History of Canada*	1958
Lower, Arthur Reginald Marsden	*Colony to Nation: A History of Canada**	1946
MacKay, Robert Alexander	*Newfoundland: Economic, Diplomatic, and Strategic Studies*	1946
Martin, Chester	*Foundations of Canadian Nationhood*	1955
McInnis, Edgar	*Canada: A Political and Social History*	1947
Morton, William Lewis	*Manitoba: A History*	1957
Ormsby, Margaret A.	*British Columbia: A History*	1958
Stanley, George	*Canada's Soldiers, 1604–1954: The Military History of an Unmilitary People*	1954
Talman, James J.	*Basic Documents in Canadian History*	1959
Wade, Mason	*The French Canadians, 1760–1945*	1955
Wright, James	*Saskatchewan: The History of a Province*	1955
	Total, History:	25

LITERATURE – PROSE

Allen, Ralph	*Peace River Country*	1958
Barbeau, Marius	*The Tree of Dreams*	1955
Callaghan, Morley	*The Loved and the Lost**	1951
Carr, Emily	*Klee Wyck**	1941

Davies, Robertson	*Leaven of Malice*	1954
Elie, Robert	*Il suffit d'un jour*	1957
Grove, Frederick P.	*Over Prairie Trails*	1922
Guèvremont, Germaine	*Le survenant**	1945
Guèvremont, Germaine	*Marie-Didace**	1947
Haliburton, Thomas C.	*The Clockmaker, or The Sayings and Doings of Samuel Slick of Slickville*	1837
Hémon, Louis	*Maria Chapdelaine**	1916
Kirby, William	*Le chien d'or (The Golden Dog): A Legend of Québec*	1877
Langevin, André	*Poussière sur la ville*	1953
Leacock, Stephen	*Sunshine Sketches of a Little Town*	1912
Leacock, Stephen, and John Boynton Priestley, ed.	*The Best of Leacock*	1957
Lemelin, Roger	*Au pied de la pente douce*	1944
Lemelin, Roger	*Les Plouffe*	1948
MacLennan, Hugh	*The Watch that Ends the Night**	1958
MacLennan, Hugh	*Two Solitudes**	1945
Mitchell, W.O.	*Who Has Seen the Wind*	1947
Raddall, Thomas	*The Wings of Night*	1956
Richler, Mordecai	*Son of a Smaller Hero*	1955
Ringuet	*Trente arpents*	1938
Robins, John D., and Margaret V. Ray	*A Book of Canadian Humour*	1951
Roy, Gabrielle	*La petite poule d'eau*	1950
Roy, Gabrielle	*Rue Deschambault**	1955
Roy, Gabrielle	*Street of Riches**	1957
Roy, Gabrielle	*The Tin Flute**	1945
Savard, Félix-Antoine	*Menaud, maître-draveur*	1937
Thériault, Yves	*Aaron*	1954
Weaver, Robert, and Helen James	*Canadian Short Stories*	1952
Wilson, Ethel	*Love and Salt Water*	1956
Wiseman, Adele	*The Sacrifice**	1956
	Total, Literature – Prose:	33

LITERATURE – POETRY

Choquette, Robert	*Oeuvres poétiques*	1956
de Saint-Denys Garneau, Hector	*Poésies complètes*	1949

Grandbois, Alain	L'Etoile pourpre	1957
Hébert, Anne	Le tombeau des rois	1953
Layton, Irving	The Improved Binoculars	1956
LePan, Douglas	The Net and the Sword*	1953
Livesay, Dorothy	Selected Poems of Dorothy Livesay, 1926–1956	1957
McPherson, Jay	The Boatman*	1957
Nelligan, Émile	Poésies complètes	1952
Page, P.K.	The Metal and the Flower	1954
Pratt, E.J., and Northrop Frye, ed.	The Collected Poems of E.J. Pratt	1958
Roy, George Ross	Douze poètes modernes du Canada français	1958
Scott, Francis Reginald	Events and Signals	1954
Scott, Francis Reginald, and Arthur James Marshall Smith	The Blasted Pine	1957
Service, Robert M.	Collected Poems	1940
Souster, Raymond	The Selected Poems	1956
	Total, Literature – Poetry:	16

PERIODICALS

Canadian Art

Canadian Commentator

Canadian Forum

Canadian Geographical Journal

Canadian Historical Revue

Canadian Journal of Economics and Political Science

Canadian Literature

Canadian Music Journal

Cité libre

Culture

Écrits du Canada-français

Financial Post

Globe and Mail, Weekly Overseas Edition

International Journal

Journal of the Royal Architectural Institute of Canada

La Revue de L'Université d'Ottawa

La vie des arts

Liberté 59

MacLean's

Queen's Quarterly
Relations
Saturday Night
Tamarack Review
University of Toronto Quarterly

                                                              Total, Periodicals: 24

POLITICAL BIOGRAPHIES

Bissell, Claude	*Our Living Tradition: Seven Canadians*	1957
Creighton, Donald	*John A. Macdonald: The Old Chieftain**	1955
Creighton, Donald	*John A. Macdonald: The Young Politician**	1952
Dawson, Robert MacGregor	*William Lyon Mackenzie King: A Political Biography, 1874–1923*	1958
Hutchison, Bruce	*The Incredible Canadian: A Candid Portrait of Mackenzie King**	1952
Kilbourn, William	*The Firebrand: William Lyon Mackenzie and the Rebellion in Upper Canada*	1956
McNaught, Kenneth	*A Prophet in Politics: A Biography of J.S. Woodsworth*	1959

                                         Total, Political Biographies: 7

STUDIES OF THE ROYAL COMMISSION ON CANADA'S ECONOMIC PROSPECTS

Anderson, Roger	*The Future of Canada's Export Trade*	1957
Brecher, Irving, and Sol Simon Reisman	*Canada-United States Economic Relations*	1957
Davis, John	*Mining and Mineral Processing in Canada*	1957
Davis, John	*The Canadian Chemical Industry*	1957
Davis, John, et al.	*The Outlook for the Canadian Forest Industries*	1957
Dept. of Fisheries	*The Commercial Fisheries of Canada*	1956
Dept. of Labour	*Skilled and Professional Manpower in Canada*	1957
Drummond, William Malcolm, and William Mackenzie	*Progress and Prospects of Canadian Agriculture*	1957
Dubé, Yves, et al.	*Housing and Social Capital in Canada*	1957
Fullerton, Douglas H., and H. Anthony Hampson	*Canadian Secondary Manufacturing*	1957
Hood, William C., and Anthony Scott	*Output, Labour and Capital in the Canadian Economy*	1957
Howland, Robert Dudley	*Some Regional Aspects of Canada's Economic Development*	1957
Lessard, Jean-Charles	*Transportation in Canada*	1956

Royal Bank of Canada	*The Canadian Construction Industry*	1956
Slater, David W.	*Canada's Imports*	1957
Slater, David W.	*Consumption Expenditures in Canada*	1957
Smith, J.M.	*Canadian Economic Growth and Development, 1939–1955*	1957
Young, John H.	*Canadian Commercial Policy*	1957
Total, Studies of the Royal Commission on Canada's Economic Prospects:		18

* Won Governor General's Award.

Note: Typographical errors have been corrected when relevant. Categories are transcribed from the original list. Year of first publication has been added.

Source: Annex A: A List of Canadian Books and Periodicals for Inclusion in Major Presentations Under the Annual Book Presentation Programme, 1959, vol. 7797, file 125-2-40, 1.2, DEA-LAC.

Appendix B

Selections for the Special Book Presentation Programme, by Language

Table B.1   English-language publications selected for the Special Book Presentation Programme for Colombo-Plan Area Countries (1956–59)

Author	Title	First year of publication
Bailey, Sydney D., ed.	Parliamentary Government in the Commonwealth	1951
Barnard, Chester	The Functions of the Executive	1938
Beach, Earl Francis	Economic Models: An Exposition	1957
Beloff, Max	The Debate on the American Revolution, 1761–1783	1949
Bennett, George	The Concept of Empire: Burke to Attlee, 1774–1947	1953
Bissell, Claude T.	Our Living Tradition: Seven Canadians	1957
Bladen, Vincent W.	An Introduction to Political Economy	1941
Brady, Alexander	Democracy in the Dominions: A Comparative Study in Institutions	1947
Brierly, James L.	The Law of Nations	1928
Brinton, Crane	Ideas and Men: The Story of Western Thought	1950
Brogan, Denis W.	The Price of Revolution	1951
Bullock, Allan, and Maurice Shock, eds.	The Liberal Tradition: From Fox to Keynes	1956
Butterfield, Herbert	Christianity, Diplomacy, and War	1953
Butterfield, Herbert	George III and the Historians	1956
Campbell, Marjorie W.	The North West Company	1957
Carter, Gwendolen	The British Commonwealth and International Security: The Role of the Dominions, 1919–1939	1947
Chase, Stuart	Roads to Agreement: Successful Methods in the Science of Human Relations	1951

Author	Title	First year of publication
Clark, John M.	*Economic Institutions and Human Welfare*	1957
Clark, William	*Less Than Kin: A Study of Anglo-American Relations*	1957
Cobban, Alfred	*The Debate on the French Revolution 1789–1800*	1950
Corry, James A.	*Democratic Government and Politics*	1946
Creighton, Donald	*John A. MacDonald: The Old Chieftain*	1955
Creighton, Donald	*John A. MacDonald: The Young Politician*	1952
Crosland, Anthony	*The Future of Socialism*	1956
Dales, John	*Hydroelectricity and Industrial Development: Quebec, 1898–1940*	1957
Djilas, Milovan	*The New Class: An Analysis of the Communist System*	1957
Dray, William	*Laws and Explanation in History*	1957
Elliott, George	*Tariff Procedures and Trade Barriers: A Study of Indirect Protection in Canada and the United States*	1955
Flew, Antony	*Logic and Language* (first series)	1951
Fowke, Vernon	*The National Policy and the Wheat Economy*	1957
Frye, William	*A United Nations Peace Force*	1957
Glazebrook, George P. de Twenebroker	*A Short History of Canada*	1950
Green, Thomas H.	*Lectures on the Principles of Political Obligation*	1895
Hatt, Paul, and Albert Reiss, eds.	*Cities and Society: The Revised Reader in Urban Sociology*	1957
Hearnshaw, Fossey J.C., ed.	*The Social and Political Ideas of Some Great Thinkers of the Sixteenth and Seventeenth Centuries*	1926
Heckscher, Gunnar	*The Study of Comparative Government and Politics*	1957
Hutchison, Bruce	*The Struggle for the Border*	1955
Jamieson, Stuart	*Industrial Relations in Canada*	1957
Jaques, Elliott	*The Changing Culture of a Factory*	1951
Johnson, Wendell	*People in Quandaries: The Semantics of Personal Adjustment*	1946
Jouvenel, Bertrand de	*Sovereignty: An Inquiry into the Political Good*	1957
Laslett, Peter, ed.	*Philosophy, Politics and Society: A Collection*	1956
LeRoy Burt, Alfred	*The Evolution of the British Empire and Commonwealth from the American Revolution*	1956

Author	Title	First year of publication
Lipson, Leslie	*The Great Issues of Politics*	1958
Livingston, William S.	*Federalism and Constitutional Change*	1956
Lower, Arthur R.M.	*Colony to Nation: A History of Canada*	1946
Lower, Arthur R.M.	*This Most Famous Stream: The Liberal Democratic Way of Life*	1954
Maccoby, Simon	*The English Radical Tradition, 1763–1914*	1952
MacGregor Dawson, Robert	*The Government of Canada*	1946
MacIver, Robert	*Democracy and the Economic Challenge*	1952
MacKenzie, Robert T.	*British Political Parties: The Distribution of Power Within the Conservative and Labour Parties*	1955
Magnus, Philip	*Gladstone: A Biography*	1954
Mannheim, Karl	*Essays on Sociology and Social Psychology*	1953
Mansergh, Nicholas	*The Commonwealth and the Nations: Studies in British Commonwealth Relations*	1948
Mansergh, Nicolas	*Survey of British Commonwealth Affairs*, vols 3 and 4	1952, 1958
Marrow, Alfred J.	*Living Without Hate: Scientific Approaches to Human Relations*	1951
McRuer, James C.	*The Evolution of the Judicial Process*	1957
Morpurgo, Jack, ed.	*The Pelican History of England*, 6 vols	1950–55
Morrison, Herbert	*Government and Parliament: A Survey from the Inside*	1954
Mowat, Charles Loch	*Britain Between the Wars: 1918–1940*	1955
Mumford, Lewis	*The Condition of Man*	1944
Mumford, Lewis	*The Culture of Cities*	1938
Mumford, Lewis	*Technics and Civilization*	1934
Nef, John U.	*Industry and Government in France and England, 1540–1640*	1940
Nef, John U.	*War and Human Progress: An Essay on the Rise of Industrial Civilization*	1950
Neufeld, Edward P.	*Bank of Canada Operations and Policy, 1935–54*	1958
Neumann, Franz	*The Democratic and the Authoritarian State: Essays in Political and Legal Theory*	1954
Nicolson, Harold	*Diplomacy*	1939
Park, Robert E.	*Human Communities: The City and Human Ecology*	1952
Park, Robert E.	*Race and Culture*	1950
Pearson, Lester B.	*Democracy in World Politics*	1955

Author	Title	First year of publication
Pelling, Henry	The Challenge of Socialism	1954
Plamenatz, John	German Marxism and Russian Communism	1954
Plunkett, Thomas J.	Municipal Organization in Canada: A Study of the Structure and Forms of Municipal Government Organization in Canada	1955
Popper, Karl R.	The Open Society and its Enemies, vol. 1	1945
Popper, Karl R.	The Open Society and its Enemies, vol. 2	1945
Pryce-Jones, Alan, ed.	The New Outline of Modern Knowledge	1956
Robbins, Lionel	The Theory of Economic Policy in English Classical Political Economy	1947
Robertson, Denis H.	Lectures on Economic Principles, vol. 1	1957
Robinson, Joan	The Accumulation of Capital	1956
Rosenbluth, Gideon	Concentration in Canadian Manufacturing Industries	1957
Ross, Murray	Community Organization: Theory, Principles and Practice	1955
Ross, Murray, and Charles Hendry	New Understandings of Leadership: A Survey and Application of Research	1957
Royal Society of Canada	Studia Varia: Literary and Scientific Papers	1957
Russell, Bertrand	Human Knowledge: Its Scope and Limits	1948
Russell, Bertrand	Human Society in Ethics and Politics	1954
Ryle, Gilbert	Dilemmas: The Tarner Lectures, 1953	1954
Saywell, John T.	The Office of Lieutenant-Governor: A Study in Canadian Government and Politics	1957
Schumpeter, Joseph	Capitalism, Socialism and Democracy	1950
Sirois, Joseph, and Newton W. Rowell	Report of the Royal Commission on Dominion-Provincial Relations	1940
Talmon, Jacob L.	The Origins of Totalitarian Democracy	1952
Taylor, Overton H.	Economics and Liberalism: Collected Papers	1955
Thistlethwaite, Frank	The Great Experiment: An Introduction to the History of the American People	1955
Thomson, David	Europe Since Napoleon	1957
Tomlin, Eric W.F.	Living and Knowing	1955
Toynbee, Arnold	The World and the West	1953
Trevor-Roper, Hugh	Historical Essays	1957
Underhill, Frank H.	The British Commonwealth: An Experiment in Co-Operation Among Nations	1956
Usher, Abbott	A History of Mechanical Inventions	1929
Vereker, Charles	The Development of Political Theory	1957

Author	Title	First year of publication
Wallace, Elisabeth	*Goldwin Smith, Victorian Liberal*	1957
Watkins, Frederick	*The Political Tradition of the West*	1948
Watson, George	*The Unservile State: Essays in Liberty and Welfare*	1957
Weber, Max	*The Protestant Ethic and the Spirit of Capitalism*	1930 (transl.)
Weldon, Thomas D.	*The Vocabulary of Politics*	1953
Wheare, Kenneth C.	*Federal Government*	1946
Wheare, Kenneth C.	*Government by Committee: An Essay on the British Constitution*	1955
Wheare, Kenneth C.	*Modern Constitutions*	1951
White, Reginald J., ed.	*The Conservative Tradition*	1950
Wilkinson, Anne	*Lions in the Way: A Discursive History of the Oslers*	1956
Woodhouse, Arthur S.P.	*Puritanism and Liberty*	1951
Young, George M.	*Portrait of an Age: Victorian England*	1936
	Total, English-language selections	112

Note: Typographical errors have been corrected when relevant. Year of first publication has been added.

Source: English and French Books Presented Under the Special Book Presentation Programme for Colombo Plan Area Countries, 1959, vol. 7797, file 125-2-40, 1.2, DEA-LAC.

Table B.2 French-language publications selected for the Special Book Presentation Programme for Colombo-Plan Area Countries (1956–59)

Author	Title	First year of publication
Aron, Raymond	*Espoir et peur du siècle*	1957
Aron, Raymond	*Les guerres en chaîne*	1951
Aron, Raymond	*L'opium des intellectuels*	1955
Bailey, Sidney D.	*Naissance de nouvelles démocraties*	1953
Barnérias, J.S.	*L'équilibre économique international*	1952
Barre, Raymond	*Économie politique*, 2 vols	1955
Barrère, Alain	*Théorie économique et impulsion keynésienne*	1952
Bartoli, Henri	*Science économique et travail*	1957
Berger, Gaston	*Le fédéralisme*	1956
Berger, Gaston	*L'opinion publique et les gouvernements*	1957
Bergson, Henri	*Les deux sources de la morale et de la religion*	1932
Bigo, Pierre	*Marxisme et humanisme*	1953
Bréhier, Émile	*Histoire de la philosophie*, 9 vols	1930
Brochier, Hubert	*Finances publiques et redistributions des revenus*	1950
Brunschvicg, Léon	*Le progrès de la conscience dans la philosophie occidentale*	1927
Burdeau, Georges	*Traité de science politique*, 6 vols	1949–56
Cadart, Jacques	*Régime électoral et régime parlementaire en Grande Bretagne*	1948
Calvez, Jean-Yves	*La pensée de Karl Marx*	1956
Campion, Gilbert F.M., and David W.S. Lidderdale	*La procédure parlementaire en Europe*	1955
Chapman, Brian	*L'administration locale en France*	1955
Chevalier, Jacques	*Histoire de la pensée*, 2 vols	1955–56
Chevallier, Jean-Jacques	*Les grandes oeuvres politiques; de Machiavel à nos jours*	1949
Coyle, David C.	*Le système politique des États-Unis et son fonctionnement*	1955
Cros, Jacques	*Le néo-libéralisme; étude positive et critique*	1951
D'Hérouville, Hubert	*L'économie de la nouvelle Europe*	1958
Djilas, Milovan	*La nouvelle classe dirigeante*	1957
Dolléans, Édouard	*Histoire du mouvement ouvrier*, 3 vols	1936–53
Ducros, Bernard	*L'action des grands marchés financiers sur l'équilibre monétaire*	1950

Author	Title	First year of publication
Durand, Charles	*Confédération d'états et état-fédéral*	1955
Durkheim, Émile	*Montesquieu et Rousseau: précurseurs de la sociologie*	1953
Durkheim, Émile	*Les règles de la méthode sociologique*	1895
Duverger, Maurice	*Les partis politiques*	1951
Etcheverry, Auguste	*Le conflit actuel des humanismes*	1955
Febvre, Lucien	*La terre et l'évolution humaine*	1922
Finance, Joseph de	*Existence et liberté*	1955
Fourastié, Jean	*Machinisme et bien-être*	1951
Galbraith, John Kenneth	*Le capitalisme américain*, translated into French by Marie-Thérèse Génin	1956 (transl.)
Gehmähling, Paul	*Les grands èconomistes*	1925
Goguel, François	*Nouvelles études de sociologie électorale*	1954
Goguel, François	*Le régime politique français*	1955
Gottman, Jean	*La politique des états et leur géographie*	1952
Grosser, Alfred	*L'allemagne de l'Occident*	1953
Grousset, René, and Émile G. Léonard, eds	*Histoire universelle*, 2 vols	1956–57
Guitton, Henri, and Gaëtan Pirou	*Les fluctuations économiques*	1951
Gurvitch, Georges	*Déterminismes sociaux et liberté humaine*	1955
Gurvitch, Georges	*La vocation actuelle de la sociologie*	1950
Halphen, Louis, and Philippe Sagnac, eds	*Peuples et civilisations*, 14 vols	1926–?
Hoffman, Stanley	*Organisations internationales et pouvoirs politiques des états*	1954
James, Émile	*Histoire de la pensée économique au XXe siècle*, 2 vols	1955
Jeanselme, Paul	*La démocratie, sa nature et son évolution*	1952
Jouvenel, Bertrand de	*De la souveraineté*	1955
Jouvenel, Bertrand de	*Du pouvoir*	1945
Keynes, John Maynard	*Théorie générale de l'emploi, de l'intérêt, et de la monnaie*, translated into French by Jean de Largentaye	1949 (trans.)
Laski, Harold	*Le gouvernement parlementaire en Angleterre*, translated into French by Jacques Cadart and Jacqueline Prélot	1950 (transl.)
Lévi-Strauss, Claude	*Les structures élémentaires de la parenté*	1949
Locke, John	*Traité du gouvernement civil*, translated into French by David Mazel	1795 (transl.)

Author	Title	First year of publication
Mabileau, Albert	*Le parti libéral dans le système constitutionnel britannique*	1953
Madariaga, Salvador de	*Portrait de l'europe*, translated into French by Marie-Louise Garvague	1952 (transl.)
Magaud, Charles	*L'Équilibre économique à travers la pensée moderne*	1950
Marchal, André	*Méthode scientifique et économique*, 2 vols	1952, 1955
Marchal, Jean	*Cours d'économie politique*	1950
Marchal, Jean	*Le méchanisme des prix*	1946
Maritain, Jacques	*L'homme et l'état*	1953
Marrou, Henri I.	*De la connaissance historique*	1954
Mathiot, André	*Le régime politique britannique*	1955
Mauss, Marcel	*Sociologie et anthropologie*	1950
Mendès-France, Pierre, and Gabriel Ardent	*La science économique et l'action*	1954
Mirkine-Guetzévitch, Boris	*Les constitutions européennes*, 2 vols	1951
Montesquieu	*De l'esprit des lois*, 2 vols	1748
Morazé, Charles	*Essai sur la civilisation d'Occident*	1950
Morazé, Charles	*La France bourgeoise, XVIIIe–XXe siècles*	1946
Morazé, Charles	*Introduction à l'histoire économique*	1943
Moret, Michel	*L'échange international*	1956
Mosca, Gaetano	*Histoire des doctrines politiques*, translated into French by Gaston Bouthoul	1955 (transl.)
Mounier, Emmanuel	*Qu'est-ce que le personnalisme?*	1946
Naville, Pierre	*La vie du travail et ses problèmes*	1954
Pelloux, Robert	*Libéralisme, traditionalisme, décentralisation*	1952
Perry, Ralph B.	*Puritanisme et démocratie*, translated into French by François Meaulnes	1952 (transl.)
Picon, Gaëtan, ed.	*Panorama des idées contemporaines*	1957
Pie XII [Pope Pius XII]	*Relations humaines et société contemporaine*, 2 vols	1956
Piettre, André	*Economie allemande contemporaine*	1952
Plato	*Le politique*, translated into French by Auguste Diès	1567 (transl.)
Renouvin, Pierre	*Histoire des relations internationales*, 6 vols	1954–55
Reuter, Paul	*Institutions internationales*	1955
Ripert, Georges	*Régime démocratique et le droit civil moderne*	1936
Rougemont, Denis de	*L'aventure occidentale de l'homme*	1957

Author	Title	First year of publication
Rousseau, Jean-Jacques	*Du contrat social*	1762
Rousseau, Pierre	*Histoire des techniques*	1956
Sauvy, Alfred	*Théorie générale de la population*, 2 vols	1952
Schumpeter, Joseph	*Capitalisme, socialisme et démocratie*, translated into French by Gaël Fain	1942 (transl.)
Seurin, Jean-Louis	*La structure interne des partis politiques americains*	1953
Simon, Pierre-Henri	*L'esprit et l'histoire: essai sur la conscience historique dans la littérature du XXe siècle*	1954
Sorre, Max	*Les fondements de la géographie humaine*, 4 vols	1950–54
Soto, Jean de	*La Communauté européenne du charbon et de l'acier*	1958
Tocqueville, Alexis de	*De la démocratie en Amérique*, 2 vols	1835, 1840
Tunc, André, and Suzanne Tunc	*Le droit des États-Unis d'Amérique*	1955
Vincent, André L.A.	*Initiation à la conjoncture économique*	1947
Visscher, Charles de	*Théories et réalité en droit international public*	1953
	Total, French-language selections	98

Note: Typographical errors have been corrected when relevant. Year of first publication has been added.

Source: English and French Books Presented Under the Special Book Presentation Programme for Colombo Plan Area Countries, 1959, vol. 7797, file 125-2-40, 1.2, DEA-LAC.

Notes

Introduction

1. Tavia Grant, "Hollow Core," *Globe and Mail*, 1 April 2023, A12–14.
2. See, for example, Fuller and Sedo, "A Reading Spectacle for the Nation," 5–36; Kamboureli, "The Culture of Celebrity and National Pedagogy," 35–55; Roberts, *Prizing Literature*.
3. Sachs, "Introduction," xv.
4. Davis, "The Origins of the Third World," 54. This essay is an excerpt from Davis's book, first published in 2001, *Late Victorian Holocausts*.
5. Fanon, *The Wretched of the Earth*, 102–3, 207–8; Rist, *The History of Development*, 25–46, 57–62; Esteva, "Development," 3–6; Sachs, "Introduction," xv–xx; Jerónimo, "Repressive Develpmentalism," 540. Other scholars' works that have been central to my thinking about the continuities between colonialism and development include Baughan, *Saving the Children*; Cooper, "Modernizing Colonialism and the Limits of Empire"; McCarthy, *Race, Empire, and the Idea of Human Development*; and Unger, *International Development*. For poststructuralist critiques that attend to the continuities between imperial and colonial governmentality, see Duffield and Hewitt, *Empire, Development, and Colonialism*; Escobar, *Encountering Development*; and Tlostanova and Mignolo, *Learning to Unlearn*.
6. Williams, *Keywords*, 64; Rist, *The History of Development*, 71, 75–6; Escobar, *Encountering Development*, 3, 23–4, 4.
7. Unger, *International Development*, 61; Williams and Young, "The International Politics of Social Transformation," 105; Rist, *The History of Development*, 83–6, 145, 162; Leyes, *The Rise and Fall of Development Theory*, 11–12. Rist insists that the non-aligned movement was not especially radical because its 1974 Declaration called for no more than a reinforcement of the "existing order of things" (i.e., economic growth, an expansion of world trade, and increased aid by industrial nations) (149). For a discussion

of critiques of modernization theory that emerged from the right, see McCarthy, *Race, Empire*, 209–13. On "high modernism" and modernization theory, see Scott, *Seeing like a State*.

8   Sachs, "Introduction," xvi–xviii.
9   Slaughter, *Human Rights, Inc.*, 272, 275.
10 Benjamin, "The Power of Books," 155–9; Altbach and Rathgeber, *Publishing in the Third World*, 7–8; Laugesen, "Books for the World," 136–7. See also Barnhisel, *Cold War Modernists*; and Laugesen, *Taking Books to the World*.
11 Behrstock, "Books for All?," 29–36; Behrstock, "National Book Development Councils in Africa," 78–88.
12 Brouillette, UNESCO *and the Fate of the Literary*, 94; Escarpit, *Trends in Worldwide Book Development*, 3–5.
13 For earlier book historical work on Cold War book development, see Barnhisel, *Cold War Modernists*; Laugesen, "Books for the World"; and Laugesen, *Taking Books to the World*. This scholarship has been supplemented more recently by studies such as Davis, *African Literature and the CIA*; Kalliney, *The Aesthetic Cold War*; and Popescu, *At Penpoint*. The different approaches to UNESCO are best exemplified in Slaughter, *Human Rights, Inc.*; and Brouillette, UNESCO *and the Fate of the Literary*.
14 Meren, "'Commend Me to the Yak,'" 345; Morrison, *Aid and Ebb Tide*, 2–3; Brushett, "'Trotsky in Pinstripes,'" 163–85. For a slightly different argument about what he understands to be the delayed emergence of diplomatic and international history in Canada, see Meren, "The Tragedies of Canadian International History," 534–66. Monographs on the Canadian history of development assistance include: Barry-Shaw, *Paved with Good Intentions*; Compton Brouwer, *Canada's Global Villagers*; Langford, *The Global Politics of Poverty in Canada*; Morrison, *Aid and Ebb Tide*; Muirhead and Harpelle, *IDRC*; and Webster, *Fire and the Full Moon*. This historiography is growing rapidly. Articles, edited collections, and dissertations that deal with the history broadly include: Brown, *Struggling for Effectiveness*; Brown, "Canada's Foreign Aid Before and After CIDA," 501–12; Cogan, "Sharing the Nation's Heart Globally?"; Donaghy and Webster, *A Samaritan State Revisited*; and Kane, "Canada and the Third World," 88–119. Spicer's key publication is *A Samaritan State?* For a recent assessment of the legacy of Spicer's book for Canadian historians, see Donaghy and Webster, *A Samaritan State Revisited*.
15 Development Education Centre and Latin American Working Group, "Corporate Power, the Canadian State, and Imperialism," 58–65; Swift, "Introduction," 15; Kane, "Canada and the Third World," 100. For critical evaluations of Canadian foreign policy and CIDA from the political economy tradition, see Carty, Smith, and LAWG, *Perpetuating Poverty*; Morrison, *Aid and Ebb Tide*; Swift and Clark, *Ties that Bind*; and Swift and Tomlinson,

Conflicts of Interest. For a history of CIDA's NGO division that nuances the critique of CIDA, see Brushett, "'Trotsky in Pinstripes.'" For a broader critique of the history of development that insists on the fact that the development paradigm has not narrowed the inequalities between the North and the South, see Rist, *The History of Development*. In *Aid and Ebb Tide*, Morrison notes that western donors agreed in 1969 to define Official Development Assistance as "flows to developing nations and multilateral institutions *provided by official agencies*, including state and local governments, or by their executive agencies" with the aim of promoting the economic development and welfare of developing countries and as being "concessional in character" (i.e., with a grant element of at least 25 per cent) (4).

16 Morrison, *Aid and Ebb Tide*, 13–14, 25; Langford, *The Global Politics*, 7. For the "domestic and foreign entanglements" of development, see also Meren, "'Commend Me to the Yak'"; and, in the US context, Immerwahr, *Thinking Small*. Immerwahr contends that, alongside its commitment to modernization in the postwar decades, the US was the "chief international bankroller of community development in the South. The communitarian projects and strategies it financed in India and the Philippines, for instance, ultimately returned home in the mid-1960s to inform the American War on Poverty" (9). For a full discussion of the Colombo Plan, see the section "Books as Colombo Plan Aid" in this book's chapter 2.

17 Morrison, *Aid and Ebb Tide*, 2.

18 Campbell-Miller, "Encounter and Apprenticeship," 37.

19 Bryant, *The Homing Place*, 20, 76–7, 65; Coleman, *White Civility*; Fee, *Literary Land Claims*. There are many versions of American exceptionalism, but the one most relevant to Bryant's argument is linked to Puritan thinkers such as John Winthrop, who propounded the belief that America's democratic promise had been granted to settlers as the chosen people of God. See Bremer, *John Winthrop*. See chapter 2 in Fee's *Literary Land Claims* for a discussion of John Richardson's conviction that the moral superiority of British North Americans over Americans rested on the former's treatment of Indigenous Peoples.

20 Bryant, *The Homing Place*, 79–80; Regan, *Unsettling the Settler Within*; Webster, "Foreign Policy, Diplomacy, and Decolonization," 155–92. Lester B. Pearson was awarded the Nobel Peace Prize in 1957 for his work on the Suez Canal Crisis, a fact that came to shape both domestic and international conceptions of Canada's relation to foreign affairs. The identification of Pearson with a legacy of "humane internationalism" was further assured by his role as chair of the World Bank's Commission on International Development, which produced *Partners in Development* (1969), a report that, according to Molly Kane, contributed to Canada's reputation as a "keen

player in international cooperation for development." See Kane, "Canada and the Third World," 95, as well as Brushett, "Partners in Development?," 84–102. On the question of the Cold War–era belief that Canada's associations with the Commonwealth, the UN, and the North Atlantic Treaty Alliance could counter the effects of American hegemony, see Meren, "The Tragedies of Canadian International History," 547–8.

21 Madokoro and McKenzie, "Introduction," 5, 11. See also the essays collected in Madokoro et al., *Dominion of Race*; and Meren, "The Tragedies of Canadian International History" (as well as a response from Marshall, "Réponse à 'The Tragedies of Canadian International History,'" 583–89).

22 Chapnick, "The Canadian Middle Power Myth," 23; Rubboli, "Canada, Peacekeeper to the World?," 149; Razack, *Dark Threats and White Knights*. For a slightly different reading of the peacekeeping narrative that emphasizes its erasure during the Stephen Harper years, see also McKay and Swift, *Warrior Nation*. Swift notes that this image of Canada has "helpful fixer" became especially "fraught with paradox" in the context of the American-led reorganization, during the 1980s, of development priorities to the benefit of multinational corporations and local elites (23).

23 Nguyen and Phu, *Refugee States*, 3–4, 11; Tunnicliffe, *Resisting Rights*, 5; Bryant, *The Homing Place*, 81.

24 Bryant, *The Homing Place*, 4; Fee, "Decolonizing Indigenous Oratures," 562; Street, *Social Literacies*, 3, 153–8; Gee, *Social Linguistics*; Fee, *Literary Land Claims*, 207. Walter Ong's *Orality and Literacy* has become central to the discipline of book history, as evidenced in its inclusion in canonical collections such as Finkelstein and McCleery, *The Book History Reader*. On the relationship between Ong's work and the Toronto School of Communication, see Fee, *Literary Land Claims*, 183.

25 Lowman and Barker, *Settler Identity and Colonialism in 21st-Century Canada*, 31; Veracini, *Settler Colonialism*, 46.

26 Benjamin, *U.S. Books Abroad*, 53–7; Benjamin, "The Power of Books," 159. For a full description of the various American book-related assistance programs of the second half of the twentieth century, see parts 5 and 6 of Benjamin, *U.S. Books Abroad*; Benjamin's book cites a 1981 USIA study that indicates that Soviet cultural and information work, including book export and media-related activity, was focused on sub-Saharan Africa and South Asia (53–4).

27 O'Sullivan, *The NGO Moment*.

28 Denning, *Culture in the Age of Three Worlds*, 2; Swift, "Introduction," 9; Escobar, *Encountering Development*, 31; Davis, "The Origins of the Third World," 55. See also Sauvy, "Trois mondes, une planète," 81–3 (originally published in 1952).

Chapter One

1. Johnson and Davis, "Introduction," 1–4; Fee, "Decolonizing Indigenous Oratures," 563. For scholarship that explores preprint manuscript traditions on the African continent and their relation to both oral and print cultures, see part 1 of Davis and Johnson, *The Book in Africa*.
2. Zell, "Introduction," 19; Peterson and Hunter, "Print Culture in Colonial Africa," 7, 12; Peterson, "Vernacular Language and Political Education," 165.
3. Wrong, Africa and the Making of Books, 3; Compton Brouwer, *Modern Women, Modernizing Men*, 96–7.
4. Registrar, University College to Prof. George M. Wrong, 25 May 1948, box 018, file 14, "Correspondence with George, Letters of sympathy re Margaret's death, 1948," George M. Wrong Family fonds, B2004-0010, University of Toronto (hereafter cited as GMW-UT); Wrong Armstrong, "There's Too Much Waiting to Be Done," 99. For information about Wrong's hiring by the ICCLA (her Canadian identity was considered an asset because it would please the American missionary societies), see box 1, file titled "African Literature Bureau Correspondence," GB 102, International Commission on Christian Literature for Africa fonds, School of Oriental and African Studies, University of London (hereafter cited as ICCLA-SOAS); and box 1, file titled "African Literature Bureau Papers, Etc," ICCLA-SOAS. Information related to contributions to ICCLA work can be found in the association's minutes; see box 2, ICCLA-SOAS. For information related to the role of the Inter Church Council of Canada in the "Books for Africa" project, see box 14, file titled "Books for Africa (Reports, etc.)," ICCLA-SOAS.
5. O'Sullivan, *The NGO Moment*, 2, 5, 8; Compton Brouwer, "When Missions Became Development," 663; Mason, *Home Feelings*. For an overview of the many nonstate actors (including missionaries) involved in literacy work in Canada in the late nineteenth century, see the Preface to Mason, *Home Feelings*. On the tensions produced by the overlapping efforts of Canadian churches and NGOs in 1960s Canada, as well as the "newer kind of church experience" that became useful to Canada's NGO movement after 1965, see Marshall and Sterparn, "Oxfam Aid to Canada's First Nations, 1962–1975," 314, 322.
6. Rist, *The History of Development*, 44–5, 37. As we will see, most scholarship on book development emphasizes its postwar history and the postwar institutions (state and international institutions as well as NGOs) central to this history. Chapters 2 and 3 of this book discuss both state and international institutions and the relevant scholarship; chapter 3 also focuses on NGOs and the relevant scholarship, and NGOs are the focus of chapter 4.
7. The quotation from the Le Zoute report is taken from Matasci, Jerónimo, and Dores, "Introduction," 13.

8   Cooper, *Africa Since 1940*, 27; Allshorn, *King Khama*, 20. The complete "Little Books for Africa" can be found in box 40, ICCLA-SOAS. The complete "African Home Library" can be found in box 41, ICCLA-SOAS. The ICCLA sought manuscripts from Africa, Europe, and North America for these series and contributed to the cost of their publication.

9   Hodge, "Beyond Dependency, 621–2, 624–5; Bonneuil, "Development as Experiment," 259, 269; Cooper, *Decolonization and African Society*, 18, 68; Van Beusekom and Hodgson, "Lessons Learned?," 31. On the new pressures that colonies placed on the British metropole in the immediate postwar period and the reforms that the Colonial Office instituted in response, see Cooper, *Africa Since 1940*; Cooper, "Modernizing Colonialism and the Limits of Empire," 63–72; and Unger, *International Development: A Postwar History*, 50–5.

10 Compton Brouwer, *Modern Women, Modernizing Men*, 98; Compton Brouwer, "Margaret Wrong's Literacy Work and the 'Remaking of Woman' in Africa, 1929–1948," 430; King, *Pan-Africanism and Education*, 74, 22, 103; Küster, "'Book Learning' versus 'Adapted Education,'" 85. On the Phelps-Stokes Commission and its influence on missionary organizations and colonial governments in the interwar period, see also Kallaway, *The Changing Face of Colonial Education in Africa*. For DuBois's criticism of the Phelps-Stokes Commissions, see DuBois, "Education in Africa," 86–9. As King points out in chapter 6 of *Pan-Africanism and Education*, the second Phelps-Stokes Commission (in East Africa) was indeed guilty of the charges DuBois was making: the commission's findings affirmed the value of industrial education for the needs of the European economy, diminished the importance of higher education for Africans, and aimed to suppress emergent African dissent.

11 Berman, "American Influence on African Education," 133–4, 138, 132; Groves, *The Planting of Christianity in Africa*, 110, 115. The quotation from the 1925 Memo issued by the Advisory Committee on Native Education in British Tropical Africa is quoted in Küster, "'Book Learning' versus 'Adapted Education,'" 85. For a summary of the education policy produced by an Advisory Committee of the Colonial Office after 1923, see *African Education*, 2–5. This history notes that the Colonial Office first established the Advisory Committee on Native Education in the British Tropical African Dependencies in 1923; although it changed names, it continued to function into the period of the Second World War (3–4).

12 Groves, *The Planting of Christianity in Africa*, 82, 134. I take the information about the ICCLA's funding from Wrong, *Africa and the Making of Books*, 3. This information is confirmed in Wrong's reports on her various tours of Africa, which can be found in box 018, files 01–04, GMW-UT.

13 Margaret Wrong, "Outline of Report," 7 October 1933, box 018, file 01, "ICCLA, 1930–1935," GMW-UT; Margaret Wrong, "Report No. 1," 9 March 1933, box 018, file 01, "ICCLA, 1930–1935," GMW-UT; Margaret Wrong, "Report on Tours in Africa 1936 and 1939," undated, box 018, file 02, "ICCLA, 1936–1938," GMW-UT. On the recommendations made by the two Education Commissions of the Phelps-Stokes Fund, see Berman, "American Influence" and Groves, *The Planting of Christianity in Africa*, 108–10.

14 Margaret Wrong, "Report on Tours in Africa, 1936 and 1939," box 018, file 02, "ICCLA, 1936–1938," GMW-UT; Margaret Wrong, "Secretary's Tour in Africa: Notes on Some Aspects of Literature Policy Arising Out of the Tour," 1939, box 018, File 03, "ICCLA, 1939," GMW-UT. For Wrong's letters related to her 1939 tour, see box 018, file 03, "ICCLA, 1939," GMW-UT.

15 Margaret Wrong, "Memorandum with regard to a grant from the Carnegie Corporation," 12 April 1935, box 018, file 01, "ICCLA, 1930–1935," GMW-UT; Cooper, *Africa Since 1940*, 30–4; Margaret Wrong, "Letter IV," 30 Oct 1936, file 02, "ICCLA, 1936–1938," GMW-UT; Higginson, "Liberating the Captives," 70; Cooper, *Decolonization and African Society*, 58–60, 130; Wrong, *The Land and Life of Africa*, 3. In *Decolonization and African Society*, Cooper describes "stabilization" as the strategy adopted by the British colonial bureaucracies in Africa after the mid-1930s; unlike previous approaches to African migrant labour, which had emphasized the importance of frequent return to the village as a means of preventing "detribalization," "stabilization" aimed to bring male labourers and their wives to urban and industrial sites of labour on a permanent basis, as a means of building a more "stable, more acculturated, more experienced labor force" (2).

16 Wrong, *Africa and the Making of Books*, 29.

17 "Biographies of Africans," 7; "Notices of Books," 14; Wrong, "Reading Matter for Literacy Campaigns," 10–12. A discussion of the four "simples" and their relation to missionary fear regarding political protest in Kenya can be found in King, *Pan-Africanism and Education*, 73, 138. Wrong's bibliography was printed as an appendix to *Mass Education in African Society*, which I discuss later in this chapter.

18 *Phelps-Stokes Reports on Education in Africa*, abridged with introduction by L.J. Lewis, 63–6. Ngũgĩ wa Thiong'o, baptized James Ngũgĩ, is a Kenyan writer and academic known for his turn away in the late 1960s from literary production in English to work in Kikuyu. See Ngũgĩ, "On the Abolition of the English Department," 438-2.

19 Compton Brouwer, *Modern Women, Modernizing Men*, 101; Margaret Wrong, "The Importance of Literatures in African Languages," undated address to the Royal Anthropological Society, box 9, file titled "Articles, 1940–1945," ICCLA-SOAS. Colonial governments in Africa differed on

the question of language and education: under the policy of indirect rule, governments in British territories developed systems of education in the late colonial period that favoured African languages for the first six years, but the French and Portuguese favoured education in European languages. On this point, see *African Education*, 79–84.

20 Cooper, *Africa Since 1940*, 20–65; Cooper, "Modernizing Colonialism," 70.
21 Jones, "Introduction," 13; "Report 1939–1940," box 14, file titled "Listen 1931–40," ICCLA-SOAS; Margaret Wrong, "Circular Letter," 26 December 1941, box 018, file 04, "ICCLA, 1940–1948," GMW-UT; Margaret Wrong, "Circular Letter," 10 February 1941, box 018, file 04, "ICCLA, 1940–1948," GMW-UT; Margaret Wrong, "The ICCLA, 1939–1945," 30 November 1945, box 018, file 04, "ICCLA, 1940–1948," GMW-UT; Wrong, *Five Points for Africa*, 89; Groves, *The Planting of Christianity in Africa*, 281. The British Council's support of *Listen* appears to have significantly increased its circulation, or at least it meant that more copies were being sent to Africa; the periodical's annual reports put circulation at 3,500 copies a year in 1938–39 and at over thirteen thousand in 1944–45. "Report 1938–1939," box 14, file titled "Listen, 1930–40," ICCLA-SOAS; and "Report on Listen, News from Far and Near, 1944–1945," box 14, file titled "Listen, 1941–50," ICCLA-SOAS.
22 Wrong, *Five Points*, 96; Colonial Office, *Mass Education in African Society*, 48–9; Huxley, "Colonies and Freedom," 106–9; Sluga, "UNESCO and the (One) World of Julian Huxley," 407. For other wartime essays by Wrong on the topic of educating the community outside of schools, see box 10, file titled "Articles on Colonial Development, 1940–1945," ICCLA-SOAS.
23 Davis, Campbell, and Wrong, *Africa Advancing*, 78–9, 81–4. For further biographical information on Wrong's African American collaborators Jackson Davis and Thomas M. Campbell, see Davis et al., *Africa Advancing*, 3–4.
24 Berman, "American Influence on African Education," 144; Küster, "'Book Learning' Versus 'Adapted Education,'" 85; *African Education*, 3–4.
25 Wrong, *Five Points*, 91; Davis et al., *Africa Advancing*, 143–4, 154–5, 165, 125. On the "Antigonish Way," see Sacouman, "Underdevelopment and the Structural Origins of Antigonish Movement Co-Operatives in Eastern Nova Scotia," 66–85.
26 Challiss, "Phelps-Stokeism and Education in Zimbabwe," 116–18; Küster, "'Book Learning' versus 'Adapted Education,'" 82–3, 92–3; Davis et al., *Africa Advancing*, 142–3.
27 T.M. Campbell, "Miss Margaret Wrong: A few notes on my travels with her and Jackson Davis in West Africa, 1944–45," 22 September 1948, box 018, file 04, "ICCLA, 1940–1948," GMW-UT.
28 Earle, *Colonial Buganda and the End of Empire*, 90–1, 103–7; Challiss, "Phelps-Stokeism," 119–22; Lewis and Wrong, *Towards a Literate Africa*;

Lewis, *Education and Political Independence in Africa and Other Essays*, 55, 39–63, 91. For a full history of the Margaret Wrong Memorial Fund prizes and their relation to late colonial development (as well as an appendix that lists all winners), see Mason, "The Margaret Wrong Memorial Fund," 26–55.

29 Wrong's work in support of African authorship was demonstrated in many ways through her career. Both ICCLA periodicals, *Listen* and *Books for Africa*, supported African writing (contributions from African authors, promotion of African-authored materials, and, in the latter case, the promotion of the International African Institute's vernacular literary competition for African authors). In the report of her first (1933) ICCLA tour, *Africa and the Making of Books*, Wrong argues that "creative work by Africans who will express the genius of their race in their mother-tongue is essential" (24–5). As Compton Brouwer notes in *Modern Women*, Wrong's second (1936) ICCLA tour demonstrates her increasing interest in the question of African authorship; at a meeting of black South African writers that she attended on this tour, she met a number of African writers whose work she later featured in *Books for Africa* (108–9).

30 Margaret Wrong, "Outline of Report," 7 October 1933, box 018, file 01, "ICCLA, 1930–1935," GMW-UT; Margaret Wrong, "Secretary's Tour in Africa: Notes on Some Aspects of Literature Policy Arising out of the Tour," 1939, box 018, file 03, "ICCLA, 1939," GMW-UT; Margaret Wrong, "The ICCLA, 1939–1945," 30 November 1945, box 018, file 04, "ICCLA, 1940–1948," GMW-UT.

31 Groves, *The Planting of Christianity in Africa*, 291; Oduyoye, "The Role of Christian Publishing Houses Today," 229–30.

32 Davis, "Creating A Book Empire: Longmans in Africa," 135–6.

33 Ritter, *Imperial Encore*, 48–51; Wrong, *Africa and the Making of Books*, 9; Charles Granston Richards, "Notes on Adult Literacy: Outlines of a Scheme for Bookshop Contribution," 25 April 1944, box 26, file titled "East African Literature Bureau, 1944–54," ICCLA-SOAS.

34 Ritter, *Imperial* Encore, 54–8, 62–71. While publishers' memoirs and company histories have tended to narrate the history of British commercial publishers in late twentieth-century Africa as, in Davis's words, a "cultural mission, vital to the education and enlightenment of Africa," African publishers and postcolonial scholars have cast these same publishers as "agents of neocolonialism or cultural imperialism that served to prevent the growth of an indigenous publishing industry." Davis, "Creating A Book Empire," 128; Bejjitt, "Heinemann's African Writers Series and the Rise of James Ngugi," 224. The former category includes books such as Hill, *In Pursuit of Publishing* and company histories such as Sutcliffe's *The Oxford University Press*. The latter category includes Makotsi and Nyariki, *Publishing and the Book Trade in Kenya*; Nottingham, "Establishing an

African Publishing Industry," 139–44; and Onibonoje, "Wanted! A Cultural Revolution, Not a Dialogue!" 262–76. For scholarship on Oxford University Press's Three Crowns Series and Heinemann's African Writers Series that is generally critical, see part 2 of Davis, *Creating Postcolonial Literature*; chapters 2 and 3 of Ching-Liang Low, *Publishing the Postcolonial*; Lizarríbar, *Something Else Will Stand Beside It*; and chapter 5 of Ritter, *Imperial Encore*.

35 Allison, "State Participation in Publishing," 59–65; Onibonoje, "Wanted! A Cultural Revolution, Not a Dialogue!" 268–9, 272. See chapter 4 of this book for a discussion of post-independence educational policy in Zambia.

36 Sluga, "UNESCO and the (One) World," 410–12. The groundnut scheme in British Tanganyika (now Tanzania) was a late colonial development plan that was meant to ease food shortages in postwar Britain. Led by a private company with support from UNESCO, the scheme was a failure because of planners' inadequate knowledge of local conditions. See Unger, *International Development*, 52–4.

37 Alfred Moore to Wrong, 26 June 1946, box 23, file titled "Literacy: Correspondence, 1938–1950," ICCLA-SOAS; Dorn and Ghodsee, "The Cold War Politicization of Literacy," 373–98.

38 Barker and Escarpit, *The Book Hunger*, 11–25. Wrong's references to "famine of books" can be found, for example, in Wrong, *West African Journey*. The collaboratively authored *Mass Education in African Society* (published one year prior) employs the phrase "famine of reading material."

Chapter Two

1 Mount, *Arrival*; Broten, *The Lumberjack Report*, 31–2; Escarpit, *Trends in Worldwide Book Development*, 3.
2 Johnston and Lawson, "Settler Colonies," 369, 370.
3 Litt, "The State and the Book," 39–40.
4 Parker, "The Agency System and Branch-Plant Publishing," 166–7. The report of the Ontario Royal Commission on Book Publishing notes that, in 1970, foreign-owned firms produced only 27 per cent of all Canadian literature (including fiction, poetry, and criticism). Ontario, *Canadian Publishers and Canadian Publishing*, 59–62. In a 1996 study, Rowland Lorimer states that Canadian-owned publishers produce nearly 90 per cent of Canadian-authored books. Lorimer, "Book Publishing," 6. For more recent statistics on this question, see Lorimer, *Ultra Libris*, 161–2.
5 Ninkovich, *The Diplomacy of Ideas*, 167, 154, 156.
6 Lacy, "The Overseas Book Program of the United States Government," 191; Barnhisel, *Cold War Modernists*, 12–13, 97, 118, 13–20, 99–111, 98. The term "vital center" was coined by historian Arthur Schlesinger in his 1949 book of the same name.

7   Laugesen, *Taking Books to the World*, 3, 6; Laugesen, "Books for the World," 126–44; Brouillette, *UNESCO and the Fate of the Literary*, 149–56, 31, 33, 42–3.
8   Unger, *International Development*, 55–8, 67.
9   Ekbladh, *The Great American Mission*, 74; Cullather, "Development and Technopolitics," 107; Scott, *Seeing like a State*, 4; Oakman. *Facing Asia*, 142–9. On the relevance of high modernism to Canadian aid efforts in the postwar period, see Meren, "'Commend me to the Yak,'" 349–50.
10 Stephens, *Study of Canadian Government Information Abroad, 1942–1972*, 1–48 (chapter 2), 4–9 (chapter 3), 1–18 (chapter 4), 2 (chapter 3); Hilliker and Barry, *Canada's Department of External Affairs*, 29–30. Gary Evans documents John Grierson's unprecedented success in connecting international audiences to Canadian materials. During Grierson's tenure at the head of the WIB, for instance, the global audience for NFB newsreels was estimated at forty to fifty million a week. Evans, *John Grierson and the National Film Board*, 224–5.
11 Rushton, "The Origins and Development of Canada's Public Diplomacy," 84; Tippett, *Making Culture*, 181; Druick, "International Cultural Relations as a Factor in Postwar Canadian Cultural Policy," 181, 185.
12 Berland, "Nationalism and the Modernist Legacy," 18; Litt, *The Muses, the Masses, and the Massey Commission*, 17; Litt, "The State and the Book," 39. Through the 1931 Statute of Westminster, Britain granted Canada full legislative independence, excepting the repeal, amendment, or alteration of the British North America Act. Canada did not immediately take up all of these new powers; it was not until 1949 that Britain's Judicial Committee of the Privy Council ceased to be the nation's highest court. Andrew McIntosh and Norman Hillmer, "The Statute of Westminster," *Canadian Encyclopedia*, updated 29 April 2020, https://www.thecanadianencyclopedia.ca/en/article/statute-of-westminster. For Dowler's argument, see Dowler, "The Cultural Industries." On the enmeshment of the national cultural institutions that emerged in Canada in the postwar decades and the same period's internationally oriented security state, see Kristmanson, *Plateaus of Freedom*, 86–94.
13 Canada, "The Projection of Canada Abroad," in *Report of the Royal Commission on National Development*, 253–67, https://www.collectionscanada.gc.ca/massey/h5-437-e.html.
14 Stephens, *Study of Canadian Government*, 2–18 (chapter 4); N.A. Robertson, "Memorandum for the Minister," vol. 7797, file 12569-2-40, Department of External Affairs fonds, RG 25, Library and Archives Canada (hereafter cited as DEA-LAC). Through the latter half of the 1950s, receiving nations/regions included Japan, India, Brazil, Chile, Colombia, Ghana, the West Indies, Spain, Poland, Belgium, Southern Rhodesia, and Iceland. The 1954 restructuring of the program coincided with the arrival of Archibald Day as head of the Information Division. Focusing book donations on particular

nations would, Day hoped, establish "the nuclei of future nationally-known centres of knowledge about Canada," serving also as potential future "institutes of Canadian studies." Cavell, "Canadiana Abroad," 86.

15 Cavell, "Canadiana Abroad," 84; "Annex A: A List of Canadian Books and Periodicals for Inclusion in Major Presentations Under the Annual Book Presentation Programme," vol. 7797, file 125-2-40, 1.2, DEA-LAC; Canada and Pierre Berton, *Canada from Sea to Sea*, 102.

16 Norman Hillmer, "Douglas Valentine LePan," *Canadian Encyclopedia*, updated 25 February 2015, https://www.thecanadianencyclopedia.ca/en/article/douglas-valentine-lepan"; LePan, *The Net and the Sword*, 18, 19. LePan's External Affairs career stretched from 1945 to 1959. During these years, he published his first two books of poetry – *The Wounded Prince and Other Poems* (Chatto & Windus, 1948) and *The Net and the Sword* (Clarke, Irwin, 1953). From 1959 to 1979, LePan taught English literature at Queen's University and the University of Toronto. As LePan makes clear in his chapter on Eliot in *Bright Glass of Memory*, his early devotion to Eliot's poetry led him, through Wyndham Lewis, to a 1943 meeting in London with Eliot at Faber and Faber. The two formed an acquaintance that endured through the war and into the immediate postwar period when LePan was still frequently in London. Though an avid admirer of Eliot's oeuvre, LePan's essay quibbles with Eliot's theory of impersonality and with his insistence that a poet's biography is irrelevant to the work. The very things he admires most in Eliot's poetry are the qualities of nostalgia, enigma, precision, and "perfection of form and finish" that he admired in the man. LePan, *Bright Glass of Memory*, 144. The moccasin flower (*cypripedium acaule*, also commonly known as pink lady's slipper or whip-poor-will shoes) is native to the eastern United States and eastern and central Canada. It boasts three pink petals, the largest of which resembles a slipper or moccasin. LePan's use of the name draws on the associations the name carries with the word for "footwear" in many Algonquian languages: Plains Ojibwe (makisin or makizinan), Siksika (niitsitsikin) and Plains Cree (maskisin). René R. Gadacz, "Moccasin," *Canadian Encyclopedia*, updated 19 June 2020, https://thecanadianencyclopedia.ca/en/article/moccasin.

17 N.A. Robertson, 31 August 1959, "Memorandum for the Minister," vol. 7797, file 12569-2-40, DEA-LAC; Benjamin, *U.S. Books Abroad*, 60–2.

18 Brooks, "Uncertain Embrace," 7–9; Robertson, "Memorandum for the Minister," vol. 7797, file 12569-2-40, DEA-LAC.

19 Cavell, "Canadiana Abroad," 81; Ritchie, "Economic Division, to D.W. Bartlett, Dept. of Trade and Commerce," 12 December 1956, vol. 7797, file 12569-2-40, 1.1, DEA-LAC. Laura Beattie's 1953 memorandum regarding Jean Bruchési's *Le Canada* expressed alarm at the high price ($6.75 for

a paperback) of its English-language edition, published in 1952 by the domestically owned Ryerson Press; she suggested that her colleagues should investigate the cost of the book in France because "it is printed there." The department opted to purchase only two copies of the book (probably because the Quebec government ordered two thousand copies), but this order was for the French-language edition published by F. Nathan in Paris and was placed with Paillard, a French publishing house, an arrangement that produced a significant discount. Laura Beattie, "Memorandum for E.H. Norman," 17 February 1953, vol. 4433, file 12569-40, DEA-LAC; Paul Malone, Information Division, to Supplies and Properties Division, Department of External Affairs Memorandum, 16 September 1953, vol. 4433, file 12569-40, DEA-LAC.

20 Denning, *Culture in the Age of Three Worlds*, 79, 76–81; Berland, "Nationalism and the Modernist Legacy," 22; Litt, "The State and the Book," 36; Litt, *The Muses*, 85. A corollary of this valuing of folk culture can be found in UNESCO's first major book industry program, the Collection of Representative Works, which was created in 1948 to support the translation and cross-border dissemination of the world's classic literature. A collection of global "classics" in translation (mostly into English and French), the Collection of Representative Works aimed to grant what were cast as less developed cultures access to the best of western literature, while making folk cultures accessible to those nations where industrialized life threatened high culture. Brouillette, *UNESCO and the Fate of the Literary*, 11–12, 29.

21 Cavell, "Canadiana Abroad," 84; Joshee, "The Federal Government and Citizenship Education for Newcomers," 110.

22 Tory, "Introduction," v; P.C. Dobell, Information Division, "Memorandum for Supplies and Properties Division," 22 November 1952, vol. 4433, file 12569-40, DEA-LAC; Bruce Keith, Information Division, "Requisition for Books and Publications," 25 November 1952, vol. 4433, file 12569-40, DEA-LAC; Paul Malone, Information Division, to Supplies and Properties Division, Department of External Affairs Memorandum, 3 June 1953, vol. 4433, file 12569-40, DEA-LAC; Paul Malone, Information Division, to Supplies and Properties Division, Department of External Affairs Memorandum, 20 May 1953, vol. 4433, file 12569-40, DEA-LAC; Canada, "Canadian Council for Reconstruction Through UNESCO," in Report of the Royal Commission on National Development in the Arts, Letters and Sciences, 1949–51, https://collectionscanada.ca/massey/h5-318-e.html (hereafter cited as "Canadian Council for Reconstruction"), 4; Gerson, "Design and Ideology," 67. For more information on the CCRU, see chapter 3 of this book.

23 Rampure, "'Harlequin Has Built an Empire,'" 186; "Margaret Paull," 20; Brouillette and Michon, "Control and Content in Mass-Market Distribution,"

405; Campbell, "William Collins During World War II," 58; Gerson, "Design and Ideology," 68–9. For a useful history of the White Circle series, including a partial bibliography that clearly demonstrates the dominance of British writers, see Doug Sulipa, "Collins White Circle 1942–1952," *Doug Sulipa's Comic World*, accessed 9 July 2024, http://www.dougcomicworld.com/inventory/INVENTORY-CollinsPaperbackSite.html. As Gerson notes in "Design and Ideology," due to the fact that the papers of the Canadian Collins subsidiary were destroyed, the information regarding the print runs for any of the versions of *A Pocketful* is unavailable. Gerson, "Design and Ideology," 67. Gerson's essay provides important details regarding differences among the three editions of *A Pocketful*, as well as a description of the physical book, which is indeed a "pocketful" (the hardback measures 7.5 inches by 4.5 inches, not much bigger than the paperback and much smaller than a standard hardback). Gerson, "Design and Ideology," 68–9.

24 Gerson, "Design and Ideology," 72–3; Veracini, *Settler Colonialism*, 46. It is important to note that the style of engraving that Hyde used for the images in *A Pocketful* is associated not merely with fine-press work but also with the visual style of Anglo-American leftist publications of the 1930s, including Canadian publications such as *New Frontier* (1936–37), a magazine that featured Hyde's work. For examples of Hyde's engravings for *New Frontier* see Senechal Carney, "*New Frontier* (1936–1937) and the Antifascist Press in Canada," 232–56. Hyde's use of wood engravings for leftist critique is also exemplified in his 1951 "wordless novel," *Southern Cross: A Novel of the South Seas*, which visually narrates American postwar nuclear testing in the South Pacific. On settler "disavowal," see Veracini, *Settler Colonialism*, 75–86. One of these strategies is to disallow the existence or the claims of Indigenous Peoples; many of the texts collected in *A Pocketful* might be read as exemplifications of this strategy, including the excerpt from L.C. Douthwaite's 1939 *The Royal Canadian Mounted Police*.

25 Tory, "Introduction," v; Johnston and Lawson, "Settler Colonies," 365. In "William Collins During WWII," Grant Campbell documents the unusually high production standards of Collins's Canadian branch during the Second World War. Under Frank Appleton, the firm advocated high-quality production (standards of layout and typography, wide margins, large type, etc.), despite wartime shortages of paper and other materials. Campbell contends that Appleton and other Canadian publishers resented poor British production standards and saw higher standards in Canada as a sign of growing national pride (56–8). Campbell does not discuss an obvious exception to this line of thinking – the White Circle paperbacks. In "Design and Ideology," Gerson notes that postwar shortages of paper likely account for the low quality of *A Pocketful* (69).

26 Lecker, *Keepers of the Code*, 14, 190; Pacey, *A Book of Canadian Stories*, xvi, 17. John Howe was in fact one of the earliest printers in the region and in British North America and, with his two eldest sons and his brother-in-law, went on to dominate Halifax printing. Lockhart Fleming, "First Printers and the Spread of the Press," 61, 65. For further information regarding Joseph Howe's 1835 libel case, see Parker, "Joseph Howe and the Freedom of the Press," 330–1.

27 Lois Kernaghan, "Novascotian," *Canadian Encyclopedia*, updated 4 March 2015, https://thecanadianencyclopedia.ca/en/article/novascotian; Pacey, *A Book of Canadian Stories*, xxxvi. A notable exception to my point about the invisibility of economic relations to early scholarship on literature in Canada is E.K. Brown's *On Canadian Poetry*, which acknowledges that "economic" factors help to explain the "difficulties" faced by English Canadian writers. Brown, *On Canadian Poetry*, 6.

28 Spicer, "Clubmanship Upstaged," 23–33. For the war debt argument, see Cogan, "Sharing the Nation's Heart Globally?," 29–33; and LePan, *Bright Glass*, 171. For the decolonization argument, see Unger, *International Development*, 65.

29 Hilliker and Barry, *Canada's Department*, 82–3; Canada, *Canada and the Colombo Plan*, 3; LePan, *Bright Glass*, 213.

30 LePan, *Bright Glass*, 212–18; Hilliker and Barry, *Canada's Department*, 83–5; Spicer, "Clubmanship Upstaged," 29, 31–2. Spicer's essay, published in 1970, condemns the Colombo Plan as a Victorian hangover that could not survive the modern era of foreign aid represented by, for instance, the establishment of the Canadian International Development Agency in 1968. Spicer, "Clubmanship Upstaged," 28–33. Canada withdrew from the plan in 1992.

31 Meren, "'Commend Me to the Yak,'" 348–51; LePan, *Bright Glass*, 150; Canada, *Canada and the Colombo Plan*, 13–24. On the general lack of Canadian experience in 1950 with bilateral aid for the purposes of development in the global South, see Campbell-Miller, "Encounter and Apprenticeship," 27–52. On the "tied aid" that characterized bilateral agreements under the Colombo Plan, see also Campbell-Miller, "Encounter and Apprenticeship," 35–6.

32 Scurr, "Cold War by 'Other Means,'" 31, 83–138, 128, 107, 134; Vorano, "Inuit Art," 423–8; "Notes for the Under-Secretary's Statement Before the Standing Committee on External Affairs," 20 February 1956, vol. 7797, file 12569-2-40, 1.1, DEA-LAC. For a full history of the involvement of the Department of External Affairs in the "Canadian Eskimo Art" touring exhibit of the later 1950s and early 1960s, see chapters 5 and 6 of Vorano, "Inuit Art," as well as Wakeham, "At the Intersection."

33 M.Q. Dench, Information Division to W.M. Agnes, Establishments and Organization Division, 30 May 1956, vol. 7797, file 12569-2-40, DEA-

LAC; "Extract from the Minutes of the Standing Committee on External Affairs," 17 May 1956, vol. 4433, file 12569-1-40, DEA-LAC; J.F.M. Newton, Information Division, to Mr Mathews, 27 February 1958, vol. 7797, file 12569-2-40, 1.1, DEA-LAC; E.R. Bellemare to W.K. Lamb, 20 December 1957, vol. 7797, file 12569-2-40, 1.1, DEA-LAC; "Draft Memorandum: Special Book Presentation Programme for the Colombo Plan," 24 May 1957, vol. 7797, file 12569-2-40, 1.1, DEA-LAC.

34 Marcuse and Whitaker, *Cold War Canada*, 33–57.

35 Cavell, "Introduction," 8. For information regarding co-publication arrangements, see Young, "The Macmillan Company of Canada in the 1930s," 119–20. The United States did not recognize Canadian copyright until the late twentieth century; from 1790 to 1962, editions "first published in Canada automatically forfeited copyright protection in the United States." MacLaren, *Dominion and Agency*, 11. For a thorough discussion of the possibility that *The Fall of a Titan* was ghostwritten, see Sawatsky, *Gouzenko*. Sawatsky's text, which compiles assorted testimony from those who had contact with Gouzenko, offers ample evidence of Gouzenko's considerable literary ambitions. Journalist Willson Woodside recalls, for instance, that Gouzenko "wanted the Nobel prize for the book and went through some considerable effort to get it." RCMP officer and friend Don Fast notes that Gouzenko was not impressed by the Governor General's Award and quotes him as saying "This is just a minor prize. There should be more" (148). For reviews of *The Fall of a Titan*, see Granville Hicks, "Decline and Fall of a Russian Idol," *New York Times*, 18 July 1954, BR1; and Glendy Culligan, "Gouzenko Turns Novelist: Intellectual Conflict in Russia," *Washington Post and Times Herald*, 18 July 1954, B6.

36 Canadian Embassy in Washington, DC, to Under-Secretary of State, Department of External Affairs, 1 February 1957, vol. 7797, file 12569-2-40, 1.1, DEA-LAC. The USIA program in question is not named, but it is likely the Books in Translation Program. As Barnhisel explains in *Cold War Modernists*, the Books in Translation Program, like its sister USIA book programs in this decade, eschewed the "polemic anti-Communist tracts popular among conservative readers in the United States" but admitted books such as George Orwell's *Animal Farm* or Czeslaw Milosz's *Captive Mind* because, like *The Fall of a Titan*, these books "attacked the lack of intellectual freedom in the Communist world without the hysterical tone of many domestic anti-Communist publications" (116–17).

37 Meren, "'Commend me to the Yak,'" 345–6, 353–4; Farish and Lackenbauer, "High Modernism in the Arctic," 517–44; Canada, *Canada and the Colombo Plan*, 2. The 1968 Colombo Plan Report is quoted in Campbell-Miller, "Encounter and Apprenticeship," 46. While the federal government largely

ignored the Inuit until the end of the Second World War, the high modernist thinking that informed Indian Affairs' policy after 1945 came to bear during the late 1940s on Inuit populations, as well. Frank Tester and Peter Kulchyski outline the complicated history of the relation of Inuit to the Government of Canada: a 1939 Supreme Court decision rendered the Inuit a federal responsibility (a responsibility the federal government had long rejected based on the argument that the British North America Act of 1867 included a clause referring to "Indians" but not to the Inuit, whose territory was not located in the area recognized by the act). The federal government did not begin to assume this responsibility until the early 1950s. Tester and Kulchyski, *Tammarniit*, 13–42.

38 Tester and Kulchyski, *Tammarniit*, 56. According to Tester and Kulchyski, the Department of Resources and Development (renamed Northern Affairs and National Resources in December of 1953) and its minister were "swamped" by angry letters responding to *The People of the Deer*; these came not only from Canada, but also Britain, Europe, New Zealand, and the United States (56–7). Reviews tended to be less indignant and more critical of Mowat's assertions. Two scientists (a botanist and an anthropologist) from the National Museum of Canada published reviews that discredited many of the claims in the book; see A.E. Porsild, "Review of *People of the Deer*, by Farley Mowat," *The Beaver*, June 1952, 47–9; and Douglas Leechman, "Review of *People of the Deer*," *Canadian Geographical Journal* nos 44–45, August 1952, v–vi. P.G. Downes of *The New York Times* was impressed by the book's style but feared that "more informed and critical evaluation will not be kind." P.G. Downes, "Sanctuary of the North: *People of the Deer* by Farley Mowat," *New York Times*, 24 February 1952, p. BR4, ProQuest Historical Newspapers. Mowat uses the term "Ihalmuit" to refer to the inland Inuit around Ennadai Lake; historians Tester and Kulchyski use the term "Ennadai Lake Inuit." Following the practice of the community, I use the term "Ahiarmiut."

39 Mowat, *The People of the Deer*, 302–3, 191, 304, 305–6, 312, 318. Mowat's *The Desperate People* (1959) offers a kind of tragic sequel to his first book in that it offers an account of the 1957 government relocation of the Ennadai Lake Inuit to Henik Lake.

40 Canada, *House of Commons Debates*, vol. 1, 768–74; Canada, *House of Commons Debates*, vol. 2, 1244–45, 1679; Tester and Kulchyski, *Tammarniit*, 218–20, 56, 58; Meren, "'Commend Me to the Yak,'" 356–7. Tester and Kulchyski focus on government relocations in the eastern Arctic but turn to the relocations of the Ennadai Lake Inuit in chapter 5. As they note, the 1957 relocation to Henik Lake was a disaster; a subsequent forced relocation to Eskimo Point (now Arviat) followed in 1958 (218–37).

41 Harvey Hickey, "Provinces Need Aid: Smallwood," *Globe and Mail*, 19 October 1955, 1, ProQuest Historical Newspapers. On surging public support for the Colombo Plan in the mid-1950s, see Cogan, "Sharing the Nation's Heart," 56–71.

42 Greer, "1837–38," 2; Lower, *Colony to Nation*, 362. On Diefenbaker's "northern vision," see Farish and Lackenbauer, "High Modernism in the Arctic," 518. On Berton's "cultural brand" and the North, see A.B. McKillop, "Books, Brands, and Berton," *The Underhill Review: A Forum of History, Ideas, and Culture*, Fall 2009, https://www3.carleton.ca/underhillreview/09/fall/essays/mckillop.htm.

43 LePan, *Bright Glass*, 224, 223, 226; Cogan, "Sharing the Nation's Heart," 62–3; Gorman, "Race, the Commonwealth, and the United Nations," 141, 153.

44 Cavell, "Canadiana Abroad," 88. For information regarding the Canada Council's Aid to Publications program or its later Book Purchases, see "Corporate Reports: Annual Reports," *Canada Council for the Arts*, accessed 9 July 2024, https://canadacouncil.ca/about/governance/corporate-reports. For contemporary studies of the Canadian government's uses of books as instruments of cultural diplomacy, see, for instance, Fuller and Billingham, "CanLit(e): Fit for Export?," 114–27.

Chapter Three

1 On book "dumping" as an early twentieth-century practice of American publishers that Canadian publishers decried, see Parker, "Trade and Regional Book Publishing in English," 165. On the continued relation of northern-based book donation programs to Africa and "book dumping" in the present (and on the role that northern-based conglomerate publishers play in this practice), see Zell, "Book Donation Programmes," 12.

2 Louise Rohonczy, "Discussion Paper on Special Grants Policy," 4 March 1974, vol. 37, file 26, "Overseas Book Centre, 1973–74," MG28 I323, Canadian University Service Overseas/Service Universitaire Canadien Outre-Mer fonds, Library and Archives Canada (hereafter cited as CUSO/SUCO-LAC).

3 Carty, Smith, and LAWG, *Perpetuating Poverty*, 28; Druick, "International Cultural Relations as a Factor in Postwar Canadian Cultural Policy," 184; Tippett, *Making Culture*, 181; Canada, "UNESCO," in Report of the Royal Commission on National Development in the Arts, Letters and Sciences, 1949–1951, 247, https://www.collectionscanada.gc.ca/massey/h5-436-e.html.

4 Goldthorp, "Reluctant Internationalism," 72–86; "Canadian Council for Reconstruction," 1–3. The council was built on the existing organizational capacity of the United Nations Association in Canada.

5   "Canadian Council for Reconstruction," 3. According to Druick, the NFB was well-placed in the 1940s to help UNESCO realize its educational goals through film: NFB initiatives in film and citizenship "melded well with the postwar institutionalization of interwar international liberal philosophy of education in UNESCO." Indeed, John Grierson (the first Government Film Commissioner) went to work for UNESCO after he left the NFB in 1945, as did his successor Ross McLean in 1950. Druick, *Projecting Canada*, 93–4, 189–90.

6   "Canadian Council for Reconstruction," 4–6, 13; Canada, "Literature," in Report of the Royal Commission on National Development in the Arts, Letters and Sciences, 1949–1951, 225, https://collectionscanada.ca/massey/h5-430-e.html.

7   Scott, *Seeing like a State*, 4–5; Canada, *Canada from Sea to Sea*, 5, 22. Scott's aim in *Seeing like a State* is not to denounce high modernism – indeed, he concedes that in liberal democracies, high modernism could "spur reform" (5). But he also does not discuss the relation of settler-colonial nations to the twentieth century's instances of "late colonial rule." As the discussion in the preceding chapter of high modernism in the Arctic during the 1950s indicates, the Government of Canada's high modernist ideology was indeed imbricated in the kinds of ill-fated, large-scale social engineering that Scott explores in his book, even if it was not an authoritarian state (one of the elements Scott considers crucial to the social-planning failures of the last century).

8   "Books for Hungry Minds," *Toronto Daily Star*, 9 March 1949, 1, ProQuest Historical Newspapers; "Canadian Council for Reconstruction," 7–8; "To Revive Learning in Europe," *Globe and Mail*, 8 March 1949, 6, ProQuest Historical Newspapers; "Any Books to Give?," *Globe and Mail*, 15 January 1949, 10, ProQuest Historical Newspapers; "Canada UN Body Denies Criticism of High Overhead," *Globe and Mail*, 26 August 1949, 3, ProQuest Historical Newspapers; "French Grateful for 6,000 Books," *Globe and Mail*, 8 April 1950, 5, ProQuest Historical Newspapers; "Canadian Book Centre Cumulated Statement of Items Filled by Recipient Country to March 31, 1950," vol. 1, file titled "Reports and Minutes of the Executive and Operating Committees, 1950–1951 (1)," MG28 145, Canadian Council for Reconstruction Through UNESCO fonds, Library and Archives Canada. For an example of the argument that cast European libraries – and hence knowledge – as victims of the Nazis, see W.A. Deacon, "The Fly Leaf," *Globe and Mail*, 12 February 1949, 12, ProQuest Historical Newspapers.

9   "Canadian Council for Reconstruction," 12; "Canadian Council for Reconstruction Through UNESCO, Minutes of the Third Annual Meeting of the Council at the Royal York Hotel, Toronto, May 29, 1950," vol. 1, file titled "Reports and Minutes of the Executive and Operating Committees, 1950–1951 (2)," MG28 145, Canadian Council for Reconstruction Through UNESCO fonds, Library and Archives Canada.

10 "To Revive Learning in Europe," *Globe and Mail*, 8 March 1949, 6, ProQuest Historical Newspapers. For an account of the tension that arose between the CCRU and the Department of External Affairs after 1947 or so and that led to the relinquishment of its operating Charter in 1953, see Goldthorp, "Reluctant Internationalism," 81–3.

11 Kidd, "Canada's Stake at UNESCO," 249; Druick, "International Cultural Relations," 182; Druick, *Projecting Canada*, 75, 77; Tippett, *Making Culture*, 183–4.

12 Goldthorp, "Reluctant Internationalism"; Kidd, "Canada's Stake at UNESCO," 263. Founded in 1936 when a number of adult education organizations joined forces, the CAAE was patterned after its American predecessor and funded by the Carnegie Corporation – the pocketbook that paid for a slew of Canadian arts and education initiatives after 1926, including the Banff School of Fine Arts and the National Film Society. Administered by a "Canadian Committee" of nine (including Robert Wallace and Vincent Massey), Carnegie dollars were meant to assist in bringing Canadian life to maturity. The Carnegie Corporation, and to a lesser extent the Rockefeller Foundation, were crucial sources of support for Canadian cultural life in the prewar years. Maria Tippett's history – and she is one of the few historians to have documented the extent to which cultural life in prewar Canada was underwritten by American philanthropy – shows how Canadian artists, writers, musicians, and educationalists came in this period to be beholden to organizations that wished to ameliorate the deleterious effects of industrial capitalism with the balm of culture. Tippett, *Making Culture*, 145–51, 153.

13 "Draft Constitution: Overseas institute of Canada Institut canadien d'outre mer," container B286880, file F1204-4-0-2 (file 1 of 4), "Overseas Institute of Canada," J.R. Kidd fonds, F 1204-4, Archives of Ontario; Richards, "From Giving to Helping," 26–7; "Background Notes on the Overseas Book Centre," vol. 37, file 22, "Overseas Book Centre, 1969–70," CUSO/SUCO-LAC. The details regarding Campbell's work with Voice of Women and the quotation of Campbell from a 1984 correspondence with W.A. Teager come from Teager, "Cultural and Humanitarian," 122–3.

14 Kidd, *Roby Kidd*, 7, 99, 46–7. For details regarding Kidd's career during the period of 1950 to 1966 (when he became the first chairperson of the Department of Adult Education at the Ontario Institute for Studies in Education), see Teager, "Cultural and Humanitarian"; and Kidd, *Roby Kidd* (especially chapters 5–7).

15 Teager, "Cultural and Humanitarian," 112–35; "CODE Remembers Co-Founder Harry Campbell," *CODE*, updated 20 August 2009, https://web.archive.org/web/20160304100129/http://www.codecan.org/fr/nouvelles/code-remembers-co-founder-henry-campbell. McFarland is also recognized

in the minutes of the OBC Annual General Meeting for 1970 "for gracious leadership of the program in Ontario since its inception." "Minutes: Annual and Special Meeting of the OBC," 6 May 1970, vol. 37, file 19, "Overseas Book Centre, 1969–70," CUSO/SUCO-LAC.

16 "In Memoriam: Henry C 'Harry' Campbell (1919–2009)," 188.
17 "Kurt Swinton, 73, Leading Educator," *Toronto Star*, 9 December 1987, A16, ProQuest; "Obituary: Kurt Swinton Designed Allied Radio Gear After Fleeing Native Austria," *Globe and Mail*, 9 December 1987, C9, ProQuest.
18 Compton Brouwer, *Canada's Global Villagers*, 2–4. Oxfam, for instance, started in 1942 as an Oxford University–based group working to help wartime refugees in Greece; many other NGOs that predate the Second World War were affiliated with religious organizations. See "Our Story," Oxfam Canada, accessed 25 March 2021, https://www.oxfam.ca/who-we-are/about-oxfam/our-story.
19 Slaughter, *Human Rights, Inc.*, 272, 275, 281–2; Benjamin, "The Power of Books," 156; Benjamin, *U.S. Books Abroad*, 71–2.
20 Kidd, *Roby Kidd*, 62–4, 102; J.R. Kidd, "An International Development Program for Canada," February 1961, vol. 43, file 15, "JRK – 1950s and 1960s (Cultural Background), 1950–61," ICAE-LAC; Teager, "Cultural and Humanitarian," 127, 122, 128. The Bon Echo Foundation – focused on domestic adult and citizenship education – was transformed into the OIC in 1962, a shift that is suggestive of the energy that was coalescing around international development in this period. See container B286880, file F1204-4-0-1, "Overseas Institute and Bon Echo," J.R. Kidd fonds, Archives of Ontario; container B286880, files F1204-4-0-2 (file 1 of 4), "Overseas Institute of Canada," J.R. Kidd fonds, Archives of Ontario. After its first year of operation, the CAAE's National Commission for Aboriginal Peoples became an autonomous organization, the Indian-Eskimo Association of Canada. According to Hugh Shewell, it remained a largely non-Indigenous organization with strong ties to the international adult education movement that was so central to Kidd's career. See Shewell, "'Bitterness Behind Every Smiling Face,'" 63.
21 Cogan, "Sharing the Nation's Heart Globally?," 147–55, 162–3. As Cogan's tables indicate, foreign aid expenditure grew across all metrics between 1963 and 1976. See Tables 4.1–4.3 in Cogan, "Sharing the Nation's Heart Globally?," 189–90; and appendix A in Morrison, *Aid Ebb and Tide*, 453–4.
22 Cogan, "Sharing the Nation's Heart Globally?," 161; Teager, "Cultural and Humanitarian," 129–31.
23 Kidd, *Education for Perspective*, 89–91; Teager, "Cultural and Humanitarian," 129. According to its website, the Coady Institute "is a world-renowned centre of excellence in community-based development and leadership

education." It was established at St Francis Xavier University in 1959. Its roots lie in the Rev. Francis Coady's interwar Antigonish Movement. "About Coady Institute," Coady International Institute, St Francis Xavier University, 2024, https://coady.stfx.ca/coady. On the Antigonish Movement, see Sacouman, "Underdevelopment and the Structural Origins," 66–85.

24 Massey, *On Being Canadian*, 99–109, 133–4; Kidd, *Roby Kidd*, 80; Kidd, *Education for Perspective*, 335–6, 340.

25 Kidd, *Education for Perspective*, 335–6, 340; Bryant, *The Homing Place*, 65; J.R. Kidd, "An International Development Program for Canada," February 1961, p. 2, 15, vol. 43, file 15, "JRK – 1950s and 1960s (Cultural Background), 1950–61," ICAE-LAC. When liberal internationalists like Massey articulated Canada's position in the new internationalism, they drew on the interwar English Canadian concept of the Dominion as a "sisterhood," an idea that replaced older paternalistic figurations of the relation. This unique blending of national status and imperial identity may not have resulted in material commitments to the centralization of empire (in the form of common imperial foreign policy, for instance), but it was a powerful idea with tremendous cultural importance. On this idea of the "Third British Empire," see Thompson, "Canada and the 'Third British Empire,'" 64–87.

26 Laugesen, "Books for the World," 131–2, 134. For further discussion of the "race question" in American book programs during the early Cold War, see Barnhisel, *Cold War Modernists*, 126–34.

27 Freeman-Maloy, "The International Politics of Settler Self-Governance," 86, 88–9; Gendron, *Towards a Francophone Community*, 83. As Gendron notes, federal educational assistance to French Africa expanded in the early Pearson years to a broader range of assistance, including technical assistance, food aid, and even capital assistance. He also observes the continuing dominance of the French government in these nations and the fact that "many French agencies and officials resented Canada's intrusion into their spheres of influence" (87). Quebec's paradiplomatic activity grew through the 1960s, culminating the 1965 Gérin-Lajoie doctrine; meanwhile, the Pearson government attempted to soothe Quebec in various ways, beginning with the Royal Commission on Bilingualism and Biculturalism, which was struck in 1963.

28 Kidd, *Education for Perspective*, 248, 258, 261. Article 22 of the League's Covenant required member nations to accept a "sacred trust of civilization" – a duty to promote the well-being of the Indigenous populations of those "colonies and territories that remained under their control." The Haudenosaunee appeal to the League of Nations, "The Red Man's Appeal for Justice," sought the League's recognition of the Six Nations Confederacy's "independent right of home-rule," in addition to the protection of the League of Nations "if the Imperial Government of

Great Britain shall avow its unwillingness to continue to extend adequate protection or withhold guarantees of such protection." The League declined this request, judging the claims of the Haudenosaunee to be "domestic" and thus outside its jurisdiction. Youngblood Henderson, *Indigenous Diplomacy and the Rights of Peoples*, 24, 29–34; Hoyaneh Levi General (Deskaheh), "The Redman's Appeal for Justice," 1–3, *Charles B. Sears Law Library*, accessed 12 February 2021, https://law.lib.buffalo.edu/pdf/Redmanappeal.pdf.

29 Kidd, *Roby Kidd*, 48–166; Kapoor, Kidd, and Touchette, *Functional Literacy*.
30 Jones and Coleman, *The United Nations and Education*, 60–2; Dorn and Ghodsee, "The Cold War Politicization of Literacy," 389–95; Kapoor, Kidd, and Touchette, *Functional Literacy*, 12, 35. Dorn and Ghodsee explain that UNESCO's promotion of "fundamental education" during its earliest years was abandoned in 1958 under the director-generalship of the American Luther Evans. Increasing suspicion in the US government and at the World Bank of literacy work was fuelled by the "mass literacy" campaign undertaken in Cuba in the early 1960s, an important factor in UNESCO's turn to "functional literacy" through its Experimental World Literacy Program.
31 Kidd, *Education for Perspective*, 254–5; Reid, *The Leopard*, 18. Michael G. Cooke points out that through the 1960s and early '70s Reid also published novels for Jamaican schoolchildren that represent Jamaican history, culture, and language from a black Jamaican perspective; his *Sixty-Five* (1960) takes up the subject of his first novel, *New Day* (1949), recounting the Morant Bay Rebellion of 1865. In this sense, Reid was attempting to supplant the "white man's book" in post-independence Jamaican classrooms. Cooke, "Vic(tor) (Stafford) Reid."
32 Kidd, *Roby Kidd*, 101, 104, 109; Kapoor, Kidd, and Touchette, *Functional Literacy*, 12, 23. See also Kidd, *Adult Education in the Caribbean*.
33 Kapoor, Kidd, and Touchette, *Functional Literacy*, 27.
34 Kidd, *Roby Kidd*, 105; Kidd, *Education for Perspective*, 93–5; Abrahams, *Tell Freedom*, 171–4, 280; UNESCO, *Experimental World Literacy Programme*, 138.
35 Teager, "Cultural and Humanitarian," 132–3; Cogan, "Sharing the Nation's Heart Globally?," 334–5, 328, 338–9; Compton Brouwer, *Canada's Global Villagers*, 135. On the shifting priorities of Canadian NGOs in the last half of the twentieth century, see also Murphy, "Canadian NGOs and the Politics of Participation," 161–212; and chapter 3 of O'Sullivan, *The NGO Movement*.
36 Cogan, "Sharing the Nation's Heart Globally?," 238, 247–9, 356, 431; Compton Brouwer, *Canada's Global Villagers*, 108–24.
37 "Overseas Book Centre: Statement of Revenue and Expenditures," 30 September 1969, vol. 37, file 21, "Overseas Book Centre, 3 of 4," CUSO/SUCO-LAC; "Background Notes on the Overseas Book Centre," vol. 37, file 22, "Overseas Book Centre, 1969–70," CUSO/SUCO-LAC; "Overseas Book

Centre, Annual Report 1975–76," vol. 104, file 15, "OBC (Overseas Book Centre), 1974–76," ICAE-LAC. For an account of the NGO division at CIDA under the leadership of Lewis Perinbam that emphasizes the division's "permissive approach" and the "humane internationalism" of Perinbam, see Brushett, "'Trotsky in Pinstripes,'" 163–85. The Miles for Millions walkathon, launched in Canada as part of the 1967 centennial celebrations, was spearheaded by Oxfam Canada, CUSO, and other Canadian NGOs; it lasted more than a decade. It was an important source of funding for the OBC, which became an associate member of the National Miles for Millions Walk Committee in the fall of 1969. See W.A. Teager, "Memo re: Miles for Millions," 20 November 1969, vol. 37, file 20, "Overseas Book Centre, 1969–70," CUSO/SUCO-LAC; and chapter 3 of O'Sullivan, *The NGO Moment*.

38 "Overseas Book Centre, Pamphlet #1," vol. 37, file 22, "Overseas Book Centre, 1969–70," CUSO/SUCO-LAC; Teager, "Cultural and Humanitarian," 132–3; "Minutes of the Meeting of the Board of Directors," 4 October 1974, vol. 37, file 23, "Overseas Book Centre, 1973–74," CUSO/SUCO-LAC. Information regarding the incorporation of the OBC and its changing structure after 1968 is taken from vol. 37, files 19–22, CUSO/SUCO-LAC; and vol. 38, files 1–3, CUSO/SUCO-LAC. In 1974, a new bilingual Comité de la francophonie was created to replace the distinct English and French committees in Montreal; this merger created significant friction within the organization and indicates its growing bureaucratic complexity, as do the documents from this period that outline the responsibilities and duties of each local committee and the policies related to the organization's paid employees. For le Comité, see vol. 37, files 23–4, CUSO/SUCO-LAC; for local committees, see "Overseas Book Centre Committees," vol. 37, file 25, "Overseas Book Centre, 1973–74," CUSO/SUCO-LAC; for paid employees, see, for example, "OBC Personnel Policy," vol. 37, file 23, "Overseas Book Centre 1973–74," CUSO/SUCO-LAC.

39 W.A. Teager, "Report of Trip to Africa," January–March 1971, vol. 95, file 22, "Overseas Book Centre to: 1973, 1967–1973," ICAE-LAC. See comments regarding the irrelevance of "cast-off" Canadian books in W.A. Teager, "Report of the Director's Trip to the Caribbean Area," 31 March 1970, vol. 37, file 20, "Overseas Book Centre, 1969–70," CUSO/SUCO-LAC; see comments regarding the "increasingly specific" character of requests for books in OBC/CLO reports from 1969–70, vol. 37, file 22, "Overseas Book Centre, 1969–70," CUSO/SUCO-LAC; see Teager's repetition of the problem of quantity over quality and the perils of sending books to Africa that will not be used in W.A. Teager, "Report of Visits to Ghana and Nigeria, November and December, 1973," vol. 38, file 1, "Overseas Book Centre, 1973–74," CUSO/SUCO-LAC.

40 Ian Young to CUSO Field Staff, 3 June 1970, vol. 24, file 20, "Overseas Book Centre, 1969–70," CUSO/SUCO-LAC; "Executive Newsletter," February 1974,

vol. 104, file 15, "OBC (Overseas Book Centre), 1974–1976," ICAE-LAC; "Books and Educational Aids for Developing Countries," undated, vol. 108, file 13, "ICAE (International Council for Adult Education) General Files 1976–80 International Organizations – Society for International Development 1976–80 Overseas Book Centre, 1976–80" (hereafter cited as "ICAE General Files 1976–80"), ICAE-LAC; "Executive Newsletter," April 1976, vol. 104, file 15, "OBC (Overseas Book Centre), 1974–76," ICAE-LAC. There are three volumes (vols 37, 38, 24) in the CUSO/SUCO fonds that contain information about its relation to the OBC/CLO from 1968 to the mid-1970s.

41 Brouillette, UNESCO and the Fate of the Literary, 82–6.

42 Dorn and Ghodsee, "The Cold War Politicization of Literacy," 396–7; UNESCO, Experimental World Literacy Programme, 121–2, 143. Following the Cuban Revolution, a 1961 mass literacy campaign managed in less than a year to reduce that nation's illiteracy rate from 23 per cent to less than 4 per cent. For a discussion of this campaign and the Iranian one that was modeled on it, see Dorn and Ghodsee, "The Cold War Politicization of Literacy," 385–9. For a further critique of the inadequacy of the concept of functional literacy, see the final report on the EWLP, M'Bow and Peterson, *The Experimental World Literacy Programme*.

43 Barker and Escarpit, *The Book Hunger*, 24–7; Altbach and Rathgeber, *Publishing in the Third World*, 12; Altbach and Gopinathan, "Textbooks in the Third World, 18; UNESCO, *Book Development in Africa*, 29; Hoggart, *An Idea and Its Servants*, 194; Brouillette, UNESCO and the Fate of the Literary, 88–90.

44 "UNESCO Committee of Experts in Book Promotion and Development," 28–30 May 1973, vol. 37, file 25, "Overseas Book Centre, 1973–74," CUSO/SUCO-LAC; Louise Rohonczy, "Discussion Paper on Special Grants Policy," 4 March 1974, vol. 37, file 26, "Overseas Book Centre, 1973–74," CUSO/SUCO-LAC; "OBC Annual Report, 1976–77," vol. 108, file 13, "ICAE General Files 1976–80," ICAE-LAC; and "Executive Newsletter," April 1976, vol. 104, file 15, "OBC (Overseas Book Centre), 1974–76," ICAE-LAC. Book shipments in the 1976–77 Annual Report are measured in tons, which have been converted to tonnes.

45 "The Overseas Book Centre in the Near Future," vol. 108, file 13, "ICAE General Files 1976–80," ICAE-LAC; "Executive Newsletter," December 1976, vol. 108, file 13, "ICAE General Files 1976–80," ICAE-LAC. The recipient's response is quoted in Richards, "From Giving to Helping," 27, but is not attributed to a source.

46 Richards, "From Giving to Helping," 26–8; *NGOMA* 3, no. 2, June 1980, vol. 108, file 13, "ICAE General Files 1976–80," ICAE-LAC; "OBC Annual Report, 1976–77," vol. 108, file 13, "ICAE General Files 1976–80," ICAE-LAC; *NGOMA*, 7, no. 1, Spring 1984, vol. 129, file 3-5, "Canadian Organization

for Development Through Education (CODE) (Former OBC, Overseas Book Centre), Canada), 1984," ICAE-LAC; "OBC Annual Report, 1980–81," vol. 2, file 3-2, "000C-Canadian Organization for Development Through Education CODE, (Former OBC – Overseas Book Centre) – Canada, 1983," ICAE-LAC. OCED was the French organizational name used in the period following the name change, but this title is no longer featured on the organization's unilingual website. See https://code.ngo/.

47 "Paper Supply Problems and Education in the Third World," May 1981, vol. 2, file 3-2, "000C-Canadian Organization for Development Through Education CODE, (Former OBC – Overseas Book Centre – Canada), 1983," ICAE-LAC; *NGOMA*, 6, no. 4, Winter 1983, vol. 2, file 3-2, "000C-Canadian Organization for Development Through Education CODE, (Former OBC – Overseas Book Centre – Canada), 1983," ICAE-LAC; "Paper Support Programme," vol. 129, file 3-5, "Canadian Organization for Development Through Education (CODE) (Former OBC, Overseas Book Centre), Canada, 1984," ICAE-LAC; Rathgeber, "The Book Industry in Africa, 1973–1983," 63; Francisco Via Grossi to Francis Childe, 13 November 1980, vol. 108, file 13, "ICAE General Files 1976–80," ICAE-LAC; Francis Childe to Francisco Vio Grossi, 31 August 1981 and Lyne Denis to Francisco Vio Grossi, 21 September 1983, vol. 2, file 3-2, "000C-Canadian Organization for Development Through Education CODE, (Former OBC – Overseas Book Centre – Canada), 1983," ICAE-LAC; Richards, "From Giving to Helping," 27.

48 Richards, "From Giving to Helping," 27–31.

49 Rosi, *Book Donations for Development*, 5, 13, 17, 51–3. On the state of the publishing industry in Canada in the three decades after the Second World War, see the section "Publishing in Canada at Mid-Century" in this book's chapter 2. For an assessment of book donation schemes operating in English- and French-speaking Africa in the present, see Zell and Thierry, "Book Donation Programmes for Africa."

50 Kidd, "Still On Our Agenda," 30–7; Minutes from "Sub-Commission on Education," Canadian Commission for UNESCO, 1 April 1976, vol. 105, file 7 "UNESCO – J. Roby Kidd Adult Education File, 1974–77," ICAE-LAC; Kidd, *Roby Kidd*, 158.

51 Hoggart, *An Idea and Its Servants*, 194; Huggan, *The Postcolonial Exotic*, 35; Donaghy, "A Wasted Opportunity," 183–207. On the withdrawal of the United States and Britain from UNESCO, see chapter 3 of Giffard, *UNESCO and the Media*. For a discussion of the negative domestic media coverage of CIDA and of its president Paul Gérin-Lajoie in the years after 1975, see Morrison, *Aid and Ebb Tide*, 136–40.

52 Zell, "Book Donation Programmes," 36; "Teaching and Learning in Fragile Contexts (2022–2026)," CODE, updated 2025, https://code.ngo/tlfc;

"Research Initiatives," CODE, updated 2025, https://code.ngo/approach/research-initiatives; "Literary Awards," CODE, updated 2025, https://code.ngo/approach/literary-awards. According to this page, the literary award program ceased in 2020 due to lack of funding (it was privately funded by William Burt). According to Burt's obituary notice in *Quill & Quire*, he was a commodities broker who retired in his early forties, "turning his attention toward literacy in Africa." Sue Carter, "William Burt, International Literacy Philanthropist, Dies at 71," *Quill & Quire*, 20 November 2017, https://quillandquire.com/omni/william-burt-international-literacy-philanthropist-dies-at-71. The Burt Award for First Nations, Inuit, and Métis Young Adult Literature was awarded to three titles per year from 2013 to 2016 (these winning authors received prizes of twelve, eight, and five thousand dollars each). Between 2016 and 2018, there was one winner and one or more "Honour" prizes (worth twelve thousand and two thousand dollars, respectively). Likely due to the pandemic, the 2019 and 2020 awards were combined, and awarded in three categories, Indigenous-language, English-language, and "Honour" English-language (these winning authors received six thousand each, and the "Honour" winner received three thousand dollars). It is no longer possible to consult the list of past winners of the Burt Award on the CODE website, but the Wikipedia entry for the prize lists the winners from the award's inception in 2013 to 2019. See "Burt Award for First Nations, Inuit, and Métis Literature," Wikipedia, https://en.wikipedia.org/wiki/Burt_Award_for_First_Nations,_Inuit_and_M%C3%A9tis_Literature. I have verified each of these winning titles as correct using publishers' websites.

53 "Literary Awards," CODE, updated 2025, https://code.ngo/approach/literary-awards. For CODE funding information, see "Accountability: Annual Reports," CODE, updated 2025, https://code.ngo/about/accountability. (CIDA contributed just over 64 per cent of CODE's annual budget in 2011/12, but by 2014/15, only 38 per cent of CODE's budget came from the Department of Foreign Affairs, Trade, and Development, which absorbed CIDA after 2013). For the argument regarding CODE's domestic turn as a cost-saving measure, and for a critique of the CODE Burt Award for First Nations, Inuit, and Métis, Young Adult Literature as biased toward "firmly established presses" that points to the limitations of identifying structural dispossession as a literacy or book supply problem, see Bayrock and Brouillette, "Who Wins? The Politics of Prize Culture," 86–95. For scholarship on literary prizes in Canada that demonstrates the privileging of the multinationals, see Mason, "'Capital Intraconversion,'" 424–46; and Scott and Tucker-Abramson, "Banking on a Prize," 5–20. BookNet Canada shows that Canadian-owned publishers sold just over three million units in 2018 (Canadian publisher

sales for an average week in 2018 were 59,902 units). Annick Press, an independent Canadian publisher of children's and young adult literature, sold approximately 250,000 units in 2018. BookNet Canada, *The Canadian Book Market 2018*, 16.

Chapter Four

1. Mount, *Arrival*, 8–9.
2. Important studies of Canadian literature from a postcolonial perspective include Brydon, "Testing the Limits"; Moss, *Is Canada Postcolonial?*; Sugars, *Home-Work*; and Sugars, *Unhomely States*.
3. Litt, "The State and the Book," 36–7; Edwardson, *Canadian Content*, 159. On the field-altering institutions of this period, see the following chapters in Gerson and Michon, *History of the Book in Canada*, vol. 3, *1918–1980*: Litt, "The State and the Book"; Robert, Verduyn, and Friskney, "Canadianization of the Curriculum"; Davey, "Economics and the Writer"; Steele, "Case Study: Collecting Canadian Manuscripts"; and Earle, "Case Study: The Canada Council."
4. Atwood, *Survival*, 177–94; Lee, "Cadence, Country, Silence," 155; Sugars, "Introduction," xxi. Northrop Frye's theory of the "garrison mentality" can be found in his "Conclusion" to the *Literary History of Canada*, originally published in 1965 but reprinted in *The Bush Garden*, 213–51. The John Moss editorial Sugars refers to can be found in *Journal of Canadian Fiction* 1–2.
5. Azzi, "The Nationalist Moment in English Canada," 218, 225. On Walter Gordon, the Waffle, and the Committee for an Independent Canada, see Azzi, "The Nationalist Moment," 222–5, as well as note 60 of this chapter. For a list of the members of the Committee for an Independent Canada, as well as its statement of purpose, see appendix 2 of Resnick, *The Land of Cain*, 226–28. Resnick's Marxist critique of late twentieth-century English Canadian nationalism contends in its fifth chapter that not all nationalism in this era was leftist and very little of it was working-class.
6. Purdy, "Introduction," iv, ii; Walker, *Racial Discrimination in Canada*, 6; Godfrey, "The Generation of Hunters," 112–15; Laurence, "Open Letter to the Mother of Joe Bass," 34–7; Livesay, "New Jersey: 1935," 110–11.
7. Dean, "Canadianization, Colonialism, and Decolonization," 31, 34, 43; Mathews, *Canadian Literature*, 4, 1–2. Important studies related to the dearth of Canadian materials in classrooms include A.B. Hodgetts's *What Culture? What Heritage?* (1968), which prompted the Association of Universities and Colleges in Canada to sponsor a commission, which produced a report, T.H.B. Symons's *To Know Ourselves: The Report of the Commission on Canadian Studies*, in 1975.

8   Resnick, *The Land of Cain*, 202; Palmer, *Canada's 1960s*, 248. On the importance of anti-racist and anti-colonial thought to the anglophone nationalisms and New Left thought of the late 1960s and '70s, see also Azzi, "The Nationalist Moment," 213–28. There were, to be sure, some New Left attempts to forge networks of solidarity with Indigenous Peoples, particularly among students, who were the most ardent anti-imperialists. As Peter Graham and Ian McKay's history of the Toronto New Left indicates, black New Leftists in Toronto (in groups such as the Black Liberation Front) made alliances with Indigenous Peoples in Ontario. The Student Union for Peace Action, a key New Left organization of the 1960s and the main Canadian student movement in the period, cultivated ties with Indigenous activists, creating in the mid-1960s the Student Neestow Partnership Project, which took as its goal the establishment of contact between Student Union for Peace Action activists and Indigenous communities in Saskatchewan. Graham with McKay, *Radical Ambition*, 143, 296–7; Palmer, *Canada's 1960s*, 264–6.

9   Mills, *The Empire Within*, 104–8; Austin, "All Roads Led to Montreal," 518–29, 535; Graham with McKay, *Radical Ambition*, 289–90, 291–300. For a more detailed examination of black activism in 1960s Montreal, see Austin, *Moving Against the System*; and James, *You Don't Play with Revolution*. On Quebecois nationalisms and the influence of Third World decolonization movements, see also Lachaîne, "Black and Blue." As in anglophone Canada, an indigenizing rhetoric in Quebec did not necessarily entail actual political solidarity with Indigenous Peoples. See Giroux, *L'Oeil du maître*, 41–78.

10 Veracini, *Settler Colonialism*, 21–2.

11 Godard, *Audrey Thomas and Her Works*, 5; Vincent, "Peripheral Visions," 7–8.

12 Livesay, "Song and Dance," 40–8; Laurence, "Ten Years' Sentences," 10–16.

13 New, "Africanadiana," 33–8; New, "Canadian Literature and Commonwealth Responses," 17; Donald Cameron, "The Mysterious Literary Fondness for Darkest Africa," *Maclean's*, 1 August 1971, 64, *Periodicals Archive Online*; Downey, "The Canadian Identity and African Nationalism," 16. See also George Woodcock, "Savoring Love and Life in Sex and Death," *Maclean's*, 1 February 1974, 80, *Periodicals Archive Online*; and Monk, "Shadow Continent: The Image of Africa in Three Canadian Writers," 3–7, 19. W.H. New's "Africanadiana" essay and his 1972 review of *Mrs. Blood* and *The New Ancestors* (originally published in the *Journal of Commonwealth Literature* in 1972) were slightly revised and published together in 1972. See New, "Equatorial Zones and Polar Opposites," in New, *Articulating West*, 216–33.

14 David Knight was also in Africa in the 1960s but not with an NGO; a professor of English at the University of Toronto, he spent 1965 at the University of Ibadan (Nigeria) on exchange. Mark Lovewell, "David James Knight," accessed 10 July 2024, http://marklovewell.com/articles/knight.htm.

15 Millman, *British Somaliland*, 1–5.
16 Osborne and Kingsley Kent, *Africans and Britons*, 174; Millman, *British Somaliland*, 192–5, 230, 201.
17 Millman, *British Somaliland*, 235–8; Somaliland Protectorate, *Annual Review of the Development Plan, 1954*, 2, 5.
18 Laurence's story "Uncertain Flowering" was published in the American magazine *Story* in 1953. For a (not quite complete) bibliography of Laurence's writing, see Nancekivell, "Margaret Laurence," 263–85; for an account of the writing that Laurence did while in Somaliland and the Gold Coast that was not published, including several attempts at novels, see King, *The Life of Margaret Laurence*, 94–6, 106–9. In 1968, Laurence also published a critical study of Nigerian writing, *Long Drums and Cannons: Nigerian Dramatists and Novelists*. Studies that dwell on the anti-imperialism of Laurence's African oeuvre include Davis, *Margaret Laurence Writes Africa and Canada*; Roy, "Anti-Imperialism and Feminism," 33–42; and Sparrow, *Into Africa with Margaret Laurence*. For Laurence's own ruminations on her "white liberal" anti-imperialism, see Laurence, *Dance on the Earth*, 152–3; as well as her essays in *Heart of a Stranger*, particularly "The Very Best Intentions."
19 Laurence, *The Prophet's Camel Bell*, 56–8. Millman's *British Somaliland* gives more detail regarding the school for girls in *The Prophet's Camel Bell*: the first secular girls' school in the Protectorate, the Girls' Central Boarding School was established at Burao in 1952; as Laurence's anecdote suggests, it focused on "practical skills" (e.g., preparation as teachers or as nurses) so as not to render the girls "unmarriageable" (242).
20 Laurence, *The Prophet's Camel Bell*, 72–6; Osborne and Kingsley Kent, *Africans and Britons*, 174–5. Laurence's views on the emergent development paradigm are similarly evident in the stories collected in 1963 in *The Tomorrow-Tamer* (especially the title story), all of which are set in the territory that became the Republic of Ghana in 1957.
21 Margaret Laurence to Adele Wiseman, 4 September 1951, 1991-012/043, file 6, "Correspondence-Margaret Laurence," Adele Wiseman fonds, F0477, Clara Thomas Archives and Special Collections, York University; Laurence, *The Prophet's Camel Bell*, 245–7. The Canadian writer Adele Wiseman was an important interlocutor for Laurence's development as a writer during her years in Africa. Their correspondence from these years (1951–56) can be found in Wiseman's papers at York University, referenced above. As Millman documents in *British Somaliland*, E.P.S. Shirley served as chief secretary of the Protectorate (the highest office in the Protectorate) from 1952–54 and had by the early 1950s spent a large part of his career in Somaliland, first in the Somaliland Camel Corps and then, after 1930, in the Administrative Service (194).

22 *A Tree for Poverty*, 3; Millman, *British Somaliland*, 246–7. Laurence critiques the use of British materials in African classrooms in stories such as "The Rain Child" (from *The Tomorrow-Tamer*); in *This Side Jordan*, Laurence prioritizes the sceptical view of a curriculum based on memorization of British texts that students and teachers alike fail to understand. All citations in this book's notes to *A Tree for Poverty* refer to the 1970 reprint listed in the bibliography.

23 Laurence, *The Prophet's Camel Bell*, 226–7, 46; *A Tree for Poverty*, 1, 5; Richards, "'Leave the Dead Some Room to Dance!,'" 28; Sparrow, *Into Africa with Margaret Laurence*, 53. Despite the differences that Sparrow finds in the translations produced by Laurence, on one hand, and by Andrzejewski and Lewis, on the other, Lewis's 1955 review of *A Tree for Poverty* is glowing: he agrees, for example, with the praise of those Somali poets "whose knowledge of English is sufficiently good for them to judge of the quality of the translations" and calls the book "a work of high literary quality." Lewis, "*A Tree for Poverty*," 305. In *A Tree for Poverty*, Laurence describes a belwo as a "farily recent form," a "short lyric love poem" (5).

24 Millman, *British Somaliland*, 230–2; Somaliland Protectorate, *Annual Review of the Development Plan, 1953*, 17; Laurence, *The Prophet's Camel Bell*, 45; *A Tree for Poverty*, ix, 3.

25 Ritter, *Imperial Encore*, 54–66.

26 *A Tree for Poverty*, v; King, *The Life of Margaret Laurence*, 230. Of the 178 extant copies of the first edition of *A Tree for Poverty* listed in WorldCat, 164 are located in North America and western Europe; however, WorldCat tends to document the holdings of libraries in these regions better than anywhere else, so this concentration may only be a reflection of this fact.

27 New, "Africanadiana," 36; Laurence, *The Prophet's Camel Bell*, 10. Laurence identified as a Christian socialist in the tradition of Tommy Douglas; she was a member of the Cooperative Commonwealth Federation from her student days and, later, a member of the New Democratic Party of Canada. McDonald, "Margaret Laurence and the NDP," 23–4.

28 Laurence, *The Prophet's Camel Bell*, 251, 25; Laurence, "Ivory Tower or Grassroots?," 17, 22. On Laurence's reading of Mannoni, see Sparrow, *Into Africa with Margaret Laurence*, 31–2. For criticism that frames African nations and Canada as emerging from comparable experiences of colonization, see Abraham, "Margaret Laurence and the Ancestral Tradition," 137–42; Gross, "Margaret Laurence's African Experience," 73–81; Killam, "Third World Aspects of Canadian Literature," 214–21; Ravenscroft, "Africa in the Imagination of Margaret Laurence," 35–50; Thomas, *The Manawaka World of Margaret Laurence*. George Woodcock notes the confluence of African and Métis values in Laurence's writing.

Woodcock, "Speaker for the Tribes," 30–2. It was not until after 2000 or so that scholarship on Laurence's African writing began to treat Canada as a settler colonial nation, though there are some earlier exceptions, such as Vincent's "Peripheral Visions."

29 Laurence's extensive library of African fiction, history, sociology, and anthropology can be consulted in her archival fonds at the William Ready Division of Archives and Research Collections, McMaster University, Hamilton, Ontario.

30 *Right Hand Left Hand* offers Livesay's recollections of her years of involvement with the Communist Party of Canada. It is best understood in relation to Livesay's efforts in the 1970s to cast her involvement with the Old Left as one of her "past sins," part of her dialogue in that decade with the New Left. See Livesay, *Right Hand Left Hand*; and Livesay, "Early Days," 34–5.

31 Livesay, *Journey with My Selves*, 189–92, 198, 211; J.R. Kidd to Mrs Calais Calvert-Marty, UNESCO, 26 August 1958, box 9, folder 3, "UNESCO and Africa Teaching, 1958–63: Correspondences, Reports, Documents," MSS 37, Dorothy Livesay fonds, University of Manitoba (hereafter cited as DL-UM); Notebook 1959–60, box 10, folder 2, "UNESCO and Africa Teaching, 1958–63: Teaching-Related Material," MSS 37, DL-UM; "UNESCO Technical Assistance, Briefing Specialist at Headquarters, 15–18 Nov. 1960," box 9, folder 3, "UNESCO and Africa Teaching, 1958–63: Correspondences, Reports, Documents," MSS 37, DL-UM. I constructed the narrative of Livesay's appointments in Northern Rhodesia from her reports to UNESCO, located in box 9, folder 3, "UNESCO and Africa Teaching, 1958–63: Correspondences, Reports, Documents," MSS 37, DL-UM.

32 Jones and Coleman, *The United Nations and Education*, 52, 61–2. On the shift in late twentieth-century UNESCO approaches to education and literacy, see also UNESCO, *50 Years for Education*, and this book's chapter 3.

33 Matasci, "Assessing Needs, Fostering Development," 37–41, 43–4; Watras, "UNESCO's Programme of Fundamental Education," 220–1. As Matasci points out, however, only 18 per cent of the total number of UNESCO missions went to Africa. One of the effects of UNESCO's work on measuring inequality in education was to demonstrate the fact that "nations still under colonial rule, were disproportionately affected by 'educational underdevelopment.' Sub-Saharan Africa was the most striking example." Not surprisingly, colonial powers France, Belgium, and Britain initially responded negatively to UNESCO's data-gathering in Africa and to its attempts in 1949 establish a fundamental education centre in sub-Saharan Africa. They were obliged to respond defensively to UNESCO's work, undertaking independent efforts related to education as a means of "avoiding international criticism." "Closely guarded by the colonial powers,"

Africa thus remained largely excluded from UNESCO's campaign to globalize the right to education, though this began to change in 1959, when the General Conference at UNESCO requested the undertaking of a major survey on the educational needs of sub-Saharan Africa (43–5, 47).

34 Larmer, *Rethinking African Politics*, 23–5; Osborne and Kingsley Kent, *Africans and Britons*, 180–1; Mulford, *Zambia*, 5–6, 48–9. For a fuller account of African opposition to Federation, see Mulford, *Zambia*, 13–48. Larmer's recent history revises the historiographical tendency to emphasize the political unity of Africans in the territory that became Zambia. The classic account is Mulford's. Mulford notes that white settlers did not arrive in what became Northern Rhodesia until the turn of the century (following Cecil Rhodes's establishment of a white settlement in what became Southern Rhodesia in 1890); as the railway opened southern Africa as far north as the Copperbelt in the first decade of the twentieth century and copper deposits were discovered by the British South Africa Company, the white population expanded. By the 1950s, there were roughly seventy thousand white settlers in Northern Rhodesia and approximately three million Africans (belonging to at least six major linguistic groups) (1–3).

35 Larmer, *Rethinking African Politics*, 26–43. Larmer recounts that Kaunda had been secretary-general of Nkumbla's African National Congress but left the party when the Zambian African National Congress merged with other groups to form the UNIP in 1959. In the elections of 1962, the UNIP and the African National Congress were able to form a coalition government under the authority of the Colonial Office; in the elections of January 1964, the UNIP won 51 of 65 seats (26–33, 47–50). According to Larmer, the "Cha Cha Cha" erupted in July 1961 in the wake of Secretary of State for the Colonies Iain Macleod's proposal for a new Northern Rhodesian constitution in June 1961. This proposal was accompanied by a plan for elections that would give African voters exclusive power over fifteen seats of a forty-five-seat legislative council. This was rejected by local UNIP officials and activists, who unleashed "a wave of unofficial protest action" (including the destruction of bridges and schools and the blockading of roads) during July and August of 1961 (37–43).

36 Dorothy Livesay, "UNESCO Mission to Northern Rhodesia," 30 December 1960, box 9, folder 3, "UNESCO and Africa Teaching, 1958–63: Correspondences, Reports, Documents," MSS 37, DL-UM; "CUSO Backgrounder on Northern Rhodesia," box 9, folder 3, "UNESCO and Africa Teaching, 1958–63: Correspondences, Reports, Documents," MSS 37, DL-UM; Dorothy Livesay to Sophie Livesay Stewart, 8 February 1961, box 39, folder 7, "Dorothy Livesay's Letters to Sophie Livesay Stewart, 1960–61," MSS 37, DL-UM; Dorothy Livesay to Sophie Livesay Stewart, 26 August 1961, box 39, folder 7, "Dorothy Livesay's Letters to Sophie Livesay Stewart,

1960–61," MSS 37, DL-UM. Livesay's African journals are full of anecdotes that demonstrate her discomfort with the racism of white settlers in Northern Rhodesia. See, for instance, her account of her interactions with a South African car dealer, whose racist views move her "more to sorrow than to anger." Dorothy Livesay, "Kwatcha! A UNESCO Sojourn: First Impressions: Northern Rhodesia, 1960," 1 December 1960, box 3, folder 4, MSS 37, DL-UM.

37 Dorothy Livesay, "Personal Diary: Chalimbana Training College, Lusaka, Northern Rhodesia," 14 July 1962, box 3, folder 4, "Diaries," MSS 37, DL-UM; Dorothy Livesay to Sophie Livesay Stewart, 26 August 1961, box 39, folder 7, "Dorothy Livesay's Letters to Sophie Livesay Stewart, 1960–61," MSS 37, DL-UM; Livesay, *Journey with My Selves*, 215–17. The versions of "Prophet"/"The Prophet" and "U.N.I.P. Meeting" (including those published in *Canadian Forum* and *Cyclic*) can be found in box 82, folder 5, "Poems: 1965 (Undated)," MSS 37, DL-UM; and box 83, folder 1, "Poems: 1960s," MSS 37, DL-UM. *The Colour of God's Face* is a chapbook, likely published in 1964 by the Unitarian Church of Vancouver. I quote here from the version of "The Leader" published in Livesay, *Collected Poems*, 310. Upon returning to Vancouver in 1963 and before Zambian independence was finalized in 1964, Livesay drafted a proposal for a radio show that would profile Kaunda; the proposal emphasizes the leader's philosophy of passive resistance, insisting that Kaunda "is a man of unswerving purpose who will not let violence take the upper hand if he can possibly forestall it." Dorothy Livesay, "A Profile of Kenneth Kaunda (Northern Rhodesia)," box 106, folder 15, "A Profile of Kenneth Kaunda (Northern Rhodesia)," MSS 37, DL-UM. As I note, Livesay was also clearly sympathetic to the women who were publicly identified with the politics of decolonization in Zambia, as her poems "Politics" and "The Prophetess" (both included in *Collected Poems*) demonstrate. Alice Lenchina (sometimes spelled "Lenshina") was the leader of the Lumpa Church and was associated with actions opposing white settler authority in the years leading up to independence; after Livesay's return to Vancouver and the elections of January 1964 that brought Kaunda's UNIP government to power, Lenchina led an uprising against the UNIP government. Whether or not Livesay knew about that uprising when she drafted "The Prophetess" in 1964 is unclear. Type and manuscript versions of "The Prophetess" can be found in box 82, folder 5, "Poems: 1965 (Undated)," MSS 37, DL-UM. Livesay's *The Unquiet Bed* reverses the order of "The Leader" and "The Prophetess" in *The Colour of God's Face*, placing the latter poem last in the "Zambia" suite (an order respected in her 1972 *Collected Poems*).

38 Jones, *International Policies for Third World Education*, 116, 119.

39 UNESCO, *Meeting of Ministers of Education of African Countries*, 10, 27; Mwanakatwe, *The Growth of Education in Zambia*, 43–89. As Larmer's

Rethinking African Politics makes clear, the UNIP vision for post-independence Zambia was by no means uncontested; challenges to its governance led UNIP to establish a one-party state in 1972. Mwanakatwe's history is clearly a defence of the UNIP's post-independence educational plan, a plan that was being challenged in the late 1960s by ANC and UNIP members alike for its failure to provide, for instance, more secondary school places for primary school leavers (53–61).

40   Mwanakatwe, *The Growth of Education in Zambia*, 31, 107.
41   Ching-Liang Low, *Publishing the Postcolonial*, 73; Allison, "State Participation in Publishing," 59–69.
42   Dorothy Livesay, "UNESCO Mission to Northern Rhodesia," 30 December 1960, box 9, folder 3, "UNESCO and Africa Teaching, 1958–63: Correspondences, Reports, Documents," MSS 37, DL-UM; Livesay, "Copperbelt," 247–48; Dorothy Livesay, "The Teaching of English in the Junior Secondary School – Some Suggestions for a Syllabus," box 9, folder 3, "UNESCO and Africa Teaching, 1958–63: Correspondences, Reports, Documents," MSS 37, DL-UM; Dorothy Livesay, "English S2 Course: Note on the Work Covered, January to May 1962; August to October 1962," box 9, folder 4, "UNESCO and Africa Teaching, 1958–63: Correspondences, Reports, Documents," MSS 37, DL-UM. For Livesay's complaints about the problem of books for classroom use, see, for example, Dorothy Livesay, "Report to UNESCO – Six Months Period, May, 1961 to November, 1961," box 9, folder 3, "UNESCO and Africa Teaching, 1958–63: Correspondences, Reports, Documents," MSS 37, DL-UM; "Annual Report, UNESCO Mission to Northern Rhodesia, Nov. 30, 1961," box 9, folder 3, "UNESCO and Africa Teaching, 1958–63: Correspondences, Reports, Documents," MSS 37, DL-UM; and "UNESCO Draft Final Report, Mission to Northern Rhodesia, November 1960–May 1963," box 9, folder 3, "UNESCO and Africa Teaching, 1958–63: Correspondences, Reports, Documents," MSS 37, DL-UM.
43   Ritter, *Imperial Encore*, 4, 7, 17–46; Dorothy Livesay, "UNESCO Draft Final Report, Mission to Northern Rhodesia, November 1960–May 1963," box 9, folder 3, "UNESCO and Africa Teaching, 1958–63: Correspondences, Reports, Documents," MSS 37, DL-UM; Dorothy Livesay, "Annual Report, UNESCO Mission to Northern Rhodesia," 30 November 1961, box 9, folder 3, "UNESCO and Africa Teaching, 1958–63: Correspondences, Reports, Documents," MSS 37, DL-UM; play program for *Androcles and the Lion*, box 10, folder 1, "UNESCO and Africa Teaching, 1958–63: Teaching-Related Material," MSS 37, DL-UM; Joe Mulenga to Dorothy Livesay, 14 August 1961, box 49, folder 38, "Chalimbana Training College, Correspondence from Students and Staff, 1961–69," MSS 37, DL-UM; Dorothy Livesay to "The Editor, UNESCO Features," 1 August 1961, box 73, folder 2, "UNESCO,

Teaching Services Commission, 1961–63," MSS 37, DL-UM; Dorothy Livesay, "English s2 Course: Note on the Work Covered, January to May 1962; August to October 1962," box 9, folder 4, "UNESCO and Africa Teaching, 1958–63: Correspondences, Reports, Documents," MSS 37, DL-UM. In *Imperial Encore*, Ritter notes that Oxford University Press published Julius Nyerere's Swahili translation of *Julius Caesar* in 1963 and of *The Merchant of Venice* in 1969; Nyerere's Swahili-language introduction to the former promotes Swahili – not English – as the language that African students need for their futures (68–9).

44 Livesay, *Journey with My Selves*, 217. Additionally, Livesay published a version of "Village" (which first appeared in the 1964 chapbook *The Colour of God's Face*) in *Prism International* 4, no. 1 (Summer 1964). Revised versions of this poem were later published as parts of sequences in the periodical *Cyclic* (1965), in Livesay, *Collected Poems*, and Livesay, *The Self-Completing Tree*.

45 Livesay, "Foreword," in Livesay, *Collected Poems*, v; Livesay, "Song and Dance," 46.

46 Beardsley and Sullivan, "An Interview with Dorothy Livesay."

47 Livesay, "Song and Dance," 46–7, 41; Beardsley and Sullivan, "An Interview with Dorothy Livesay"; *Songs of Ukraina*; Livesay, *Journey with My Selves*, 213. Randal Livesay also translated a novel (*Marusia*, 1940) from Ukrainian to English. In the 1980s, Livesay collaborated with Louisa Loeb to publish her mother's Ukrainian material posthumously; see Livesay, Livesay, and Loeb, *Down Singing Centuries*. The tapes that contain Livesay's African recordings can be found in reels 1 and 14, box 1, TC 31, DL-UM.

48 Barber, "An Interview with Dorothy Livesay," 21; Briscoe Thompson, *Dorothy Livesay*, 8. For other critics who connect the second "season" of Livesay's poetics to her time in Africa, see Denham, *Dorothy Livesay and Her Works*, 6, 29–31; and McInnis, *Dorothy Livesay's Poetics of Desire*, 56. Briscoe Thompson (among others) also attributes the shift in Livesay's poetics to her affair in the 1960s with a younger man – an affair that is widely understood to be the motivation for what Briscoe Thompson calls the "fresh, frank, spare" poems in *The Unquiet Bed* (1967).

49 Rauwerda, "Upsetting an Already Unquiet Bed"; Briscoe Thompson, *Dorothy Livesay*, 94; Sparrow, "The Self-Completing Tree: Livesay's African Poetry"; Dorothy Livesay, "Kwatcha! A UNESCO Sojourn: First Impressions: Northern Rhodesia, 1960," 2 December 1960, box 3, folder 4, "UNESCO and Africa Teaching, 1958–63: Correspondences, Reports, Documents," MSS 37, DL-UM. See also Livesay, *Journey with My Selves*, 203.

50 Livesay, *Journey with My Selves*, 208–17; Livesay, "The Second Language," in Livesay, *Collected Poems*, 258–9. Note that "Politics" appears in typescript

form in Livesay's archival fonds as "Before Independence (Zambia)," box 82, folder 3, "Poems, 1964," MSS 37, DL-UM; "The Second Language" can be found in box 83, folder 1, "Poems: 1960s," MSS 37, DL-UM. For Livesay's correspondence with Ralph Chbota, see box 49, folder 38, Chalimbana Training College, Correspondence from Students and Staff, 1961–69," MSS 37, DL-UM.

51 Dorothy Livesay, "Zambia," box 91, folder 26, "'Zambia,' 1972," MSS 37, DL-UM.
52 O'Sullivan, *The NGO Moment*, 2, 5, 8. On the NGO movement in Canada, see Murphy, "Canadian NGOs and the Politics of Participation," 161–212.
53 Compton Brouwer, *Canada's Global Villagers*, 216–17, 6, 28–32; "Minutes of the Meetings of the Executive Committee of the Canadian University Service Overseas, held on Sunday and Monday, November 14th and 15th, 1965," vol. 49, folder 25, "Minutes: CUSO Executive Committee Meetings, 1962–1965," CUSO/SUCO-LAC; "Canadian University Service Overseas: Report of the Executive Secretary, 1963–64," vol. 75, folder 6, "Annual CUSO/SUCO Reports, 1963," CUSO/SUCO-LAC. As Compton Brouwer notes in *Canada's Global Villagers*, CUSO was paralleled in French-speaking Canada by Service Universitaire Canadien Outre-Mer (SUCO); the organizations split in 1980 (120).
54 For details of the early funding CUSO received from the federal government, see Compton Brouwer, *Canada's Global Villagers*, 21–5.
55 Compton Brouwer, *Canada's Global Villagers*, 216–17, 32–3; Godfrey, "It's Going to Be a Good Summer," 33; Owram, *Born at the Right Time*, 219. On the social gospel roots of Frontier College, see Morrison, *A Pictorial History of Frontier College*; and Mason, *Home Feelings*. On the relationship of churches to the development paradigm, including assessments of late twentieth-century patterns of secularization, see Clarke and Jennings, *Development, Civil Society, and Faith-Based Organizations*; and, for the Canadian context, Compton Brouwer, "When Missions Became Development," 661–93; and Flatt, *After Evangelicalism*.
56 McWhinney and Godfrey, *Man Deserves Man*, 147–8; Osborne and Kingsley Kent, *Africans and Britons*, 178–9; Laurence, *Dance on the Earth*, 153.
57 Osborne and Kingsley Kent, *Africans and Britons*, 201–9; Nkrumah, *Neo-Colonialism*, xi; James, *Nkrumah and the Ghana Revolution*, 135–48.
58 Thomas's first story with an African setting was published in *The Atlantic* while she was still in Ghana. See Thomas, "If One Green Bottle," 83. Her African stories include the ones collected in *Ten Green Bottles* (1967), as well as "Joseph and His Brother," "Two in the Bush," and "Rapunzel" (*Ladies and Escorts*, 1977); "Out in the Midday Sun" and "Timbuktu" (*Real Mothers*, 1981); and "Degrees," included in Robert Weaver's 1982 anthology *Small Wonders: New Stories By Twelve Distinguished Canadian Authors*. Her novels

with African settings include *Mrs. Blood*, *Blown Figures*, and *Coming Down from Wa*. *Mrs. Blood* is a reshaping of "If One Green Bottle."

59 James Adams, "Late Writer Dave Godfrey Created Three Publishing Houses," *Globe and Mail*, 3 July 2015, https://www.theglobeandmail.com/arts/books-and-media/late-writer-dave-godfrey-created-three-publishing-houses/article25269903/; Gibson, "David Godfrey," 176–7; Compton Brouwer, *Canada's Global Villagers*, 32. The Adams obituary suggests that Godfrey earned a PhD before going to Africa but that is not accurate, as the interview with Gibson makes clear. For more information on Ellen (Swartz) Godfrey, see "Ellen Godfrey," 441.

60 MacSkimming, *The Perilous Trade*, 175–6, 187. For accounts of the late twentieth-century emergence of the teaching of Canadian literature as its own subject in postsecondary institutions in Canada, see Sugars, "Postcolonial Pedagogy"; and King, "An Uncomfortable Match."

61 MacSkimming, *The Perilous Trade*, 175–95; Cameron, "Dave Godfrey," 40. Godfrey co-edited *Gordon to Watkins to You* with Mel Watkins, political economist and founder and co-leader with James Laxer of the Waffle, a left-wing formation within the New Democratic Party. Watkins's 1968 report on the federal Task Force on Foreign Ownership and the Structure of Canadian Investment called for strict federal regulation of foreign ownership; *Gordon to Watkins to You* reviews the findings of this report. See Godfrey and Watkins, *Gordon to Watkins to You*.

62 Independent Publishers' Association, *Submission to the Ontario Royal Commission on Book Publishing*, 8, 10–12; UNESCO, *Book Development in Africa*, 17–19.

63 Lorimer, *Ultra Libris*, 87, 89, 98–100.

64 Godfrey and Lorimer, "Publishing in Canada," 265–6; Independent Publishers' Association, "Submission to the Ontario Royal Commission," 16; Ontario, *Canadian Publishers and Canadian Publishing*, 123; MacLaren and Vincent, "Book Policies and Copyright in Canada and Quebec," 63–8.

65 Altbach, Arboleda, and Gopinathan, "Publishing in the Third World," 3–4; Altbach, "Literary Colonialism," 226–36; Suzack, "Publishing and Aboriginal Communities," 292–7. For one account of the challenges faced by Indigenous-owned publishing companies in Canada in the early twenty-first century, see Sabine Milz's 2009 interview with Kateri Akiwenzie-Damm (Chippewas of Nawash Unceded First Nation, Saugeen Ojibway Nation): Milz, "Aboriginal Publishing in Contemporary Canada," 213–26.

66 Cameron, "The Three People Inside David Godfrey," 22; Margaret Laurence, "Caverns to the Mind's Dark Continent," *Globe and Mail*, 5 December 1970, A18, ProQuest Historical Newspapers; Laurence, "Ivory Tower or Grassroots," 16–17. While the critical response to *The New Ancestors*

contemporary to Laurence's review tends to reiterate her interest in the archetypal structures that link the novel to settler Canadian society, later twentieth-century analyses draw on postcolonial theory to explore what Vincent in "Peripheral Visions" calls the novel's resistance to "traditional representations of Africa" and its "violent denunciation of colonialism" (219, 222). Critical responses from the 1970s that reiterate Laurence's interest in archetypal structures include Lecker, "Locating *the New Ancestors*," 82–94; and Monk, "Shadow Continent."

67 Gibson, "David Godfrey," 163–4; Cameron, "Dave Godfrey: Myths and Gardens," 39.

68 Godfrey, "Figments of the Northern Mind,"; Godfrey, "River Two Blind Jacks," 4–7; Godfrey, "Gossip," 6, 10, 20–21. On Canadian imperialist thought, see Berger, *The Sense of Power*.

69 Godfrey, "Letter From Africa," 57–80; Gibson, "David Godfrey," 176, 163–64.

70 Atwood, *Survival*, 241; Godfrey, "The Hard-Headed Collector," 13, 12, 10. Godfrey recalls finding the story of Hirshhorn in the *New York Times* in his interview with Donald Cameron. See Cameron, "Dave Godfrey: Myths and Gardens," 44–45. "The Hard-Headed Collector" attracted the most critical attention of all the stories that appeared in *Death Goes Better with Coca-Cola*, including Atwood's analysis in *Survival* and two essays by New: "Godfrey's Uncollected Artist," 5–15; and "Godfrey's Book of Changes," 375–85.

71 Godfrey, "The First Encountering of Mr. Basa-Basa," 116, 118; Godfrey, "Letter From Africa," 60; New, "Godfrey's Uncollected Artist," 6; Cameron, "Dave Godfrey: Myths and Gardens," 36–7. In "Equatorial Zones," a 1972 review of *The New Ancestors* originally published in the *Journal of Commonwealth Literature* and reprinted in *Articulating West*, W.H. New identifies Godfrey's interest in the fact that both Canada and Africa are "permeated by a foreign (American) culture to the point of selfconscious uncertainty" (233).

72 Godfrey, "Elephant He Go Come Here Plenty," 55–7; Godfrey, "Escape from My Winter Pent House," 44; Godfrey, "Of Bucks and Death," 44. "The Generation of Hunters" and "Up in the Rainforest" keep their original titles in *Death Goes Better with Coca-Cola*; "Of Bucks and Death" becomes "Mud Lake: If Any"; "Elephant He Go Come Here Plenty" becomes "Fulfilling Our Foray"; "The Big Game Fisherman in Florida" becomes "Flying Fish"; and "Pheasants in the Corn" becomes "An Opening Day." New discusses some of the minor changes that occur across this transition, as well as some of the changes made in the 1973 edition of *Death Goes*. See New, "Godfrey's Book of Changes," 375–6; and Godfrey, *Death Goes Better with Coca-Cola*.

73 Gonick, "Enlightened (?) Self-Interest of the U.S.," 163–4; Development Education Centre and Latin American Working Group, "Corporate Power,

the Canadian State, and Imperialism," 65, 58–61. The New Left coalition that formed as Between the Lines Press (publisher of *Imperialism, Nationalism, and Canada*) in Toronto in the late 1970s produced other critiques of the development paradigm; see note 15 in this book's introduction.

74 Kidd and Byram, "The Performing Arts and Community Education in Botswana," 171, 173; Kidd and Kumar, "Co-opting Freire," 28; Kidd, "Popular Theatre and Nonformal Education in the Third World," 266. Kidd also analyzed the successes and limitations of theatre for development in Kidd, "Theatre for Development," 179–204; Kidd, *The Popular Performing Arts*; and Kidd, "The Performing Arts and Development in India," 95–125.

75 Kidd and Byram, "The Performing Arts," 177.

Chapter Five

1 Van Beusekom and Hodgson, "Lessons Learned?," 33, 29–30.
2 Cardinal, *The Unjust Society*, 3.
3 Edwards, "'A Most Industrious and Far-Seeing Mohawk Scholar,'" 90–5; Edwards, *Paper Talk*, 101–6, 89–93, 121, 125–30, 166. For the history of library service to Indigenous communities after 1960, see Edwards, "Reading on the 'Rez,'" 501–5; Lee and Kumarin, *Aboriginal and Visible Minority Librarians*; and Feather Maracle, "A Brief History of Ontario's First Nations Public Libraries," *This Magazine*, 12 May 2020, https://this.org/2020/05/12/a-brief-history-of-ontarios-first-nations-public-libraries.
4 Meren, "'Commend me to the Yak,'" 343–70; Meren, "Lessons Learned," 45; Marshall and Sterparn, "Oxfam Aid to Canada's First Nations, 1962–1975," 298–343.
5 Shewell, "Bitterness Behind Every Smiling Face," 61; Weaver, *Making Canadian Indian Policy*, 12–20; Angus Mowat to Editors of *The Star* et al., 13 March 1959, vol. B1877, file B126-B220, "Correspondence Related to Indian Affairs 1958–1959," Angus McGill Mowat Collection, Archives and Special Collections, D.B. Weldon Library, Western University (hereafter cited as AMM-WU). Mowat's other correspondence in this same file indicates that he also used the occasion of a television appearance in March 1959 to condemn the RCMP raid. See Angus Mowat to Fred Greene, 18 March 1959, vol. B1877, file B126-B220, "Correspondence Related to Indian Affairs 1958–1959," AMM-WU. Mowat's 1959 scrapbook also contains newspaper clippings and photographs related to the raid, though it is not clear where he obtained these since he was not present. See "1959 Scrapbook," vol. B1875, AMM-WU. For an abbreviated form of Mowat's letter see Mowat, "Attack on Indians a Thing of Shame," *Toronto Daily Star*, 19 March 1959, 6.
6 Slaughter, *Human Rights, Inc.*, 278, 280; Graff, *The Literacy Myth*, 5–6; Gee, *Social Linguistics and Literacies*, 38; Angus Mowat to J.J. Honigmann,

16 January 1959, vol. B1877, file B126-B220, "Correspondence Related to Indian Affairs 1958-1959," AMM-WU; Angus Mowat to Sarah Cowley, 2 June 1959, vol. B1877, file B126-B220, "Correspondence Related to Indian Affairs 1958-1959," AMM-WU. Mowat's correspondence from these years suggests that he did not keep abreast of UNESCO literacy work. In a 1959 letter, Mowat reports that "UNESCO want a librarian to go to Indonesia for a year to start libraries." He declined the invitation but recommended his colleague Grace Crooks. Angus Mowat to Gilbert Faries, 16 June 1959, vol. B1877, file B126-B220, "Correspondence Related to Indian Affairs 1958-1959," AMM-WU. Given his support for the principle of Indigenous-run services, it is unsurprising that Mowat was "suspicious" of the settler-led organizations devoted to Indigenous Peoples that began to emerge in the late 1950s, such as the CAAE's National Commission on the Indian Canadian, established in 1957, while the CAAE was still under the leadership of J.R. Kidd. Mowat to Leslie Claus, 14 November 1958, vol. B1877, file B126-B220, "Correspondence Related to Indian Affairs 1958-1959," AMM-WU.

7 W.A. Roedde, "Angus Mowat: Speech at Mowat Luncheon, Ontario Library Association Conference, London, 25 October 1978," vol. B1874, file 1584, "W.A. Roedde: A.M. Correspondence, 1957-77," AMM-WU; Angus Mowat to Ethel Brant Monture, 4 November 1958, vol. B1877, file B126-B220, "Correspondence Related to Indian Affairs 1958-1959," AMM-WU. Information on Mowat's work with the Moose Factory and Shoal Lake libraries, as well as his efforts to extend travelling library service to reserves across Ontario, can be found in vol. B1877, file B126-B220, "Correspondence Related to Indian Affairs 1958-1959," AMM-WU; vol. B1877, file B222-B318, "Indian Affairs-Libraries 1958-1966," AMM-WU; and vol. B1877, file B319-B321, "Angus C.O. Director of Provincial Library Service on Moose Factory Library Project 1958, 1959, 1961," AMM-WU. For information on Mowat's biography, see chapter 3 of Cummings, "Angus McGill Mowat and the Development of Ontario Public Libraries." Travelling library service to "New Ontario" (the northern part of the province) was provided by the Education Department of the Ontario government beginning in 1901. See Bruce, *Free Books for All*, 114-15, 126-8. Though clearly influenced by developmentalist thinking as this was being applied to Indigenous Peoples in the 1950s, Mowat rejected out of hand the premise of second hand books for reserves, despite the fact that book developmentalism was in this period very much oriented to book donation schemes. In a 1959 report to Indian Affairs, he insists that "secondhand or obsolete or merely run-of-the-mill books are not good enough and will not do." Angus Mowat, "Public Library Service: Indians," 1 October 1959, vol. B1877, file B222-B318, "Indian Affairs-Libraries 1958-1966," AMM-WU.

8   For Mowat's correspondence in the late 1950s with Greene, Monture, and Faries, see vol. B1877, file B126-B220, "Correspondence Related to Indian Affairs 1958-1959," AMM-WU; vol. B1877, file B222-B318, "Indian Affairs-Libraries 1958-1966," AMM-WU; and vol. B1877, file B319-B321, "Angus C.O. Director of Provincial Library Service on Moose Factory Library Project 1958, 1959, 1961," AMM-WU. Mowat refers to his adopted children in more than a few of these letters. See, for example, Angus Mowat to Mr and Mrs Pratt, 16 October 1958, vol. B1877, file B126-B220, "Correspondence Related to Indian Affairs 1958-1959," AMM-WU. (The Pratts were the adoptive parents of Kunee, the young woman who features in *The People of the Deer*. They lived in Churchill, Manitoba).

9   Angus Mowat to Ethel Brant Monture, 11 February 1958, vol. B1877, file A918-A986, "Correspondence Related to Indian Affairs c. 1960s," AMM-WU; Angus Mowat to Gilbert Faries, 25 May 1959, vol. B1877, file A918-A986, "Correspondence Related to Indian Affairs c. 1960s," AMM-WU; Sarah Cowley to Angus Mowat, 20 May 1959, vol. B1877, file A918-A986, "Correspondence Related to Indian Affairs c. 1960s," AMM-WU; Mowat, *The People of the Deer*, 304-12, 309; and Scott, *Seeing like a State*, 88. See the section "Books as Colombo Plan Aid" in this book's chapter 2 for a discussion of the role of high modernist thinking in the federal government's approach to the Arctic and its people after 1950.

10 Angus Mowat to Gilbert Faries, 16 June 1959, vol. B1877, file B126-B220, "Correspondence Related to Indian Affairs 1958-1959," AMM-WU; Meren, "Lessons Learned," 45; "Harry Bertram Hawthorn," Archives at the Museum of Anthropology, University of British Columbia, https://atom.moa.ubc.ca/index.php/harry-bertram-hawthorn.

11 Hawthorn, Belshaw, and Jamieson, *The Indians of British Columbia*, 12-13, 268, 312-13; Angus Mowat to Fred Greene, 17 June 1958, vol. B1877, File B126-B220, "Correspondence Related to Indian Affairs 1958-1959," AMM-WU; Angus Mowat, "Public Library Service: Indians," 1 October 1959, vol. B1877, file B222-B318, "Indian Affairs-Libraries 1958-1966," AMM-WU; Angus Mowat to H.M. Jones, 16 December 1962, vol. B1877, file B222-B318, "Indian Affairs-Libraries 1958-1966," AMM-WU.

12 Shewell, "'Bitterness Behind Every Smiling Face,'" 65; R.F. Davey to Angus Mowat, 4 February 1964, vol. B1877, file B222-B318, "Indian Affairs-Libraries 1958-1966," AMM-WU; Angus Mowat to H.B. Rodine, 2 May 1965, vol. B1877, file B222-B318, "Indian Affairs-Libraries 1958-1966," AMM-WU; R.F. Davey to Angus Mowat, 18 June 1969, vol. B1877, file B056-B125, "Correspondence Related to Indian Affairs 1965-1972," AMM-WU; Adamson, "Public Library Service to the Indians of Canada," 48-9.

13 "Opening of the Six Nations Public Library," *Tekawennake News*, 18 June 1969, 5, Six Nations Public Library Digital Collections; Richard Pilant

to Angus Mowat, 6 November 1960, vol. B1877, file A918-A986, "Correspondence Related to Indian Affairs c. 1960s," AMM-WU; Angus Mowat to H.M. Jones, 30 October 1961, vol. B1877, file B222-B318, "Indian Affairs-Libraries 1958-1966," AMM-WU; Angus Mowat to C.W. Booth, 17 October 1958, vol. B1877, file B319-B321, "Angus C.O. Director of Provincial Library Service on Moose Factory Library Project 1958, 1959, 1961," AMM-WU; Edna Hampton, "Library on Six Nations Reserve a Victory for Women," *Globe and Mail*, 23 January 1969, W5, ProQuest Historical Newspapers; "Coming Events," *New Credit Reporter*, 27 January 1968, 2, Six Nations Public Library Digital Collections. For more on the history of the Six Nations Library, see "About," Six Nations Public Library, updated 2021, https://snpl.ca/board-and-staff.

14 Cardinal, *The Unjust Society*, 3. On Canadian NGOs turning to domestic development initiatives after 1970, see Marshall and Sterparn, "Oxfam Aid"; O'Sullivan, *The NGO Moment*, 70; and Murphy, "Canadian NGOs and the Politics of Participation," 161–212. On CUSO's hesitation to expand its domestic work for fear of spreading its resources too thinly, see Compton Brouwer, *Canada's Global Villagers*, 29, 101, 207–8. Marshall and Sterparn include a brief discussion of how settler Canadians' preference for development in the global South, particularly in Biafra, was noticed by the Edmonton-based Indigenous newspaper *The Native People* in 1970 (320). Marshall and Sterparn also point out that encounters between "lay charities," such as anti-slavery organizations and, later, NGOs such as Oxfam Canada, and Indigenous communities in Canada preceded the 1960s, though their focus also falls on the period contemporary with development's second wave (300).

15 Kapoor, Kidd, and Touchette, *Functional Literacy and International Development*, 14–15; "Background Notes on the Overseas Book Centre," vol. 37, file 21, "Overseas Book Centre, 1969–70," CUSO/SUCO-LAC; Marshall and Sterparn, "Oxfam Aid," 322–9.

16 E.W. Robinson to Jean Chrétien, 5 February 1969, vol. 304, file 7, "Fort Hope Project, Correspondence, 1968," Frontier College fonds, MG28 I124, Library and Archives Canada (hereafter cited as FC-LAC); Ian Morrison to Mrs D. Hovorka, 12 January 1970, vol. 334, file 5, "Department of Indian Affairs and Northern Development Correspondence, 1970," FC-LAC; Mrs D. Hovorka to Director, 9 December 1969, vol. 334, file 5, "Department of Indian Affairs and Northern Development Correspondence, 1970," FC-LAC.

17 Ian Morrison to F.A. Clark, 14 May 1971, vol. 336, file 28, "Department of Indian Affairs and Northern Development Correspondence, 1971," FC-LAC; Drew Lamonte, "Frontier College Community Education Project in Amaranth, Manitoba," vol. 427, file 30, "Community Education Program-Reports," FC-LAC. For information about the programs in Fort Hope, Lennox Island, and Frobisher Bay, see vol. 304, file 7, "Fort Hope

Project, Correspondence, 1968," FC-LAC; vol. 305, files 6 and 7, Lennox Island Project, Correspondence 1969–70," FC-LAC; and vol. 334, file 26, "Governments-NWT-Correspondence, 1970," FC-LAC. On the history of Frontier College and its traditional labourer-teacher model, see Mason, *Home Feelings*; on Frontier College as an important element in the pre-1950 voluntary sector that shaped the emergence of the NGO movement in Canada, see the introductory section to this book's chapter 1 and the section "The 'NGO Moment': CUSO and Settler Literatures of the 1960s and '70s" in this book's chapter 4. Frontier College's community education workers were also tasked with distributing the infamous "Statement of the Government of Canada on Indian Policy, 1969," though, as Morrison's 1970 correspondence with Jean Chrétien makes clear, he understood this task less as promotion than as information sharing. He urged the department to ensure that the wishes of Indigenous Peoples "were taken into account before the proposals were acted upon in any way." Ian Morrison to Jean Chrétien, 26 January 1970, vol. 334, file 5, "Department of Indian Affairs and Northern Development Correspondence, 1970," FC-LAC.

18 Bob Holmes to Eric Robinson, 29 January 1970, vol. 334, file 5, "Department of Indian Affairs and Northern Development Correspondence, 1970," FC-LAC; Compton Brouwer, *Canada's Global Villagers*, 206–7; "Frontier College: Inuit Management Training Project, Stage 1," vol. 284, file "Inuit Tapirisat of Canada-Correspondence and Publicity, 1971–1976 (2 of 2)", FC-LAC; and "Memorandum of Agreement," 3 October 1975, vol. 285, file "Inuit Management Training Project, Part One (1976) (2 of 5)," FC-LAC. Most of the material related to the Inuit Management Training Program (1971–1976), including notes from some nineteen community visits, can be found in volumes 284 and 285, FC-LAC. For a discussion of Frontier College veterans in CUSO, see chapter 4 of this book.

19 George Manuel (Secwépemc) offers an important corrective to histories that suggest that Indigenous activism in North America began with the Red Power movement of the late 1960s and '70s. He insists that the cultural and political renaissance of Red Power is not a *"new Indian resistance*," noting that there was "never a time since the beginning of colonial conquest when Indian people were not resisting the four destructive forces besetting us: the state through the Indian agent; the church through the priests; the church and state through the schools; the state and industry through the traders." See Manuel and Posluns, *The Fourth World*, 69.

20 Coulthard, "Once Were Maoists," 380, 382, 384–5; Maracle, *Bobbi Lee: Indian Rebel*, 118, 81, 117. Not only does Maracle's memoir, *Bobbi Lee: Indian Rebel*, attempt to document Indigenous encounters with Third Worldist decolonization movements, the book itself is a product of them:

the narrative was recorded by the settler anthropologist Don Barnett, founder and chair of the Liberation Support Movement, the Vancouver-based organization that published Maracle's text in its "Life Histories from the Revolution" series, which also included books and pamphlets that documented the lives of Third World liberation leaders from Kenya's Mau Mau and Angola's People's Movement for the Liberation of Angola. The first edition of *Bobbi Lee* offers evidence of this publishing history, including a list of "Other Books & Pamphlets by Don Barnett"; a "Dedication" to Barnett that acknowledges his role as "comrade of the Native Study Group" and as "chairman" of the Liberation Support Movement; a list of "Selected LSM Publications" related to imperialism, revolutionary movements, and Marxist theory; and a three-point summary of the Liberation Support Movement's principles.

21 Coulthard, *Red Skin, White Masks*, 66–9; Coulthard, "Introduction," xvi–xvii; Crossen, "Another Wave of Anti-Colonialism," 533–59.
22 Crossen, "Marie Smallface-Marule," 137–40; Compton Brouwer, *Canada's Global Villagers*, 207, 29; "CUSO Programme: Zambia," September 1968, vol. 19, file 17, "Zambia: Country Plans and Budget, 1968–74," CUSO/SUCO-LAC; "CUSO Volunteer Wants More Indians to Go Overseas," *CUSO/SUCO Bulletin*, December 1968, p. 9, vol. 103, file 2, "CUSO Bulletin, 1967–1971," CUSO/SUCO-LAC. On the conflicts that arose from CUSO's relation to the politics of Tanzanian socialism during the 1960s and 70s, see Langford, "International Development and the State Question," 195–216.
23 David Beer, "Au Retour: The Thoughts of a CUSO Volunteer from Zambia," *CUSO/SUCO Bulletin*, October 1967–January 1968, p. 21, vol. 103, file 3, "CUSO Bulletin, 1967–1971," CUSO/SUCO-LAC; and "CUSO Volunteer Wants More Indians to Go Overseas," *CUSO/SUCO Bulletin*, December 1968, p. 9, vol. 103, file 2, "CUSO Bulletin, 1967–1971," CUSO/SUCO-LAC. Information about the total number of CUSO volunteers in Zambia from 1966 to 1968 comes from "1960–1970 Orientation," vol. 19, file 17, "Zambia: Country Plans and Budget, 1968, 1974," CUSO/SUCO-LAC.
24 Crossen, "Marie Smallface-Marule," 140–50; Manuel and Posluns, *The Fourth World*, xv.
25 Coulthard, "Introduction," x.
26 Coulthard, "Introduction," xiii–xx; Manuel and Posluns, *The Fourth World*, 5; Crossen, "Another Wave of Anti-Colonialism," 539–47; McFarlane with Manuel, *Brotherhood to Nationhood*,162–77; Manuel, "Presentation to the Mackenzie Valley Pipeline Inquiry," 17. The 1960 UN Declaration on the Granting of Independence to Colonial Countries and Peoples, which affirmed the right of self-determination, was accompanied by a resolution that defined a colony as "a territory which is geographically separate" and "distinct

ethnically and/or culturally from the country administering it." United Nations, "Declaration on the Granting of Independence to Colonial Countries and Peoples," General Assembly Resolution 1514 (XV), 14 December 1960, UN *Human Rights Office of the High Commissioner*, https://www.ohchr.org/en/instruments-mechanisms/instruments/declaration-granting-independence-colonial-countries-and-peoples; United Nations, "Resolution 1541 (XV): Principles Which Should Guide Members in Determining Whether or Not an Obligation Exists to Transmit the Information Called For Under Article 73 e of the Charter," *undocs.org*, https://documents.un.org/doc/resolution/gen/nro/153/15/pdf/nro15315.pdf.

27 Manuel and Posluns, *The Fourth World*, 219, 220, 217, 236–38; Manuel, "Presentation to the Mackenzie Valley Pipeline Inquiry," 17. In "Another Wave of Anti-Colonialism," Crossen cites Manuel's personal diary as evidence of his reading of Nyerere's book in 1972 (in the wake of his visit to Tanzania) (541).

28 Manuel qtd. in McFarlane, *Brotherhood to Nationhood*, 153; Manuel and Posluns, *The Fourth World*, 204, 246; Lal, *African Socialism in Postcolonial Tanzania*, 27–53. Nyerere's policy of villagization was initially voluntary; after 1973 it was not. For assessments of the increasingly authoritarian character of Nyerere's government after 1973, see Shivji, "Nationalism and Pan-Africanism," 103–16.

29 Cunningham, "Community Development," 53; United Nations Bureau of Social Affairs, *Social Progress Through Community Development*, 5–6, 11–12; Hawthorn et al., *The Indians of British Columbia*, 432; Weaver, *Making Canadian Indian Policy*, 48. The Indian Affairs July 1964 announcement is quoted in Cunningham's thesis (57). Community development was tied to the high modernist thinking of postwar developmentalism. As Antony John Lloyd, the first scholar to produce a study of community development in Canada, puts it, "community development, in short, is expected to bring a measure of material gain to compensate for old values lost due to the impact of economic, social, and technological changes." See Lloyd, *Community Development in Canada*, 11. On the Community Development program at Indian Affairs, see also Buckley, *From Wooden Ploughs to Welfare*, 102–3; and Shewell, "'Bitterness Behind Every Smiling Face.'"

30 Cunningham, "Community Development," 81; Manuel and Posluns, *The Fourth World*, 130–4, 153, 152, 154, 151, 205–6; McFarlane, *Brotherhood to Nationhood*, 89–92; Weaver, *Making Canadian Indian Policy*, 28; Manuel, "Presentation to the Mackenzie Valley Pipeline Inquiry," 15–16. In *The Unjust Society*, Cardinal makes the point that the Company of Young Canadians, a federal community development program that followed the Indian Affairs program, aimed many of its initiatives "at native

31 Manuel and Posluns, *The Fourth World*, 192. For a discussion of these shifts at UNESCO, see the section "The OBC/CLO and Development's Second Wave" in this book's chapter 3.
32 Buckley, *From Wooden Ploughs*, 97–101; Manuel and Posluns, *The Fourth World*, 121–4, 189–93, 249; McFarlane, *Brotherhood to Nationhood*, 147–52. On *Citizens Plus*, or the Indian Association of Alberta's Red Paper, see Jamie Bradburn, "Citizens Plus (The Red Paper)," *Canadian Encyclopedia*, updated 16 March 2023, https://www.thecanadianencyclopedia.ca/en/article/citizens-plus-the-red-paper.
33 Manuel and Posluns, *The Fourth World*, 249; National Indian Brotherhood/Assembly of First Nations, *Indian Control of Indian Education*.
34 Manuel and Posluns, *The Fourth World*, 204, 246–49. In 2010, the Assembly of First Nations updated *Indian Control of Indian Education*. The revisions include renewed calls for adequate federal funding to support Indigenous-controlled education at all three levels (elementary, secondary, post-secondary). See Assembly of First Nations, *First Nations Control of First Nations' Education: It's Our Vision, It's Our Time*, July 2010, https://education.afn.ca/afntoolkit/wp-content/uploads/2021/04/2010-AFN-First-Nations-Contol-of-First-Nations-Education_sm.pdf. For a review of the major challenges that have beset the principle of Indigenous control of Indigenous education since 1973, see Battiste, "Introduction," vii–xx.
35 Watson and Watson, *Indian Education Project*, 17–21, 27–27a; Williamson with Armstrong, "What I Intended Was to Connect ... and It's Happened," 121–3. On the history of Theytus Books, see Young-Ing, "Aboriginal Peoples' Estrangement: Marginalization in the Publishing Industry," 186; and "Theytus Books," 233–4.
36 Lutz, "Jeannette Armstrong," 27–9; Armstrong, *Slash*, 54. See also Maracle, *Bobbi Lee*.
37 Armstrong, *Slash*, 26, 21, 32, 23, 35.
38 Williamson with Armstrong, "What I Intended," 119; Armstrong, *Slash*, 178–9, 183. The Constitution Express was a cross-country movement organized in 1980 to protest the lack of recognition of Indigenous rights in the proposed text of the patriated Constitution. It was led by George Manuel (then-leader of the Union of British Columbia Indian Chiefs). See Erin Hanson, "Constitution Express," Indigenous Foundations, indigenousfoundations.arts.ubc.ca, 2009, https://indigenousfoundations.arts.ubc.ca/constitution_express.
39 Rist, *The History of Development*, 19, 43–5, 73; McCarthy, *Race, Empire, and the Idea of Human Development*, 183–4.

40 Esty, *Unseasonable Youth*, 4; Rist, *The History of Development*, 40–3; Slaughter, "Enabling Fictions and Novel Subjects," 1411; Cheah, *Spectral Nationality*, 243. For an extended discussion of the classic nineteenth-century bildungsroman, see Moretti, *The Way of the World*. On the postcolonial bildungsroman more generally, see Hoagland, "The Postcolonial Bildungsroman," 217–38.

41 Hay, "*Nervous Conditions*, Lukács, and the Postcolonial Bildungsroman," 322; Lutz, "Jeannette Armstrong," 15–16. *Slash* closely tracks actual historical events, which makes it an easy matter to follow its timeframe. At the opening of the novel, Tommy is in grade six (and is roughly twelve years old); this is the same year, he tells us, that "John Kennedy got killed" (1963). In the novel's final chapter, Tommy's partner Maeg travels to Europe with the Constitution Express, a trip that occurred in 1981, and Tommy recounts that the federal government cedes to their demands, which occurred in January of 1982. Armstrong, *Slash*, 15, 204–5.

42 Armstrong, *Slash*, xiii, 164–5. In her 1992 interview with Williamson, Armstrong explains her choice of a male protagonist (which some critics found odd, given that she identifies as a woman). Since men were "at the forefront and engendered the thought of the American Indian Movement," the choice made sense, but it also allowed her to comment on the "question of the breakdown in our society in relation to the male role." Williamson with Armstrong, "What I Intended," 119.

43 Slaughter, *Human Rights, Inc.*, 273, 284; Armstrong, *Slash*, 2, 21; Teuton, "Indigenous Orality and Oral Literatures," 168; Armstrong, "Traditional Indigenous Education," 15–18.

44 Jones, "Slash Marks the Spot," 48; Armstrong, *Slash*, xiii; Lutz, "Jeannette Armstrong," 14–15; Fee, "Decolonizing Indigenous Oratures and Literatures," 563; Warkentin, "Dead Metaphor or Working Model?," 48; Maracle, "Oratory on Oratory," 55–70.

45 Coulthard, *Red Skin*, 13.

46 Armstrong, "Kwtlakin? What Is Your Place?," 29–31; Armstrong, *Slash*, 190–91, 205.

47 Barnes, "We Need A Library," 1; Miller, "Kahnawake Teen Knows How to Get the Job Done," 11; Lisa Fitterman, "Teen's Library Dream Inspires Donations," *The Gazette* [Montreal], 21 September 2002, A7. In 2003, *The Gazette* reported that Barnes's campaign had attracted thirty thousand books, though the new library that opened its doors in 2003 could house only five thousand. Debbie Parkes, "Kahnawake Turns a Page," *The Gazette* [Montreal], 5 October 2003, A3.

48 Michelle Ruby, "They Are Cries of Despair," *The Brantford Expositor*, 14 November 2018, https://www.brantfordexpositor.ca/news/local-news/they-are-cries-of-despair; Roy McGregor, "Bartelman Uses Books to Help

Native Children Survive the Impossible," *Globe and Mail*, 18 March 2005, A2. See also Bartelman's memoir of his childhood in Bartelman, *Out of Muskoka*.
49 Rodney, *How Europe Underdeveloped Africa*, 246.

Conclusion

1 Rist, *The History of Development*, 140–70, 171–2, 220; Leys, *The Rise and Fall of Development Theory*, 18–26.
2 Brouillette, UNESCO *and the Fate of the Literary*, 91–4, 95. In 2025, the US once again exited UNESCO.
3 Mason, "'Capital Intraconversion,'" 436; Atkinson, "Calculating Normative Literacy," 139–42. On the instrumentalist character of the OECD literacy surveys, see Atkinson, "Grade 12 or Die," 7–21; Hamilton and Barton, "The International Adult Literacy Survey," 377–89; and Walker, "The Needy and Competent Citizen in OECD Policy Documents," 97–112.
4 Graff, *The Literacy Myth*; Watkins, *Literacy Work in the Reign of Human Capital*, 27, 9, 11, 16–17. On the New Literacy Studies and Graff's concern that its challenge to the literacy myth was "never complete," see Graff, "The New Literacy Studies and the Resurgent Literacy Myth," 47–53. On the New Literacy Studies more generally and its challenge to the basic premises of the orality-literacy binary (articulated most forcefully in the later twentieth century by Walter Ong's 1982 study *Orality and Literacy*), see Gee, *Social Linguistics*; and Street, *Social Literacies*. On platform capitalism – what Nick Srnicek has theorized as the unique capitalism that is premised on the monopolistic platforms of technology giants such as Apple and Microsoft – see Srnicek, *Platform Capitalism*.
5 Roberts, *Prizing Literature*, 4; Fuller and Sedo, "A Reading Spectacle for the Nation," 7. On the settler nationalist politics of public book performances in the era of conglomerate publishing, see also Kambboureli, "The Culture of Celebrity and National Pedagogy," 35–55; Lael Netzer, "'A VR Empathy Machine,'" 58–78; and Moss, "Canada Reads," 6–10.
6 Nguyen and Phu, *Refugee States*, 3–4; Lael Netzer, "A VR Empathy Machine."
7 Lang, "A Book That All Canadians Should be Proud to Read," 120–36; Rymhs, "Appropriating Guilt," 105–6; Lael Netzer, "'A VR Empathy Machine'"; Mason and Pelletier, "Singular Plurality," 467–96. On the "cunning of reconciliation," see Wakeham, "The Cunning of Reconciliation," 209–33; as well as Henderson and Wakeham, *Reconciling Canada*. On the "politics of recognition," see Coulthard, *Red Skin, White Masks*.
8 Fuller and Sedo, *Reading Beyond the Book*; Collins, *Bring on the Books for Everybody*.

Bibliography

Archival Sources

Angus McGill Mowat Collection. Archives and Special Collections. D.B. Weldon Library. Western University. [AMM-WU]

Canadian Council for Reconstruction Through UNESCO fonds. MG28 145. Library and Archives Canada.

Canadian University Service Overseas/Service Universitaire Canadien Outre-Mer fonds. MG28 1323. Library and Archives Canada. [CUSO/SUCO-LAC]

Department of External Affairs fonds. RG 25. Library and Archives Canada. [DEA-LAC]

Dorothy Livesay fonds. University of Manitoba. [DL-UM]

Frontier College fonds. MG28 1124. Library and Archives Canada. [FC-LAC]

George M. Wrong Family fonds. B2004-0010. University of Toronto. [GMW-UT]

International Committee on Christian Literature for Africa fonds. GB 102. School of Oriental and African Studies. University of London. [ICCLA-SOAS]

International Council for Adult Education fonds. R14041. Library and Archives Canada. [ICAE-LAC]

J.R. Kidd fonds. F-1204. Archives of Ontario.

Margaret Laurence to Adele Wiseman. 4 September 1951. 1991-012/043, file 6, "Correspondence-Margaret Laurence." Adele Wiseman fonds. F0477. Clara Thomas Archives and Special Collections. York University.

Published Sources and Dissertations

Abraham, Cecil. "Margaret Laurence and the Ancestral Tradition." In *New Perspectives on Margaret Laurence: Poetic Narrative, Multiculturalism, and Feminism*, edited by Greta M.K. McCormick Coger. Greenwood, 1996.

Abrahams, Peter. *Tell Freedom: Memories of Africa*. Alfred A. Knopf, 1954.

Adamson, Edith. "Public Library Service to the Indians of Canada." *Canadian Library Journal* 26, no. 1 (1969): 48–53.

African Education: A Study of Educational Policy and Practice in British Tropical Africa. Charles Batey, 1953.

Allison, Simon D. "State Participation in Publishing: The Zambian Experience." In Oluwasanmi et al., *Publishing in Africa in the Seventies*.

Allshorn, Florence. *King Khama*. Sheldon, 1927.

Altbach, Philip G. "Literary Colonialism: Books in the Third World." *Harvard Educational Review* 15, no. 2 (May 1975): 226–36.

Altbach, Philip G., Amadio A. Arboleda, and S. Gopinathan, eds. *Publishing in the Third World: Knowledge and Development*. Heinemann, 1985.

Altbach, Philip G., Amadio A. Arboleda, and S. Gopinathan. "Publishing in the Third World: Some Reflections." In Altbach, Arboleda, and Gopinathan, *Publishing in the Third World*.

Altbach, Philip G., and S. Gopinathan. "Textbooks in the Third World: Challenge and Response." In Altbach, Arboleda, and Gopinathan, *Publishing in the Third World*.

Altbach, Philip G., and Eva-Maria Rathgeber. *Publishing in the Third World: Trend Report and Bibliography*. Praeger, 1980.

Armstrong, Jeannette. "Kwtlakin? What Is Your Place?" In *What Is Your Place? Indigeneity and Immigration in Canada*, edited by Hartmut Lutz with Thomas R. Ruiz. Wissner-Verlag, 2007.

Armstrong, Jeannette. *Slash*. Theytus, 2011.

Armstrong, Jeannette. "Traditional Indigenous Education: A Natural Process." *Canadian Journal of Native Education* 14, no. 3 (1987): 15–18.

Atkinson, Tannis. "Calculating Normative Literacy, Constituting Human Capital." In *Governing the Social in Neoliberal Times*, edited by Deborah R. Brock. University of British Columbia Press, 2019.

Atkinson, Tannis. "Grade 12 or Die: Literacy Screening as a Tactic of Bio-Power." In *Canadian Education: Governing Practices and Producing Subjects*, edited by Brenda L. Spencer, Kenneth D. Gregory, Kari Delhi, and James Ryan. Sense, 2012.

Atwood, Margaret. *Survival: A Thematic Guide to Canadian Literature*. House of Anansi, 1972.

Austin, David. "All Roads Led to Montreal: Black Power, the Caribbean, and the Black Radical Tradition in Canada." *Journal of African American History* 92, no. 4 (2007): 516–39.

Austin, David. *Moving Against the System: The 1968 Congress of Black Writers and the Making of Global Consciousness*. Between the Lines, 2018.

Azzi, Stephen. "The Nationalist Moment in English Canada." In *Debating Dissent: Canada and the Sixties*, edited by Lara Campbell, Greg Kealey, and Dominique Clément. University of Toronto Press, 2012.

Barber, Marsha. "An Interview with Dorothy Livesay." *Room of One's Own* 5, nos 1–2 (1979): 13–34.

Barker, Ronald, and Robert Escarpit, eds. *The Book Hunger*. UNESCO, 1973.

Barnes, Skawenniio. "We Need a Library." *Eastern Door* 11, no. 5 (2002): 1.

Barnhisel, Greg. *Cold War Modernists: Art, Literature, and American Cultural Diplomacy*. Columbia University Press, 2015.

Barry-Shaw, Nikolas. *Paved with Good Intentions: Canada's Development NGOs from Idealism to Imperialism*. Fernwood, 2012.

Bartelman, James. *Out of Muskoka*. Penumbra, 2002.

Battell Lowman, Emma, and Adam J. Barker. *Settler Identity and Colonialism in 21st-Century Canada*. Fernwood, 2015.

Battiste, Marie. "Introduction." In *First Nations Education in Canada: The Circle Unfolds*, edited by Marie Battiste and Jean Barman. University of British Columbia Press, 1995.

Baughan, Emily. *Saving the Children: Humanitarianism, Internationalism, and Empire*. University of California Press, 2022.

Bayrock, Dessa, and Sarah Brouillette. "Who Wins? The Politics of Prize Culture in Canada's CODE Burt Awards." *Wasifiri* 37, no. 1 (2022): 86–94.

Beardsley, Doug, and Rosemary Sullivan. "An Interview with Dorothy Livesay." *Canadian Poetry* 3 (Fall/Winter 1978). https://canadianpoetry.org/volumes/vol3/sullivan.html.

Behrstock, Julian. "Books for All? UNESCO's Long Love Affair with the Book." *Logos* 2, no. 1 (1991): 29–36.

Behrstock, Julian. "National Book Development Councils." In Oluwasanmi et al., *Publishing in Africa in the Seventies*.

Bejjitt, Nourdin. "Heinemann's African Writers Series and the Rise of James Ngugi." In Davis and Johnson, *The Book in Africa*.

Bejjitt, Nourdin. "National Book Development Councils in Africa: A Report by UNESCO." In Oluwasanmi et al., *Publishing in Africa in the Seventies*.

Benjamin, Curtis G. "The Power of Books: National Development and International Relations." *Vital Speeches of the Day* 31 (December 1964): 155–9.

Benjamin, Curtis G. *U.S. Books Abroad: Neglected Ambassadors*. Library of Congress, 1984.

Berger, Carl. *The Sense of Power: Studies in the Ideas of Canadian Imperialism, 1867–1914*. University of Toronto Press, 1970.

Berland, Jody. "Nationalism and the Modernist Legacy: Dialogues with Innis." In *Capital Culture: A Reader on Modernist Legacies, State Institutions, and the Value(s) of Art*, edited by Jody Berland and Shelly Hornstein. McGill-Queen's University Press, 2000.

Berman, Edward H. "American Influence on African Education: The Role of the Phelps-Stokes Fund's Education Commissions." *Comparative Education Review* 15, no. 2 (June 1971): 132–45.

"Biographies of Africans." *Books for Africa* 1, no. 1 (January 1931): 7.

Bonneuil, Christophe. "Development as Experiment: Science and State Building in Late Colonial and Postcolonial Africa, 1930–1970." *Osiris* 15 (2000): 258–81.

BookNet Canada. *The Canadian Book Market 2018*. BookNet Canada, 2019.

Bremer, Francis J. *John Winthrop: America's Forgotten Founding Father*. Oxford University Press, 2003.

Briscoe Thompson, Lee. *Dorothy Livesay*. Twayne, 1987.

Brooks, Stephen. "Uncertain Embrace: The Rise and Fall of Canadian Studies Abroad as a Tool of Foreign Policy." In *Promoting Canadian Studies Abroad: Soft Power and Cultural Diplomacy*, edited by Stephen Brooks. Palgrave Macmillan, 2019.

Broten, Delores. *The Lumberjack Report: English Canadian Literary Trade Book Publishers' Sales, 1963–1972*. CANLIT, 1975.

Brouillette, Sarah. *UNESCO and the Fate of the Literary*. Stanford University Press, 2019.

Brouillette, Sarah, and Jacques Michon. "Control and Content in Mass-Market Distribution." In Gerson and Michon, *History of the Book in Canada*.

Brown, E.K. *On Canadian Poetry*. Ryerson, 1943.

Brown, Stephen. "Canada's Foreign Aid Before and After CIDA: Not a Samaritan State." *International Journal* 68, no. 3 (September 2013): 501–12.

Brown, Stephen. *Struggling for Effectiveness: CIDA and Canadian Foreign Aid*. McGill-Queen's University Press, 2012.

Bruce, Lorne. *Free Books for All: The Public Library Movement in Ontario, 1850–1930*. Dundurn Press, 1994.

Brushett, Kevin. "Partners in Development? Robert McNamara, Lester Pearson, and the Commission on International Development, 1967–1973." *Diplomacy & Statecraft* 26 (2015): 84–102.

Brushett, Kevin. "'Trotsky in Pinstripes': Lewis Perinbam, CIDA, and the Non-Governmental Organizations Program, 1968–1991." In Donaghy and Webster, *A Samaritan State Revisited*.

Bryant, Rachel. *The Homing Place: Indigenous and Settler Literary Legacies of the Atlantic*. Wilfrid Laurier University Press, 2017.

Brydon, Diana, ed. "Testing the Limits: Postcolonial Theories and Canadian Literature." Special issue, *Essays On Canadian Writing* 56 (1995).

Buckley, Helen. *From Wooden Ploughs to Welfare: Why Indian Policy Failed in the Prairie Provinces*. McGill-Queen's University Press, 1992.

Cameron, Donald. "Dave Godfrey: Myths and Gardens." In Donald Cameron, *Conversations with Canadian Novelists*. Macmillan, 1973.

Cameron, Donald. "The Three People Inside David Godfrey." *Saturday Night*, September 1971, 22.

Campbell, Grant. "William Collins During World War II: Nationalism Meets a Wartime Economy in Canadian Publishing." *Papers of the Bibliographical Society of Canada* 39, no. 1 (2001): 45–65.

Campbell-Miller, Jill. "Encounter and Apprenticeship: The Colombo Plan and Canadian Aid in India, 1950–1960." In Donaghy and Webster, *A Samaritan State Revisited*.

Canada. Department of External Affairs. *Canada and the Colombo Plan*. Queen's Printer, 1962.

Canada. *House of Commons Debates*, 22nd Parliament, 1st Session, 1953–1954, vol. 1. Queen's Printer, 1954.

Canada. *House of Commons Debates*, 22nd Parliament, 1st Session, 1953–1954, vol. 2. Queen's Printer, 1954.

Canada. *Canada from Sea to Sea*. Edmond Cloutier, Queen's Printer and Controller, 1947.

Canada and Pierre Berton. *Canada from Sea to Sea*. Edmond Cloutier, Queen's Printer and Controller, 1958.

Cardinal, Harold. *The Unjust Society: The Tragedy of Canada's Indians*. M.G. Hurtig, 1969.

Carty, Robert, Virginia R. Smith, and LAWG [Latin American Working Group]. *Perpetuating Poverty: The Political Economy of Canadian Foreign Aid*. Between the Lines, 1981.

Cavell, Janice. "Canadiana Abroad: The Department of External Affairs' Book Presentation Programmes, 1949–1963." *American Review of Canadian Studies* 39, no. 2 (June 2009): 81–93.

Cavell, Richard. "Introduction: The Cultural Production of Canada's Cold War." In *Love, Hate and Fear in Canada's Cold War*, edited by Richard Cavell. University of Toronto Press, 2004.

Challiss, R.J. "Phelps-Stokeism and Education in Zimbabwe." *Zambezia* 11, no. 2 (1983): 109–25.

Chapnick, Adam. "The Canadian Middle Power Myth." *International Journal* 55, no. 22 (Spring 2000): 188–206.

Cheah, Pheng. *Spectral Nationality: Passages of Freedom from Kant to Postcolonial Literatures of Liberation*. Columbia University Press, 2003.

Ching-Liang Low, Gail. *Publishing the Postcolonial: Anglophone West African and Caribbean Writing in the UK*. Routledge, 2020.

Clarke, Gerald, and Michael Jennings, eds. *Development, Civil Society, and Faith-Based Organizations: Bridging the Sacred and the Secular*. Palgrave Macmillan, 2008.

Cogan, Theodore. "Sharing the Nation's Heart Globally? Foreign Aid and the Canadian Public, 1950–1980." PhD diss., University of Guelph, 2018.

Coleman, Daniel. *White Civility: The Literary Project of English Canada*. University of Toronto Press, 2006.

Collins, Jim. *Bring On the Books for Everybody: How Literary Culture Became Popular Culture*. Duke University Press, 2010.

Colonial Office, Committee on Education in the Colonies. *Mass Education in African Society*. His Majesty's Stationery Office, 1944.

Compton Brouwer, Ruth. *Canada's Global Villagers: CUSO In Development, 1961–1986*. University of British Columbia Press, 2013.

Compton Brouwer, Ruth. "Margaret Wrong's Literacy Work and the 'Remaking of Woman' in Africa, 1929–1948." *The Journal of Imperial and Commonwealth History* 23, no. 3 (1995): 427–52.

Compton Brouwer, Ruth. *Modern Women, Modernizing Men: The Changing Missions of Three Professional Women in Asia and Africa, 1902–69*. University of British Columbia Press, 2002.

Compton Brouwer, Ruth. "When Missions Became Development: Ironies of 'NGOization' in Mainstream Canadian Churches in the 1960s." *Canadian Historical Review*, 4, no. 91 (2010): 661–93.

Cooke, Michael G. "Vic(tor) (Stafford) Reid." In *Twentieth-Century Caribbean and Black African Writers: Second Series*, edited by Bernth Lindfors and Reinhard Sander. Gale, 1993. *Gale Literature Resource Center*.

Cooper, Frederick. *Africa Since 1940: The Past of the Present*. Cambridge University Press, 2002.

Cooper, Frederick. *Decolonization and African Society: The Labor Question in French and British Africa*. Cambridge University Press, 1996.

Cooper, Frederick. "Modernizing Colonialism and the Limits of Empire." In *Lessons of Empire: Imperial Histories and American Power*, edited by Craig Calhoun, Frederick Cooper, and Kevin W. Moore. New Press, 2006.

Coulthard, Glen Sean. "Introduction: A Fourth World Resurgent." In Manuel and Posluns, *The Fourth World*, ix–xxxiv.

Coulthard, Glen Sean. "Once Were Maoists: Third World Currents in Fourth World Anti-Colonialism, Vancouver, 1967–1975." In *The Routledge Handbook of Critical Indigenous Studies*, edited by Brenda Hokowhitu,

Aileen Moreton-Robinson, Linda Tuhiwai-Smith, Chris Andersen, and Steve Larkin. Routledge, 2020.

Coulthard, Glen Sean. *Red Skin, White Masks: Rejecting the Colonial Politics of Recognition*. University of Minnesota Press, 2014.

Cox, James H., and Daniel Heath Justice, eds. *The Oxford Handbook of Indigenous American Literature*. Oxford University Press, 2014.

Crossen, Jonathan. "Another Wave of Anti-Colonialism: The Origins of Indigenous Internationalism." *Canadian Journal of History* 52, no. 3 (2017): 533–59.

Crossen, Jonathan. "Marie Smallface-Marule: An Indigenous Internationalist." In *Breaking Barriers, Shaping Worlds: Canadian Women and the Search for Global Order*, edited by Jill Campbell-Miller, Greg Donaghy, and Stacey Barker. University of British Columbia Press, 2021.

Cullather, Nick. "Development and Technopolitics." In *Explaining the History of American Foreign Relations*, 3rd ed., edited by Frank Costigliola and Michael J. Hogan, 102–18. Cambridge University Press, 2016.

Cummings, Stephen F. "Angus McGill Mowat and the Development of Ontario Public Libraries, 1920–1960." PhD diss., University of Western Ontario, 1986.

Cunningham, Rob. "Community Development at the Department of Indian Affairs in the 1960s: Much Ado About Nothing." Master's thesis, University of Saskatchewan, 1997.

Davey, Frank. "Economics and the Writer." In Gerson and Michon, *History of the Book in Canada*.

Davis, Caroline. *African Literature and the CIA: Networks of Authorship and Publishing*. Cambridge University Press, 2020.

Davis, Caroline. "Creating a Book Empire: Longmans in Africa." In Davis and Johnson, *The Book in Africa*.

Davis, Caroline. *Creating Postcolonial Literature*. Palgrave Macmillan UK, 2013. https://doi.org/10.1057/9781137328380.

Davis, Caroline, and David Johnson, eds. *The Book in Africa: Critical Debates*. Palgrave Macmillan, 2015.

Davis, Jackson, Thomas M. Campbell, and Margaret Wrong. *Africa Advancing: A Study of Rural Education and Agriculture in West Africa and the Belgian Congo*. Friendship, 1944.

Davis, Laura K. *Margaret Laurence Writes Africa and Canada*. Wilfrid Laurier University Press, 2017.

Davis, Mike. "The Origins of the Third World." *Antipode* 32, no. 1 (2000): 48–89.

Davis, Mike. *Late Victorian Holocausts: El Niño Famines and the Making of the Third World*. Verso, 2017.

Dean, Misao. "Canadianization, Colonialism, and Decolonization: Investigating the Legacy of 'Seventies Nationalism' in the Robin Mathews Fonds." *Studies in Canadian Literature* 41, no. 1 (2016): 27–48.
Denham, Paul. *Dorothy Livesay and Her Works*. ECW Press, 1987.
Denning, Michael. *Culture in the Age of Three Worlds*. Verso, 2004.
Development Education Centre and Latin American Working Group [LAWG]. "Corporate Power, the Canadian State, and Imperialism." In *Imperialism, Nationalism, and Canada*, edited by Craig Heron. New Hogtown Press and Between the Lines Press, 1977.
Donaghy, Greg. "A Wasted Opportunity: Canada and the New International Economic Order, 1974–1982." In *Canada and the United Nations: Legacies, Limits, Prospects*, edited by Colin McCullough and Robert Teigrob. McGill-Queen's University Press, 2017.
Donaghy, Greg, and David Webster, eds. *A Samaritan State Revisited: Historical Perspectives on Canadian Foreign Aid*. University of Calgary Press, 2019.
Dorland, Michael, ed. *The Cultural Industries in Canada: Problems, Policies and Prospects*. James Lorimer, 1996.
Dorn, Charles, and Kristen Ghodsee. "The Cold War Politicization of Literacy: Communism, UNESCO, and the World Bank." *Diplomatic History* 36, no. 2 (2012): 373–98.
Dowler, Kevin. "The Cultural Industries Policy Apparatus." In Dorland, *The Cultural Industries in Canada*.
Downey, Deane E.D. "The Canadian Identity and African Nationalism." *Canadian Literature* 75 (Winter 1977): 15–26.
Druick, Zoë. "International Cultural Relations as a Factor in Postwar Canadian Cultural Policy: The Relevance of UNESCO for the Massey Commission." *Canadian Journal of Communication* 31 (2006): 177–95.
Druick, Zoë. *Projecting Canada: Government Policy and Documentary Film at the National Film Board*. McGill-Queen's University Press, 2007.
DuBois, W.E.B. "Education in Africa: A Review of the Recommendations of the African Education Committee." *Crisis* 32, no. 2 (June 1926): 86–89.
Duffield, Mark, and Vernon Hewitt, eds. *Empire, Development, and Colonialism: The Past in the Present*. Boydell and Brewer, 2007.
Earle, Jonathan L. *Colonial Buganda and the End of Empire: Political Thought and Historical Imagination in Africa*. Cambridge University Press, 2017.
Earle, Nancy. "Case Study: The Canada Council for the Arts Writer-in-Residence Program." In Gerson and Michon, *History of the Book in Canada*.
Edwards, Brendan Frederick R. "'A Most Industrious and Far-Seeing Mohawk Scholar': Charles A. Cooke (Thawennensere), Civil Servant, Amateur Anthropologist, Performer, and Writer." *Ontario History* 102, no. 1 (Spring 2010): 81–108.

Edwards, Brendan Frederick R. *Paper Talk: A History of Libraries, Print Culture, and Aboriginal Peoples in Canada Before 1960*. Scarecrow, 2005.

Edwards, Brendan Frederick R. "Reading on the 'Rez.'" In Gerson and Michon, *History of the Book in Canada*.

Edwardson, Ryan. *Canadian Content: Culture and the Quest for Nationhood*. University of Toronto Press, 2007.

Ekbladh, David. *The Great American Mission: Modernization and the Construction of an American World Order*. Princeton University Press, 2011.

"Ellen Godfrey." In *The Encyclopedia of Literature in Canada*, edited by W.H. New. University of Toronto Press, 2002.

Escarpit, Robert. *Trends in Worldwide Book Development, 1970–1978*. UNESCO, 1982.

Escobar, Arturo. *Encountering Development: The Making and Unmaking of the Third World*. Princeton University Press, 2012.

Esteva, Gustavo. "Development." In Sachs, *The Development Dictionary*.

Esty, Jed. *Unseasonable Youth: Modernism, Colonialism, and the Fiction of Development*. Oxford University Press, 2012.

Evans, Gary. *John Grierson and the National Film Board: The Politics of Wartime Propaganda*. University of Toronto Press, 1984.

Fanon, Frantz. *The Wretched of the Earth*. Translated by Richard Philcox. Grove, 1963.

Farish, Matthew, and P. Whitney Lackenbauer. "High Modernism in the Arctic: Planning Frobisher Bay and Inuvik." *Journal of Historical Geography* 35 (2009): 517–44.

Fee, Margery. "Decolonizing Indigenous Oratures and Literatures of Northern British North America and Canada (Beginnings to 1960)." In Cox and Heath Justice, *The Oxford Handbook of Indigenous American Literature*.

Fee, Margery. *Literary Land Claims: The "Indian Land Question" from Pontiac's War to Attawapiskat*. Wilfrid Laurier University Press, 2015.

Finkelstein, David, and Alistair McCleery, eds. *The Book History Reader*. 2nd ed. Routledge, 2006.

Flatt, Kevin N. *After Evangelicalism: The Sixties and the United Church of Canada*. McGill-Queen's University Press, 2013.

Freeman-Maloy, Dan. "The International Politics of Settler Self-Governance: Reflections on Zionism and 'Dominion' Status Within the British Empire." *Settler Colonial Studies* 8, no. 1 (2018): 80–95.

Frye, Northrop. *The Bush Garden: Essays on the Canadian Imagination*. House of Anansi, 1971.

Fuller, Danielle, and Susan Billingham. "CanLit(e): Fit for Export?" *Essays on Canadian Writing* 71 (2000): 114–27.

Fuller, Danielle, and DeNel Rehberg Sedo. "A Reading Spectacle for the Nation: The CBC and Canada Reads." *Journal of Canadian Studies* 40, no. 1 (2006): 5–36.

Fuller, Danielle, and DeNel Rehberg Sedo. *Reading Beyond the Book: The Social Practices of Contemporary Literary Culture*. Routledge, 2013.

Gee, James. *Social Linguistics and Literacies*. Falmer, 1990.

Gendron, Robin. *Towards a Francophone Community: Canada's Relations with France and French Africa, 1945–1968*. McGill-Queen's University Press, 2006.

Gerson, Carole. "Design and Ideology in *A Pocketful of Canada*." *Papers of the Bibliographical Society of Canada* 44, no. 2 (June 2006): 65–85.

Gerson, Carole, and Jacques Michon, eds. *History of the Book in Canada*, vol. 3, *1918–1980*. University of Toronto Press, 2007.

Gibson, Graeme. "David Godfrey." In Graeme Gibson, *Eleven Canadian Novelists Interviewed by Graeme Gibson*. House of Anansi Press, 1973.

Giffard, C. Anthony. *UNESCO and the Media*. Longman, 1989.

Giroux, Dalie. *L'Oeil du maître: figures de l'imaginaire colonial québécois*. Mémoire d'encrier, 2021.

Godard, Barbara. *Audrey Thomas and Her Works*. ECW Press, 1994.

Godfrey, Dave. *Death Goes Better with Coca-Cola*. Press Porcépic, 1973.

Godfrey, Dave. "Elephant He Go Come Here Plenty." *Saturday Night*, February 1967.

Godfrey, Dave. "Escape from My Winter Pent House." *Saturday Night*, April 1967.

Godfrey, Dave. "Figments of the Northern Mind." *The Tamarack Review*, Spring 1964.

Godfrey, Dave. "The First Encountering of Mr. Basa-Basa and His Excellency, Ling Huo." *The Tamarack Review*, Autumn 1966.

Godfrey, Dave. "The Generation of Hunters." In Purdy, *The New Romans*.

Godfrey, Dave. "Gossip: The Birds That Flew, the Birds That Fell." *The Tamarack Review*, Winter 1964.

Godfrey, Dave. "The Hard-Headed Collector." *The Tamarack Review*, Summer 1966.

Godfrey, Dave. "It's Going to Be a Good Summer: There's a Wedding Every Night and Mostly There's Two." *The Tamarack Review*, Summer 1963.

Godfrey, Dave. "Letter from Africa, to an American Negro." *The Tamarack Review*, Winter 1966.

Godfrey, Dave. "Of Bucks and Death." *Saturday Night*, January 1967.

Godfrey, Dave. "River Two Blind Jacks." *The Tamarack Review*, Spring 1961.

Godfrey, Dave, and James Lorimer. "Publishing in Canada." In *Read Canadian: A Book About Canadian Books*, edited by Robert Fulford, David Godfrey, and Abraham Rotstein. J. Lorimer, 1972.

Godfrey, Dave, and Mel Watkins, eds., *Gordon to Watkins to You, A Documentary: The Battle for Control of Our Economy*. New Press, 1970.

Goldthorp, Linda A. "Reluctant Internationalism: Canadian Approaches to UNESCO, 1946–1987." PhD diss., University of Toronto, 1991.

Gonick, Cy. "Enlightened (?) Self-Interest of the US." In Purdy, *The New Romans*.

Gorman, Dan. "Race, the Commonwealth, and the United Nations: From Imperialism to Internationalism in Canada, 1940–60." In Madokoro et al., *Dominion of Race*.

Graff, Harvey J. *The Literacy Myth: Cultural Integration and Social Structure in the Nineteenth Century*. Routledge, 2017.

Graff, Harvey J. "The New Literacy Studies and the Resurgent Literacy Myth." *Literacy in Composition Studies* 9, no. 1 (January 2022): 47–53.

Graham, Peter, with Ian McKay. *Radical Ambition: The New Left in Toronto*. Between the Lines, 2019.

Greer, Alan. "1837–38: Rebellion Reconsidered." *Canadian Historical Review* 76, no. 1 (1995): 1–18.

Gross, Konrad. "Margaret Laurence's African Experience." In *Encounters and Explorations: Canadian Writers and European Critics*, edited by Franz K. Stanzel and Waldemar Zacharasiewicz. Königshausen & Neumann, 1986.

Groves, C.P. *The Planting of Christianity in Africa*, vol. 4, *1914–1954*. Lutterworth, 1958.

Hamilton, Mary, and David Barton. "The International Adult Literacy Survey: What Does It Really Measure?" *International Review of Education* 46, no. 5 (2000): 377–89.

Hawthorn, H.B., C.S. Belshaw, and S.M. Jamieson. *The Indians of British Columbia: A Study of Contemporary Social Adjustment*. University of Toronto Press, 1958.

Hay, Simon. "*Nervous Conditions*, Lukács, and the Postcolonial Bildungsroman." *Genre* 46, no. 3 (Fall 2013): 317–44.

Henderson, Jennifer, and Pauline Wakeham, eds. *Reconciling Canada: Critical Perspectives on the Culture of Redress*. University of Toronto Press, 2013.

Higginson, John. "Liberating the Captives: Independent Watchtower as an Avatar of Colonial Revolt in Southern Africa and Katanga, 1908–1941." *Journal of Social History* 26, no. 1 (Fall 1992): 55–80.

Hill, Alan. *In Pursuit of Publishing*. John Murray, 1988.

Hilliker, John, and Donald Barry. *Canada's Department of External Affairs*, vol. 2, *Coming of Age, 1946–1968*. McGill-Queen's University Press, 1995.

Hoagland, Ericka A. "The Postcolonial Bildungsroman." In *A History of the Bildungsroman*, edited by Sarah Graham. Cambridge University Press, 2019.

Hodge, Joseph Morgan. "Beyond Dependency: North-South Relationships in the Age of Development." In *The Oxford Handbook of the Ends of*

Empire, edited by Martin Thomas and Andrew S. Thompson. Oxford University Press, 2018.

Hodgetts, A.B. *What Culture? What Heritage? A Study of Civic Education in Canada*. Ontario Institute for Studies in Education, 1968.

Hoggart, Richard. *An Idea and Its Servants: UNESCO from Within*. Oxford University Press, 1978.

Huggan, Graham. *The Postcolonial Exotic: Marketing the Margins*. Routledge, 2001.

Huxley, Julian. "Colonies and Freedom." *The New Republic* 110, no. 4 (January 1944): 106–9.

Immerwahr, Daniel. *Thinking Small: The United States and the Lure of Community Development*. Harvard University Press, 2015.

Independent Publishers' Association. *Submission to the Ontario Royal Commission on Book Publishing from the Independent Publishers' Association*. Independent Publishers' Association, 1971.

"In Memoriam: Henry C 'Harry' Campbell (1919–2009)." *Feliciter* 55, no. 5 (2009): 188.

James, C.L.R. *Nkrumah and the Ghana Revolution*. Duke University Press, 2022.

James, C.L.R. *You Don't Play with Revolution: The Montréal Lectures of C.L.R. James*. Edited by David Austin. AK Press, 2009.

Jerónimo, Miguel Bandeira. "Repressive Developmentalism: Idioms, Repertoires, and Trajectories in Late Colonialism." In *The Oxford Handbook of the Ends of Empire*, edited by Martin Thomas and Andrew S. Thompson. Oxford University Press, 2018.

Johnson, David, and Caroline Davis. "Introduction." In Davis and Johnson, *The Book in Africa*.

Johnston, Anna, and Alan Lawson. "Settler Colonies." In *A Companion to Postcolonial Studies*, edited by Henry Schwarz and Sangeeta Ray. Blackwell, 2000.

Jones, A. Creech. "Introduction." In *Fabian Colonial Essays*, edited by Rita Hinden. Routledge, 2023.

Jones, Manina. "Slash Marks the Spot: 'Critical Embarrassment' and Activist Aesthetics in Jeanette Armstrong's *Slash*." *West Coast Line* 33, no. 3 (2000): 48–62.

Jones, Phillip W. *International Policies for Third World Education: Unesco, Literacy, and Development*. Routledge, 1988.

Jones, Phillip W., and David Coleman. *The United Nations and Education: Multilateralism, Development, and Globalization*. Routledge, 2005.

Joshee, Reva. "The Federal Government and Citizenship Education for Newcomers." *Canadian and International Education* 25, no. 2 (1996): 108–27.

Kallaway, Peter. *The Changing Face of Colonial Education in Africa*. African Sun Media, 2021.

Kalliney, Peter J. *The Aesthetic Cold War: Decolonization and Global Literature*. Princeton University Press, 2022.

Kamboureli, Smaro. "The Culture of Celebrity and National Pedagogy." In Sugars, *Home-Work*.

Kane, Molly. "Canada and the Third World: Development Aid." In *Canada and the Third World*, edited by Karen Dubinsky, Sean Mills, and Scott Rutherford. University of Toronto Press, 2016.

Kapoor, S., J.R. Kidd, and C. Touchette. *Functional Literacy and International Development: A Study of Canadian Capability to Assist with the World Campaign to Eradicate Illiteracy*. Canadian National Commission for UNESCO, 1968.

Kidd, J.R. *Adult Education in the Caribbean*. University College of the West Indies, Extra Mural Department, 1958.

Kidd, J.R. "Canada's Stake at UNESCO." *Queen's Quarterly* 63, no. 2 (1956): 249.

Kidd, J.R. *Education for Perspective*. Indian Adult Education Association, 1969.

Kidd, J.R. *Roby Kidd: Adult Educator, 1915–1982*. OISE Press, 1995.

Kidd, J.R. "Still On Our Agenda." *Continuous Learning* 5 (1966): 30–37.

Kidd, Ross. "The Performing Arts and Development in India: Three Case Studies and a Comparative Analysis." In *Continuity and Change in Communications Systems: An Asian Perspective*, edited by Georgette Wang and Wimal Dissanayake. Ablex, 1984.

Kidd, Ross. *The Popular Performing Arts, Non-Formal Education and Social Change in the Third World: A Bibliography and Review Essay*. Centre for the Study of Education in Developing Countries, 1982.

Kidd, Ross. "Popular Theatre and Nonformal Education in the Third World: Five Strands of Experience." *International Review of Education* 30, no. 3 (1985): 27–36.

Kidd, Ross. "Theatre for Development: Diary of a Zimbabwe Workshop." *New Theatre Quarterly* 1, no. 2 (1985): 179–204.

Kidd, Ross, and Martin Byram. "The Performing Arts and Community Education in Botswana." *Community Development Journal* 13, no. 3 (1978): 170–8.

Kidd, Ross, and Krishna Kumar. "Co-opting Freire: A Critical Analysis of Pseudo-Freirian Adult Education." *Economic and Political Weekly* 16, nos 1–2 (1981): 27–36.

Killam, G.D. "Third World Aspects of Canadian Literature." In *Language and Literature in Multicultural Contexts*, edited by Santendra Nandan. University of the South Pacific and ACLALS, 1983.

King, James. *The Life of Margaret Laurence*. Alfred A. Knopf Canada, 1997.

King, Kenneth James. *Pan-Africanism and Education: A Study of Race, Philanthropy, and Education in the Southern States of America and East Africa*. Diasporic Africa Press, 2016.

King, Sarah. "An Uncomfortable Match: Canadian Literature and English Departments in Canada, 1919–1965." PhD diss., University of Western Ontario, 2003.

Kristmanson, Mark. *Plateaus of Freedom: Nationality, Culture, and State Security in Canada, 1940–1960*. University of Toronto Press, 2003.

Küster, Sybille. "'Book Learning' Versus 'Adapted Education': The Impact of Phelps-Stokeism on Colonial Education Systems in Central Africa in the Interwar Period." *Paedagogica Historica* 43, no. 1 (2007): 79–97.

Lachaîne, Alexis. "Black and Blue: French Canadian Writers, Decolonization, and Revolutionary Nationalism in Quebec, 1960–1969." PhD diss., York University, 2007.

Lacy, Dan. "The Overseas Book Program of the United States Government." *Library Quarterly* 24, no. 2 (April 1954): 178–91.

Lael Netzer, Orly. "'A VR Empathy Machine': Testimony, Recognition, and Affect on Canada Reads 2019." *Canadian Literature* 242 (2020): 58–78.

Lal, Priya. *African Socialism in Postcolonial Tanzania: Between the Village and the World*. Cambridge University Press, 2015.

Lang, Anouk. "'A Book That All Canadians Should be Proud to Read': Canada Reads and Joseph Boyden's *Three Day Road*." *Canadian Literature* 215 (Winter 2012): 120–36.

Langford, Will. *The Global Politics of Poverty in Canada: Development Programs and Democracy, 1964–1979*. McGill-Queen's University Press, 2020.

Langford, Will. "International Development and the State Question: Liberal Internationalism, the New Left, and Canadian University Service Overseas in Tanzania, 1963–1977." In *Undiplomatic History: The New Study of Canada and the World*, edited by Philip Van Huizen and Asa McKercher. McGill-Queen's University Press, 2019.

Larmer, Miles. *Rethinking African Politics: A History of Opposition in Zambia*. Routledge, 2016.

Laugesen, Amanda. "Books for the World: American Book Programs in the Developing World, 1948–1968." In *Pressing the Fight: Print, Propaganda, and the Cold War*, edited by Greg Barnhisel and Catherine Turner. University of Massachusetts Press, 2010.

Laugesen, Amanda. *Taking Books to the World: American Publishers and the Cultural Cold War*. University of Massachusetts Press, 2017.

Laurence, Margaret. *Dance on the Earth: A Memoir*. McClelland & Stewart, 1989.

Laurence, Margaret. *Heart of a Stranger.* McClelland & Stewart, 1976.
Laurence, Margaret. "Ivory Tower or Grassroots? The Novelist as Socio-Political Being." In *A Political Art: Essays and Images in Honour of George Woodcock*, edited by W.H. New. University of British Columbia Press, 1978.
Laurence, Margaret. "Open Letter to the Mother of Joe Bass." In Purdy, *The New Romans.*
Laurence, Margaret. *The Prophet's Camel Bell.* McClelland & Stewart, 1988.
Laurence, Margaret. "Ten Years' Sentences." *Canadian Literature* 41 (Summer 1969): 10–16.
Lecker, Robert. *Keepers of the Code: English-Canadian Literary Anthologies and the Representation of Nation.* University of Toronto Press, 2013.
Lecker, Robert. "Locating *The New Ancestors*." *Studies in Canadian Literature* 2, no. 1 (1977): 82–94.
Lee, Deborah, and Mahalakshi Kumarin. *Aboriginal and Visible Minority Librarians: Oral Histories from Canada.* Rowman & Littlefield, 2014.
Lee, Dennis. "Cadence, Country, Silence: Writing in Colonial Space." *boundary 2*, vol. 3, no. 1 (Autumn 1974): 151–68.
LePan, Douglas. *Bright Glass of Memory: A Set of Four Memoirs.* McGraw-Hill Ryerson, 1979.
LePan, Douglas. *The Net and the Sword.* Clarke, Irwin, 1953.
Lewis, I.M. "*A Tree for Poverty: Somali Poetry and Prose*, Collected by Margaret Laurence." *Africa: Journal of the International African Institute* 25, no. 3 (1955): 305–6.
Lewis, L.J. *Education and Political Independence in Africa and Other Essays.* Thomas Nelson, 1962.
Lewis, L.J., and Margaret Wrong. *Towards a Literate Africa.* Longman's, Green, 1948.
Leyes, Colin. *The Rise and Fall of Development Theory.* James Currey, 1996.
Litt, Paul. *The Muses, the Masses, and the Massey Commission.* University of Toronto Press, 1992.
Litt, Paul. "The State and the Book." In Gerson and Michon, *History of the Book in Canada.*
Livesay, Dorothy. *Collected Poems: The Two Seasons.* McGraw-Hill Ryerson, 1972.
Livesay, Dorothy. "Copperbelt: A Letter from Northern Rhodesia." *Canadian Forum* (February 1961): 247–8.
Livesay, Dorothy. "Early Days." *Canadian Forum* (April/May 1970): 34–5.
Livesay, Dorothy. *Journey with My Selves.* Douglas & McIntyre, 1991.
Livesay, Dorothy. "New Jersey: 1935." In Purdy, *The New Romans.*
Livesay, Dorothy. *Right Hand Left Hand: A True Life of the Thirties.* Press Porcépic, 1977.

Livesay, Dorothy. *The Self-Completing Tree: Selected Poems.* Press Porcépic, 1986.
Livesay, Dorothy. "Song and Dance." *Canadian Literature* 41 (Summer 1969): 40–8.
Livesay, Florence Randal, Dorothy Livesay, and Louisa Loeb. *Down Singing Centuries: The Folk Literatures of the Ukraine.* Hyperion, 1981.
Lizarríbar, Camille. *Something Else Will Stand Beside It: The African Writers Series and the Development of African Literature.* University of Michigan Press, 1998.
Lloyd, Antony John. *Community Development in Canada.* St Paul University, 1967.
Lockhart Fleming, Patricia. "First Printers and the Spread of the Press." In *History of the Book in Canada*, vol. 1, *Beginnings to 1840*, edited by Patricia Lockhart Fleming, Gilles Gallichan, and Yvan Lamonde. University of Toronto Press, 2004.
Lorimer, Rowland. "Book Publishing." In Dorland, *The Cultural Industries in Canada.*
Lorimer, Rowland. *Ultra Libris: Policy, Technology, and the Creative Economy of Book Publishing in Canada.* ECW Press, 2012.
Lower, Arthur R.M. *Colony to Nation: A History of Canada.* Longmans, Green, 1946.
Lutz, Hartmut. "Jeannette Armstrong." In *Contemporary Challenges: Conversations with Canadian Native Authors*, edited by Hartmut Lutz. Fifth House Publishers, 1991.
MacLaren, Eli. *Dominion and Agency: Copyright and the Structuring of the Canadian Book Trade, 1867–1918.* University of Toronto Press, 2011.
MacLaren, Eli, and Josée Vincent. "Book Policies and Copyright in Canada and Quebec: Defending National Cultures." *Canadian Literature* 204 (Spring 2010): 63–82.
MacSkimming, Roy. *The Perilous Trade: Publishing Canada's Writers.* McClelland & Stewart, 2003.
Madokoro, Laura, David Meren, and Francine McKenzie, eds. *Dominion of Race: Rethinking Canada's International History.* University of British Columbia Press, 2017.
Madokoro, Laura, and Francine McKenzie. "Introduction." In Madokoro et al., *Dominion of Race.*
Makotsi, Ruth, and Lily Nyariki. *Publishing and the Book Trade in Kenya.* East African Educational Publishers, 1997.
Manuel, George. "Presentation to the Mackenzie Valley Pipeline Inquiry." *This Magazine* 10, no. 3 (June–July 1976): 14–17.
Manuel, George, and Michael Posluns. *The Fourth World: An Indian Reality.* University of Minnesota Press, 2019.

Maracle, Lee. *Bobbi Lee: Indian Rebel.* LSM Press, 1975.
Maracle, Lee. "Oratory on Oratory." In *Trans.Can.Lit: Resituating the Study of Canadian Literature*, edited by Smaro Kamboureli and Roy Miki. Wilfrid Laurier University Press, 2007.
Marcuse, Gary, and Reginald Whitaker. *Cold War Canada: The Making of a National Insecurity State, 1945–1957.* University of Toronto Press, 2000.
"Margaret Paull: 42 Years with Collins." *Quill & Quire* 51 (May 1985): 20.
Marshall, Dominique. "Réponse à 'The Tragedies of Canadian International History': un autre survol historiographique." *Canadian Historical Review* 96, no. 4 (December 2015): 583–9.
Marshall, Dominique, and Julia Sterparn. "Oxfam Aid to Canada's First Nations, 1962–1975: Eating Lynx, Starving for Jobs, and Flying a Talking Bird." *Journal of the Canadian Historical Association* 23, no. 2 (2012): 298–343.
Mason, Jody. "'Capital Intraconversion' and Canadian Literary Prize Culture." *Book History* 20 (2017): 424–46.
Mason, Jody. *Home Feelings: Liberal Citizenship and the Canadian Reading Camp Movement.* McGill-Queen's University Press, 2019.
Mason, Jody. "The Margaret Wrong Memorial Fund, Late Colonial Development, and the Prizing of African Literatures, 1950–1962." *Research in African Literatures* 54, no. 4 (Winter 2024): 26–55.
Mason, Jody, and Sarah Pelletier. "'Singular Plurality': Settler Colonial Transcendence and Canada's 2021 Guest-of-Honour-Campaign at the Frankfurt Book Fair." *Book History* 26, no. 2 (Fall 2023): 467–96.
Massey, Vincent. *On Being Canadian.* J.M. Dent, 1948.
Matasci, Damiano. "Assessing Needs, Fostering Development: UNESCO, Illiteracy, and the Global Politics of Education (1945–1960)." *Comparative Education* 53, no. 1 (2017): 35–53.
Matasci, Damiano, Miguel Bandeira Jerónimo, and Hugo Gonçalves Dores. "Introduction: Historical Trajectories of Education and Development in (Post)Colonial Africa." In *Education and Development in Colonial and Postcolonial Africa*, edited by Matasci et al. Palgrave Macmillan, 2020.
Mathews, Robin. *Canadian Literature: Surrender or Revolution.* Steel Rail, 1978.
Mathews, Robin, and James Steele, eds. *The Struggle for Canadian Universities.* New Press, 1969.
M'Bow, Amadou-Mahtar, and Rudolph A. Peterson. *The Experimental World Literacy Programme: A Critical Assessment.* UNESCO, 1976.
McCarthy, Thomas. *Race, Empire, and the Idea of Human Development.* Cambridge University Press, 2009.
McDonald, Lynn. "Margaret Laurence and the NDP." *Canadian Women's Studies* 8, no. 3 (1985): 23–4.

McFarlane, Peter, with Doreen Manuel. *Brotherhood to Nationhood and the Making of the Modern Indian Movement*. 2nd ed. Between the Lines, 2020.

McInnis, Nadine. *Dorothy Livesay's Poetics of Desire*. Turnstone, 1994.

McKay, Ian, and Jamie Swift. *Warrior Nation: Rebranding Canada in an Age of Anxiety*. Between the Lines, 2012.

McWhinney, Bill, and Dave Godfrey, eds. *Man Deserves Man: CUSO in Developing Countries*. Ryerson Press, 1968.

Meren, David. "'Commend Me to the Yak': The Colombo Plan, the Inuit of Ungava, and 'Developing' Canada's North." *Histoire sociale / Social History* 50, no. 102 (November 2017): 343–70.

Meren, David. "Lessons Learned: Settler Colonialism, Development, and the UN Regional Training Centre in Vancouver, 1959–62." *BC Studies*, no. 208 (Winter 2020/21): 45–72.

Meren, David. "The Tragedies of Canadian International History." *Canadian Historical Review* 96, no. 4 (December 2015): 534–66.

Miller, Heather A. "Kahnawake Teen Knows How to Get the Job Done." *Windspeaker* 20, no. 10 (February 2003): 11.

Millman, Brock. *British Somaliland: An Administrative History, 1920–1960*. Routledge, 2013.

Mills, Sean. *The Empire Within: Postcolonial Thought and Political Activism in Sixties Montreal*. McGill-Queen's University Press, 2010.

Milz, Sabine. "Aboriginal Publishing in Contemporary Canada: Kateri Akiwenzie-Damm and Kegedonce Press." *Essays on Canadian Writing* 84 (Fall 2009): 213–26.

Monk, Patricia. "Shadow Continent: The Image of Africa in Three Canadian Writers." *ARIEL: A Review of International English Literature* 8, no. 4 (1977): 3–25.

Moretti, Franco. *The Way of the World: The Bildungsroman in European Culture*. Translated by Albert Sbraglia. Verso, 2000.

Morrison, David R. *Aid and Ebb Tide: A History of CIDA and Canadian Development Assistance*. North-South Institute, 2011.

Morrison, James H. *A Pictorial History of Frontier College: Camps and Classrooms*. Frontier College, 1989.

Moss, John. "Editorial." *Journal of Canadian Fiction* 3, no. 4 (1975): 1–2.

Moss, Laura. "Canada Reads." *Canadian Literature*, no. 182 (2004): 6–10.

Moss, Laura. *Is Canada Postcolonial? Unsettling Canadian Literature*. Wilfrid Laurier University Press, 2003.

Mount, Nick. *Arrival: The Story of CanLit*. House of Anansi, 2017.

Mowat, Farley. *The People of the Deer*. Little, Brown, 1952.

Muirhead, Bruce, and Ronald N. Harpelle. *IDRC: 40 Years of Ideas, Innovation, and Impact*. Wilfrid Laurier University Press, 2010.

Mulford, David C. *Zambia: The Politics of Independence, 1957–1964*. Oxford University Press, 1967.
Murphy, Brian K. "Canadian NGOs and the Politics of Participation." In Swift and Tomlinson, *Conflicts of Interest: Canada and the Third World*.
Mwanakatwe, J.M. *The Growth of Education in Zambia Since Independence*. Oxford University Press, 1968.
National Indian Brotherhood / Assembly of First Nations. *Indian Control of Indian Education*. Assembly of First Nations, 2001.
Nancekivell, Sharon. "Margaret Laurence: Bibliography." *World Literature Written in English* 22, no. 2 (Autumn 1983): 263–85.
New, W.H. "Africanadiana: The African Setting in Canadian Literature." *Journal of Canadian Studies* 6, no. 1 (February 1971): 33–8.
New, W.H. *Articulating West: Essays on Purpose and Form in Modern Canadian Literature*. New Press, 1972.
New, W.H. "Canadian Literature and Commonwealth Responses." *Canadian Literature* 66 (Autumn 1975): 14–30.
New, W.H. "Godfrey's Book of Changes." *Modern Fiction Studies* 22, no. 3 (Fall 1976): 375–85.
New, W.H. "Godfrey's Uncollected Artist." *ARIEL: A Review of International English Literature* 4, no. 3 (1973): 5–15.
Ngũgĩ wa Thiong'o. "On the Abolition of the English Department." In *The Post-Colonial Studies Reader*, edited by Bill Ashcroft, Gareth Griffiths, and Helen Tiffin. Routledge, 1995.
Nguyen, Vinh, and Thy Phu. *Refugee States: Critical Refugee Studies in Canada*. University of Toronto Press, 2021.
Ninkovich, Frank. *The Diplomacy of Ideas: US Foreign Policy and Cultural Relations, 1938–1950*. Cambridge University Press, 1981.
Nkrumah, Kwame. *Neo-Colonialism: The Last Stage of Imperialism*. International Publishers, 1966.
"Notices of Books." *Books for Africa* 1, no. 1 (January 1931): 14.
Nottingham, John. "Establishing an African Publishing Industry: A Study in Decolonization." *African Affairs* 68, no. 271 (April 1969): 139–44.
Oakman, Daniel. *Facing Asia: A History of the Colombo Plan*. Australian National University Press, 2010.
Oduyoye, Modupe. "The Role of Christian Publishing Houses Today." In Oluwasanmi et al., *Publishing in Africa in the Seventies*.
Oluwasanmi, Edwina, Eva McLean, and Hans Zell, eds. *Publishing in Africa in the Seventies*. University of Ife Press, 1975.
Onibonoje, G.O. "Wanted! A Cultural Revolution, Not a Dialogue!" In Oluwasanmi et al., *Publishing in Africa in the Seventies*.
Ong, Walter. *Orality and Literacy: The Technologizing of the Word*. Routledge, 2002.

Ontario. *Canadian Publishers and Canadian Publishing: Royal Commission on Book Publishing*. Queen's Printer for Ontario, 1972.

Osborne, Myles, and Susan Kingsley Kent. *Africans and Britons in the Age of Empires, 1660–1980*. Routledge, 2015.

O'Sullivan, Kevin. *The NGO Moment: The Globalisation of Compassion from Biafra to Live Aid*. Cambridge University Press, 2021.

Owram, Doug. *Born at the Right Time: A History of the Baby-Boom Generation*. University of Toronto Press, 1996.

Pacey, Desmond, ed. *A Book of Canadian Stories*. Ryerson, 1947.

Palmer, Bryan. *Canada's 1960s: The Ironies of Identity in a Rebellious Era*. University of Toronto Press, 2009.

Parker, George L. "The Agency System and Branch-Plant Publishing." In Gerson and Michon, *History of the Book in Canada*.

Parker, George L. "Joseph Howe and Freedom of the Press." In *History of the Book in Canada*, vol. 1, *Beginnings to 1840*, edited by Patricia Lockhart Fleming, Gilles Gallichan, and Yvan Lamonde. University of Toronto Press, 2004.

Parker, George L. "Trade and Regional Book Publishing in English." In Gerson and Michon, *History of the Book in Canada*.

Peterson, Derek R. "Vernacular Language and Political Education." In *Tracing Language Movement in Africa*, edited by Ericka A. Albaugh and Kathryn M. de Luna. Oxford University Press, 2018.

Peterson, Derek R., and Emma Hunter. "Print Culture in Colonial Africa." In *African Print Cultures: Newspapers and Their Publics in the Twentieth Century*, edited by Derek R. Peterson, Emma Hunter, and Stephanie Newell. University of Michigan Press, 2016.

Phelps-Stokes Reports on Education in Africa. Abridged with an introduction by L.J. Lewis. Oxford University Press, 1962.

Popescu, Monica. *At Penpoint: African Literatures, Postcolonial Studies, and the Cold War*. Duke University Press, 2020.

Purdy, Al. "Introduction." In Purdy, *The New Romans*.

Purdy, Al., ed. *The New Romans: Candid Canadian Opinions of the U.S.* M.G. Hurtig, 1968.

Rampure, Archana. "'Harlequin Has Built an Empire.'" In Gerson and Michon, *History of the Book in Canada*.

Rathgeber, Eva-Maria. "The Book Industry in Africa, 1973–1983: A Decade of Development?" In Altbach, Arboleda, and Gopinathan, *Publishing in the Third World*.

Rauwerda, Antje M. "Upsetting an Already Unquiet Bed: Contextualizing Dorothy Livesay's 'Zambia.'" *Canadian Poetry* 43 (Fall/Winter 1998). https://canadianpoetry.org/volumes/vol43/rauwerda.html.

Ravenscroft, Arthur. "Africa in the Imagination of Margaret Laurence." *The Literary Criterion* 21, no. 3 (1986): 35–50.

Razack, Sherene. *Dark Threats and White Knights: The Somalia Affair, Peacekeeping, and the New Imperialism*. University of Toronto Press, 2004.

Regan, Paulette. *Unsettling the Settler Within: Indian Residential Schools, Truth Telling, and Reconciliation in Canada*. University of British Columbia Press, 2011.

Reid, V.S. *The Leopard*. Heinemann, 1980.

Resnick, Philip. *The Land of Cain: Class and Nationalism in English Canada, 1945–1975*. New Star Books, 1977.

Richards, David. "'Leave the Dead Some Room to Dance!': Margaret Laurence in Africa." In *Critical Approaches to the Fiction of Margaret Laurence*, edited by Colin Nicholson. Macmillan, 1990.

Richards, Tony. "From Giving to Helping: The Evolution of a Development Agency." *Logos* 4, no. 1 (January 1993): 26–32.

Rist, Gilbert. *The History of Development: From Western Origins to Global Faith*. Translated by Patrick Camiller. Zed Books, 1997.

Ritter, Caroline. *Imperial Encore: The Cultural Project of the Late British Empire*. University of California Press, 2021.

Robert, Lucie, Christl Verduyn, and Janet B. Friskney. "Canadianization of the Curriculum." In Gerson and Michon, *History of the Book in Canada*.

Roberts, Gillian. *Prizing Literature: The Celebration and Circulation of National Literature*. University of Toronto Press, 2011.

Robins, John D., ed. *A Pocketful of Canada*. Collins, 1946.

Rodney, Walter. *How Europe Underdeveloped Africa*. Pambazuka Press and CODESRIA, 2012.

Rosi, Mauro. *Book Donations for Development*. UNESCO, 2005.

Roy, Wendy. "Anti-Imperialism and Feminism in Margaret Laurence's African Writings." *Canadian Literature*, no. 169 (2001): 33–42.

Rubboli, Massimo. "Canada, Peacekeeper to the World? Myths, Values, and Reality in Canadian Foreign Policy." In *Building Liberty: Canada and World Peace, 1945–2005*, edited by Conny Steenman-Marcusse and Aritha van Herk. Barkhuis Publishing, 2005.

Rushton, Sean. "The Origins and Development of Canada's Public Diplomacy." In *Branding Canada: Projecting Canada's Soft Power Through Public Diplomacy*, edited by Evan Potter. McGill-Queen's University Press, 2009.

Rymhs, Deena. "Appropriating Guilt: Reconciliation in an Aboriginal Canadian Context." *English Studies in Canada* 32, no. 1 (2006): 105–23.

Sachs, Wolfgang, ed. *The Development Dictionary*. Zed Books, 2010.

Sachs, Wolfgang. "Introduction." In Sachs, *The Development Dictionary*.

Sacouman, James R. "Underdevelopment and the Structural Origins of Antigonish Movement Co-Operatives in Eastern Nova Scotia." *Acadiensis* 7, no. 1 (1977): 66–85.

Sauvy, Alfred. "Trois mondes, une planète." *Vingtième siècle, revue d'histoire* 12 (1986): 81–3.

Sawatsky, John. *Gouzenko: The Untold Story*. Macmillan, 1984.

Scott, James C. *Seeing like a State: How Certain Schemes to Improve the Human Condition Have Failed*. Yale University Press, 1998.

Scott, Jennifer, and Myka Tucker-Abramson. "Banking on a Prize: Multicultural Capitalism and the Canadian Literary Prize Industry." *Studies in Canadian Literature* 32, no. 1 (2007): 5–20.

Scurr, Cory. "Cold War by 'Other Means': Canada's Foreign Relations with Communist Eastern Europe, 1957–1963." PhD diss., Wilfrid Laurier University, 2017.

Senechal Carney, Laura. "*New Frontier* (1936–1937) and the Antifascist Press in Canada." In *Sketches from an Unquiet Country: Canadian Graphic Satire, 1840–1940*, edited by Dominic Hardy, Annie Gérin, and Laura Senechal Carney. McGill-Queen's University Press, 2018.

Shewell, Hugh. "'Bitterness Behind Every Smiling Face': Community Development and Canada's First Nations." *Canadian Historical Review* 83, no. 1 (2002): 58–84.

Shivji, Issa G. "Nationalism and Pan-Africanism: Decisive Moments in Nyerere's Intellectual and Political Thought." *Review of African Political Economy* 39, no. 131 (2012): 103–16.

Slaughter, Joseph. "Enabling Fictions and Novel Subjects: The *Bildungsroman* and International Human Rights Law." *PMLA* 121, no. 5 (2006): 1405–23.

Slaughter, Joseph. *Human Rights, Inc.: The World Novel, Narrative Form, and International Law*. Fordham University Press, 2007.

Sluga, Glenda. "UNESCO and the (One) World of Julian Huxley." *Journal of World History* 21, no. 3 (2010): 393–418.

Somaliland Protectorate. *Annual Review of the Development Plan, 1953*. Government of the Somaliland Protectorate, 1954.

Somaliland Protectorate. *Annual Review of the Development Plan, 1954*. Government of the Somaliland Protectorate, 1955.

Songs of Ukraina, with Ruthenian Poems. Translated by Florence Randal Livesay. J.M. Dent & Sons, E.P. Dutton, 1916.

Sparrow, Fiona. *Into Africa with Margaret Laurence*. ECW Press, 1992.

Sparrow, Fiona. "The Self-Completing Tree: Livesay's African Poetry." *Canadian Poetry* 20 (1987). https://canadianpoetry.org/volumes/vol20/sparrow.html.

Spicer, Keith. "Clubmanship Upstaged: Canada's Twenty Years in the Colombo Plan." *International Journal: Canada's Journal of Global Policy Analysis* 25, no. 1 (March 1970): 23–33.

Spicer, Keith. *A Samaritan State? External Aid in Canada's Foreign Policy.* University of Toronto Press, 1966.

Srnicek, Nick. *Platform Capitalism.* Polity Press, 2016.

Steele, Apollonia. "Case Study: Collecting Canadian Manuscripts at the University of Calgary." In Gerson and Michon, *History of the Book in Canada.*

Stephens, L.A.D. *Study of Canadian Government Information Abroad, 1942–1972: The Development of the Information, Cultural and Academic Divisions and Their Policies.* Department of External Affairs, 1977.

Street, Brian. *Social Literacies: Critical Approaches to Literacy in Development, Ethnography, and Education.* Routledge, 2013.

Sugars, Cynthia, ed. *Home-Work: Postcolonialism, Pedagogy & Canadian Literature.* University of Ottawa Press, 2004.

Sugars, Cynthia. "Introduction." In Sugars, *Unhomely States.*

Sugars, Cynthia. "Postcolonial Pedagogy and the Impossibility of Teaching: Outside in the (Canadian Literature) Classroom." In Sugars, *Home-Work.*

Sugars, Cynthia, ed. *Unhomely States: Theorizing English-Canadian Postcolonialism.* Broadview, 2004.

Sutcliffe, Peter. *The Oxford University Press: An Informal History.* Oxford University Press, 1978.

Suzack, Cheryl. "Publishing and Aboriginal Communities." In Gerson and Michon, *History of the Book in Canada.*

Swift, Jamie. "Introduction." In Swift and Tomlinson, *Conflicts of Interest.*

Swift, Jamie, and Brian Tomlinson, eds. *Conflicts of Interest: Canada and the Third World.* Between the Lines, 1991.

Swift, Richard, and Robert Clark, eds. *Ties That Bind: Canada and the Third World.* Between the Lines, 1982.

Teager, W.A. "Cultural and Humanitarian Activities Leading to an International Role and Focus." In *J. R. Kidd: An International Legacy of Learning*, edited by Nancy J. Cochrane. Centre for Continuing Education, University of British Columbia, 1986.

Tester, Frank, and Peter Kulchyski. *Tammarniit (Mistakes): Inuit Relocation in the Eastern Arctic, 1939–1963.* University of British Columbia Press, 2014.

Teuton, Christopher B. "Indigenous Orality and Oral Literatures." In Cox and Heath Justice, *The Oxford Handbook of Indigenous American Literature.*

"Theytus Books." CM: *A Reviewing Journal of Canadian Materials for Young People* 12, no. 6 (1984): 233–4.

Thomas, Audrey. *Blown Figures*. Knopf, 1974.
Thomas, Audrey. *Coming Down from Wa*. Penguin Books Canada, 1995.
Thomas, Audrey. "If One Green Bottle." *The Atlantic*, June 1965, 83.
Thomas, Audrey. *Mrs. Blood*. Talonbooks, 1970.
Thomas, Clara. *The Manawaka World of Margaret Laurence*. McClelland & Stewart, 1975.
Thompson, John Herd. "Canada and the 'Third British Empire,' 1901–1939." In *Canada and the British Empire*, edited by Phillip Buckner. Oxford University Press, 2010.
Tippett, Maria. *Making Culture: English-Canadian Institutions and the Arts Before the Massey Commission*. University of Toronto Press, 1990.
Tlostanova, Madina V., and Walter D. Mignolo. *Learning to Unlearn: Decolonial Reflections from Eurasia and the Americas*. Ohio State University Press, 2012.
Tory, H.M. "Introduction." In Robins, *A Pocketful of Canada*, v–vi.
A Tree for Poverty: Somali Poetry and Prose. Collected by Margaret Laurence. Irish University Press and McMaster University Library Press, 1970.
Tunnicliffe, Jennifer. *Resisting Rights: Canada and the International Bill of Rights, 1947–76*. University of British Columbia Press, 2019.
UNESCO. *50 Years for Education*. UNESCO, 1997.
UNESCO. *Book Development in Africa: Problems and Perspectives*. UNESCO, 1969.
UNESCO. *Meeting of Ministers of Education of African Countries Participating in the Implementation of the Addis Ababa Plan: Final Report*. UNESCO House, 1962.
Unger, Corrina R. *International Development: A Postwar History*. Bloomsbury Academic, 2018.
United Nations Bureau of Social Affairs. *Social Progress Through Community Development*. United Nations, 1955.
Van Beusekom, Monica M., and Dorothy L. Hodgson. "Lessons Learned? Development Experiences in the Late Colonial Period." *Journal of African History* 41 (2000): 29–33.
Veracini, Lorenzo. *Settler Colonialism: A Theoretical Overview*. Palgrave Macmillan, 2010.
Vincent, Kerry. "Peripheral Visions: Postcolonial Images of Africa in the Fiction of Margaret Laurence, Audrey Thomas, and Dave Godfrey." PhD diss., Dalhousie University, 1994.
Vorano, Norman David. "Inuit Art in the *Qallunaat* World: Modernism, Museums, and the Popular Imaginary, 1949–1962." PhD diss., University of Rochester, 2007.

Wakeham, Pauline. "The Cunning of Reconciliation: Reinventing White Civility in the Age of Apology." In *The Shifting Ground of Canadian Literary Studies*, edited by Smaro Kamboureli and Robert Zacharias. Wilfrid Laurier University Press, 2012.

Wakeham, Pauline. "At the Intersection of Apology and Sovereignty: The Arctic Exile Monument Project." *Cultural Critique* 87 (Spring 2014): 84–143.

Walker, James W. St G. *Racial Discrimination in Canada: The Black Experience*. Canadian Historical Association, 1985.

Walker, Judith. "The Needy and Competent Citizen in OECD Policy Documents." In *The State, Civil Society, and the Citizen: Exploring Relationships in the Field of Education in Europe*, edited by Michal Bron Jr., Paula Guimarães, and Rui Viera de Castro. Peter Lang, 2009.

Warkentin, Germain. "Dead Metaphor or Working Model?" In *Colonial Mediascapes: Sensory World of the Early Americas*, edited by Matt Cohen and Jeffrey Glover. University of Nebraska Press, 2014.

Watkins, Evan. *Literacy Work in the Reign of Human Capital*. Fordham University Press, 2015.

Watras, Joseph. "UNESCO's Programme of Fundamental Education, 1946–1959." *History of Education* 39, no. 2 (March 2010): 219–37.

Watson, Kenneth, and Vinita Watson. *Indian Education Project*, vol. 4. Evaluation and Strategic Management Associates, 1983.

Weaver, Sally M. *Making Canadian Indian Policy: The Hidden Agenda, 1968–70*. University of Toronto Press, 1981.

Webster, David. *Fire and the Full Moon: Canada and Indonesia in a Decolonizing World*. University of British Columbia Press, 2009.

Webster, David. "Foreign Policy, Diplomacy, and Decolonization." In *Canada and the Third World*, edited by Karen Dubinsky, Sean Mills, and Scott Rutherford. University of Toronto Press, 2016.

Williams, David, and Tom Young. "The International Politics of Social Transformation: Trusteeship and Intervention in Historical Perspective." In Duffield and Hewitt, *Empire, Development, and Colonialism*.

Williams, Raymond. *Keywords: A Vocabulary of Culture and Society*. Oxford University Press, 2015.

Williamson, Janice, with Jeannette Armstrong. "What I Intended Was to Connect ... and It's Happened." *Tessera* 12 (Summer 1992): 111–29.

Woodcock, George. "Speaker for the Tribes." *Canadian Women's Studies* 8, no. 3 (1987): 30–2.

Wrong Armstrong, Agnes. "There's Too Much Waiting to Be Done." *Food for Thought* (March 1956): 258–63.

Wrong, Margaret. *Africa and the Making of Books: Being A Survey of Africa's Need of Literature*. ICCLA, 1934.

Wrong, Margaret. *Five Points for Africa*. Edinburgh House Press, 1942.
Wrong, Margaret. *The Land and Life of Africa*. Edinburgh House Press, 1935.
Wrong, Margaret. "Reading Matter for Literacy Campaigns." *Books for Africa* 13 (January 1943): 10–12.
Wrong, Margaret. *West African Journey: In the Interests of Literacy and Christian Literature, 1944–45*. Edinburgh House Press, 1945.
Young, David. "The Macmillan Company of Canada in the 1930s." *Journal of Canadian Studies* 30, no. 3 (Fall 1995): 117–33.
Youngblood Henderson, James (Sa'ke'j). *Indigenous Diplomacy and the Rights of Peoples: Achieving UN Recognition*. University of British Columbia Press, 2008.
Young-Ing, Greg. "Aboriginal Peoples' Estrangement: Marginalization in the Publishing Industry." In *Looking at the Words of Our People: First Nations Analysis of Literature*, collected by Jeannette Armstrong. Theytus, 1993.
Zell, Hans S. "Book Donation Programmes in English-Speaking Africa." *African Research and Documentation*, no. 127 (2015): 4–130.
Zell, Hans S. "Introduction." In *The Book Trade of the World*, vol. 4, *Africa*, edited by Sigfred Taubert and Peter Weidhass. K.G. Saur München, 1984.
Zell, Hans S., and Raphaël Thierry. "Book Donation Programmes for Africa: Time for a Reappraisal? Two Perspectives." Special Issue of *African Research and Documentation* no. 127 (2015).

Index

Abrahams, Peter, 112–13; *Tell Freedom*, 112–13
Achebe, Chinua, 146, 148, 158, 168, 178; *No Longer at Ease*, 158; *Things Fall Apart*, 158, 159
Adamson, Edith, 196, 197, 199
adult education and developmentalism, 98–101, 103, 110–13, 125–6, 200–1; and continuing education, 106, 109–10; demeaning effect of, 110–11; and functional literacy, 109–10, 125; and "Open University" concept, 111; vocational, 34, 103, 110, 200; in the West Indies, 103, 111. *See also* Canada and adult education, community development in; Canadian Association for Adult Education; Frontier College; International Council for Adult Education; UNESCO education policy, initiatives of
Africa, 129–86; Christian missionaries in, 25–6, 34–5, 42–3, 112; decolonization movements in, 15, 25, 41, 134, 207; literacy in, 25–56, 223; racism in, 204–5; women's education in, 149–51; in the writing of English Canadian settler authors, 135–7, 139–48
Africa, book development in, 25–56, 175; and book donations to, 29–30, 115–16, 119–20, 126; and book shortages, 119–20, 223; as impediment to change, 27, 32; late-colonial, 25–56
Africa, book publishing in, 49–54, 123, 128, 176–7; in African vernaculars, 26, 36, 40–1, 47–8, 51–2; and African writers, 11, 127, 158–9; and British publishers, 49, 50–1, 158; and book printers, 49; and funding dependency, 53–4; and mission presses, 49, 51–2; and paper shortages, 123
Africa, education initiatives in, 33–5, 42–3, 46, 156–61; responsibility for, 42–3; and role of missionary groups, 22, 25–8, 30, 40, 42–3, 47–50; vocational emphasis in, 32, 34, 45, 46–7, 49
African Literature Committee, 36, 50
African National Congress (ANC), 153, 205, 283n35, 284n39
African People's Union. *See* African National Congress

Aggrey, James, 39–40
American Indian Movement (AIM), 216
Andrzejewski, B.W., 141, 143–4, 146, 281n23
Annual Book Presentation Programme (External Affairs), 22, 58, 66–7, 86–7, 89; aims of, 66, 70; book selection list, 67, 76, 86–7, 231–40; exclusion of Indigenous presence from, 67; funding of, 69
Antigonish Movement, 46, 271n23
Appleton, Franklin, 73–4, 264n25
Armstrong, Jeannette, 213–21, 223, 298n42; and Okanagan Indian Curriculum Project, 213–15; and scholarship on Syilx Okanagan thought, language, 215; *Slash*, 213–21, 298n41; and traditional Indigenous education, 220–1
Assembly of First Nations, 127, 213, 297n34
Association of Canadian Publishers, 127, 175
Atwood, Margaret, 131, 133, 180; *The Circle Game*, 175; *Survival*, 131, 175, 180, 289n68
Audley, Paul, 60
Australia, 63, 78, 107, 206; book donation in, 69; Colombo Plan initiatives of, 63

Bacque, Jim, 175
Bandung Conference (1955), 7, 16
Barbeau, Marius, 72, 75; "Indian Art and Myth," 75; *The Tree of Dreams*, 75
Barker, Robert, 10; *The Book Hunger*, 10, 55–6, 119; *Books for All*, 10
Barnes, Skawenniio, 222, 298n47

Bartelman, James, 222–3
Behrstock, Julian, 10
Belshaw, Cyril S., 190, 193, 194–5; and film as instrument of "social development," 195; *The Indians of British Columbia*, 193, 194–5, 208–9
Benjamin, Curtis G., 9, 20, 69, 102; "Benjamin Report" (*U.S. Books Abroad*), 20, 102, 254n26
Berton, Pierre, 67, 87; *Canada from Sea to Sea*, 67, 94–5, 96; *The Mysterious North*, 87
Birney, Earle, 67
Blake, Sophia Hume, 28
Bodet, Jaime Torres, 60, 96
Bon Echo Foundation, 100, 103, 271n20
book, role of in development, 8–12, 15, 19, 102–3, 225, 255n6; creating opportunity for foreign investment, 55, 61; as instrument of settler exceptionalism, 4, 15, 19–20, 107, 225, 230; as instrument of settler indigenization, 15, 19–20, 75, 131, 135; promoting ideology, trade, technology, 102; serving the aid-disbursing nation, 54. *See also* book diplomacy
book diplomacy, 21–2, 57–89, 90–128; in Canada, 22, 58, 71, 76, 89–90; in the US, 22, 60–1
book donation, 9–10, 29, 90–1, 95–6, 99, 105, 115, 119–20, 124, 126, 222–3, 291n7; and "book dumping," 91; to Indigenous communities, 222–3; responsive, 95–6, 116–17, 120, 122, 124; role of in developing overseas markets, 9, 102; undermining local publishing, 120

"book hunger," 29, 55–6. *See also* Escarpit, Robert: *The Book Hunger*

book publishing, 10–12, 121–4; and copyright, 10, 59, 77, 83, 177, 266n35; and domestic textbook publication, 115, 119–20; impact of book donation on, 69–70, 90–1, 120; missionary involvement in, 25–6, 28–9; and paperbacks, 11, 129; in the Third World, 14, 55–6, 120, 123. *See also* Africa, book publishing in; Canada, book publishing in; International Committee on Christian Literature for Africa

Book Publishing Industry Development Program, 59–60, 176

Books for Africa, 28, 39–40

Botswana, 185; and Laedza Batanani ("Community Awakening"), 185

Boyden, Joseph, 229; *Three Day Road*, 229

Britain, 9, 11, 55; book development in, 9, 102, 120; NGOs in, 169; and withdrawal from UNESCO, 126. *See also* Colonial Office (Britain)

Britain and colonial policy in Africa, 32–3, 41–2, 138–9, 144, 159, 172, 257n15; Development Plan in British Somaliland, 138, 143; and labour unrest, strikes, 32, 41. *See also* Colonial Office (Britain)

British Colonial Film Unit, 54

British Council, 42, 159, 258n21

British South Africa Company, 46, 153, 157, 283n34; Native Affairs Department, 46

Buckler, Ernest, 131; *The Mountain and the Valley*, 131

Bunumbu Press, 123

Campbell, Harry, 99, 100–1

Campbell, Thomas, 44, 47; *Africa Advancing*, 44–5, 47

Canada: book diplomacy in, 22, 58, 71, 76, 89–90; cultural diplomacy in, 58, 63–5, 68–9, 80–1, 87–9; foreign policy in, 63, 69, 78, 253n20; and "humanitarian" exceptionalism, 16–18, 88, 184, 228–9; internal colonization in, 4, 15, 20, 22, 58, 84, 134; as a middle power, 16–17, 20, 64, 107; national identity, mythmaking in, 4, 16–18, 23, 89, 229; and peacekeeping, 16–17, 254n22; and settler colonialism, 4, 12–24, 71, 89, 107, 129–37, 147–8, 188, 228–9; and settler exceptionalism, 4, 15–16, 18–19, 90–1, 106–8, 130, 134–5; and settler indigenization, 15, 19–20, 68, 74–6, 131, 135, 137, 178–9

Canada, book development in, 12–24, 57–89, 92, 225–6; and book diplomacy programs, 22, 57–89; and book donation programs, 12, 19, 20–1, 66–88, 89; and missionary, service tradition, 21, 225; and NGOs, 22–3, 90–128, 226; oriented externally vs. internally, 12, 23. *See also* Canada, NGO book development in

Canada, book donation in, 66–88, 105, 226; and Annual (Canadiana) Book Presentation Programme, 22, 68, 69; funding for, 69, 89; and Indigenous communities, 222–3; and Special Book Presentation Programme for Colombo Plan Area Countries, 22, 58, 68, 70. *See also* Overseas Book Centre

Canada, book publishing in, 14–15, 22, 58–60, 83–4, 90–1, 124, 174–7; and the agency system, 59–60, 74, 77, 83; and branch plants, 59–60, 74, 132, 176; and Canadian-owned publishers, 59–60, 69, 174–8, 277n53; vs. book publishing in Africa and Third World nations, 14–15, 176–7; and copyright, 59, 77, 83, 177, 266n35; and federal block grants, 59–60, 91, 176; and foreign domination of domestic market, 14, 74, 76, 82, 127, 175–6, 260n4; impact of book donation programs on, 69–70; and Indigenous-owned publishers, 127, 177, 214; and mass-market book production, 73, 76; overseas promotion of, 70–7, 229

Canada, book publishing programs in: Book Publishing Industry Development Program, 59–60, 176; Ontario Book Publishers' Assistance Program, 176. *See also* Canada Council

Canada, cultural policy in: asserting sovereignty, 65, 71, 87; and aversion to mass culture, 71, 75, 76; and state-sponsored culture, 64–5; and threat of American hegemony, 65–6, 71; and threat of Soviet communism, 65, 68, 77, 80. *See also* Massey Commission

Canada, literary culture in, 130–1, 227–30; and Canada Reads (CBC), 228–9; and the "CanLit boom," 57, 129; disputed advent of, 57–8, 76–7; effect of American hegemony on, 133, 174; and the English Canadian canon, 168, 184; and the Giller Prize, 228; and Indigenous writers, 213–14, 229; moralizing rhetoric of, 3–4, 228–30; performative nature of, 228–30; and postsecondary institutions, 130–1, 174; presence of Africa in, 135–7; state support for, 57, 59–60, 65, 69, 89, 130. *See also* Canada Council

Canada, NGO book development in, 21–3, 90–128, 226; and Indigenous communities, 198–201; and the "NGO moment," 21, 23, 130,168–83. *See also* Overseas Book Centre; Canadian University Students Overseas

Canada, postwar national identity and mythmaking in, 16–18; and "friend of the Third World," 16; and international humanitarianism, 17–18; and international human rights,18; and "middlepowerhood," 16–17; and peacekeeping, 16–17; and "peacemaker myth," 16

Canada and adult education, community development in, 19, 21, 28–9, 103, 109, 225–6; and adult literacy programs, 21, 28–9, 109, 225–6; and extension education, 21, 225; and National Literacy Secretariat, 226

Canada Council, 59–60, 89, 92, 149, 162, 175; author grants, 59, 149; block grants, 59–60, 91; Book Purchase Program, 89; and Governor General's Literary Awards, 67, 83, 87, 135, 149, 178, 266n35

Canada Reads (CBC), 228–9

Canadian Appeal for Children (Canadian United Nations), 93

Canadian Association for Adult Education (CAAE), 98, 100,

103, 109, 270n12; and National Commission on the Indian Canadian (Indian-Eskimo Association of Canada), 103, 271n20, 291n6; and study in the Caribbean, 100, 103
Canadian Citizenship Council, 100, 109
Canadian Council for International Cooperation, 113. *See also* Overseas Institute of Canada
Canadian Council for Reconstruction Through UNESCO (CCRU), 72, 91, 92–8, 268n4; funding for, 92; objectives of, 93, 98
Canadian Council for Reconstruction Through UNESCO (CCRU), book programs of, 94, 99; Joint Canadian Book Project Committee, 95–6; periodical reprint project, 96–7; "school-box" project, 94–5. *See also* Joint Canadian Book Project Committee
Canadian Council of Education for Citizenship, 71
Canadian Film Institute, 100, 109
Canadian Forum, 155, 174; "Piquefort's Column," 175
Canadian Information Service (CIS), 63, 66, 94
Canadian International Development Agency (CIDA), 12–13, 88, 101, 104, 113–14, 126, 128, 265n30; and funding for Overseas Book Centre, 114, 122; NGO division of, 13, 113, 169
Canadian Library Association, 95, 100–1; Joint Canadian Book Project Committee, 95–6
Canadian Organization for Development in Education (CODE), 100, 122–8; and Burt Award for First Nations, Inuit, and Métis, 127–8, 276nn52–3; and Burt Literary Awards, 126–7; and literacy projects, research, 126–8; and support for local publishing, 123. *See also* Overseas Book Centre
Canadian Organization for Development in Education (CODE), teacher training and book donation programs, 123–6; *Book Donations for Development*, 124; "Context Matters," 126; "Teaching and Learning in Fragile Contexts," 126
Canadian Reading Camp Movement. *See* Frontier College
Canadian United Allied Relief Fund, 92
Canadian University Students Overseas (CUSO), 21, 78, 101, 113–16, 154, 168–83, 198, 200, 203–6, 273n37; CIDA funding of, 169; and distancing from mission work tradition, 170–1; and the "NGO moment," 168–83; radicalism in, 114; volunteers of, 169–71, 184–5, 201, 203–6
Canadian University Students Overseas (CUSO) publications: CUSO/SUCO *Bulletin*, 203–5, *204*; "SUCO et Vous" ("CUSO and You") booklet, 170, *171*
Canadiana program. *See* Annual Book Presentation Programme
Cardinal, Harold, 188, 198; on developmentalism and the settler-colonial context, 188; response of to White Paper, 198; *The Unjust Society*, 188, 296n30
Carnegie Corporation, 35, 36, 157,

270n12; and funding for African libraries, 42
Carr, Emily, 75; "Blunden Harbour," 75; *Klee Wyck*, 75
Central African Federation, 153–4
Chrétien, Jean, 199, 293n17
Christian Missionary Society (CMS) Bookshop (Kenya), 51, 52, 144
Coady Institute, 105, 271n23
Cold War, 7, 23–4, 61, 78, 83, 86, 106–7, 173; and book as instrument of cultural diplomacy, 9, 11, 61–2, 80, 83, 88, 107
Colombo Plan for Co-Operative Development in South and Southeast Asia, 13, 15, 22, 63, 67, 68, 78–81, 87, 95, 100, 104, 265n30; and benefits to contributing nations, 80; Canada's involvement in, 79–80, 84, 85, 87–8; cultural initiatives of, 63, 80; economic development projects of, 63, 79–80; genesis of, 78–9; goals of, 78–9, 86; US involvement in, 79
Colonial Development Act (1929), 32
Colonial Development and Welfare Act (1940, 1945), 32, 38, 41–2, 44, 138; funding initiatives of, 50, 52, 144
Colonial Literature Bureaus, 27; East Africa Literature Bureau (EALB), 50–2, 144–5, *145*; Joint Publications Bureau (Northern Rhodesia and Nyasaland), 50
Colonial Office (Britain), 33, 35, 37–8, 41–2, 141, 145, 153, 256n11; and Advisory Committees on Education in Africa, 45; and African education, literacy policy, 34–5, 43, 47; and colonial self-government, 44–5; and Committee on Education in the Colonies, 54; and literacy, publication in Africa, 49–50, 52; and *Mass Education in African Society*, 43, 45, 46, 51, 55; and subcommittee on mass education, 43–4; and UNESCO, 54–5
Comeau, Napoleon A., 183; *Life and Sport on the North Shore*, 183
Committee for an Independent Canada, 132–3
Commonwealth of Nations, 13, 17, 45, 58, 79, 107–8; and Commonwealth Aid Program, 78–9; and liberal internationalism, 22; and racialization, 108
Company of Young Canadians, 209, 296n30
Connor, Ralph, 75; *Postscript to Adventure*, 75
Convention People's Party (Ghana), 172, 181
Cooke, Charles Angus, 188
Copway, George, 193; *Traditional History and Characteristic Sketches of the Ojibway Nation*, 193
Cowichan Reserve, 209–10
Cuba, mass literacy campaign in, 55, 119, 273n30, 275n42
cultural diplomacy, 61–2; and the "'vital center' argument," 61, 260n6. *See also* book diplomacy
"cunning of reconciliation," 229
CUSO. *See* Canadian University Students Overseas

Danquah, Joseph, 172; and United Gold Coast Convention, 172

Index

Davey, R.F., 196–7
Davis, Jackson, 44, 50–1, 259n34; *Africa Advancing*, 44–5, 47
Daystar Press, 50
Deane, Phyllis, 44; *The Future of the Colonies*, 44
decolonization movements, 20, 103, 130, 134, 149, 187; in Africa, 15, 25, 41, 134, 207; influence of on Indigenous activism, 134, 188, 201–2, 206, 214; influence of Marxism on, 173, 208; in the Third World 15, 125
de Gaspé, Philippe Aubert, 67; *Les Anciens canadiens*, 67
Dene Nation, 202; Dene Declaration (Mackenzie Valley Pipeline project), 202–3
dependency theory, 7, 113, 117, 125, 198
Development Education Centre, 184
developmentalism, 4–8; and the bildungsroman, 217–20; and Cold War anticommunism, 7, 61, 83; and community development, 55, 99, 185, 208–10, 213–16, 296n29; and dependency theory, 7, 113, 117, 125, 187; end phase of, 224–30; "fourth world" challenge to, 187–223; and Indigenous Peoples, 12, 15, 18, 20, 22–3, 198–223; and modernization theory/high modernism, 7, 9, 62–3, 87–8, 95, 189, 194, 224; and NGOs, 9, 13, 21–3, 90–128, 168–83; and post-development theory, 5–6; and "second wave," 103, 113–17, 187, 198, 200, 208–9, 224; and Structural Adjustment Programs, 8, 13, 224; and technical assistance, 8–10, 61–3, 99, 151–2, 156–7, 208; and Truman's inaugural address ("Four Point"), 6, 7, 62; and the UN's first Development Decade, 101, 103–6, 109, 118, 172. *See also entries under* developmentalism in Canada
developmentalism, late colonial, 5–6, 15–16, 22, 142–6, 168; in Africa, 25–56; and Colonial Development Act (1929), 32; and Colonial Development and Welfare Act (1940, 1945), 32, 38, 41–2, 44, 50, 52, 138; role of the book in, 27, 32
developmentalism, late twentieth-century, 8, 22, 29, 129–86, 187–223; in Africa, 129–86; and global decolonization movements, 130, 134, 149, 187, 198; and the New Left, 133–5, 146, 175; and outward-oriented development, 188, 189; and post-development theory, 5–6; and policy related to Indigenous Peoples, 189–90; premises of, 8; role of the book in, 8–12, 90–128
developmentalism, postwar, 5–9, 101–3, 139, 193, 219; in Africa, 32–3; and high modernism, 7, 9, 63, 94–5, 189–90, 224, 296n29; and modernization theory, 62–3, 87–8, 95; and rise of NGOs, 101–3, 129; role of the book in, 10, 27, 29, 32, 57–89
developmentalism in Canada, 4, 12–24, 28–9; and foreign aid, 12, 84, 87–88, 104, 113–14, 252n15; and northern development, 86; objectives of, 13–14, 23; and parallels with Third World

nations, 14–15; and policy concerning Indigenous Peoples, 84, 86; and "underdevelopment" at home, 87
developmentalism in Canada, late twentieth-century, 14, 21–2; and Indigenous Peoples, 187–223; and internal colonization, 4, 15, 20, 22, 58, 84, 134; and the "NGO moment," 21, 23, 130, 168–83; role of the book in, 3–4, 14–15, 19, 21–3, 90–128, 129–86
developmentalism in Canada, postwar, 11, 14–17, 21, 57–89, 225–6; and Colombo Plan initiatives, 63, 79–80, 84, 85, 87–8; and Indigenous Peoples, 189–95; role of the book in, 22, 57–89, 225
Diefenbaker, John, 87, 190; government of, 80, 211; "northern vision" of, 87
DuBois, W.E.B., 34, 256n10

Eagle Press, 144, *145*
East Africa Literature Bureau (EALB), 50–2, 144–5, *145*; funding for, 52, 144; missionary roots of, 144; as publisher, 50, 144–5
East African High Commission, 144
Éditions Beauchemin, 69
Eisen, Max, 228; *By Chance Alone*, 228
Ekwensi, Cyprian, 158; *Burning Grass*, 158, 159; *The Drummer Boy*, 159
En'owkin Centre, 213–14
Escarpit, Robert, 10; *The Book Hunger*, 10, 55–6, 119; *La Révolution du livre*, 10, 11
Experimental World Literacy Programme (EWLP), 109–10, 111–13, 118–19, 125, 273n30; evaluation of by Expert Group, 118–19, 125; and locally sourced, produced educational materials, 119
External Affairs, 22, 57–89, 92, 104; Economic Division, 69–70; External Aid Office, 104
External Affairs, book initiatives of, 22, 57–89, 92; and Annual Book Presentation Programme, 22, 58, 66–7, 69, 70–7, 86–7, 89; and impact of book purchasing, 69–70; and Information Division, 63–4, 66–7, 68, 71–2, 81, 261n14; and Special Book Presentation Programme for Colombo Plan Area Countries, 22, 58, 68, 70, 77–88, 194, 241–5

Fabian Colonial Bureau, 42, 195
Fanon, Frantz, 5, 202; *Black Skin, White Masks*, 202; *The Wretched of the Earth*, 202
Fitzpatrick, Alfred, 29
Ford Foundation, 61, 102, 103
Foreign Missions Conference of North America, 55
"fourth world," 206–7; challenge of to developmentalism, 201–13
Fourth World: An Indian Reality, The, 205–13, 223; on education, 211–3; and paternalism, 223; on Third World decolonization, 206–8
Franklin Book Programs, 10, 61–2, 91, 102, 120–1; mission of, 62
Freire, Paulo, 113, 185; *Pedagogy of the Oppressed*, 113
Frontier College, 19, 100, 109, 127, 170, 174, 226, 293n17; and

"Anglophone tradition of aid,"
28–9; and community education
programs, 200; and initiatives
with Indigenous Peoples, 199–201
Frye, Northrop, 131; *The Bush
Garden*, 135, 175; and "garrison
mentality" archetype, 131
Frye, William, 82; *A United Nations
Peace Force*, 82
*Functional Literacy and
International Development*, 109

Galal, Musa H.I., 143–4
Galbraith, John Kenneth, 81
General, Cayuga Hoyaneh Levi, 109
Germany, book as instrument of
development in, 9, 102, 120
Ghana, 135, 136, 169–70, 172–3,
178; independence in, 172–3,
181–2; publishing in, 174. See also
Gold Coast
Gibson, Graeme, 131; *Five Legs*, 131;
interview with Dave Godfrey, 178,
180–1
Godfrey, Dave, 23, 129, 132–3,
135–7, 173–83, 288n58; African-
influenced writing of, 178–83; and
Frontier College, 170, 174; and
House of Anansi Press, 174–5;
and Independent Publishers'
Association, 175–6; and New
Press, 175; and "Piquefort's
Column," 175; and Press
Porcépic, 175, 181; and settler
indigenization, 178–9, 180–3;
and study of Canadian publishing
(with J. Lorimer), 176; and work
for CUSO in Ghana, 169–70, 172,
173–4, 178
Godfrey, Dave: "The Big Game
Fisherman in Florida," 182; *Death
Goes Better with Coca-Cola*, 175,
178–83, *182*, 289n68, 289n70;
"Elephant He Go Come Here
Plenty," 182–3; "Escape from My
Winter Pent House," 182–3; "The
First Encountering of Mr. Basa-
Basa and His Excellency, Ling
Huo," 179, 181; "The Generation
of Hunters," 132, 182; *Gordon to
Watkins to You, A Documentary*
(with Mel Watkins), 175, 288n60;
"Gossip: The Birds That Flew,
the Birds That Fell," 179; "The
Hard-Headed Collector," 180–1,
289n68; "Letter from Africa, to
an American Negro," 180, 181;
"Of Bucks and Death," 182–3;
"Pheasants in the Corn," 182;
"River Two Blind Jacks," 179; *The
New Ancestors*, 135, 178, 181,
183, 288n64, 289n69 "Up in the
Rainforest," 182–3
Godfrey, Ellen (Swartz), 174, 175,
288n58
Gold Coast, 41, 44, 136, 137–48,
172. See also Ghana
Gonick, Cy, 183
Gordon, Walter, 132
Gouzenko, Igor, 82–3, 266n35; *The
Fall of a Titan*, 82–4, 266nn35–6;
This Was My Choice, 83
Governor General's Literary Awards.
See Canada Council
Graff, Harvey J., 191, 226–7; and
"the literacy myth," 191; *The
Literacy Myth*, 226–7
Grant, George, 131; *Lament for a
Nation*, 131
Grierson, John, 63, 261n10, 269n5
"grounded normativity," 220–1

Harris, Lawren, 72
Hassan, Mohamed Abdullah, 138, 142, 146
Haudenosaunee, 109, 272n28
Hawthorn, Harry, 193, 194–5; Hawthorn Report, 195; *The Indians of British Columbia*, 193, 194–5, 208–9
Heinemann, 52, 158–9; African Writers Series, 158
high modernism, 7–9, 63, 70–1, 94–5, 189–90, 224, 296n29; in Canada's North, 86, 189, 194, 266n37, 269n7; in postwar era, 7, 60–70, 102
Hoffman, Stanley, 82; *Organisations internationals et pouvoirs politiques des états*, 82
Hoggart, Richard, 120, 125
Homes, Bob, 200–1
Hood, Hugh, 135, 137; *You Can't Get There From Here*, 135
House of Anansi Press, 174–5
Howe, John, 76–7, 264n26; and the *Novascotian*, 77
Howe, Joseph, 76–7
Hungry Minds (NFB film), 93
Hurtig, Mel, 132
Huxley, Julian, 43–4, 54; "Colonies and Freedom," 44; *The Future of the Colonies*, 44
Hyde, Laurence, 74, 75, 264n25

Independent Publishers' Association, 60, 175–6; recommendations of, 177. *See also* Association of Canadian Publishers
India, 63, 78, 79–80, 81, 84, 108, 177; and Canada-India Atomic Reactor, 63, 79

Indian Affairs (and Northern Development), 188–90, 192–3, 196–7, 199–201, 213–14, 291n7; Community Development program of, 208–9, 213; and Economic Development Fund loans, 210; and "Indian National Library of literature," 188–9; and integration/assimilation, 189–90, 196–7, 199, 211, 215; Joint Committee of Senate and House of Commons to investigate, 190, 211; and libraries, 188–9; perceived paternalism of, 209; and welfare provision, 190, 196
Indian Affairs (and Northern Development), education policies of, 199, 200–1, 211–14; and Adult Education for Arctic Quebec, 201; curriculum project of, 213–14; and integration, 211, 215; and Okanagan Indian Curriculum Project, 213–15; and partnership between Indigenous Peoples and government, 212
Indian Association of Alberta, 210, 212; and response to White Paper, 212
Indian Brotherhood of the Northwest Territories. *See* Dene Nation
Indian Control of Indian Education, 212–13, 214
Indian-Eskimo Association of Canada, 199
Indians of British Columbia, The, 193, 194–5, 208–9; and education of Indigenous children, 195
Indigenous activism, 201–23, 294n19; and education, 211–14, 297n34; influence of African

liberation movements on, 202–6; influence of Mao Zedong on, 202, 208; and Tanzanian socialism, 202, 206, 223; and Third World decolonization movements, 201–2, 214. See also Red Power movement
Indigenous Peoples, Canada, 12, 18, 67, 108–9, 186, 187–223; and anglophone settler nationalisms, 21,135; and critique of developmentalism, 15, 23; federal policy concerning, 23, 58, 188, 190, 198, 209, 212–15; influence of global decolonization on, 134, 188, 201–2, 206, 214; and integration/assimilation, 189–90, 196–7; and racism, 190–1, 211; relevance of developmentalism to, 22–3, 198–201; and resource extraction, 15, 18, 84, 86, 195; and settler-Indigenous reconciliation, 229; and sovereignty, 18, 223. See also Canada: internal colonization in; Canada: and settler indigenization; Indigenous activism
Indigenous Peoples, Canada, and book development, 22, 128, 177; book and library services for, 23, 188–98, 222–3; book donations to, 222–3; and literacy rates, 22, 128, 199
Indigenous Peoples, Canada, and education, 103, 211–14, 297n34; graduation rates, 211; and residential schools, 107, 211; vocational, 103, 200
Indigenous Peoples, Canada, and publishing: Indigenous-owned publishers, 127–8, 177, 214;

Indigenous writers, 213–14, 223; Native Communications Program, 177; and recommendations of the Independent Publishers Association, 177
Inhabit Media, 127
Inkster, Tim, 175
Innis, Harold, 67
Institute for Iroquoian Studies, 197
Inter Church Council of Canada, 28
Interior Tribes of British Columbia, Aboriginal Native Rights Committee, 211
International Committee on Christian Literature for Africa (ICCLA), 22, 26–55; formation of, 34–5; funding for, 35; and ideology of the book, 38–9; mandate of, 26–7, 35; and publishing in Africa, 49–54; and influence of Phelps-Stokeism, 35–6, 39–40, 45, 51; and relationship with British Colonial Office, 35, 37–8; and responsibility for education in Africa, 42–3
International Committee on Christian Literature for Africa (ICCLA), publications of, 30–2; "African Home Library," 30, 39, 40; Books for Africa, 28, 39–40; King Khama, 30, 31; Listen, 39, 40–1, 42, 258n21; "Little Books for Africa," 30, 31, 39, 40
International Co-operation Year program, 100
International Council for Adult Education (ICAE), 101, 109, 121, 125
International Missionary Council (IMC), 26, 28, 33
International Working Group for

Indigenous Affairs, 206
Inuit, 84–6, 266n37; Ahiarmiut, 85–6, 194; literacy rates of, 199; relocation of, 194, 267nn39–40. *See also* Inuit Tapirisat of Canada
Inuit Tapirisat of Canada (Inuit Tapiriit Kanatami), 127, 201; Inuit Management Training Project, 201
Iron Curtain, The (film and memoir), 83

James, C.L.R., 134, 173
Jameson, Anna Brownell, 15, 18; *Winter Studies and Summer Rambles*, 18
Jamieson, Stuart M., 193, 194; *The Indians of British Columbia*, 193, 194–5, 208–9
Jardine, Douglas, 142; *The Mad Mullah of Somaliland*, 142
Jenness, Diamond, 67, 193; *The Indians of Canada*, 67, 193
Joint Canadian Book Project Committee, 95–6, 97; and Canadian Book Centre, 95–6; goals of, 95; and "March of Books / En avant les livres," 95–6, 97, 98
Jonas, George, 175; *The Absolute Smile*, 175
Jones, Thomas Jesse, 33, 46

Kahnawà:ke, 222; public library for, 222
Kanai News, 203, 205
Kaunda, Kenneth, 153–6, 163, 203, 283n35, 284n37; *Zambia Shall Be Free*, 158
Kegedonce Press, 127
Kenneth Kaunda Foundation, 158
Kenya, 47, 50, 52, 144, 158

Keynes, John Maynard, 62, 81
Kidd, James Robbins (J.R.), 19–21, 91, 98–103, 105–13, 121, 125, 149, 198; and adult education movement, 98–101, 106, 110–13, 125–6; and Canada's "special mission," 107, 109, 129; and "functional literacy," 110; and settler exceptionalism, 106–7
Kidd, James Robbins (J.R.), organizational affiliations of: Canadian Association for Adult Education, 98, 103, 109, 291n6; International Council for Adult Education, 109, 121; Overseas Book Centre, 91, 99, 102–3; Overseas Institute of Canada, 100, 105, 109; UNESCO, 98, 100, 109–10
Kidd, James Robbins (J.R.), writings of: *Adult Education in the Caribbean*, 111; "Canada's Stake at UNESCO," 99; "Continuing – Not Fundamental Education Only," 108; "The Creative Crusade," 108; *Functional Literacy and International Development*, 109, 111–12, 198–9; *An International Development Program for Canada*, 103
Kidd, Margaret, 125
Kidd, Ross, 170, 184–5; and CUSO, 170, 184; and Frontier College, 170; and theatre of development, 185
King, Mackenzie, 82
Klein, A.M., 67, 131; "A Portrait of the Poet as Landscape," 131
Knight, David, 135, 279n14; *Farquarson's Physique and What It Did to His Mind*, 135

Lamb, W.K., 81
Lamming, George, 134
Latin American Working Group, 184
Laurence, Jack, 138–41, 144
Laurence, Margaret, 23, 132–3, 135–48, 172–3, 178, 281n27, 288n64; African writing of, 129, 135, 139–48, 280n18, 280n21, 281n28; and critique of colonialism, 147–8; *The Diviners*, 147–8; "The Drummer of All the World," 139; *Heart of a Stranger*, 147; "Ivory Tower or Grassroots," 148, 178; and late colonial development paradigm, 141–3; *Long Drums and Cannons*, 148, 280n18 "Mask of Beaten Gold," 139; "Open Letter to the Mother of Joe Bass," 132–3; "The Poem and the Spear," 146–8; poetry translation project of (*A Tree for Poverty*), 141–6, 145, 281n23, 281n26; *The Prophet's Camel Bell*, 129, 139–41, 142–4, 146–7, 280n19; *The Stone Angel*, 146; *This Side Jordan*, 139, 281n22; "The Tomorrow-Tamer," 173; *The Tomorrow-Tamer and Other Stories*, 139, 146, 179, 280n20, 281n22; "Uncertain Flowering," 139, 280n18
League of Nations, 6, 62, 109, 272n28; and the mandate system, 6, 44; and status of Indigenous nations, 109, 272n28
Lee, Dennis, 131, 133, 174–5; "Cadence, Country, Silence," 131; *Civil Elegies*, 175; and House of Anansi Press, 174–5; *Kingdom of Absence*, 175
Léger, Jules, 80

Lenchina, Alice, 155, 284n37
LePan, Douglas, 67–8, 79, 88, 262n16; Colombo Plan Report (1950), 79; *The Net and the Sword*, 67–8
Lesage, Jean, 86
Levine, Norman, 136
Lewis, Leonard John, 47–8, 50; "Anglo-American University Co-Operation in the Changing World," 48; "The British Contribution to Education in Africa," 48; and Phelps-Stokeism, 48; *Towards a Literate Africa*, 48
Le Zoute conference (1926), 30, 34, 35
liberal internationalism, 90, 92, 101, 104, 108–9; and Indigenous internationalism, 108
libraries in Indigenous communities, 188–97; cultural relevance of, 195–6; and Indigenous-authored materials, 189; selection of materials for, 189, 192, 195; travelling, 192, 196, 197, 291n7
literacy, 8–9, 119, 127, 191, 219, 223, 273n30; adult literacy programs, 28–9, 170; and denigration of nontextual knowing, 191; "functional," 55, 109–12, 117–19, 125, 152, 211; and literacy myths, 226–7; and New Literacy Studies, 226; and orality, 18–19, 25, 191, 219–20; role of in developmentalism, 4, 8–9, 191, 198, 219. *See also* Canada and adult education; Experimental World Literacy Programme; Frontier College; UNESCO book and literacy policy, initiatives of

Livesay, Dorothy, 23, 129, 132–3, 135–7, 149–68, *150*, *151*, 284n37, 286n48; and adult education, 149–51; African poetry of, 154–5, 161–8; *Collected Poems*, 155, 161–2, 166; *The Colour of God's Face*, 155, 165; *Day and Night*, 149; education of, 149; *Journey with My Selves*, 161, 166–7; "The Leader" ("U.N.I.P. Meeting," "Prophet"), 155–6, 163; "The Land," 165; "New Jersey: 1935," 133; in Northern Rhodesia for UNESCO, 154, 156, 158–9, 167, 283n36; in Paris for UNESCO, 149, 162; *Poems for People*, 149; "Politics," 166; "The Prophetess," 155; *Right Hand, Left Hand*, 149, 282n30; "The Second Language," 166–7; *Selected Poems*, 149; *The Self-Completing Tree*, 161, 166; "Song and Dance," 162–4; teacher at Chalimbana Training College, 151, 154, 156, 157–61, 167; teacher at Kitwe Training College, 151, *151*, 159, 165, 167; teaching British canon, 149, 158–61; "The Teaching of English in the Junior Secondary School," 158; *The Unquiet Bed*, 149, 155, 161;"The Wild Fig Tree," 166; "Zambia" (versions of poem cycle), 155, 166; "Zambia: The Land," 166

Longmans, 50–1; *African Participation in Government*, 51; *African Trade Unions*, 51; "Pathfinder Books," 50–1

Loram, Charles T., 46

Lorimer, James, 176

Lower, Arthur R.M., 82; *Colony to Nation*, 82, 87

Macdonald, John A., 82, 87

MacLennan, Hugh, 74, 136; *Two Solitudes*, 74

Macmillan, 50, 53, 59, 158

MacSkimming, Roy, 174; and New Press, 175

Maheu, René, 109

Malcolm X Speaks, 202

Manitoba Métis Federation, 177

Mannoni, Octave, 146, 147–8; *Prospero and Caliban*, 147; *The Psychology of Colonization*, 146

Manuel, George, 203, 205–13, 223, 294n19, 297n38; and authentic community development, 213, 214, 216; and Community Development program, Indian Affairs, 208–10; and the "fourth world," 206–7; and Mackenzie Valley Pipeline Inquiry, 206–7, 210; and National Indian Brotherhood, 206–7; and relationship of economic development to land, 207–8, 211; and response to *Indian Control of Indian Education*, 212–13. See also *Fourth World: An Indian Reality, The*

Maracle, Lee, 202, 207, 220; *Bobbi Lee: Indian Rebel*, 214, 294n20

Marchal, André, 81–2

Martin, Paul, 104

Marule, Jacob, 205

Marx, Karl, 14, 133, 173, 202, 208, 221

Massey, Vincent, 98, 105, 107, 270n12, 272n25; *On Being Canadian*, 105–6

Massey Commission, 58, 64–6, 67, 71, 75, 94; and "high-culture nationalism," 131; impact of,

59–60, 65; influence of UNESCO on, 92; report of, 57, 59, 65–6, 91
Mathews, Robin, 132, 133–4; *Canadian Literature*, 133; *The Struggle for Canadian Universities*, 133, 175
M'Bow, Amadou-Mahtar, 110, 117, 211
McClelland & Stewart, 59, 69, 85, 175; Canadian Writers' Series, 175
McFarland, Marion, 99, 100
McGraw-Hill Publishing Co., 9, 20, 59, 69, 175
Mennonite Central Committee, 101
Métis National Council, 127
missionaries and education in colonial Africa, 22, 25–6, 30, 33–4, 36, 51; British state support for, 33. See also Le Zoute conference
missionaries as publishers, 25–6; and African Literature Subcommittee, 26; in African vernaculars, 26; secular nature of, 28–9
modernization theory, 62–3, 87–8, 95, 125
Monture, Ethel Brant, 192, 193
Moose Factory Reserve (Moose Cree First Nation), 192; library at, 188–97, 192, 195–6, 291n7
Morceaux choisis d'auteurs canadiens, 94
Morrison, Ian, 199, 293n17
Moss, John, 131
Mowat, Angus McGill, 189, 190–8, 222, 291n6; library career of, 192–3, 197, 198; as literacy advocate, 191; and library at Moose Factory, 192, 195–6, 291n7; and library at Shoal Lake Reserve, 291n7; and travelling library to Ontario reserves, 196–7

Mowat, Farley, 84–7, 107, 267nn38–9; *The People of the Deer*, 84–7, 107, 193–4, 267n38; and representation of Inuit, 85–6
Mulira, Eridadi M.K., 47–8; *Teefe*, 47; *The Vernacular in African Education*, 47
Mwanakatwe, J.M., 156–7, 284n39

National Association of Friendship Centres, 127
National Council of Education, 98
National Film Board (NFB), 63, 74, 92, 93, 100, 195, 261n10, 269n5
National Film Society, 98, 270n12
National Indian Brotherhood (NIB), 198, 205–7, 212, 216; Education Committee, 212; and *Indian Control of Indian Education*, 212–13, 214, 297n34
National Indian Council, 203
National Seminar on Adult Basic Education, 199
Native Alliance for Red Power (NARP), 202, 208; Native Study Group, 202, 208
Native Communications Program, 177
Native People's Friendship Delegation (to China, 1975), 202
New Left movement, 133–5, 149, 175, 183–4, 279n8; and critique of US racism, imperialism, 133; influence of Third World anti-imperialism on, 201; and politics of decolonization, 146
New Press, 175
New Zealand (Aotearoa), 78, 207; and Maori participation in government, 207
Ngũgĩ wa Thiong'o, 40, 52, 219,

257n18; *Caitaani mütharaba-Inĩ* (Devil on the Cross), 218
Nigeria, 41, 48, 50, 136, 172; Hausa Translation Bureau, 41, 50; Nigerian writers, 148, 178
Nkrumah, Kwame, 172–3, 181; and Convention People's Party, 172
Nkumbla, Harry, 153, 283n35
Northern Rhodesia, 36, 38, 47, 50, 135–6, 149–68, 283nn34–6; and Four-Year Capital Plan (1961–65), 156–7; and movement to independence, 153–5. *See also* Zambia
"North Star myth," 132
Northwestern Regional Library Cooperative, 192
Nyasaland, 37, 38, 47, 50, 153
Nyerere, Julius, 157, 203, 207–8, 212, 285n43, 296nn27–8; *Uhuru Na Ujamaa* (Freedom and Socialism), 207

Oduyoye, Modupe, 50
Okanagan Nation Alliance, 213–14
Okigbo, Christopher, 146
Oldham, Joseph, 33–4; *Education in Africa*, 34; and International Missionary Council (IMC), 33
Ondaatje, Michael, 228; *The English Patient*, 228
Ong, Walter, 19; *Orality and Literacy*, 19, 254n24; and Toronto School of Communication, 254n24
Onibonoje, G.O., 53–4
Ontario: Department of Education, 192–3, 195, 291n7; and General Welfare Assistance Act, 196; and Lieutenant-Governor's Book Program, 222–3; literacy policy in, 226; and Ontario Book Publishers' Assistance Program, 176; and Ontario Royal Commission on Book Publishing, 175–7, 260n4
Ontario, library services in: and grants, 193; and Indigenous communities, 188–97; and Provincial Library Service, 189; and Public Library Act, 196
Organisation for Economic Co-Operation and Development (OECD), 226; and international literacy surveys, 226
Overseas Book Centre (OBC/CLO), 21, 23, 90–1, 98–106, 110, 113–17, *116*, *118*, 129, 139; book donation program of, 115–17, 120, 126, 189; and "Books for Developing Countries," 99; and development's "second wave," 113–17; funding for, 114; goals of, 91, 99, 120–2; and "Miles for Millions," 114, 273n37; and "The Overseas Book Centre in the Near Future," 121; paper program of, 122–4; and support for indigenous publishing, 120–2; and work with Indigenous communities, 199. *See also* Canadian Organization for Development in Education, 122
Overseas Institute of Canada (OIC), 100, 103–5, 109, 113, 271n20; and "Conference on Overseas Aid," 104; funding for, 103; and Second National Workshop on Canada's Participation in International Development, 104
Oxfam Canada, 101, 190, 199, 271n18, 273n37, 293n14; and starvation among Nisichawayasihk

Cree Nation, 190; and support for Indian-Eskimo Association of Canada, 199
Oxford University Press, 50, 52, 59, 145, 158, 159, 285n43; *Oxford English Course*, 52

Pacey, Desmond, 71, 76–7; *A Book of Canadian Stories*, 71, 76–7
Page, P.K., 67, 136
Paton, Alan, 159; *Cry, the Beloved Country*, 159
Pearson, Lester B., 16, 64, 82, 85, 104, 253n20, 272n27; *Democracy in World Politics*, 82; government of, 108; and Nobel Peace Prize, 16, 253n20
Pemmican Publications, 177
Penguin Random House Canada, 127, 229
Phelps-Stokes Fund, 33, 35, 44–6, 49
Phelps-Stokes Fund, Educational Commissions, 33–5, 39–40, 44, 46, 256n10; *Education in Africa* (report), 40; and emphasis on vocational training, 45, 46–7; findings of, 35–6; and Phelps-Stokeism, 40, 45, 46–8, 51; and promotion of traditional African life, 40. *See also* Le Zoute conference
Pierce, Lorne, 72; "The Underlying Principle of Confederation," 72
Pilant, Richard, 197
Pocketful of Canada, A, 71–7, 73, 94, 263nn23–4; as instrument of postwar cultural diplomacy, 72, 74
Popper, Karl, 82
Press Porcépic, 175, 181
Progressive Workers' Movement, 202

Publishers' Association of Great Britain, 10
Purdy, Al, 132–3, 136; *The New Romans*, 132–3, 183

Quebec, 13, 108, 169, 279n9; black activist movement in, 134; sovereignty movement in, 108, 126, 134, 148

Randal Livesay, Florence, 163–4, 286n47; *Songs of Ukraina*, 164
Read, Margaret, 43, 170
Reagan, Ronald, 126
Reaney, James, 131, 136; "The Upper Canadian," 131
Red Power movement, 201–2, 214, 294n19; influence of Third World decolonization movements on, 201–2
Reid, V.S., 110–11, 273n31; *The Leopard*, 110–11
Renaud, André, 103
Reuter, Paul, 82; *Institutions internationals*, 82
Richards, Charles Granston, 51–2
Richler, Mordecai, 136
Rist, Gilbert, 5–7, 29, 216–17, 224–5, 251n7; and "linear reading of world history," 29
Rivard, Adjutor, 75; "The Cradle," 75
Robins, John D., 71; *The Incomplete Anglers*, 75; *A Pocketful of Canada*, 71–7, 73, 263nn23–4
Robinson, Eric, 199
Robinson, Harry, 19
Robinson, Joan, 81
Rockefeller Foundation, 44, 270n12
Rodney, Walter, 134, 187, 223; *How Europe Underdeveloped Africa*, 187

Ross, Sinclair, 131; *As for Me and My House*, 131
Royal Commission on Canada's Economic Prospects, 67, 87, 239
Royal Commission on Development in the Arts, Letters and Sciences. *See* Massey Commission
Ryerson Press, 69, 149, 175, 262n19

Sachs, Wolfgang, 3, 8; and "age of development," 3, 5
Salamé, N., 119
Saturday Night, 132, 174, 178, 182, 198
Sauvy, Alfred, 24
Scott, Duncan Campbell, 188–9
settler colonialism, 4, 14–15, 21, 90, 229; and indigenization, 19–20; role of book in, 19–20, 75; and settler cultural nationalism, 90; and settler disavowal, 18–19, 76, 107, 129, 264n24. *See also* settler exceptionalism; settler indigenization
settler colonialism, in Canada, 4, 12–24, 71, 89, 107, 129–37, 147–8, 188, 228–9; anti-Americanism of, 131; and appropriation of Indigenous lifeways, 58, 74–6, 89; and centennial period, 129, 130, 273n37; and cultural nationalism, 21, 129–37, 147–8, 175, 228, 278n5; and internal colonization, 4, 15, 20, 22, 58, 90, 134, 184, 202; and settler exceptionalism, 106–7, 130, 230; and settler indigenization, 178–9
settler exceptionalism, 15–17, 18–20, 106–7, 130; book as representative of, 4, 15, 230; and Indigenization, 19–20; and settler disavowal, 18–19

settler indigenization, 15, 19–20, 75, 135–7, 186; and indigenizing rhetoric, 131
settler nationalism, in Canada, 12–24, 74, 129–86; and anti-Americanism, 59, 131–3; and New Left, 133–5, 175; and settler indigenization, 58, 75, 135, 137, 178–9, 186
Shea, Jack, 199
Sherlock, Philip, 111
Shirley, Philip, 141, 144, 280n21
Shoal Lake Reserve (Shoal Lake 40 First Nation), 192; library at, 291n7
Six Nations: Band Council, 191; Public Library, 197; RCMP raid on (1959), 191; *Tekawennake News*, 197; Women's Institute, 197
Six Nations Confederacy, 108–9
Slash (Jeannette Armstrong), 213–21, 298n41; as bildungsroman, 217–21
Smallface-Marule, Marie, 203–7, 204, 207, 223; and CUSO, 203–6; and educational institutions for Indigenous Peoples, 206
Smallface, Marie. *See* Smallface-Marule, Marie
Smallwood, Joey, 87
Smith, Edwin W., 39; *Aggrey of Africa*, 39
Somaliland, 136, 137–48; as British Protectorate, 137–41; literacy in, 142–3; and scarcity of reading materials, 142
Somali Republic. *See* Somaliland
South Africa, 39, 153; Canadian foreign policy in, 114; education in, 112–13; publishing in, 49
South and Southeast Asia, 5, 78–9, 84; publishing in, 177

Southern Rhodesia, 46–7, 108, 153, 283n34; Government Industrial Schools, 46. *See also* Zimbabwe
Soviet Union, 43, 60, 80, 138; and espionage, 82–3; influence of, 7, 9, 62; threat of, 8, 61, 65
Soviet Union, book as instrument of development in, 9, 102, 254n26; and book donation, 20, 61, 68, 77, 89, 120; and book export, 9
Special Book Presentation Programme (External Affairs), 22, 68, 70, 77–88; and American-authored selections, 82; and French-language selections, 82; funding for, 81, 84; goal of, 77, 81; selected book list for, 81–2, 83, 86, 241–5
Spicer, Keith, 12, 78, 79, 265n30
St Laurent, Louis, 71
Standing, T.W., 197
Steele, James, 134; *The Struggle for Canadian Universities*, 133
Structural Adjustment Programs, 8, 13, 224–5
Swinton, Kurt, 99, 101

Tamarack Review, 139, 174, 178–81
Tanganyika, 50, 144; and groundnut scheme, 54, 260n36
Tanzania, 115, 203–4, 208, 223; and Arusha Declaration (1967), 7, 203, 207; education in, 157
Theytus Books, 127, 177, 214
Thomas, Audrey, 135–6; and African fiction, 135, 173, 287n57; and CUSO, 169–70, 172, 173; and second-wave settler feminism, 173
Thomas, Audrey, writings of: *Blown Figures*, 173; *Mrs. Blood*, 135, 173; "Ten Green Bottles" (story), 135; *Ten Green Bottles*, 135

Thomas, Ian, 173
Toombs, Farrell, 209
Tory, H.M., 71–2, 76
Trotsky, Leon, 202; *Permanent Revolution*, 202
Trudeau, Justin, 17
Trudeau, Pierre, 126
Truman, Harry, 6, 7; inaugural address of, 6, 7, 42
Trump, Donald, 17; and ban on Syrian refugees, 17
Tuskegee Institute, 44, 47
Tutola, Amos, 158; *The Palm Wine Drinkard*, 158

Uganda, 50, 144
UNESCO, 92–3, 98–9, 102, 117–19, 151–2, 225, 282n33; British, US withdrawal from, 126, 225; developmentalist ethos of, 62; influence of on Canadian cultural policy, 64–5, 92; influence of US on, 60, 62; and New International Economic Order, 117, 125–6; and New World Information and Communications Order, 120, 125, 152, 225; and Technical Assistance Program, 151, 152, 156
UNESCO, book and literacy policy initiatives of, 9–11, 55–6, 119–20, 152, 198, 210–11, 263n20; and Accra Conference (1968), 176; and "book hunger," 29, 55–6; Canada's influence on, 226; and copyright, 10; and Florence Agreement (1950), 10; and functional literacy, 55, 109–10, 117, 152, 211, 273n30; and International Book Year (1972), 10, 55, 176; and library division, programs, 96, 100; Meeting of Experts on Book Development

in Africa, 120; meeting on "Book Promotion and Development," 120; World Conference of Ministers on the Eradication of Illiteracy, 109. *See* Canadian Council for Reconstruction Through UNESCO; Experimental World Literacy Programme

UNESCO, education policy, initiatives of, 152, 269n5, 273n30; on adult education, 100, 106, 109–10, 125–6; on fundamental education, 10, 54–5; Meeting of Ministers of Education of African Countries, 157; Recommendation on Development of Adult Education, 125; on right to free, compulsory education, 152, 156, 157, 168, 282n33; World Conference on Adult Education, 106, 109

UNESCO, publications of: *Book Donations for Development*, 124; *The Book Hunger*, 10, 55–6, 119; *Facilities for Education in Rural Areas*, 151; *Functional Literacy and International Development*, 109, 111–12, 198–9; *Meeting of Ministers of Education of African Countries Participating in the Implementation of the Addis Ababa Plan: Final Report*, 157; *World Illiteracy at Mid-Century*, 151–2

Union of British Columbia Indian Chiefs, 216, 297n38

United Gold Coast Convention, 172

United National Independence Party (UNIP), 153–4, 156–7, 158, 203, 283n35, 284n37, 284n39; protest movement of, 154

United Nations, 6, 24, 62, 64, 108–9, 206, 295n26; Conference on the Human Environment (1972), 206; Conference on Trade and Development (1964), 7, 104; Declaration on the New International Economic Order, 7, 117, 125–6; and development as economic growth, 117–18; First Development Decade, 101, 103–6, 109, 118, 172; and International Bill of Rights, 18; and International Co-operation Year, 104–5; Peacekeeping Force, 16; *Social Progress Through Community Development*, 208

United Nations Association, 100, 101, 268n4

United Nations Development Agency, 119

United Nations Educational, Scientific, and Cultural Organization. *See entries for* UNESCO

United States, 6–7, 11, 15, 23, 138; cultural and economic hegemony of, 11, 15, 16, 65, 71, 89, 133; and cultural diplomacy, 22, 58, 60–6, 70, 75; and "functional literacy," 55, 109–10, 125, 211, 273n30; settler exceptionalism in, 16, 253n19; and withdrawal from UNESCO, 126, 225

United States, book as instrument of development in, 9, 10–11, 102; and impact on emerging markets, 9, 61–2. *See also* United States Information Agency

United States, book donation in, 11, 20, 82, 89, 102, 107, 120; and Bookshelf USA, 107; and Books

USA, 107; and Franklin Book Programs, 10, 61–2, 91, 102
United States, foreign policy goals of, 62–3, 78; and foreign aid, 102; role of the State Department, 60–1; and the Truman Doctrine, 78
United States Agency for International Development (USAID), 10, 102; and funding for book programs, 10, 61
United States Information Agency (USIA), 20, 61, 69, 83, 107; and funding for book programs, 61–2, 69, 83–4

Vallières, Pierre, 134; *Les n— blancs d'amérique*, 134
Voice of Women Canada, 99

Waffle movement (New Democratic Party), 132–3, 288n60
Wallace, Robert, 98, 270n12
Wartime Information Board (WIB), 63, 66, 261n10
Washington, Booker T., 34; *Up from Slavery*, 39
Watch Tower Bible and Tract Society, 38
Weaver, Robert, 174
"white civility," 16
William Collins Sons & Company Canada, 72–4, 263n23, 263n25; White Circle Pocket Editions, 72–4, 73, 76, 264n25
Winslow, Bernice Loft, 197
Wiseman, Adele, 141, 280n21
Woodcock, George, 136, 281n28
World Bank, 6, 7, 102, 117, 273n30; and "basic needs," 7–8, 224; and definition of poverty, 6; and

"functional literacy," 55, 109–10, 125, 211, 273n30
World Conference of the Organization of the Teaching Profession, 100
World Council of Indigenous Peoples, 205, 206
Wrong, George MacKinnon, 28
Wrong, Margaret, 27–9, 35–43, 36, 37, 55; *Africa Advancing*, 44–6; *Africa and the Making of Books*, 51, 259n29; and book selection, curation, 39–40; education of, 28; and encouragement of African authorship, languages, 40–1, 47–8, 49, 259n29; and "famine of books," 55; *Five Points for Africa*, 42–3, 45; and the ICCLA, 27–9, 35–42, 45, 49–51; "The Importance of Literatures in African Languages," 41; *The Land and Life of Africa*, 39; legacy of, 47, 50–2; and Phelps-Stokeism, 39–40, 46, 48–9; and promotion of African publishing, 49–54; *Towards a Literate Africa*, 48

Yukon Native Brotherhood, 199

Zambia, 50, 53, 185, 203–5; adult literacy program in, 203; educational publishing in, 53, 158; nationalizing of educational publishing in, 53; shortage of teachers and schools in, 157; and universal primary education, 157. *See also* Northern Rhodesia
Zanzibar, 50, 144
Zedong, Mao, 202
Zimbabwe, 46, 185, 204

Rethinking Canada in the World

SERIES EDITORS: IAN MCKAY AND SEAN MILLS

1 Canada and the United Nations
 Legacies, Limits, Prospects
 Edited by Colin McCullough and
 Robert Teigrob
2 Undiplomatic History
 The New Study of Canada and
 the World
 Edited by Asa McKercher and Philip
 Van Huizen
3 Revolutions across Borders
 Jacksonian America and the
 Canadian Rebellion
 Edited by Maxime Dagenais and
 Julien Mauduit
4 Left Transnationalism
 The Communist International
 and the National, Colonial, and
 Racial Questions
 Edited by Oleksa Drachewych and
 Ian McKay
5 Landscapes of Injustice
 A New Perspective on the
 Internment and Dispossession of
 Japanese Canadians
 Edited by Jordan Stanger-Ross
6 Canada's Other Red Scare
 Indigenous Protest and Colonial
 Encounters during the Global Sixties
 Scott Rutherford
7 The Global Politics of Poverty
 in Canada
 Development Programs and
 Democracy, 1964–1979
 Will Langford
8 Schooling the System
 A History of Black Women Teachers
 Funké Aladejebi
9 Constant Struggle
 Histories of Canadian
 Democratizatin
 Edited by Julien Mauduit and
 Jennifer Tunnicliffe
10 The Racial Mosaic
 A Pre-history of Canadian
 Multiculturalism
 Daniel R. Meister
11 Dominion over Palm and Pine
 A History of Canadian Aspirations
 in the British Caribbean
 Paula Hastings
12 Harvesting Labour
 Tobacco and the Global Making of
 Canada's Agricultural Workforce
 Edward Dunsworth
13 Distant Stage
 Quebec, Brazil, and the Making of
 Canada's Cultural Diplomacy
 Eric Fillion
14 Repenser l'Acadie dans le monde
 Études comparées, études
 transnationales
 Sous la direction de Clint Bruce et
 Gregory Kennedy
15 Books for Development
 Canada in the Late Twentieth-
 Century World
 Jody Mason